BTEC Level 2

HOSPITALITY LEVEL 2

BTEC First

Stephen Batten | Carol Carysforth | Gillian Dale
Sue Holmes | Steven Ingle | Tracay Mead
Mike Neild | Wilf Richer | Paul Wilson

Published by Pearson Education Limited, a company incorporated in England and Wales, having its registered office at Edinburgh Gate, Harlow, Essex, CM20 2JE. Registered company number: 872828

www.pearsonschoolsandfecolleges.co.uk

Edexcel is a registered trademark of Edexcel Limited

Text © Pearson Education Limited 2011

First published 2011

13 12 11 10

10 9 8 7 6 5 4 3 2 1

British Library Cataloguing in Publication Data
A catalogue record for this book is available from the British Library.

ISBN 978 0 435026 59 2

Edited by Paul Stirner and Andy Lowe

Designed by Wooden Ark

Typeset by Tech-Set Ltd, Gateshead

Original illustrations © Saxon Graphics Ltd, Derby

Cover design by Visual Philosophy

Picture research by Katharine Oakes

Cover photo/illustration © Getty Images: BLOOMimage

Back cover photos © Pearson Education Ltd: Gareth Boden, Debbie Rowe; The Hilton Group

Printed in Spain by Grafos

Hotlinks
There are links to relevant websites in this book. In order to ensure that the links are up to date, that the links work, and that the sites are not inadvertently linked to sites that could be considered offensive, we have made the links available on the Pearson website at www.pearsonschoolsandfecolleges.co.uk/hotlinks. When you access the website, search for the title (*BTEC Level 2 First Hospitality Student Book*) or ISBN (978 0 435026 59 2).

Disclaimer
This material has been published on behalf of Edexcel and offers high-quality support for the delivery of Edexcel qualifications. This does not mean that the material is essential to achieve any Edexcel qualification, nor does it mean that it is the only suitable material available to support any Edexcel qualification. Edexcel material will not be used verbatim in setting any Edexcel examination or assessment. Any resource lists produced by Edexcel shall include this and other appropriate resources.

Copies of official specifications for all Edexcel qualifications may be found on the Edexcel website: www.edexcel.com

Contents

The following optional units are available on the Pearson Education website.

Credits

The authors and publisher would like to thank the following organisations for their kind permission to reproduce material:

Sodexo, a food and facilities management services company (p9); Whole School Meals (p9); The Compass Group (p9); The Dorchester (p37); Frankie & Benny's (p37); Thomas Cook (p48)

The authors and publisher would like to thank the following individuals and organisations for their permission to reproduce photographs:

(Key: b-bottom; c-centre; l-left; r-right; t-top)

Alamy Images: Beyondfotomedia GmbH 107, Blend Images 59, 305, Bon Appetit 294, Brendan MacNeill 109, 136, Buzzshotz 185, Cultura 349, David J Green 397, David R Frazier Photolibrary Inc 371, England / Alan King 382, Foodimage Collection 262, Ian Trower 324, Image Source Black 128, Image State 290, Itanistock 229, Larry Lilac 27, Liz Bond 273, Luca Di Cecco 147, Malcolm Cochrane 291, MBI 281, Michele Molinari 151, Moodboard 249, Peter Noyce 45, Photosindia.com LLC 181, Radius Images 301, Robert Stainforth 69, RT Images 323, Simon Holdcroft 331r, Solaria 345, T.M.O.Buildings 37bl; **Arnos Design Ltd:** 210br, 227, 258, 320bl, 333; **The Dorchester Collection:** 46; **Corbis:** Brigitte Sporres / Zefa 303, 322, FusionPix / Corbis 334, Erik K K Yu 97, Juice Images 297, Michael Jenner 338br, Nogues / Sygma 326bl, Radius Images 149; **Debenhams:** 210bl; **Fotolia.com:** Natalie Bratslavsky 366, Pius Lee 111, Yuri Arcurs 205; **Getty Images:** PunchStock / Bananastock 355, PunchStock / Upper Cut Images 329, Photonica 243br, PunchStock / Thinkstock 347, 357; **Image courtesy of The Advertising Archives:** 160; **Compass Group UK & Ireland:** 9bl; **iStockphoto:** ALEAIMAGE 284, Anne Trautmann 157b, diego cervo 183, ImagesbyTristo 394, Lars Christiansen 159, Myles Dumas 157bl, Shanekato 157br, Surakit Harntongkul 279, Ryan KC Wong 55; **The Ritz Hotel London:** 7, 40; **Whole School Meals :** 9br; **Pearson Education Ltd:** Ben Nicholson 172, 231, 237tr, 237br, 240tl, 240bl, 251, 254, 256, 261, 337, 338tl, Gareth Boden 3, Rob Judges 31, Jules Selmes 8, 11, 25, 225, MindStudio 51, Debbie Rowe 17, 48; Photodisc. Don Tremain 277; **Photolibrary.com:** 243tr, Fresh Food Images / John Carey 331, Fresh Food Images / Robert Lawson 320br, Joyce Lockhead 1, 37br; **Press Association Images:** ABACA / Gregorio Binuya 165, Empics / Paul Faith 129; **Keith Prowse:** 9bc; **Rex Features:** Geoff Moore 162; **Sodexo:** 9b; **The Hilton Group:** 57, 63, 77, 88, 100, 259, 326tl, 353

All other images © Pearson Education

Every effort has been made to trace the copyright holders and we apologise in advance for any unintentional omissions. We would be pleased to insert the appropriate acknowledgement in any subsequent edition of this publication.

About the authors

Stephen Batten is a Senior Standards Verifier for Hospitality. He has taught for 28 years in colleges across a range of Hospitality and Tourism subjects and is currently Deputy Head of Faculty of Professional and Vocational Studies at Southampton City College.

Carol Carysforth had a successful business career before entering Further Education. As a lecturer, Divisional Head and then Deputy Dean of Faculty, she gained extensive experience of teaching, managing, assessing and verifying BTEC courses. She has been writing for Heinemann for over 20 years and is the author of over 40 best-selling textbooks.

Gillian Dale has many years' experience teaching travel and tourism and running BTEC programmes, and has written textbooks for various qualifications. She is an educational adviser, coach and additional inspector. Her main focus is curriculum design and programme development and her recent projects include developing courses in customer service for frontline personnel who will encounter Olympic visitors and the design and delivery of coaching skills courses.

Sue Holmes is the Hospitality and Travel Coordinator at a large FE college. She has taught for over 15 years on a range of programmes from Entry Level to BA (Hons). Sue has extensive experience writing units and teacher support material for Edexcel.

Steve Ingle has over ten years' experience in the post-compulsory education and training sector and is currently a Senior Lecturer, Course Leader and accredited Ofsted Additional Inspector. A Fellow of the Chartered Institute of Educational Assessors, Steve also has an extensive background in quality assurance and assessment, working with Edexcel as Senior Examiner, Principal Moderator, BTEC Standards Verifier and Centre Quality Reviewer.

Tracay Mead was Head of Department for over 10 years and taught for over 17 years in an FE college across a range of travel, leisure and hospitality qualifications. She is also an experienced internal verifier. Tracay is a seasoned external moderator and has marked a variety of exam papers since 2000. She vets exam papers and has worked with awarding bodies to write units for travel and tourism and hospitality qualifications. She is now a self-employed lecturer, assessor, internal and external verifier and moderator.

Mike Neild worked in Production Management before entering teaching. As a Course Director, Senior Tutor and Centre Manager at Blackburn College, he taught, assessed and managed a wide range of business and management programmes. He has been co-writing successful business resources with Carol Carysforth for over 15 years.

Wilf Richer has been teaching in secondary schools for over nine years. He is a Programme Leader for BTEC Level 2 Hospitality in his centre, and also works as a Standards Verifier for Edexcel. He is a course tutor for a graduate teacher training programme, training teachers within technology. Prior to teaching he has had many years of experience within the hospitality and catering industry.

Paul Wilson is a consultant in education and hospitality as well as a Senior Examiner for an Edexcel exam board. Paul has worked extensively in the hospitality industry as well as having his own catering business. Paul taught in further and higher education, becoming a Vice Principal of a further education College as well as an Inspector of Education.

The publishers would also like to thank Frances Ovenden and Sarah Warnes for their permission to update their materials from the first edition of this book.

v

About your BTEC Level 2 First Hospitality

Choosing to study for a Level 2 BTEC First Hospitality qualification is a great decision to make for lots of reasons. Hospitality is an exciting and diverse industry. It provides food, drink and accommodation for people who are away from home, whether travelling, working or on holiday. You will learn a variety of skills such as how to prepare a meal, how to look after customers and how to plan for a special event. These skills can be used when working in many settings, including hotels, restaurants, bars and catering businesses, and can lead to great job satisfaction and perhaps the chance to travel.

Your BTEC Level 2 First in Hospitality is a **vocational** or **work-related** qualification. This doesn't mean that it will give you *all* the skills you need to do a job, but it does mean that you will have the opportunity to gain specific knowledge, understanding and skills that are relevant to your chosen subject or area of work.

What will you be doing?

The qualification is structured into **mandatory units (M)** (ones that you must do) and **optional units (O)** (ones that you can choose to do).

- BTEC Level 2 First **Certificate** in Hospitality: 2 mandatory units and optional units that provide a combined total of 15 credits
- BTEC Level 2 First **Extended Certificate** in Hospitality: 2 mandatory units and optional units that provide a combined total of 30 credits
- BTEC Level 2 First **Diploma** in Hospitality: 4 mandatory units and optional units that provide a combined total of 60 credits

Unit	Credit value	Unit name	Cert	Ex. Cert	Diploma
1	4	Investigate the catering and hospitality industry	M	M	M
2	1	Products, services and support in the hospitality industry	M	M	M
3	1	Principles of customer service in hospitality, leisure, travel and tourism	O	O	M
4	4	Providing customer service in hospitality	O	O	M
5	10	Planning and running a hospitality event	O	O	O
6	1	Healthier food and special diets	O	O	O
7	3	Applying workplace skills	O	O	O
8	4	Prepare cook and finish food	O	O	O
9	10	Contemporary world food	O	O	O
10	5	Alcoholic drinks	O	O	O
11	1	Service of food at table	O	O	O
12	1	Service of alcoholic and non-alcoholic drinks	O	O	O
13	5	Accommodation services in hospitality	O	O	O
14	5	Hospitality front office operations	O	O	O
15	5	Bookkeeping for business	O	O	O
16	5	Consumer rights	O	O	O
17	5	The UK travel and tourism sector	O	O	O
18	5	Hospitality operations in travel and tourism	O	O	O

How to use this book

This book is designed to help you through your BTEC Level 2 First Hospitality course. It is divided into 9 chapters to reflect the units in the specification; some chapters contain more than one unit, as outlined on the contents page (page iii). This is because they contain similar or linked topics.

There are three units that have not been printed in the book. These are available on our website. You can print these out or read them on screen. The units are:

- Unit 16 Consumer rights
- Unit 17 The UK travel and tourism sector
- Unit 18 Hospitality operations in travel and tourism

This book contains many features that will help you to use your skills and knowledge in work-related situations and assist you in getting the most from your course.

Assessment and grading criteria

These introductions give you a snapshot of what to expect from each unit – and what you should be aiming for by the time you finish it.

These tables explain what you must do in order to achieve each of the assessment criteria for each unit. Each unit contains a number of assessment activities to help you with the assessment criteria, shown by the grade button (e.g. **P1**).

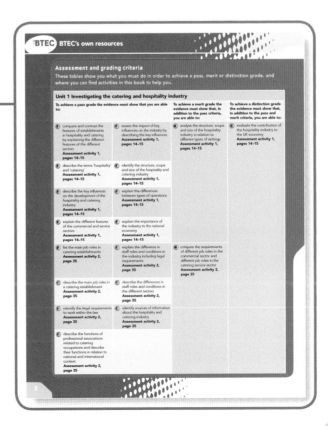

Assessment

Your tutor will set **assignments** throughout your course for you to complete. These may take the form of projects where you research, plan, prepare, make and evaluate a piece of work or an activity, case study or presentation. The important thing is that you collect evidence of your skills and knowledge to date.

Stuck for ideas? Daunted by your first assignment? These students have all been through it before…

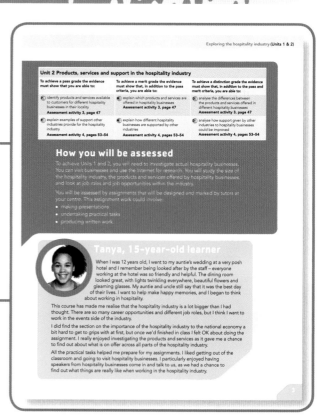

Activities

There are different types of activities for you to do: **assessment activities** are suggestions for tasks that you might do as part of your assignments and will help you to develop your knowledge, skills and understanding. Each one has **grading tips** that clearly explain what you need to do in order to achieve a pass, merit or distinction grade.

Assessment activity 4

Unit 4 P M D   BTEC

You have been asked to monitor and evaluate the customer service provision in two hospitality businesses. You must first select two businesses. These could be the two organisations you investigated for the earlier assessment activities in these units or they could be different organisations.

Next, visit these businesses to find out the methods that they use to monitor and evaluate customer service. You need to focus on:
- what information is gathered
- how the information is obtained
- how it is used to improve customer service.

1 Based on your visits and investigations, produce a report identifying the methods of monitoring and evaluating customer service used in the two businesses. P

2 Following your investigations, produce a set of guidelines that analyses the strengths and weaknesses of each method you identified in Task 1. M

3 Produce a further report that evaluates the customer service provision in both hospitality businesses, making suggestions for improvement. D

Grading tips

P Investigate each organisation before each visit. Prepare some questions to ask the staff about how they monitor customer service and how they use the information gathered to improve customer service.

M When determining the strengths and weaknesses of different methods of monitoring customer service, consider factors such as ease of use, the cost of obtaining the information and how easy it would be to analyse the information gathered. Does the information allow the hospitality business to recognise areas for improvement? Is it reliable?

D You could collect information from tourist boards, such as brochures and leaflets, and do some research on the Internet to find out more about the type of service that each business aims to provide. You might be able to find on the Internet some opinions from customers of their provision. You could also do your own mystery customer exercise. The recommendations you suggest can be minor, but all should be realistic and in line with each organisation's customer service policies. You must justify your recommendations by relating them to existing customer service policies, general industry practice or the potential benefit to the business.

There are also suggestions for **activities** that will give you a broader grasp of the industry and develop your skills.

Activity: Understanding prices

In small groups, discuss these questions and agree on a set of answers.
- Why is a B&B cheaper than a five-star hotel?
- Why can a top restaurant charge more for dinner than a country hotel, even if the food is of the same standard?
- Why are some hotel rooms cheaper at the weekend?
- Why are prices for guest houses in Blackpool different to those in the Cotswolds?
- Why do some pubs offer '2 for 1' prices for meals?
- Why do children eat for free in some restaurants?

Assessment and grading criteria

These tables show you what you must do in order to achieve a pass, merit or distinction grade, and where you can find activities in this book to help you.

Unit 1 Investigating the catering and hospitality industry

To achieve a pass grade the evidence must show that you are able to:		To achieve a merit grade the evidence must show that, in addition to the pass criteria, you are able to:	To achieve a distinction grade the evidence must show that, in addition to the pass and merit criteria, you are able to:
P1 compare and contrast the features of establishments in hospitality and catering by explaining the different features of the different sectors **Assessment activity 1, pages 14–15**	**P2** assess the impact of key influences on the industry by describing the key influences **Assessment activity 1, pages 14–15**	**M1** analyse the structure, scope and size of the hospitality industry in relation to different types of settings **Assessment activity 1, pages 14–15**	**D1** evaluate the contribution of the hospitality industry to the UK economy **Assessment activity 1, pages 14–15**
P3 describe the terms 'hospitality' and 'catering' **Assessment activity 1, pages 14–15**	**P4** identify the structure, scope and size of the hospitality and catering industry **Assessment activity 1, pages 14–15**		
P5 describe the key influences on the development of the hospitality and catering industry **Assessment activity 1, pages 14–15**	**P6** explain the differences between types of operations **Assessment activity 1, pages 14–15**		
P7 explain the different features of the commercial and service sectors **Assessment activity 1, pages 14–15**	**P8** explain the importance of the industry to the national economy **Assessment activity 1, pages 14–15**		
P9 list the main job roles in catering establishments **Assessment activity 2, page 35**	**P10** explain the difference in staff roles and conditions in the industry including legal requirements **Assessment activity 2, page 35**	**M2** compare the requirements of different job roles in the commercial sector and different job roles in the catering service sector **Assessment activity 2, page 35**	
P11 describe the main job roles in a catering establishment **Assessment activity 2, page 35**	**P12** describe the differences in staff roles and conditions in the different sectors **Assessment activity 2, page 35**		
P13 identify the legal requirements to work within the law **Assessment activity 2, page 35**	**P14** identify sources of information about the hospitality and catering industry **Assessment activity 2, page 35**		
P15 describe the functions of professional associations related to catering occupations and describe their functions in relation to national and international context. **Assessment activity 2, page 35**			

1 & 2 Exploring the hospitality industry

Most people have experienced the hospitality industry. The industry is vast, and constantly changing to meet customer expectations. It is also a very diverse industry, ranging from stays in a five-star hotel to meals in a fast-food outlet.

In these two units, you will develop your knowledge and understanding of this exciting and fast-moving industry. You first consider the different types of business in hospitality industry at national and local levels. You will explore the types of hospitality jobs, and the skills needed to work in the industry.

You will then go on to look at the products and services offered in different hospitality settings, and how other businesses, such as those in the travel sector, support the hospitality industry.

Learning outcomes

After completing this unit, you should:

Unit 1 Investigating the catering and hospitality industry

1 Understand the hospitality and catering industry

2 Understand the national and international employment opportunities available in the hospitality industry.

Unit 2 Products, services and support in the hospitality industry

1 Know the products and services offered in the hospitality industry

2 Understand support given by other industries to hospitality businesses.

Just checking

When you see this sort of activity, take stock. These quick questions are there to check your knowledge. You can use them to see how much progress you have made or as a revision tool.

BTEC BTEC's own resources

Just checking

1 Explain what is meant by the term 'the commercial sector'.
2 Give examples of two settings in the commercial sector.
3 List the different types of businesses that make up the hospitality sector.
4 What types of staff work in a hotel?
5 What are some of the job roles these staff might have?
6 List three qualities that people need to have when working in the hospitality industry.
7 Explain why teamwork is important in the hospitality industry.
8 Explain why personal appearance is important.
9 Explain the role of Staffing agencies.
10 List three other industries that support the hospitality industry.

edexcel

Assignment tips

- Spend some time researching and reading the reports and profiles on the People 1st website.
- Visit as many different types of hospitality businesses as you can. Find out if each is a local or national business.
- Talk to people who work in the hospitality industry. Discuss their job role, and find out what qualities they need to do their job and what the requirements of their job are.
- Start your research into hospitality jobs early in these units so you have plenty of examples to chose from when you come to do your assignment.
- When you do assessment activity 3, make sure that you chose businesses from different parts of the industry so you can cover all types of hospitality products and services.
- Practise your presentation for assessment activity 4. You will feel less nervous and appear more confident. It will also help you know what you need to say so that you don't just read your notes.
- When you do assessment activity 4 task 3, base your suggestions for improvements on the weaknesses you have identified. Remember to be realistic.

56

Edexcel's assignment tips

At the end of each chapter, you will find hints and tips to help you get the best mark you can, such as the best websites to go to, checklists to help you remember processes and really useful facts and figures.

Don't miss out on these resources to help you.

Have you read your BTEC Level 2 First Study Skills Guide? It's full of advice on study skills, putting your assignments together and making the most of being a BTEC Hospitality student.

Your book is just part of the exciting resources from Edexcel to help you succeed in your BTEC course. Visit www.edexcel.com/BTEC or www.pearsonfe.co.uk/BTEC2010 for more details.

Personal, learning and thinking skills (PLTS)

Throughout your BTEC Level 2 First Hospitality course, there are lots of opportunities to develop your personal, learning and thinking skills. Look out for these as you progress.

Functional skills

It is important that you have good English, maths and ICT skills – you never know when you'll need them, and employers will be looking for evidence that you've got these skills too.

Key terms

Technical words and phrases are easy to spot, and definitions are included. You can also use the glossary at the back of the book.

WorkSpace

These case studies provide snapshots of real workplace issues, and show how the skills and knowledge you develop during your course can help you in your career.

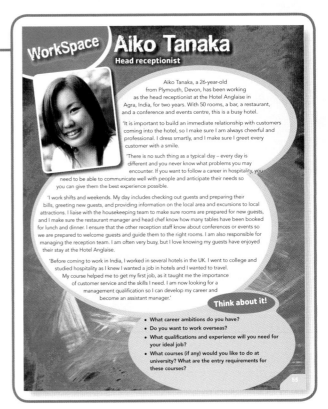

WorkSpace **Aiko Tanaka**
Head receptionist

Aiko Tanaka, a 26-year-old from Plymouth, Devon, has been working as the head receptionist at the Hotel Anglaise in Agra, India, for two years. With 50 rooms, a bar, a restaurant, and a conference and events centre, this is a busy hotel.

'It is important to build an immediate relationship with customers coming into the hotel, so I make sure I am always cheerful and professional. I dress smartly, and I make sure I greet every customer with a smile.

'There is no such thing as a typical day – every day is different and you never know what problems you may encounter. If you want to follow a career in hospitality, you need to be able to communicate well with people and anticipate their needs so you can give them the best experience possible.

'I work shifts and weekends. My day includes checking out guests and preparing their bills, greeting new guests, and providing information on the local area and excursions to local attractions. I liaise with the housekeeping team to make sure rooms are prepared for new guests, and I make sure the restaurant manager and head chef know how many tables have been booked for lunch and dinner. I ensure that the other reception staff know about conferences or events so we are prepared to welcome guests and guide them to the right rooms. I am also responsible for managing the reception team. I am often very busy, but I love knowing my guests have enjoyed their stay at the Hotel Anglaise.

'Before coming to work in India, I worked in several hotels in the UK. I went to college and studied hospitality as I knew I wanted a job in hotels and I wanted to travel. My course helped me to get my first job, as it taught me the importance of customer service and the skills I need. I am now looking for a management qualification so I can develop my career and become an assistant manager.'

Think about it!

- What career ambitions do you have?
- Do you want to work overseas?
- What qualifications and experience will you need for your ideal job?
- What courses (if any) would you like to do at university? What are the entry requirements for these courses?

Unit 2 Products, services and support in the hospitality industry

To achieve a pass grade the evidence must show that you are able to:	To achieve a merit grade the evidence must show that, in addition to the pass criteria, you are able to:	To achieve a distinction grade the evidence must show that, in addition to the pass and merit criteria, you are able to:
P1 identify products and services available to customers for different hospitality businesses in their locality **Assessment activity 3, page 47**	**M1** explain which products and services are offered in hospitality businesses **Assessment activity 3, page 47**	**D1** analyse the differences between the products and services offered in different hospitality businesses **Assessment activity 3, page 47**
P2 explain examples of support other industries provide for the hospitality industry **Assessment activity 4, pages 53–54**	**M2** explain how different hospitality businesses are supported by other industries **Assessment activity 4, pages 53–54**	**D2** analyse how support given by other industries to hospitality businesses could be improved **Assessment activity 4, pages 53–54**

How you will be assessed

To achieve Units 1 and 2, you will need to investigate actual hospitality businesses. You can visit businesses and use the Internet for research. You will study the size of the hospitality industry, the products and services offered by hospitality businesses, and look at job roles and job opportunities within the industry.

You will be assessed by assignments that will be designed and marked by tutors at your centre. This assignment work could involve:

- making presentations
- undertaking practical tasks
- producing written work.

Tanya, 15-year-old learner

When I was 12 years old, I went to my auntie's wedding at a very posh hotel and I remember being looked after by the staff – everyone working at the hotel was so friendly and helpful. The dining room looked great, with lights twinkling everywhere, beautiful flowers and gleaming glasses. My auntie and uncle still say that it was the best day of their lives. I want to help make happy memories, and I began to think about working in hospitality.

This course has made me realise that the hospitality industry is a lot bigger than I had thought. There are so many career opportunities and different job roles, but I think I want to work in the events side of the industry.

I did find the section on the importance of the hospitality industry to the national economy a bit hard to get to grips with at first, but once we'd finished in class I felt OK about doing the assignment. I really enjoyed investigating the products and services as it gave me a chance to find out about what is on offer across all parts of the hospitality industry.

All the practical tasks helped me prepare for my assignments. I liked getting out of the classroom and going to visit hospitality businesses. I particularly enjoyed having speakers from hospitality businesses come in and talk to us, as we had a chance to find out what things are really like when working in the hospitality industry.

1.1 Understand the hospitality and catering industry

Welcome

How many hospitality businesses can you name?

In pairs, think of at least ten hospitality businesses that can be found all over Britain. Once you have finished, compare your list with those produced by the other groups in the class. Combine the lists to produce one long list of national hospitality businesses.

Now repeat the exercise, again starting in pairs, but this time come up with a list of smaller independent hospitality businesses that just operate in your local area. Again, combine your ideas to produce a long list of local hospitality businesses.

This section covers:

- the hospitality industry
- hospitality industry businesses
- types of settings
- influences on the industry
- the economic importance of the hospitality industry.

The hospitality and catering industry includes hotels, guest houses, bed and breakfasts (B&Bs), inns and pubs, restaurants, cafés and takeaways, contract catering (such as catering in hospitals), catering in leisure attractions (such as museums) and motorway service areas. It also includes private clubs (such as the Royal Automobile Club) and mobile catering services.

There are many definitions of hospitality and catering. However, we shall use the following definitions in this book.

- Hospitality is the provision of accommodation, food and drink, entertainment and other services for guests, visitors, travellers and tourists.
- Catering is that part of the hospitality industry that provides customers with food and drink.

Hospitality and catering organisations aim to make profit in return for the supply of their products and services.

The hospitality industry

The hospitality industry in the UK consists of thousands of businesses. Many are small local businesses, but some are national operations.

Local

There are many hospitality businesses that are unique to a particular town or area. These are independent businesses. They are owned by individuals or partners and are not part of a national chain.

Although the experience for the customer is less predictable than with a national chain, local hospitality outlets can offer specialised and interesting menus, and a range of accommodation at various prices.

National

There are many hospitality companies that have chains of outlets around the UK. Some well-known examples are:

- Burger King
- Pizza Hut
- Yates's
- Starbucks
- Nando's
- Premier Inn.

One of the advantages of visiting a chain outlet is that you know what you will be getting. All the outlets of the chain look similar, with the same style of furnishing, menus and pricing.

Location

The location of hospitality businesses is very important. Unlike a business selling goods that can be sold in a shop or on the Internet, customers need to visit the hospitality business to experience its goods and services.

The location of a hospitality business influences the types of products and services on offer and the prices that are charged. A hotel located in the highlands of Scotland is unlikely to able to attract business customers for half-day meetings as it would be too far for most people to travel there and back in a day. However, the hotel could attract tourists for walking and sightseeing holidays.

Catering businesses also need to take location into account. A fast-food restaurant needs to be situated where people are likely to need a quick food stop. This could be in town centres, beside tourist attractions or on busy roads.

Size of businesses

Another way of looking at the hospitality industry is by the size of businesses. Many hospitality businesses are very small. For example, a small independent café may only employ two or three people. It may have a relatively small **turnover**, and only generate enough profit to provide its owner with a modest income. In contrast, the hospitality

Key term

Turnover – the amount of money taken by a business in a particular period.

businesses that run the well-known national chains are multi-million pound operations and employ thousands of people. For example, Whitbread PLC employs over 40,000 people and has over 2000 outlets in the UK.

Hospitality industry businesses

There are six main types of businesses within the hospitality industry:

- hotels
- restaurants
- pubs, bars and nightclubs
- hospitality services (catering provided by a hospitality business within a non-hospitality business organisation, such as a prison or a staff canteen in a government building)
- membership clubs such as professional association and sporting clubs
- events organisers such as businesses running music events, meetings and conferences.

Let's consider some of these organisations in a little more detail.

Hotels

The hotel sector of the hospitality industry is large. There are just over 46,000 hotels and guest houses in the UK (*Trends and Statistics 2008*, British Hospitality Association). There are about a quarter of a million people employed in hotels in the UK.

Hotels can be grouped into these categories:

- bed and breakfast (B&B) accommodation
- budget hotels
- one-star to five-star hotels.

What all hotels have in common is that they offer rooms to their guests in exchange for payment. All hotels have guest bedrooms and bathrooms (although sometimes bathrooms have to be shared). Larger hotels also have public spaces such as large foyers, private meeting rooms and

Activity: Businesses in the hotel sector

Visit a local town in small groups and find businesses in the hotel sector. Note down the name of each hotel. Is it a star-rated hotel? If so, how many stars does it have? Is it a budget hotel or bed and breakfast accommodation?

Share your findings with other groups in your class. Do you think that visitors to your area have a good choice of hotel accommodation?

conference facilities for business meetings, and function rooms.

Hotels are given ratings (from one star to five star) according to the range and quality of their facilities. Budget hotels and bed and breakfasts are not categorised on the same basis but, like the one-star to five-star hotels, the price guests pay usually reflects the standard of the accommodation and facilities.

Restaurants

The restaurant sector is the largest part of the hospitality industry in terms of the number of people employed and the number of outlets. In 2008, there were approximately 70,200 restaurants in Great Britain, of which 86 per cent were in England, 9 per cent in Scotland and 5 per cent in Wales. Nearly one-fifth of all restaurants in England are in London.

A lavish suite at an expensive hotel. What kind of service do you think this hotel offers its customers?

According to the Labour Force Survey, 567,600 people work in the restaurant industry in the UK. There is a 50 : 50 between the number of men and women working in restaurants.

The restaurant industry can be grouped into several categories.

- Fast-food establishments – these include international chains such as McDonald's, Burger King and KFC, as well as fish and chip shops and sandwich bars.
- Cafés and coffee shops – again, these include big chains such as Starbucks, Costa Coffee and Caffè Nero as well as small local cafés and teashops.
- Chain restaurants – such as Caffè Uno, Pizza Hut and Nando's.
- Fine dining – these are restaurants offering high-quality food at expensive prices. An example is Gordon Ramsay's restaurant at Claridge's, the London hotel. In this restaurant, guests can expect to pay £70 per person for a three-course meal.

Restaurants can also be classified by the type of cuisine, such as Chinese, Indian and Italian.

 Did you know?

McDonald's operates over 1,250 restaurants in the UK, employing more than 1.5 million people. However, Subway is now the largest chain in the world, with 33,749 sites globally (Source: www.caterersearch.com).

 Activity: Chain restaurants

List three advantages for customers visiting a chain restaurant such as Pizza Hut or Nando's.

Pubs, bars and nightclubs

In 2007, there were 57,600 pubs, bars and nightclubs in Great Britain. Within England, the highest concentration of pubs, bars and nightclubs is in the south-east.

Pubs and bars provide alcoholic and non-alcoholic drinks, and some also provide food. Pubs can be categorised by their type of ownership.

- Managed houses are owned by a brewery, which employs managers and staff who work in the outlet.
- Tenanted or leased pubs are owned by a brewery but occupied by a licensee, who holds the licence for the pub and serves the brewery's own beer.
- Free houses are owned and managed by the licensee, who is free to serve beer and alcoholic drinks from any supplier.

Nightclubs are establishments that play music and have dance areas, and where food and drink can also be consumed. Clubs charge an entrance fee. Some large hotels have clubs within them. Many social clubs, for example rugby clubs, have bars and restaurants that provide important additional funding.

What sort of food is served in a typical pub?

Types of settings

One way of grouping these industries is to divide them into the commercial sector, the catering services sector and contract catering in the workplace.

Commercial sector

The commercial sector includes any hospitality and catering businesses that have as their main source of income the sale of food and drink and/ or accommodation. Businesses such as hotels, restaurants and fast-food outlets, and pubs and bars fall into this category.

Catering services sector

Some organisations have to provide food and drink for their workers, clients, residents or visitors even though this is not their primary purpose. For example, all hospitals and prisons and many schools and colleges provide catering. The catering services sector includes businesses that offer catering outside the workplace, for example at events, in theatres or at sports venues.

The catering services sector provides food and drink services within these organisations. According to the latest survey by the British Hospitality Association, 1.607 billion meals were served by UK contract caterers in 2009.

Contract catering in the workplace

Some organisations run their own in-house catering operations. However, the catering services in many schools, colleges, universities, hospitals, prisons, residential and nursing homes and large private companies are managed by a contract catering company. Major contract catering companies include Aramark, Compass Group and Sodexo.

Contract catering companies manage the catering in many different types of organisation. For example, the refectory or restaurant in many colleges will be run and managed by a contract catering company. This company will be responsible for providing food and drink to people on the premises, including students, lecturers and visitors.

Contract catering companies are often invited to tender (bid) for the contract to run the catering services within an organisation. Usually there will be some competition, so a contract caterer must try to offer a quality service at the best possible price. The winner of the tender will then run the catering provision for the organisation for a fixed period of time, which will be set out in a contract for the service.

Unlike hotels, restaurants, pubs and clubs, which expect employees to work evenings and weekends, employees of a contract catering company are less likely to be required to work weekends or evenings on a regular basis. Many contract caterers are only required to provide a service during office or normal business hours. However, some contract catering businesses are also involved in events management and offer corporate packages for concerts and sporting events, as well as bespoke packages to meet the individual needs of a client.

Activity: Contract catering companies

Find out if your school or college has a contract caterer. If so, find out the name of this caterer. How big is this contract catering company?

Below are the logos of three well-known contract catering companies. Can you name four more?

Activity: Sectors of the hospitality industry

Draw up two posters, one that clearly explains the commercial sector of the hospitality industry and the other the catering services sector. In both posters describe the types of setting that businesses in each sector operate in.

Influences on the industry

The economic climate has a direct impact on all industries. If potential customers are earning good wages and their rent or mortgage, and their food, fuel and utility bills, are affordable, they will have spare money to spend. This is called disposable income. There are many things competing for this disposal income. For example, you might spend your spare money on:

- music downloads
- DVDs
- games
- clothes
- new gadgets
- going out.

We all make choices about how we spend our money. These are influenced by the media (what we read in magazines and newspapers and see on television), by our friends and by our particular interests.

The hospitality industry is also subject to many influences. Hospitality businesses must take these influences into account when planning their operations and delivering their services. The influences on the hospitality industry can be categorised as:

- social
- political
- economic
- technological
- environmental
- legal.

Let's consider one example of each of these influences.

Social influences concern people's attitudes, tastes and opinions. Today more people want to eat organic food and know how food is produced. Many hospitality businesses are changing their menus to reflect this trend.

Economic factors can influence demand for hospitality services. During a **recession** or periods of low economic growth, people do not have as much disposable income as in times of an economic boom. People become

Key terms

Recession – a downturn in the activity of the economy. Spending slows and demand for goods and services is reduced, and unemployment can increase.

Responsible sourcing – a policy by companies to take social and environmental considerations into account when dealing with suppliers.

Fair trade – a movement that aims to help producers in developing countries obtain better trading conditions and promote sustainability.

more interested in value for money. Pubs and restaurants need to offer money-off vouchers and discounts to encourage people to eat out more.

Political campaigns and government decisions can impact on the hospitality industry. Celebrity chef Jamie Oliver has raised awareness of the nutritional value of school meals. His campaign has led to government pressure to change the school meals menu. This has had an impact on contract caterers.

Technology plays a role in how people access hospitality services. Customers can now book restaurant tables, hotel rooms or spa days 24 hours a day from their computers or phones. Most hospitality businesses need an online presence.

Environmental changes can impact on the hospitality industry. Climate change could affect the tourist industry. Some hospitality businesses are being proactive by adopting a policy of **responsible sourcing** or by using **fair trade** products.

How has the Internet influenced the hospitality industry?

All industries must be concerned for the health and safety of their employees and customers, and must meet their legal obligations. Hospitality is no exception. Businesses are bound by the law. There is often a cost to the business in meeting its legal requirements, but this can save thousands of pounds in damages that might result from a negligence claim.

Case study: The cost of poor health and safety

A kitchen worker who suffered a serious leg break and concussion in an accident at work will walk with a limp for the rest of her life. The worker slipped and her leg crashed into the dishwasher. This caused some trays full of crockery to fall and they landed on the employee's leg, breaking it in two places. She hit her head on the hard tiled floor.

In court, her employer was ordered to pay over £36,000 including prosecution costs. The judge hearing the case ruled that the serious accident could have been prevented easily if the employer had taken the correct steps to comply with the law and protect its employees from physical harm.

The court heard that four other accidents that had taken place in this kitchen in the previous eight months. The health and safety inspector who visited the restaurant after the worker broke her leg discovered that the kitchen floor became very slippery when even small amounts of water or grease were spilled. Mats had been put down in some parts of the kitchen, such as in the dish wash area, but even these did not provide safe walking conditions. Scientists examined the tiled floor surface and the matting. They found that that risk of slipping was extremely high. The floor surface was clearly not fit for the purpose.

The inspector served an improvement notice on the company that require it to deal with the slip risks to employees at all its sites. The company eventually had to replace the floor surface in its kitchens. The new flooring provides enough grip when wet, greasy or soiled by food contaminates.

The case study shows what can happen if a business fails to provide a safe working environment and one of its employees is seriously injured. Not only does the company have to take action to sort out the problem, it has to pay compensation to the injured employee as well as its own legal expenses.

Businesses need to be aware of all legislation and regulations that govern their operations. This includes legislation relating to:

- the minimum wage
- the licensing of any premises serving alcohol
- terms of employment, including maternity leave and redundancy
- discrimination in the workplace.

Activity: Do we really care?

In groups, consider some of the possible influences on the hospitality industry by discussing these questions.

- Do you think television cookery shows encourage people to cook and eat at home rather than going out for a meal?
- Do you think people are really interested in where their food comes from? Do we truly care if food is healthy?
- Do all employers really provide a safe environment for employees and customers? Why is it in an employer's own interests to pay attention to health and safety?

Make some notes on your group's conclusions.

The economic importance of the hospitality industry

The hospitality, leisure, travel and tourism sector is one of the UK's largest employers. It employs almost two million people, which equates to about 7 per cent of the UK workforce. Other areas that are directly linked to hospitality, such as gambling, holiday parks, youth hostels and visitor attractions, employ another 270,500 people.

Economic value of the industry

The hospitality industry contributes over 8 per cent of the UK's gross domestic product (GDP). It generated £114 billion in sales in 2010.

As well as this direct contribution to the UK economy, the hospitality industry also supports economic activity in two other ways. First, it supports the tourist industry directly. Both UK and overseas tourists rely on the hospitality industry for accommodation (hotels and B&Bs) and food and drink (restaurants and cafés).

Second, it supports other UK industries indirectly. The nearly two million people who work in hospitality spend their wages on goods and services. This provides business for companies in other sectors. This creates a virtuous circle as these companies can employ more staff, who then spend their wages on goods and services including those offered by hospitality outlets.

Relative size of the sectors within the hospitality industry

In 2010, in the UK, there were approximately:

- 30,000 hotels
- 19,000 types of other accomodation
- 49,000 pubs
- 30,000 restaurants.

A consultancy firm called Horizons regularly publishes data about the hospitality industry. From their data, we can work out which types of hospitality business are most numerous (see Figure 1). Pubs and hotels are the largest settings.

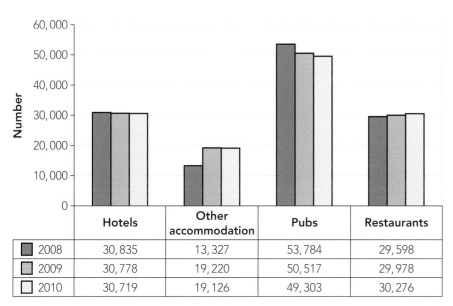

	Hotels	Other accommodation	Pubs	Restaurants
2008	30,835	13,327	53,784	29,598
2009	30,778	19,220	50,517	29,978
2010	30,719	19,126	49,303	30,276

Figure 1: The hospitality industry, 2008–2010.

Activity: Why are there fewer public houses?

Although pubs are still numerous, their numbers have declined in recent years. Discuss why the pub sector has been badly affected by the recent economic downturn.

Employment opportunities

People 1st estimates that, by 2017, the hospitality industry will have 69,000 more managerial jobs than in 2007. This will increase the demand for graduates. This does not mean that there will be no jobs for those without Higher National Diplomas or degrees. As we shall see when we consider jobs in the next section, there are many opportunities within the hospitality sector.

In the short term, the hospitality industry, like many others, is being affected by the uncertainties in the UK and the world economy. This means that there might be fewer opportunities than in periods of strong economic growth. However, the industry will get a boost when London hosts the Olympic Games in 2012. This will benefit the hospitality industry as people will come to London from all over the world to participate in and to watch the games. These people will spend money on accommodation, food, souvenirs, travel and entertainment. Many are likely to visit other parts of the UK. There is much to look forward to as far as the hospitality industry is concerned.

Transferability of skills to other professions

People who train for and work within hospitality have transferable skills. These are skills that can be applied in many work situations and many different sectors. People in the hospitality industry have:

- communication skills – they know how to communicate orally and in writing
- problem-solving skills – they know how to deal with issues and problems and have the ability to find a practical solution using the time and resources available
- teamwork skills – they have the ability to work well with others, to interact effectively and to co-operate productively
- information technology skills – they have the the ability to use IT tools to enhance their job role.

These skills are useful in many jobs. They will be valuable when someone moves into different roles within the hospitality industry or if they get a job in another industry. For example, a hotel receptionist has a similar set of skills to someone working in retail as a customer service adviser, to a receptionist in a medical surgery or to a flight attendant.

Assessment activity 1   Unit 1     BTEC

You are working for a national hotel chain. You have been asked to produce an article about the hospitality industry for the company's internal newsletter.

1   Start by providing a definition of the terms 'hospitality' and 'catering'. This should make it clear what these two parts of the industry are about. **P3**

2   In the next section of your article, compare and contrast hospitality businesses in each of these sectors of the industry:

- hotel
- restaurant
- pub
- bar or nightclub
- contract food service provider
- hospitality service
- membership club
- events business.

Choose one business from each sector of the industry (e.g. one hotel, one restaurant, one pub, etc.) and create a table to explain the different features of each one. Make sure you choose a mix of local and national examples. You will need to describe the location of the business, its size and whether it is a local business or part of a national chain. List any other distinctive features. For example, when describing your chosen hotel, state whether it has a star rating or is a budget hotel. **P1**

Now summarise your findings by explaining in more detail how businesses in the hospitality industry might operate. For example, you need to explain clearly how a fast-food restaurant is different from a five-star restaurant, and how a bar is different from a nightclub. Consider also the 'star' and other rating systems. Take each sector and give some examples to show how its businesses operate in different ways. **P6**

3   Explain how the commercial sector is different from the catering service sector. **P7**

4   Identify the structure, scope and size of the hospitality and catering industry. You need to list the sectors of the industry and describe the types of business in each sector. Then give an indication of the number of businesses in each sector. You could do this as a flow diagram or table. **P4**

To achieve **M1** you will need to analyse the structure, scope and size of the different settings of the hospitality industry. You should carry out some extra research so you can give more detail about the different factors that influence the structure, size and scope of business in:

- the commercial sector
- the catering and services sector. **M1**

5   Describe the influences that the following factors have on the hospitality industry:

- social factors
- economic factors
- political factors
- technological factors
- environmental factors
- legal factors.

Do some factors have a bigger impact than others? Give reasons for your answer. **P2**

Next, describe how these factors have influenced the development of the hospitality and catering industry. You need to think about how the factors will shape the future of the industry. **P5**

6   Explain the importance of the industry to the UK economy. Research how much money the hospitality industry makes and how many people it employs. Find out how many males and females work in the industry, and look for information about the typical ages of the workforce. Then look at the contribution of each sector within the industry and find out how many people each sector employs. Which sectors offer more part-time employment? Why do you think this is? **P8**

For **D1** you need to bring together all your information about the contribution of the hospitality industry to the UK economy and review it to form a conclusion. Give evidence to support each of your views or statements. You could discuss your ideas with your group before you complete this task. **D1**

Grading tips

In this assignment, you need to provide an overview of the hospitality industry and investigate the different sectors. You need to cover each task to ensure that you meet all the learning outcomes. You need to show that you understand the difference between 'hospitality' and 'catering'; the different types of organisations and the difference between the commercial and catering sectors. You need to investigate the structure, size and scale of the hospitality industry so you can show that you know the importance of hospitality to employment and income.

To obtain the higher grades, you need to analyse (examine in detail) the size and structure of the hospitality industry and the range of sectors and businesses within the industry. You also need to evaluate the contribution of the hospitality industry to the UK economy.

PLTS

Remember that good **independent enquirers** do not restrict their search to just one website. **Creative thinkers** ask questions when undertaking visits to local hospitality businesses. **Self-managers** organise time and resources, prioritising actions to manage assessment activities.

Functional skills

Using the Internet for researching the hospitality industry will help you develop your **ICT** skills. You will need to search for information, decide what information to use and evaluate the information you download.

You will be using **ICT** to do your assignment, and you will have to decide on a suitable format for your work. You may decide to use mainly text, but you may put some information in a table or use an image to make your assignment look more like a newsletter article. By doing this you will show you can develop, present and communicate information.

You will demonstrate **English** skills when you read the information you have gathered during your research and you will demonstrate your writing skills as you are preparing your article.

1.2 Understand the national and international employment opportunities available in the hospitality industry

In this section, we will consider the jobs and employment opportunities in the hospitality industry in some detail, including:

* staffing
* jobs
* job requirements
* legal requirements
* sources of information
* professional associations.

Staffing

There are many different types of jobs in the hospitality industry. All hospitality businesses require staff. Smaller businesses will naturally have fewer staff. For example, a country pub serving food and drink may only have eight staff, and a busy fast-food outlet may employ 20 staff. Contract caterers could have between 3 and 30 staff at each location at which they provide a service, depending on the size of the operation. At the other end of the scale, the five-star Bellagio Hotel in Las Vegas has over 9000 staff.

Managers

Managers are the people in charge of running and managing an outlet or a major part of a hospitality business.

Many hospitality businesses have a general manager who has overall responsibility for the business. Then there may be several department managers who report to the general manager. For example, there might be a restaurant manager, housekeeping or accommodation services manager, head chef and front of house manager.

Some of the responsibilities at managerial level are to:

- prepare staff schedules (rotas)
- carry out staff training
- help set budgets and monitor spending
- ensure that wages are paid
- ensure that all procedures are followed
- make sure the business complies with all relevant legislation
- ensure that the supervisors are doing their jobs
- ensure that all goods are ordered on time
- set and monitor standards.

A front of house manager has to make sure the hotel's reception has enough staff to cover busy periods. What are the other duties of the front of house manager?

Supervisors

The level below a manager is known as a supervisor. Supervisors report to their department managers, who will tell them what work needs to be done. Supervisors are found in hotels, restaurants and contract catering businesses.

Some of the responsibilities of a supervisor are to:

- ensure that staff are dressed appropriately
- ensure that customer needs are being met
- process customers' bills
- receive orders and deliveries
- ensure that work procedures are being followed
- supervise craft and operative staff
- deal with customer complaints
- pass on orders from managers.

Activity: A visit to a hospitality business

On your course you may have the opportunity to visit a hotel or large contract catering unit with your tutor. During this visit, try to identify the management and supervisory jobs at this business.

Craft staff

Staff who have trained to acquire specific practical skills are called craft staff. They may have trained for several years to develop these skills and achieved recognised qualifications to prove their ability.

For example, chefs and cooks are craft staff as they have trained to achieve their skills. It is also possible to train to specialise in advanced food or drink service.

Operative staff

The main responsibility of operative (or operational) staff is to carry out the day-to-day tasks needed for the business to run smoothly. The operational staff will have most contact with the guests. Operational staff include:

- bar staff, who serve drinks to guests
- waiting staff, who serve food to guests
- housekeeping staff, who clean the guest rooms
- reception staff, who welcome guests.

Figure 2 shows a typical organisation chart for a large hotel. There are several levels to the organisation. Generally the higher up you are in the organisation chart, the more you get paid and the more responsibilities you have. However, it is important to remember that people at all levels contribute to the running and the success of a hospitality business.

- How could a hotel manage without the housekeeping staff to clean the guest rooms?
- How could a hotel do without the kitchen porters who clean the pots and pans?
- How would the restaurant manager cope without waiting and bar staff to serve the guests food and drink?

The answer to all these questions is that the business could not run without these crucial operational staff.

 Activity: Operational staff

In groups, list all the responsibilities that the main operative staff, such as waiting staff, room service attendants and reception staff, have in a hotel.

Responsibilities

It is very important that everyone in a hospitality business knows their job role and understands their responsibilities at work. You may have

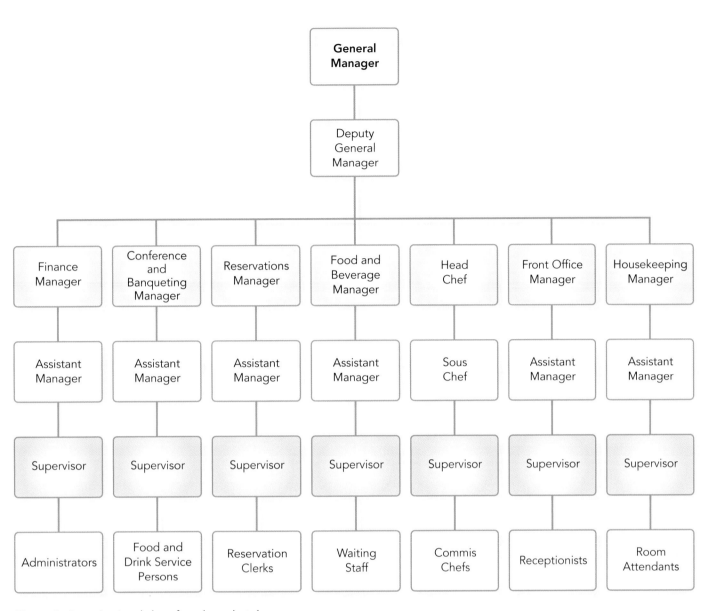

Figure 2: Organisational chart for a large hotel

daily and weekly responsibilities. If you are working in a restaurant, you will need to know the daily specials and what is in each dish on the menu. This will enable you to promote the specials and answer any questions that guests may have about the food being served. You may also need to fill the salt and pepper pots each week. If you are working in a bar, you will need to check that you have a float in the till when you open up, to ensure that the doors are open on time and that all the shelves have been restocked.

You also have a responsibility to get to work ready to start on time, and that you are in the correct uniform (if you have one) and looking presentable. You should carry out your job role to the best of your ability and ask others if you are uncertain of anything or if you cannot deal with a situation. If a customer becomes angry and starts shouting at you, it is far better to fetch your supervisor. A supervisor has the authority to deal with and resolve the complaint.

Working relationships

Relationships among staff in the hospitality industry have to be good in order for the business to run smoothly. Relationships need to be built both across the organisation and up and down the managerial chain.

Staff in different departments rely on each other to do their jobs effectively. If the departments cannot work well together and support each other, the result will be a poorly run business.

Activity: Support staff

Look at these two lists of staff. Draw up pairs of staff (with one from each list in every pair) that you think support each other most closely in their day-to-day work.

Reception staff	Chefs
Restaurant staff	Room service attendants
Conferencing and banqueting manager	Head housekeeper
Front of house manager	Head chef

Typical work routines

Work routines are planned for most operative level staff. This will vary according to the job role. Work routines may be set out on a card. This will list the tasks that need to be performed and the order in which they need to be carried out. Figure 3 gives two examples of work routines. These routines give a general insight into the types of task undertaken by operative staff in the hospitality industry. The specific tasks undertaken in these roles will vary slightly in different establishments.

The organisational structure will show to whom each member of staff should report. Most organisations have teams that work in an area together, and each team often has a supervisor. In some establishments several teams work within an area and there might be a manager overseeing these teams.

It is important to know who you need to report to, and the different roles of supervisors and managers. In general terms, supervisors will be responsible for the day-to-day running of the team and they will report to a manager. The manager will be responsible for the overall work of several teams.

This means, for example, that if you have a problem with your daily tasks – say you have run out of bathroom cleaner or you have found a stain on the carpet that you don't know how to remove – you would talk to your supervisor. However, if you have a more general issue, such as wanting to take a holiday, then you would need to ask the head of housekeeping or another manager.

Bar staff

Task 1   Stock the bar area with all the necessary drinks.

Task 2   Prepare lemons and oranges to put in drinks.

Task 3   Ensure that all glasses are clean and in the correct place.

Task 4   Fill ice buckets.

Task 5   Ensure that the float is in the till with sufficient change.

Task 6   Open the bar area and serve drinks to guests.

Task 7   Clear away and wash empty glasses.

Task 8   Close the bar, count the takings and store them correctly.

Task 9   Ensure that all glasses are cleaned and stored correctly.

Task 10 Replace drinks so that the bar is fully stocked for the next day.

Room attendant

Task 1 Ensure that the housekeeping trolley is stocked.

Task 2 Check each guest room is empty by knocking on the door before entering.

Task 3 Clean the room.

Task 4 Ensure the room has sufficient supplies such as soap and minibar items.

Task 5 Close and lock the room and inform the head housekeeper that the room is now ready.

Figure 3: Two example work routines

Hours of work

Hotels are open 24 hours a day, seven days a week, and catering businesses are often also open every day. Shift patterns are organised so that a business has staff in appropriate job roles whenever necessary. For this reason, staff in the hospitality industry tend to work nine-hour shifts. Full-time staff will usually be at work for five days a week.

These are some typical working hours in the industry:

- restaurant chef – 10 am to 2 pm (lunch); 5 pm to 10 pm (dinner)
- contract catering chef – 6.30 am to 3.30 pm
- hotel reception team – 6 am to 3 pm or 1 pm to 10 pm
- room attendant – 7 am to 4 pm five days a week
- waiting staff – 6 am to 10 am (breakfast); 6 pm to 11 pm (dinner).

Activity: The role of waiting staff

When you visit a restaurant, make a note of all the different tasks that are undertaken by the waiting staff. Remember that they will have been working before you even arrived and they will have tasks to do after you leave.

Jobs

There are many different job roles within the hospitality industry, such as:

- chef
- waiter
- bar person
- receptionist
- room service attendant.

Each job has a specific function and key tasks to carry out. For example, a head chef (sometimes also called executive chef or chef de cuisine) will be in charge of the whole kitchen. Head chefs are responsible for:

- creating innovative new food dishes
- ensuring that all ingredients and prepared food are of the highest quality
- managing the restaurant or kitchen's budget
- planning staff rotas and shift patterns
- recruiting, training and developing staff
- leading the kitchen team and managing performance
- liaising with other managers and guests.

In smaller restaurants, head chefs prepare and cook the food themselves, possibly with the help of a few assistants. They may even also serve guests and help clean up. Some chefs set up their own restaurant businesses. They are known as chef patrons and they will have responsibility for the management of their businesses as well as the cooking.

Activity: Hospitality jobs

In pairs, list as many different jobs roles in the hospitality industry as you can think of in ten minutes. Compare your list with those of other pairs in your group to see if they have come up with any different examples.

Job contracts

When you begin work in the hospitality industry, your employer will give you a contract. This has to be signed by you and the employer. Typical contracts should set out:

- hours of work
- duties expected
- whether a uniform is to be worn or any dress code
- salary or hourly rate for the job
- holiday allowance
- sick pay
- **period of notice**.

There are many different types of contracts offered to employees in the hospitality industry.

- Full-time contract – these are for people who work five or more days a week.
- Part-time contracts – this type of contract is for people who work less than a full working week. Someone working on a part-time basis may, for example, work three days a week. Part-time contracts will specify the number of days or the total number of hours to be worked each week.
- Permanent contracts – these are issued for any job offered on a permanent basis. This means that the job holder becomes a permanent member of staff. Most full-time and part-time contracts are permanent contracts.
- Temporary contracts – these are issued when a job role will only exist for a fixed period of time. For example, a temporary contract would be issued to someone working as maternity cover. The job is only available while the person normally in that job is on maternity leave.
- Seasonal contracts – the hospitality industry employs many staff on a seasonal basis to provide cover for extremely busy periods. Many students work for the hospitality industry on a seasonal basis in their Christmas, Easter and summer holidays.
- Live-in contracts – this type of contract is common in large hotels that provide accommodation for their staff. Staff on live-in contracts will have some deductions from their pay for the accommodation, and they will be given instructions on how the accommodation is to be looked after and other house rules.
- Freelance contracts – these are issued to people who are **self-employed**. For example, a hospitality business may commission a freelance person to provide some staff training. The contract will state the fee for the work, how long the work is expected to take, the number of employees to be trained and the location of the training.

Note that some staff who work in an organisation may be employed by another company. For example, contract catering companies provide services to organisations like hospitals that need to provide meals to patients and staff. Staff working in these restaurants and kitchens are employed by the contract caterers, not the hospital, so their contract is drawn up by the contract catering company. The contract catering company would also have to sign a contract with the organisation receiving the catering service.

Factors to consider in choosing jobs

The type of job you do, and the type of contract you are offered, will undoubtedly have an effect on your lifestyle. You need to take this into account when choosing a job and a career path. You also need to remember that your circumstances might change. As you get older your lifestyle will change: you may get married, have children and want to buy a house.

Key terms

Period of notice – the amount of warning employees have to give when they resign from their jobs. Typically, staff have to give one month's notice before they can leave a business. This gives their employer time to find a replacement.

Self-employed – a person is self-employed if they work for themselves rather than for one company or business. People such as electricians and window cleaners are often self-employed. They charge their customers or clients on a job-by-job basis.

As Jamal and Katrina's stories show (see the case study), our lifestyles can affect our choice of job, and equally our choice of job can affect our lifestyles. The case study clearly shows how different jobs suit different lifestyles. You must decide when you are ready to work what will be the right job for you, and which job will give you the lifestyle that you would like to have.

Case study: Jamal and Katrina

Jamal is 20, single and a full-time student studying management at Leeds University. When he is not at university he lives with his parents in his home town of Lincoln. Jamal needs to earn money in the holidays to take back to university. When he is home, he works in a restaurant and is happy to work every evening and weekend. In fact, Jamal is willing to work as many hours as possible. Most of his friends live in Leeds, so Jamal would just be bored sitting at home if he was not working.

1 In what ways does Jamal's holiday job affect his lifestyle?

2 Why is the restaurant job the right one for Jamal?

3 What type of contract would Jamal have?

Katrina is 35 and married with two children. Her younger child is only a few months old. Katrina needs to work in order to help support her family. Her husband is a nightclub manager. He starts work at 6 pm and finishes at 3 am. Katrina has applied for a part-time job as a housekeeper at a hotel, which is only 15 minutes' walk from her home. The hours of work are 7 am to 3 pm.

4 How would this job give Katrina a suitable lifestyle?

5 What type of contract would Katrina have?

Job requirements

For all the different jobs in the hospitality industry, there are certain requirements needed from the staff.

Qualities

Unit 7 covers the type of qualities that are required of staff working in the hospitality and related industries. However, it is useful to briefly set out the type of qualities required in hospitality work. These include:

- punctuality
- honesty
- personality
- efficiency.

You must be on time. If you are late, then you will be letting yourself down and those who work with you. Imagine you are the only breakfast chef in a hospital – if you are late for work, who would be available to prepare and cook breakfasts for the patients?

In any job staff must always be honest. It is very difficult to work with people who sometimes tell lies, as you never know if they are telling the truth. Some people find it hard to be honest if they have made a mistake.

Often it seems easier to tell a lie to cover up the mistake, but nine times out of ten you will be found out, so it is always better to be honest.

You will find that people working in the hospitality industry have some similar personality traits. The main factor they have in common is that they like to work with people. You tend not to get shy people working in the industry, as you really need to be outgoing and confident when dealing with the public.

Most of the jobs in the hospitality industry require staff to be able to work quickly and under pressure. A contract caterer may have to serve 500 lunches in 2 hours. Staff working in The Ballroom in the Dorchester Hotel in London could be serving drinks to 1000 people. You have to be efficient, and you have to be able to work to deadlines. To do this, you need to be organised.

Trust is an important quality in hospitality, especially when handling money. What other personal qualities are important in the hospitality industry?

Skills

In Unit 7 we will look at the many skills that staff must have when working in the hospitality industry. In this section, we will also consider some of the skills that are needed in any hospitality setting.

Using initiative

You need to have the ability to act independently. To show initiative means that you are able to think for yourself, so that when faced with a situation you have not experienced before you can work through the situation without having to ask another member of staff.

Let's consider an example of how to use initiative. Suppose a chef runs out of a product such as salmon. A hotel chef unable to use initiative would simply tell the waiting staff that the kitchen had run out and offer no alternative. A chef who uses initiative would try to source some salmon from a local shop or another restaurant. If this does not produce results, the chef would substitute the salmon with an alternative fish dish.

You will be able to show initiative more often as you gain experience. In the hospitality business unexpected situations and problems arise on a daily basis, so staff soon become very good at using their initiative.

Taking responsibility

Experienced staff generally train new members of staff. This training is usually quite brief. The new members of staff are then expected to carry out their job role.

If you are starting work in a bar, on your first day you will be shown how to work the till, the location of the different drinks and glasses, how to pour drinks and how to work the glass-washing machine. This will all be covered in a matter of hours. When the bar opens to the public, you will then be expected to start serving drinks.

Taking responsibility starts right here. You are now responsible for serving the drinks in the right glasses. You are also responsible for taking the customers' money and giving the correct change.

Following instructions

When you first start work you will be given a set of instructions. These will apply to the department in which you will be working. For example, a receptionist may be given instructions on how to:

- take or cancel bookings
- welcome guests
- answer the telephone
- deal with complaints
- deal with departures, including the paying of bills
- contact the correct taxi companies
- direct guests to local attractions.

Every department of a hospitality business will have a set of instructions that new staff have to follow. It is very important that staff follow these instructions. The instructions are issued for a purpose and if they are not followed, guests, other employees or the business itself may be at risk. If a new chef does not cook food properly, the guests in the restaurant may get food poisoning and become very ill.

There are many different rules that staff must follow concerning health, safety and security. These rules are there to protect staff and customers. When new members of staff join a company, they will always be trained in health, safety and security and told the rules and procedures that must be followed. These are rules that must not be broken. Failure to observe health, safety and security rules could result in a member of staff being asked to leave the job.

Working as a member of a team

Good working relationships and good teamwork are essential in the hospitality industry. Most jobs in a hospitality setting require teamwork:

- one chef cannot cook all the lunches
- one room attendant cannot clean all the rooms
- one waiter cannot serve all the guests
- one bar tender cannot serve all the drinks in a busy bar or club.

Teamwork is essential both within departments and also across different departments:

- reception staff need the housekeeping staff to tell them when rooms are ready for new guests
- housekeeping staff need the reception team to let them know of any early arrivals
- waiting staff need the chefs to cook the meals ordered by customers
- chefs need the waiting staff to serve the food they have prepared.

Look back at the organisation chart (Figure 2, page 19). You have to view the chart as a group people working as one team. All the people in the team have the same goal, which is to provide the best service to the guests.

Personal presentation

Most jobs in the hospitality industry require staff to wear a uniform. It is important that staff wear uniforms because:

- staff look smart if they are all dressed to the same standard
- guests can identify staff by their uniform
- uniforms can protect staff from harm – a chef's long apron and trousers are designed to protect against spillages causing burns
- staff who look smart give a good impression of the business.

It is not enough just to wear a clean uniform. Staff must also ensure that:

- they are clean
- their hair is tidy
- they do not show body piercings
- they do not wear jewellery (except a wedding ring)
- they do not wear nail varnish or too much make-up.

Employers should provide their staff with the correct uniform. Some employers also arrange for the uniforms to be cleaned.

It is important to meet customer expectations. If you go for afternoon tea at the Ritz, you would not expect to be served by waiting staff in ripped jeans and with messy hair. At the Ritz all staff are immaculately dressed in the same uniform. In restaurants such as Pizza Hut, you will also see staff in the same uniform. Often bar staff will wear the same type of shirt or identical T-shirts.

Uniforms can set the standard of a business. A member of staff who does not wear the correct uniform will stand out and will soon be asked to change.

Why is it useful for different staff members to wear different uniforms?

Activity: Interviewing members of staff

This activity requires you to interview members of staff in hospitality businesses at their work. Your tutor may need to organise these visits and may arrange for you to talk to the staff in pairs or small groups.

You should visit one business in the commercial sector and one business in the catering services sector. If your school or college uses a contract caterer, you may be able to talk to staff that work for this organisation.

You need to speak to two members of staff in each sector to find out about their job roles. Find out what tasks they are required to do. Record your answers and share them with the group when you are next in class.

Compare the jobs in the sectors, and try to see the differences and similarities. For example, how could a **commis chef**'s job role in a five-star hotel differ from that of a commis chef working for a contract caterer in a school?

Key term

Commis chef – a trainee chef. This is usually the most junior position in a kitchen.

Legal requirements

All employees need to be aware of the law as it applies to their work. It is important that businesses comply with the law. In this section, we will review some of the main laws and regulations that you will need to be aware of when working in hospitality.

Health and safety

The main legislation regulating health and safety is the Health and Safety at Work Act 1974. The legislation aims to:

- secure the health, safety and welfare of people at work
- protect other people from health and safety risks caused by work activities
- control the storage and use of explosive and dangerous substances.

Both employers and employees have responsibilities under this legislation. The main responsibilities of employers are to:

- ensure the health, safety and welfare of their employees
- provide and maintain safe equipment and systems of work
- make arrangements for the safe use, handling, storage and transport of articles and substances
- provide information, instruction, training and supervision
- provide a safe place of work and safe entrance and exit
- provide a safe working environment with adequate toilet, washing and changing facilities.

We have already seen the possible consequences of employers not taking these responsibilities seriously (see the case study on page 11). Employers are subject to routine visits by an environmental health officer. They can be served with an improvement notice if an officer spots a potential hazard on one of these visits. A follow-up visit will be made after a suitable length of time to ensure that appropriate action has been taken to minimise or reduce the risk. Typical examples of workplace hazards include trailing electrical cables that someone could easily trip over, blocked fire exits, or equipment and supplies being stacked unsafely in a storeroom regularly accessed by staff.

Employers can be prosecuted for breaches of health and safety under the Workplace (Health, Safety and Welfare) Regulations 1992 and for food hygiene offences. Heavy fines can be imposed on an offending employer. The safety of employees and customers is taken extremely seriously by the courts.

It is not just employers who have legal responsibilities for health and safety. All staff must:

- take reasonable care for their own health and safety and for others who may be affected by them

- co-operate with their employer and follow safety instructions

- not tamper with anything provided in the interests of health, safety or welfare – this is illegal and can lead to prosecution.

Employees could be liable (blamed) should their actions result in a health and safety incident. Suppose a housekeeper in a hotel mops the front hall area and forgets to put up a sign warning that the floor is wet and might be slippery. If a guest (or a fellow employee) slips on the floor and is injured, the housekeeper is responsible for the accident. This is because the housekeeper did not take the necessary steps to ensure the health and safety of others.

Hazardous substances

The Control of Substances Hazardous to Health Regulations 2002 (COSHH) covers the use and storage of dangerous substances. Examples of potentially dangerous substances include cleaning fluids, chemicals, products containing chemicals, products that produce fumes, dusts, vapours, mists and gases, and biological agents (germs).

Under this legislation, the employer is responsible for:

- assessing the risks to health from any hazardous substances used in workplace activities

- deciding on what precautions are needed, such as providing masks and goggles for employees coming into contact with the substances

- preventing or adequately controlling exposure to a dangerous substance – this could mean prevention by using safer chemicals or control by using chemicals for shorter periods of time

- ensuring that employees are properly informed, trained and supervised in the use of substances

- ensuring that substances are kept in locked storage areas

- ensuring that all substances are clearly labelled to show what they are and what they are to be used for and that instructions are provided on their safe use.

Where might you see this hazard warning sign?

Working Time Regulations

The Working Time Regulations set rules for the number of hours that can be worked in a week, about entitlements to rest breaks and about the organisation of the working week.

There are specific rules about Sunday working and night working, and about overtime work and employing part-time workers. Under this legislation, employees also have some rights to request time for training.

Lifting safely

During the working day, some hospitality employees may need to lift heavy items. Big saucepans full of water and boiled potatoes are very heavy, making beds requires bending over and lifting mattresses and working in the bar can involve lifting crates and barrels. Employees need to be trained to lift these items properly so that they do not injury themselves. The Manual Handling Operations Regulations 1992 is designed to protect employees from hurting their backs and upper limbs (arms, hands) through incorrect lifting.

Data protection

Any business that holds information about customers, such as their names, addresses and phone numbers, is required by law to keep this information safe and not pass it on to other businesses without permission. There have been several high-profile cases of employees leaving laptops on trains or losing memory sticks containing personal and sensitive information about customers. In these situations, a business can be prosecuted as it has **breached** the Data Protection Act.

The Data Protection Act 1998 is designed to make sure that any personal information you give to a business is kept safe. It should not be sold on to other organisations (without your consent), lost or misused. Businesses need to have appropriate systems in place to protect data. This means providing staff with passwords to access the information, positioning computer screens so that only authorised staff can see the personal data on the screen and training staff so that they do not give out personal information or discuss customers' personal data with anyone outside the business.

Many hospitality businesses hold personal data about not just their staff but also about their customers. A hotel or B&B, for example, will hold information about their guests' addresses, contact telephone numbers, email addresses, and credit or debit card details. All of this information has to be kept secure.

Fire prevention

Businesses have a responsibility to take measures to prevent an outbreak of a fire and to have procedures in place in case of a fire. There should be working smoke alarms, a fire alarm system and established evacuation procedures. There should also be suitable fire extinguishers in each area of all buildings. Many new hotels have also installed flashing lights and vibrating pillows in their rooms to ensure that guests with visual or hearing impairments are made aware of a fire alarm.

All staff need to be trained on how to respond when the fire alarm goes off. They need to know (and have practised) their duties during an evacuation.

The legislation concerning fire safety is the Fire Safety Regulations, Regulatory Reform (Fire Safety) Order 2005. This requires businesses

Key term

Breached – broken or disobeyed the law.

to take all practical steps to ensure safety in the event of a fire. These include having:

- a means of detection (such as smoke detectors)
- a system for giving warning in case of fire (fire alarms)
- the provision for means of escape from the buildings (marked and clear fire exits)
- the means of fighting fire (such as fire extinguishers)
- a training programme to instruct all staff in fire safety.

Employers have several responsibilities under this legislation.

- They must let their employees know of any risks to them which have been identified in the risk assessment.
- They must give new employees fire training when they start work. This should ensure that staff understand basic fire prevention and know the location of fire equipment and assembly points.
- They must ensure that all fire-fighting and detection equipment (such as smoke alarms) is maintained regularly to make sure that it is in good working order and that emergency routes are accessible and clearly marked.

Employees must co-operate with their employer to ensure the workplace is safe from fire, and must not do anything that will place themselves or other people at risk.

Personal protective equipment

Employers must provide staff with appropriate personal protective equipment (PPE). You should wear any protective equipment provided. If your employer has provided equipment and you decide not to wear the equipment, you would not be able to claim any damages from your employer if you got an injury that would have been avoided if you had been wearing the equipment. However, if an employer does not provide appropriate protective equipment, then it is breaking the law and is liable for any accidents that happen.

The law governing the provision and use of equipment is set out in the Personal Protective Equipment (PPE) at Work Regulations 1992. These are some of the guidelines that should be followed.

- Eyes – hazards to the eye include injury from chemical splash and gas. The PPE required are goggles, face shields or visors.
- Head – hazards include hair getting tangled in machinery. The PPE required are hairnets and hats to ensure that no hair is at risk of being caught in machinery.
- Hands and arms – hazards include burns, cuts, chemical splash and skin infections. The PPE required are gloves and a long-sleeved jacket for chefs.
- Feet and legs – hazards include slipping, cuts and chemical splash. The PPE required are trousers and aprons (for chefs) and safety shoes with steel toecaps.

A chef's uniform is part of their personal protective equipment. What other safety precautions should a chef take?

Reporting accidents and serious incidents

All accidents and serious incidents that happen in the work place must be reported to the Health and Safety Executive (HSE). Reporting of Injuries, Diseases and Dangerous Occurrences Regulations 1995 (RIDDOR) states that employers must report:

- work-related deaths

- major injuries – this includes amputation (loss of all or part of a limb) and loss of sight

- any accident which results in an employee being off work for more than three days

- work-related diseases – this includes some skin and lung diseases

- dangerous occurrences – this includes any collapse of a building or an explosion.

Employers have to report such occurrences so that the HSE can investigate serious accidents, identify why they occurred and recommend the necessary action to prevent them from happening again.

Food hygiene and food storage

It is very important that food is prepared and stored correctly so that customers don't become ill or get food poisoning. Research has found that each year there are 2000 cases of foreign objects, such as animal hairs, glass and metal, being found in food and medicines. This is obviously dangerous.

Food poisoning can be prevented by the correct storage, handling and cooking of food. Employers must prove that they have taken every step to prevent food becoming contaminated, otherwise they will be prosecuted under the Food Safety Act 1990.

All kitchens should have a hygienic system of the storage of dry and refrigerated goods. This is because one way to prevent food from becoming contaminated or unsafe is to store it properly.

Simple rules include:

- storing cooked meat in a separate fridge to raw or uncooked meat (or making sure that raw meat is stored at the bottom of the fridge)

- using the FIFO system (first in, first out) for all food products

- cleaning storage shelves and containers on a regular basis

- ensuring that cold food is never stored in areas that are warmer than 8°C

- keeping any hot food at a minimum 63°C before it is served.

Sources of information

There are many places you can look for information on job vacancies in the hospitality industry. These can include:

- local newspapers – as well as advertisements in the paper, they may also have an online local job search facility

- job websites – there are many websites that advertise jobs vacancies in the hospitality industry

- employers – many major employers, such as national restaurant and hotel chains, publish details of vacancies on their websites

- industry magazines – these are a good source of information about jobs and most magazines have their own websites as well.

Examples of industry publications include *Restaurant Magazine*, which is published monthly and regularly features top jobs in the industry, and *Caterer and Hotelkeeper*, which has 50 issues a year and a website for jobs.

For a list of the most useful job websites and the web addresses of some popular industry magazines, access the Hotlinks for this book (see page ii for more information).

Activity: Job search

On a weekly basis, search websites and look in your local paper for suitable hospitality jobs. Collect the adverts.

Then extend your search by looking at the websites of major employers like Best Western, McDonald's, Whitbread and JD Wetherspoon. To get the web addresses use a search engine or access the Hotlinks for this book (see page ii for more information). You may need to search each website very carefully to find the link to the careers and job vacancies section.

Professional associations

Professional associations act as the voice of their members. They raise awareness of issues that concern or affect their members. In order to join a professional association, you need to pay a membership fee. The money raised through fees is used by the association to work for its members.

A professional association may work with the government to tackle a national issue. For example, the Wine and Sprit Association has produced the drink responsibility campaign to meet government concerns about binge drinking and the misuse of alcohol. The campaign uses signs, drink mats in pubs and bars, slogans on alcohol packaging and point-of-sale displays in retailers to deliver its message. It uses the **strapline** 'Why let good times go bad?' to support the message.

Key term

Strapline – a slogan used to identify a brand.

Key term

Mandatory – compulsory so it has to be done.

Associations might lobby the government about any planned changes in the law that might affect its members. Sometimes the government might consult with a professional association if it is planning to change the law, so that new regulations get the backing of the association.

Associations keep their members aware of changes in laws that will affect them. For example, the British Institute of Innkeeping (BII) posted reminders when the second set of **mandatory** conditions for alcohol retailers came into force. These require all licensed premises and retailers to have an age verification policy and to only make certain drinks available in small measures.

We will now briefly introduce some of the associations active in the hospitality sector. The websites of these organisations can be found by going to the Hotlinks for this book (see page ii for more information).

Activity: Job search

Discuss as a group why it is important for a hospitality business to be aware of any planned changes in the law that might affect its operations.

British Hospitality Association (BHA)

This is the national trade association for hotels, restaurants and caterers. Its primary role is to lobby government across the UK and in Europe and to represent the views of the hospitality industry. The British Hospitality Association has been representing the hotel, restaurant and catering industry for over 100 years.

Association of Valuers of Licensed Property (AVLP)

This association offers its members access to specialist advice from surveyors and valuers when they want to buy a hospitality property. The surveyor will check if the building is safe and in a suitable condition to buy, and should identify any problems such as dry rot or subsidence. Valuers will estimate the market value of the property.

One of the aims of the association is to maintain some consistency in both professional standards and the approach to the valuation of licensed premises.

Association of Licensed Multiple Retailers (ALMR)

The ALMR is the association that represents the interests of the smaller independent retailers and industry supply companies that own and operate pubs, bars and restaurants in UK.

British Institute of Innkeeping (BII)

The BII has two roles. The first is to represent the licensed retail sector (such as pubs and bars). The second is to raise professional standards through its training and awarding body, the British Institute of Innkeeping Awarding Body (BIIAB). This means that the association has its own set of qualifications that are aimed specifically for people who want to work within the licensed retail trade.

Assessment activity 2

Unit 1

You work in the human resources department of a national hotel chain. You have been asked to provide a section for the new staff induction pack about national and international job opportunities in the hospitality industry. The booklet needs to help new recruits see the benefits of a career in the hospitality industry.

1   List five job roles in hospitality businesses. You need to include jobs from different sectors so that new employees can see the variety of jobs available. **P9**

   For **P11** give a description of the main job roles in a hospitality business. To do this, explain the roles of:

   • managers
   • supervisors
   • craft personnel
   • operatives. **P11**

2   Now explain the differences between the job roles you looked at in Task 1 so that the new recruits have an understanding of the demands of each role. You need to explain the different types of contract that can apply to these job roles. You also need to explain any legal requirements relevant to each role on your list. Think about the laws that could affect each job. Remember that concern for health and safety is part of every job, but the laws on data protection or hazardous substances (COSHH) may not apply in every role. **P10**

   Next, describe the differences between staff roles and conditions in the different sectors of the industry. Take each sector and look at the types of job opportunity and the typical contracts and conditions of employment in that sector. **P12**

   Show the similarities and differences between the requirements for two job roles in the commercial sector and, separately, two job roles in the catering service sector. **M2**

3   In order to raise awareness of the law, new recruits need to understand the legal requirements of hospitality businesses and why they must obey the law. You could do this by providing a list of relevant laws and regulations and by giving examples of things covered in this legislation. You could also give examples of the problems that arise, and the penalties that can be faced, if the laws are broken. **P13**

4   The next section of your booklet needs to cover how people find out about job opportunities. You need to identify three places people would look for information on job opportunities in the hospitality and catering industry. Provide examples of information and job adverts from each source. **P14**

5   Provide a description of the functions of professional associations related to hospitality and catering occupations to help the new recruits better understand their role in the industry. There will be useful information on the websites of each association, but remember to put this information into your own words. **P15**

6   Finally, you need to compare the requirements for two job roles in the commercial sector and, separately, two job roles in the catering service sector. **M2**

Grading tips

P11 You could visit a hospitality business to obtain this information.

P14 You could find a job advert from a newspaper, a job bulletin sheet from an employment agency, and a printout from the job vacancies page of a company website as your evidence.

PLTS

Independent enquirers use a variety of sources of information. **Self-managers** organise their time and resources, prioritising actions to manage assessment activities.

Functional skills

Using the Internet to search for jobs within the hospitality industry will help you to develop your **ICT** skills. When comparing job roles, you will need to search for information, decide what information to use and evaluate this information. You will also need to decide how to present your information.

You will demonstrate your **English** skills when you read the information you have gathered during your research and you will demonstrate your writing skills as you are preparing your booklet.

2.1 Know the products and services offered in the hospitality industry

Welcome

Products and services

At the start of these units, you made a list of ten hospitality businesses. Go back and look at this list. In pairs, list the products and services offered by each organisation. Compare your list with other pairs in your class and see if you have similar products on your list.

Products

The three main products offered by hotels, restaurants, pubs, clubs and contract catering businesses are:

- food
- drink
- accommodation.

Food

The type, quality and pricing of the food on offer varies enormously depending on the type of setting and the type of outlet. Some outlets pride themselves on offering a very wide choice of foods, even if their main business is in selling drinks.

Consider, for example, Starbucks. The core business is coffee, but the food products sold at a Starbucks coffee house include:

- biscuits and cookies
- cakes and muffins
- fruit salad
- pastries and scones

- sandwiches – many different types using various types of bread
- paninis – several lunch paninis with fillings such as mozzarella and tomato, falafel, and tuna and cheddar
- salads
- hot breakfasts – including different breakfast paninis with fillings such as cheese and Marmite, and egg and bacon.

Other catering outlets may offer a more limited menu because they have worked out exactly what appeals to their customers. For example, a transport café may offer a short menu, consisting mainly of varieties of the all-day breakfast. It will provide large portions at very reasonable prices.

Fine dining restaurants often change their menu frequently to offer food that is in season and to provide a range of specialities. Prices will be higher because the ingredients are more expensive and the dishes can only be made by very highly trained chefs.

Contract catering businesses provide a wide range of foods to different clients. For example, a school canteen will require a small number of popular dishes which are rotated regularly. Prices need to be kept quite low. At the other end of the scale, the directors' dining room in a City banking firm will need a varied menu of high-quality food. The prices would be much higher.

Now let's consider two specific examples. The Dorchester is a five-star hotel. Its main restaurant, Alain Ducasse at The Dorchester, has received the prestigious award of three Michelin stars. This denotes a restaurant serving exceptional cuisine. The restaurant is quite formal, and guests are expected to dress smartly and behave appropriately. The prices are quite high as two courses cost £55. However, the price reflects the setting, the skill in preparing the food and in sourcing high-quality ingredients.

Did you know?

There are only four restaurants in the UK that have been awarded three Michelin stars (as at January 2010). As well as Alain Ducasse at The Dorchester, they are Gordon Ramsay's restaurant in Chelsea and two restaurants in Bray in Berkshire: the Fat Duck and the Waterside Inn.

What differences would you expect to find between these two restaurants?

Customers choosing to dine at a Frankie & Benny's New York Italian Restaurant and Bar will have a very different experience. They can expect a relaxed and informal atmosphere, and the distinctive styling and decoration of a Frankie & Benny's restaurant. The menu is the same in every restaurant in the chain. It has variations of the meals on offer in an American diner and prices are around £8 to £17 for a main course.

You don't have to visit restaurants to see their menus as many outlets now make their menus available online. Access the Hotlinks for this book (see page ii for more information) to find links for the menus of Alain Ducasse at The Dorchester and Frankie & Benny's New York Italian Restaurant and Bar.

Activity: Food products offered by different hospitality settings

Below are two lists. List one has some typical food and drink products offered within the hospitality industry and list two has some types of hospitality settings.

Working in pairs, take each type of outlet or setting listed in list two in turn and note down which of the food and drink products in list one it is likely to offer.

List one: Food and drink	List two: Settings
Breakfast	B&Bs
Lunch	One-star hotels
Afternoon tea	Two-star hotels
Morning coffee	Three-star hotels
Dinner	Four-star hotels
Snacks such as peanuts and crisps	Five-star hotels
Fast food, sandwiches and light meals	Restaurants
Food for special events and conferences	Pubs
	Clubs
	Contract caterers

Now do some research to look in a little more detail at the food and drink offered at each of the settings in list two. Find typical menus and prices for each setting. You can find much of this information on the Internet, but you can also get details by visiting some local hospitality businesses. What do the types of food products on offer and the typical prices tell you about the standard of the setting?

Drink

Hotels, restaurants, pubs, clubs and catering services all provide drinks for their customers. There are three main categories of drink products:

- soft drinks, such as lemonade, orange juice and colas
- alcoholic drinks, such as beer, lager, wine, spirits and liqueurs
- hot drinks, such as tea, coffee and hot chocolate.

Any hospitality business may sell soft drinks and hot drinks, but a licence is needed to sell alcohol. The Licensing Act 2003 modernised the drinking laws and gave licencees more flexibility in deciding their opening hours. Before this legislation was introduced, most licensed premises had to stop serving by 11 pm. Now a licensee can apply to the local authority for an extension to stay open much later.

Prices for alcoholic drinks vary considerably. You are likely to pay more for a drink in a pub, club or restaurant in London than in an establishment in a small town. Prices even differ markedly in the same town. Pubs usually charge a little less than restaurants, and clubs often charge considerably more.

In pubs, clubs and restaurants, drinks are served in the bar and restaurant areas. In hotels, drinks can be consumed in many areas. Guests can drink in public areas, such as the restaurant, bar and lounge areas, as well as in their bedrooms.

Hot drinks

Today, there are many more coffee shops in the UK's high streets than in the 1970s. There are the major chains such as Starbucks and Costa Coffee, as well as many independent coffee shops. These serve many different coffees, teas and hot chocolate. When visiting a coffee shop, it is often difficult to decide which type of coffee or tea you want because there is such a large choice. For example, if you want a coffee at Starbucks, you can order:

- an espresso
- a caffè Americano
- a caffè latte
- a cappuccino
- a caffè mocha
- a caramel macchiato
- a freshly brewed filter coffee.

Starbucks, like its competitors, often adds new drinks to its menu to encourage customers to try new things and to provide options for people who don't like (or don't want) coffee or tea. So its drinks menu now includes a range of cold drinks, hot chocolate, specialist teas and Frappuccinos: the company's own range of blended ice beverages.

Just as most coffee shops offer a wide range of different types of coffee, customers in many outlets can now also get many different teas. Guests for afternoon tea at the Ritz in London are presented with a menu totally dedicated to a wide selection of teas. There are 17 teas on this menu, some you may know but most you are unlikely to recognise. They include:

- Ritz Royal English
- Darjeeling First Flush
- Ceylon Orange Pekoe
- Russian Caravan
- Lapsong Souchong Imperiale
- Jasmine with Flowers
- Rose Congou
- Chun Mee
- Oolong Formosa.

Activity: What drinks are on offer?

When you next visit a restaurant, café, fast-food outlet or coffee shop, note down the range of drinks on offer. You will find that in most places there will be plenty of choice of hot and cold drinks and, if you are on licensed premises, alcoholic drinks.

Accommodation

Hospitality settings offering accommodation include hotels, guest houses, bed and breakfasts and hostels. We shall concentrate here on hotels. Hotel accommodation can be divided into the bedrooms and the public areas.

The more luxurious hotels will have several features in their bedrooms that you would not expect to see in a bed and breakfast or tourist (budget) hotel. These might include:

- trouser press
- minibar
- satellite television
- DVD player
- CD player
- alarm clock
- Internet points or wireless Internet access
- private bathroom and shower.

Bedrooms that have separate but self-contained bathroom and toilet are known as en suite. Customers in bedrooms without this feature would have to use a separate bathroom, perhaps down a corridor, which they may share with other guests. Guests would expect to pay more for an en suite room. In general, the more facilities provided, the more expensive the room.

Most larger three-star, four-star and five-star hotels have public areas which are open to people who are not staying in the hotel. Hotels such as the Ritz and the Dorchester have public areas where they serve afternoon tea. This provides an opportunity to experience the quality and service of a beautiful luxurious hotel for people who do not wish (or cannot afford) to stay at such a hotel. Below is the menu for a typical afternoon tea at a leading hotel:

Where might you find a dining room like this?

> **Typical afternoon tea menu**
>
> Smoked salmon sandwiches
>
> Cucumber sandwiches
>
> Egg mayonnaise sandwiches
>
> Freshly made scones with Cornish clotted cream and strawberry preserve
>
> An assortment of afternoon tea pastries
>
> A selection of homemade cakes

Prices vary but typically start at around £35 per person. At the Ritz, traditional afternoon tea costs £40 per person, but the celebration afternoon tea including a birthday cake and a glass of champagne costs

£62 per person. As you can see, it costs a lot of money to have afternoon tea in a top London hotel. However, you are not only paying for the food, you are paying for the overall experience. The rooms where afternoon tea is served at these London hotels are pretty spectacular.

Prices

The price that a hospitality business charges for its goods and services is influenced by many different factors:

- the type of business
- the location of the business
- the quality of the goods and service
- the day of the week, the time of year and the season.

Each of these factors will have a bearing on how much a business can charge. A hospitality business will often have a range of prices for the same product. For example, many hotels often have different rates for their rooms:

- rack rate – this is the rate that is displayed in the hotel reception
- business rate – this is often a special rate for business customers
- Internet rate – this is often cheaper than the rack rate but available only to those booking online.

The online rate quoted for a bedroom can vary depending on the website used to make the booking, the day of the week and the time of year that the room is required, and the type of bedroom. For example, in August 2010, using Holiday Inn York's own website, a room for two adults for Tuesday 28 September 2010 (a midweek stay out of the main holiday period) and for Saturday 28 May 2011 (a weekend night on a bank holiday weekend) were quoted at:

- twin room – £70 for the night of 28 September 2010 and £108 for the night of 28 May 2011
- double deluxe – £86 for the night of 28 September 2010 and £126 for the night of 28 May 2011.

Note that, as you would expect, the double deluxe room is more expensive than the standard twin room. The prices for the rooms on the bank holiday weekend are much more expensive than those for a midweek stay in September. This is because hotels can charge more if there is likely to be high demand for their rooms. So, the **room tariff** will also depend on whether the hotel is likely to be busy. If a hotel is half empty, it is likely the room rate will be reduced to attract more customers. If it is nearly fully booked, the hotel will be able to charge the full rack rate.

Some hotels may have a lower rate at the weekend than during the week. There may be many business people staying on week nights who can afford higher prices. At the weekend most of the guests will be leisure guests or tourists with less money to spend.

Key term

Room tariff – another term used for the price of a room. Tariff means price or charge.

Activity: Comparing room tariffs

Compare the price of a room at a Holiday Inn in a town or location near your school or college. Choose two dates for a one-night stay. Make sure one night is during the week and the other is for a Friday or Saturday night, and that the dates are in different seasons.

Research the price for these rooms using four different booking sites, one of which must be the Holiday Inn's own website. You can find some hotel booking websites using the Hotlinks for this book (see page ii for more information). Make a note of the prices for rooms on each of your two dates.

In pairs, discuss the prices you have been quoted. Why do you think that there are different prices for the same product?

Just as the prices charged for accommodation can vary a great deal, so they can for other hospitality products and services. Christmas lunch costs a great deal more than Sunday lunch. A room in a B&B will cost much less than a room in a five-star hotel, and a cup of coffee in a café won't cost as much as in a restaurant.

Activity: Understanding prices

In small groups, discuss these questions and agree on a set of answers.

- Why is a B&B cheaper than a five-star hotel?
- Why can a top restaurant charge more for dinner than a country hotel, even if the food is of the same standard?
- Why are some hotel rooms cheaper at the weekend?
- Why are prices for guest houses in Blackpool different to those in the Cotswolds?
- Why do some pubs offer '2 for 1' prices for meals?
- Why do children eat for free in some restaurants?

Opening times

As consumers, we want to be able to buy goods and services when we want them, and this can be 24/7. There was a time when pubs closed at 3 pm, opened again at 6 pm and closed at 11pm. Things are different now. Many pubs are now open all day. Some pubs have even started to open early to serve breakfast. Restaurants are also open earlier on the morning and later at night than in previous years. Some McDonald's restaurants open at 5 am for breakfast, many stay open until midnight and a few are open 24 hours a day. Hotels often have 24-hour reception and many offer late night room service when the restaurant is closed.

The hospitality industry has responded to customer demand, with facilities opening earlier and staying open for longer hours. Hospitality businesses have had to adopt a more flexible approach. People can now get married on any day of the week and at any venue that is licensed to perform weddings, so hospitality providers have had to stop thinking of weddings as being always held on a Saturday and become ready to provide wedding banquets and receptions every day of the week.

Many hospitality providers have a seasonal business. A ski resort hotel is busiest over the winter months when there is snow. However, some have tried to develop more business during the traditional off-season period. Holiday locations like Blackpool and Brighton have developed new markets beyond the peak summer holiday season by building a reputation as great stag and hen party destinations.

For hospitality businesses offering food, opening hours depend on the type of outlet.

- Some pubs now serve food all day from 11 am (sometimes earlier for breakfast) through to 9.30 pm.
- Most coffee shops and cafés are open during the working day, so typical opening hours are 8 am to 5 pm.
- Restaurants tend to serve food from around noon to 2.30 pm and then reopen from 7 pm to 10 pm.
- Many hotels will serve breakfast from 7 am to 10 am, lunch from noon to 2.30 pm and dinner from 7 pm to 10 pm. Room service may be available 24 hours a day.

Services

Hospitality businesses try to meet the needs and expectations of their customers effectively. To do this, they offer a wide variety of services to meet the requirements of individual customers.

Levels and types of services

Wherever you go for a meal or a drink, you can expect the service to differ. Often the level of service you can expect reflects the price that you pay. For instance, guests paying £40 per person for afternoon tea at the Ritz would expect exceptional service, first due to the price they are paying and second because they will be sampling the products of the Ritz Hotel. However, someone having a cup of tea in a local café would not be expecting a high level of service and would expect to pay a much lower price.

Restaurant and catering services provide a range of experiences for customers. Traditionally, **silver service** was used in high-class restaurants and it is still the serving method used in some establishments. However, fewer restaurants now use this style of service, instead opting for the more familiar **plated service**.

Key terms

Silver service – a high-quality serving method where food is served by waiting staff at the table from service dishes on to customers' plates.

Plated service – a standard restaurant serving method where food is served on to plates in the kitchen and then brought to the customers' table by waiting staff.

Key terms

Counter service – a food service style where customers queue at a counter to select (if there is a choice) and receive their food.

Self-service – food service where customers help themselves from counters or buffets.

The level of service you would expect to find in the catering service sector will also vary. For example, a contract catering service in a prison will provide good quality food but will offer a fairly limited choice. Prisoners will not be given the wide ranging menu you might expect in a restaurant. The type of service would be **counter service**, similar to many school and college canteens.

There are contract catering services that operate within very wealthy institutions such as banks. These would provide high-quality food presented to a very high standard and would offer many choices. It is also likely that there would be a counter service or **self-service** for employees, and a plated service for higher level managers and directors who would dine in a restaurant within the building.

You will learn in more detail about styles of food and drink service in Units 11 and 12.

Business services

Four-star and five-star hotels will provide a range of business services for their guests. These services include:

- direct-dial phone
- secretarial support
- computer and internet access
- telephone messaging
- photocopying
- basic office supplies (paper and pens)
- postal services.

These services could be included in the room rate or provided at an additional cost to guests. They are often essential to business people staying in hotels. Many business people stay in hotels for several nights at a time. In effect, the hotel can become the guest's office, so the guest will expect the same business services that would normally be provided by a secretary or other support staff.

Vending machines

In hotels and some workplaces, vending machines allow guests and employees access to food and drink 24 hours a day. There may be vending machines dotted around your school or college. Vending machines can provide:

- food – sweets, biscuits, crisps, sandwiches and other snacks
- drinks – hot and cold drinks, cans or bottles of cold drinks
- items a hotel guest may have forgotten, such as toothpaste, tights, hairbrushes and razors.

An outside company usually owns the vending machines. A representative will come regularly to the premises to fill them up and collect the money that has been inserted into the machines.

Conference facilities

Another service that is provided by the hospitality industry is conference facilities. Large hotels tend to have the best conference facilities, although some restaurants may also provide a conference service.

What facilities are needed for a successful conference?

Many larger hotels will have several conference rooms. These are used by business and leisure customers. Each room is suitable for a certain number of people. The conference rooms are used for different purposes.

- Meetings – many businesses hire a meeting room at a hotel or restaurant if they don't have a suitable room at their own premises. They would expect the meeting room to be provided with stationery, an overhead projector and screen or smartboard, Internet access, a television and a DVD player, and they would expect refreshments during the meeting.

- Company promotions – some businesses will use conference facilities to promote their products or their operations. These promotions could include recruitment and careers fairs or launches of a new product range.

- Seminars – some businesses hire rooms to conduct seminars (discussions or training sessions). For a training event, a business may need a large room for lectures and several smaller rooms to allow participants to do group work.

Conferences can provide substantial income for a hospitality business. It can be very profitable. A hotel with good conference facilities is likely to attract additional customers.

Case study: Conference and business facilities at the Dorchester and at Premier Inns

The Dorchester is a very famous hotel. It is very beautifully decorated and luxurious. It is also has cutting-edge technology to meet its business customers' needs. The hotel can cater for up to 500 guests for a conference or a business meeting, but it also provides business services for small groups. The Dorchester employs banqueting managers to help guests plan every part of their event.

The Dorchester's services and facilities include:

- wireless broadband enabling up to 50 connections at a time
- complimentary refreshment bar (in the Business Suite)
- a team of e-butlers to help with technical requirements
- a team of chefs and a sommelier to create individual menus
- private cloakrooms
- vehicle access
- registration areas for business conferences and receptions.

Premier Inns offer a range of services for business customers. There are cost-effective meeting rooms in over 100 Premier Inn hotels located across the country. The hotel chain also offers what it calls Touchbase Business Centres at 15 locations in the UK. These are designed to be used as an office for a day, so they are kitted out with all the necessary office equipment, and there is space to hold meetings of up to 60 people. There is also a business lounge where tea and coffee is available all day.

Functions

Functions are another service that many hospitality settings can provide. Private function rooms are offered to guests who wish to hold a celebration, such as a wedding reception. Hotels and restaurants around Great Britain have function rooms that vary in size and style. The Dorchester Hotel, for example, has many function rooms, the largest of which is called The Ballroom and can accommodate up to 1000 guests.

The facilities that are provided at a function include:

- tables and chairs
- food and drink
- music
- decorations.

The Ballroom at the Dorchester

Activity: Celebrity weddings

Celebrities will often pay hundreds of thousands of pounds for their weddings. They want everything they can possibly have to make the perfect day.

Working in groups, imagine that you are organising a celebrity wedding. Create a list of the products and services that the couple would expect to be offered in a hotel.

Compare your list with another group. Did you include the same products and services?

Assessment activity 3

Unit 2  BTEC

You have just started working for a new magazine called *Meet the Hospitality Industry*. Its aim is to encourage people to consider a career in hospitality. It also provides information and articles about the hospitality industry that will be of interest to those new to hospitality.

You have been asked to produce an article for the next issue about products and services offered in the hospitality industry. You need to investigate the products and services of different businesses within one locality. This could be somewhere near where you live or some other resort or location you know well.

1 Investigate the products and type and level of service provided by three businesses in your chosen area. List the products and services offered by each business. Provide a map showing where these three businesses are located. **P1**

2 You now need to research another five hospitality businesses in your chosen locality. Explain the types of products and services offered by these businesses. **M1**

3 You now need to provide an explanation for the differences in the products and services offered by the five businesses you investigated in Task 2. **D1**

Grading tips

You need to investigate eight different businesses from within one locality – three for **P1** and five for **M1** and **D1**. Make sure that you choose businesses from different parts of the hospitality industry so that you can cover all types of products and services.

PLTS

Independent enquirers will use several different sources to identify products and services from different hospitality business.

Functional skills

Using the Internet for researching the hospitality industry will help you develop your **ICT** skills. You will need to search for information, decide what information to use and then evaluate that information.

You will need to decide on a suitable format for your article. You may decide to use text and you may put in a table or image to make your work look more like a newsletter article. By doing this you will develop skills in presenting and communicating information.

You will demonstrate **English** skills when you read the information you have gathered during your research and you will demonstrate your writing skills as you are preparing your article.

2.2 Understand support given by other industries to hospitality businesses

In order for hospitality businesses to function properly and to offer customers the products and services they expect, they need the support of other industries. These industries include:

- travel agents and tour operators
- banks
- phone companies
- insurance companies
- suppliers
- staffing agencies
- additional services such as hairdressing
- transport companies.

Other industries

Let's consider the role played by some of these other industries in supporting hospitality businesses.

Travel agents and tour operators

The hospitality and tourism industries work together to offer holidays. A package holiday is made up of many products and services, and these include accommodation. Tour operators put the package holidays together and travel agents sell these holidays to consumers. The sales may be made when a customer visits a travel agency, online through the Internet or over the telephone. Tour operators buy hotel rooms in bulk and put hotels in their brochures or on their website when advertising the package holidays.

In what ways do the hospitality and tourism industries work together?

Banks

Why would a hospitality business need the support of a bank? Banks provide financial services to the hospitality industry much as they do for individuals. Banks open business accounts for hospitality businesses that allow them to:

- pay in money such as its **takings**
- take money out to pay staff wages and suppliers.

You may have seen security vans pulling up outside business premises. They are collecting money from the business to pay into the bank. Small businesses will have a nominated (named) person to take cash and cheques to the bank. Usually this would be a manager.

Key term

Takings – money paid to a business through its sales.

Hospitality businesses often want to expand by opening new sites or enlarging their existing premises. A business can go to its bank and request a loan to help pay for the expansion. The bank is likely to loan the money as long as it believes that the money will be paid back in an agreed time.

Phone companies

A hospitality business could not operate without phones or other communication services. Communication systems needed by hotels include:

- telephones in guest bedrooms that can be used for calls within the hotel and outside the hotel
- internal telephones for each department within the hotel
- a reservation system to allow customers to phone to make room bookings
- Internet facilities that allow guests to access and use the Internet
- business services that require a telephone line, such as fax
- a customer service system to enable customers to ring up and ask questions about the business, such as its location and facilities.

Phone companies that can provide these services include BT, TalkTalk and Virgin Media. These companies are in competition with one another, so they all compete to offer the best package to businesses.

Many guests now have their own laptops and Internet connectivity on their mobile phones, iPads and other devices. They expect wireless Internet access in bedrooms and the public areas of the hotel. Some hotels charge for this service, while others offer it free of charge. Other hospitality outlets, such as cafés and fast-food restaurants, also offer their customers Internet access.

Activity: Internet access

Over the next few days keep an eye out for wireless Internet access at cafés and restaurants. This is often indicated by a sign or notice. You will soon learn how easy it is to access the Internet in your local town.

Insurance companies

In this book you will learn about the various security threats that face the hospitality industry. Given these threats, and in order to protect their property and that of their employees, hospitality businesses take out different types of insurance.

A business will usually have building and contents insurance. This means that if there is any damage to the property, such as broken windows, the insurance company would pay to have the damage fixed. Most insurers will also cover more serious damage caused by a fire or flood.

Contents insurance insures all the property on the business premises. If anything is stolen in a burglary, the insurance company would pay to replace the stolen items.

Suppliers

Suppliers are companies that supply hospitality businesses with the products they need to provide their services. Businesses need their suppliers to be reliable and to provide a good service. It is therefore worthwhile to build good working relationships with suppliers.

Some supplies are delivered daily, such as fresh produce to a kitchen; some weekly, such as drink stocks for the bar and linen for housekeeping. Other supplies may be delivered on a monthly basis, such as wine. When goods are delivered, there has to be someone available from the hospitality business to check them in.

Activity: Suppliers

Working in groups, choose one of these departments of a hospitality business:
- contract caterer in a school or college
- restaurant
- kitchen
- housekeeping
- bar
- B&B
- hotel.

Make a list of all the different supplies that your chosen department would need in order to function.

Make sure all departments are covered by at least one group in your class.

Staffing agencies

There will be times when hospitality businesses have a shortage of staff. This may be because:
- the business needs extra staff or more skilled staff for a large function
- employees are off sick
- staff vacancies have not yet been filled.

In all these situations there is a back-up service that the business can use. This support comes from staffing or recruitment agencies. These agencies have skilled people that they can call on at short notice who are able to work in different hospitality businesses. Staff from the agencies are loaned out to the hospitality business for an agreed time and cost. Getting staff in this way has advantages and disadvantages. The advantages are that:

- businesses can get additional staff as and when they need them
- they can get trained in specific skills that the business may only need for occasional functions or events.

The disadvantages are that:

- it can be quite costly, as the business has to pay both the agency fees and the staff salaries
- agency staff may not know how the business is run and they will not know its working practices
- it can be difficult to build a good team as the agency staff will not know the permanent members of staff.

For these reasons, many hospitality businesses use staffing agencies only when it is absolutely essential.

Additional services

Some hospitality businesses draw on other businesses to allow them to offer a wider range of products and services, such as:

- hairdressing
- beauty treatments
- souvenirs and other shopping opportunities
- ticket agency services.

In most luxury hotels guests will expect these additional services as standard. Some of these services may be provided by employees of the hotel, but it is likely that the hotel will turn to other companies to provide them.

The Ritz, five-star hotel in London, offers:

- 24-hour currency exchange
- doctor on call and medical services
- babysitting
- hairdressing
- massage and beauty treatments
- gym and fitness room
- personal trainers
- fine jewellery retail store.

It also has a service allowing guests to book tickets for London shows and tourist attractions.

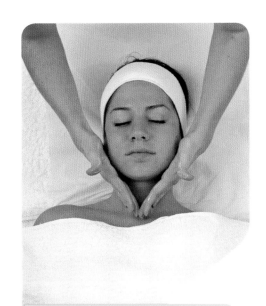

Massage and beauty treatments are an additional service offered by some hospitality businesses. What other services may be on offer?

Transport companies

Hospitality businesses need the support of transport companies. Guests going out for the evening may ask for taxis to be ordered so that they can get back to the hotel. Many hospitality businesses have a nominated taxi company that they will call on to provide this service. At the top end of the market, a business may provide its own transport for guests. The Ritz has a chauffeur-driven car service and the Dorchester has its own fleet of cars that are used to transport guests around London.

Many visitors also like to have details on local transport, which they can use throughout their stay. Hotels should also hold information on national train times. Guests may want this information if they are visiting different parts of the country. Airport information should also be accessible so that guests can easily check departure and arrival times and confirm flight bookings.

Support

The important point to understand is that other industries support hospitality businesses in providing their products and services.

Financial services

Many businesses rely on financial help and the services offered by banks and building societies. This could be for a loan as well as for banking services such as a current account. Most businesses need this kind of support. Few hospitality businesses only accept cash because many customers want to pay by credit or debit card. To provide this arrangement, a business must have a bank account.

Providing communications systems

The vast majority of people now have mobile phones and computers. We rely on phone companies to provide the network coverage to allow us to access our phones and laptops all over the country. The hospitality industry needs to keep pace with technology. Many customers want to book rooms and restaurant tables online. Businesses pay IT experts to ensure that their websites remain up to date and easy to use.

Hospitality businesses also need to have excellent internal communication systems. They will use a combination of pagers, mobile phones, internal phone systems or email. Businesses use communication companies to supply the package that suits their needs.

Delivering goods

Hospitality businesses receive many goods from their suppliers. This could be food for the kitchens; freshly laundered linen for bedrooms and the restaurant; wine, spirits and beer for the bar; and paper for the offices. These deliveries need to be dependable so the business can operate smoothly. Having fresh sheets arrive at 1 pm instead of at 7 am as expected creates problems for a busy hotel.

Removing waste

Hospitality businesses, like many other businesses, create a lot of waste, and it is important to have waste removed regularly, especially if it contains food matter. Apart from possible health and hygiene problems, uncollected waste generates a bad smell and could attract rodents. Nobody wants to eat at a restaurant that has a rat or mouse problem.

Providing staff

Staffing agencies can provide staff at short notice as well as helping a business to recruit new employees. Agencies have a bank of staff, which means a list of people, who can work at short notice and on a temporary basis in the hospitality industry. This can be a very useful, if expensive, solution to a staffing shortfall.

Personal services for customers

Customers at holiday resorts and good hotels expect a range of services in addition to accommodation and catering. In hotels, a concierge assists guests with various tasks like making restaurant reservations, arranging for spa services, recommending night life hot spots, booking transport (such as limousines, flights and boats), obtaining tickets to special events and shows, and assisting with various travel arrangements and tours of local attractions. In luxury hotels, a concierge is often expected to 'achieve the impossible', dealing with any request a guest may have, no matter how strange, and relying on an extensive list of contacts with local shops and service providers.

Assessment activity 4
Unit 2 **P2 M2 D2** BTEC

You did so well with the article for *Meet the Hospitality Industry* magazine that you have now been asked to prepare a presentation and report for a group of Year 10 children who want to find out more about the businesses that support the hospitality industry.

1 Start your presentation with a description of three examples of the support that other industries provide for the hospitality industry. You also need to include a list of the ways in which other industries support the hospitality industry. **P2**

2 Continue your presentation by clearly explaining how two different hospitality businesses are supported by other industries. **M2**

3 For this task you are going to prepare a written report or booklet. Using the same two businesses you investigated for Task 2, look at the strengths and weaknesses of the support offered to these businesses by other industries. You need to analyse these strengths and weaknesses, and then suggest some improvements in the way that the support from other industries can be provided. **D2**

For this assignment, Tasks 1 and 2 require you to deliver a presentation to your tutor and the rest of your group, and Task 3 is a written report or booklet.

Grading tips

P2 You will deliver your presentation to your tutor and (perhaps) the rest of your class. You need to use a presentation package so that you can provide handouts for your audience. You should complete your presentation at least a few days before you are to due to deliver it, so you have time to print handouts and practise your delivery.

M2 Remember that you should not just read from your slides. Your slides need to have some key points, and then you will need to prepare notes so you can provide more information for your audience. Practise your presentation and use the tone and pitch of your voice to present your information in an interesting way.

D2 You can decide with your tutor if you are going to complete a report or a booklet. Remember to look at the strengths and weaknesses of the support given to the two businesses you are investigating. Suggest how this support could be improved. These improvements must be realistic and supported by your analysis. They do not need to be big changes; sometimes little improvements can make all the difference to a hospitality business. For example, if the laundry service currently delivers fresh laundry at 9 am, an improvement may be for the delivery to happen before 8 am so fresh linen is ready for the housekeeping staff to use when they start changing rooms at 8.30 am.

PLTS

Independent enquirers will use examples from different support industries in their work for **P2**. **Creative thinkers** will ask questions when undertaking visits to hospitality businesses. **Self-managers** will organise their time and resources, prioritising actions to manage assessment activities.

Functional skills

Using the Internet for researching the hospitality industry will help you develop your **ICT** skills. You will need to search for information, decide what information to use and evaluate this information. You will do this when you are investigating the businesses that support the hospitality industry.

You will demonstrate **English** skills when you read the information you have gathered during your research and you will demonstrate your writing skills as you are preparing your presentation slides and notes and your report.

Aiko Tanaka
Head receptionist

Aiko Tanaka, a 26-year-old from Plymouth, Devon, has been working as the head receptionist at the Hotel Anglaise in Agra, India, for two years. With 50 rooms, a bar, a restaurant, and a conference and events centre, this is a busy hotel.

'It is important to build an immediate relationship with customers coming into the hotel, so I make sure I am always cheerful and professional. I dress smartly, and I make sure I greet every customer with a smile.

'There is no such thing as a typical day – every day is different and you never know what problems you may encounter. If you want to follow a career in hospitality, you need to be able to communicate well with people and anticipate their needs so you can give them the best experience possible.

'I work shifts and weekends. My day includes checking out guests and preparing their bills, greeting new guests, and providing information on the local area and excursions to local attractions. I liaise with the housekeeping team to make sure rooms are prepared for new guests, and I make sure the restaurant manager and head chef know how many tables have been booked for lunch and dinner. I ensure that the other reception staff know about conferences or events so we are prepared to welcome guests and guide them to the right rooms. I am also responsible for managing the reception team. I am often very busy, but I love knowing my guests have enjoyed their stay at the Hotel Anglaise.

'Before coming to work in India, I worked in several hotels in the UK. I went to college and studied hospitality as I knew I wanted a job in hotels and I wanted to travel. My course helped me to get my first job, as it taught me the importance of customer service and the skills I need. I am now looking for a management qualification so I can develop my career and become an assistant manager.'

Think about it!

- **What career ambitions do you have?**
- **Do you want to work overseas?**
- **What qualifications and experience will you need for your ideal job?**
- **What courses (if any) would you like to do at university? What are the entry requirements for these courses?**

Just checking

1 Explain what is meant by the term 'the commercial sector'.

2 Give examples of two settings in the commercial sector.

3 List the different types of businesses that make up the hospitality sector.

4 What types of staff work in a hotel?

5 What are some of the job roles these staff might have?

6 List three qualities that people need to have when working in the hospitality industry.

7 Explain why teamwork is important in the hospitality industry.

8 Explain why personal appearance is important.

9 Explain the role of Staffing agencies.

10 List three other industries that support the hospitality industry.

edexcel **:::**

Assignment tips

- Spend some time researching and reading the reports and profiles on the People 1st website.

- Visit as many different types of hospitality businesses as you can. Find out if each is a local or national business.

- Talk to people who work in the hospitality industry. Discuss their job role, and find out what qualities they need to do their job and what the requirements of their job are.

- Start your research into hospitality jobs early in these units so you have plenty of examples to chose from when you come to do your assignment.

- When you do assessment activity 3, make sure that you chose businesses from different parts of the industry so you can cover all types of hospitality products and services.

- Practise your presentation for assessment activity 4. You will feel less nervous and appear more confident. It will also help you know what you need to say so that you don't just read your notes.

- When you do assessment activity 4 task 3, base your suggestions for improvements on the weaknesses you have identified. Remember to be realistic.

3 & 4 Customer service in hospitality

Hospitality is about people. If you work in hospitality, you will almost certainly be involved in making sure that the needs of customers are met. You should have a passion for people and a desire to provide excellent customer service.

These units aim to develop and broaden your understanding of the principles of customer service in hospitality businesses. You will explore how hospitality staff meet the needs and expectations of different types of customers through offering a range of products and services.

Hospitality businesses understand the importance of delivering consistent and reliable customer service. You will look at how businesses monitor and evaluate their customer service by obtaining feedback from customers. This enables the businesses to make improvements to the services they provide.

In studying these units, you will have the opportunity to develop your own customer service skills.

Learning outcomes

After completing these units, you should:

Unit 3 Principles of customer service in hospitality, leisure, travel and tourism

1. Understand the importance to the organisation in providing excellent customer service in the hospitality, leisure, travel and tourism industries
2. Understand the role of the individual in delivering customer service in the hospitality, leisure, travel and tourism industries
3. Understand the importance of customers' needs and expectations in the hospitality, leisure, travel and tourism industries.

Unit 4 Providing customer service in hospitality

1. Be able to monitor and evaluate hospitality businesses' customer service
2. Be able to demonstrate customer service skills in different situations in hospitality.

Assessment and grading criteria

These tables show you what you must do in order to achieve a pass, merit or distinction grade, and where you can find activities in this book to help you.

Unit 3 Principles of customer service in hospitality, leisure, travel and tourism

To achieve a pass grade the evidence must show that you are able to:		To achieve a merit grade the evidence must show that, in addition to the pass criteria, you are able to:	To achieve a distinction grade the evidence must show that, in addition to the pass and merit criteria, you are able to:
P1 describe the role of the organisation in relation to customer service **Assessment activity 1, pages 74–75**	**P2** identify the characteristics and benefits of excellent customer service **Assessment activity 1, pages 74–75**	**M1** compare the extent to which hospitality organisations deliver consistent and reliable customer service to their internal and external customers **Assessment activity 1, pages 74–75**	
P3 give examples of internal and external customers in the industries **Assessment activity 1, pages 74–75**	**P4** describe the importance of product knowledge and sales to organisational success **Assessment activity 1, pages 74–75**		
P5 describe the importance of organisational procedures for customer service **Assessment activity 1, pages 74–75**			
P6 identify the benefits of excellent customer service for the individual **Assessment activity 2, pages 79–80**	**P7** describe the importance of positive attitude, behaviour and motivation in providing excellent customer service **Assessment activity 2, pages 79–80**	**M2** analyse the customer provision in hospitality organisations **Assessment activity 2, pages 79–80**	**D1** evaluate the effectiveness of the customer service provision in different hospitality organisations **Assessment activity 2, pags 79–80**
P8 describe the importance of personal presentation within the industries **Assessment activity 2, pages 79–80**	**P9** explain the importance of using appropriate types of communication **Assessment activity 2, pages 79–80**		
P10 describe the importance of effective listening skills **Assessment activity 2, pages 79–80**			
P11 identify what is meant by customer needs and expectations in the industries **Assessment activity 3, page 86**	**P12** identify the importance of anticipating and responding to varying customers' needs and expectations **Assessment activity 3, page 86**	**M3** analyse the ways of meeting customer needs and expectations, outlining the strengths and weaknesses of each **Assessment activity 3, page 86**	
P13 describe the factors that influence the customers' choice of products and services **Assessment activity 3, page 86**	**P14** describe the importance of meeting and exceeding customer expectations **Assessment activity 3, page 86**		
P15 describe the importance of dealing with complaints in a positive manner **Assessment activity 3, page 86**	**P16** explain the importance of complaint handling procedures **Assessment activity 3, page 86**		

Unit 4 Providing customer service in hospitality

To achieve a pass grade the evidence must show that you are able to:	To achieve a merit grade the evidence must show that, in addition to the pass criteria, you are able to:	To achieve a distinction grade the evidence must show that, in addition to the pass and merit criteria, you are able to:
P1 monitor and evaluate customer service in different hospitality businesses **Assessment activity 4, page 95**	**M1** analyse methods of monitoring and evaluating customer service, outlining the strengths and weaknesses of each **Assessment activity 4, page 95**	**D1** evaluate the customer service provision in hospitality businesses, making suggestions for improvement **Assessment activity 4, page 95**
P2 demonstrate customer service skills in different customer service situations **Assessment activity 5, page 106**	**M2** look after customers independently and confidently in different situations **Assessment activity 5, page 106**	**D2** evaluate and make recommendations to improve own performance in hospitality related customer service situations **Assessment activity 5, page 106**

How you will be assessed

These units will be assessed by one or more assignments that will be designed and marked by tutors at your centre. The assignments will be designed to allow you to show your knowledge and understanding of customer service, as well as to demonstrate your own customer service skills.

You will do this by investigating customer service provision in at least two hospitality outlets. In addition, your assignment work could involve:

- making presentations
- undertaking practical tasks
- producing written work.

Lauren, 16-year-old learner

I've decided I want to work in hospitality because I love working with people. For the last year I have been helping my mum's friend in her café at weekends and I get on really well with the customers.

Learning about customer service has helped me to understand how hard an organisation has to work to make sure that it meets the needs of its customers. It's made me much more aware of how I am treated when I am shopping or eating out. I now realise the benefits that good customer service can bring to a hospitality business.

The role plays we did in class have been great fun, and they have helped me to give better customer service when I work in the café. It is very useful to have members of the class peer assessing my performance.

Over to you

- How important do you think it is for people who work in hospitality to be good at customer service?
- Can you explain what excellent customer service actually is?
- Do you already have any customer service skills? Where have you demonstrated these skills?

3.1 Understand the importance to the organisation in providing excellent customer service in the hospitality, leisure, travel and tourism industries

Welcome

What is good customer service?

Think of an occasion when you received good customer service. In groups of two or three, share your experiences, and make a list of words and phrases that describe good customer service.

Now think of bad customer service experiences. List as many words and phrases as you can that describe bad customer service.

Hospitality is central to the travel and tourism industry as both business and leisure tourists are likely to use hospitality services during their travels. Tourists need places to stay, to eat and to drink, and their experiences of these services will have a significant impact on their overall satisfaction with their trip. Because the provision of hospitality is so important to the success of the travel and tourism industry, it is vital that the customer service we provide encourages tourists to visit again.

Good **customer service** means putting the needs of the customer first. As a member of staff in an hospitality organisation, you need to put yourself in the position of your customers. You should be aware of how you would like to be treated as a customer, and then deal with your own customers accordingly.

To start our investigation of customer service, in this section we will look at:

- the role of hospitality organisations
- the characteristics of excellent customer service
- the benefits of excellent customer service
- customer types
- product knowledge and sales
- organisational procedures.

Role of hospitality organisations

Customer service is often at the heart of a successful business. Suppose you visit a fast-food outlet for a burger and you have to queue for ages, and then you get served by staff who are rude and unfriendly. Would you go back next time you are in the area and wanted a burger? If you have had an unpleasant experience, you are much more likely to find somewhere else to go in the future. It is not enough to produce tasty burgers to be successful; the fast-food outlet must also provide a good experience for its customers.

It is important to realise that good customer service doesn't just happen by chance. As we will see in these units, hospitality businesses can take many steps to enhance the customer experience and to ensure excellent customer service.

Develop products

As a first step, of course, it is important to offer products that customers want. People's tastes are continuously changing. With this in mind, hospitality organisations regularly seek the opinions of their customers, and they develop products and services to meet their needs.

This allows a hospitality business to adapt products to suit individual requirements. For example, two customers staying in a hotel can have completely different experiences: one may book a standard room, eat in the coffee shop and not use any of the other hotel facilities, while the other may book the executive suite, eat in the fine dining restaurant and use the gym and spa.

 Did you know?

The Premier Inn hotel chain sends an email questionnaire to customers after their stay to get feedback on its services. It receives around 500,000 responses every year. The organisation also holds customer **focus groups** to help it better understand customer attitudes and opinions.

Set standards

All the time spent planning a service is wasted if it cannot be delivered to customers in a consistent and efficient way. Therefore, everyone involved in serving customers must know exactly what they should be achieving. All members of staff must be aware of the standards of performance that they are expected to deliver. All staff must also have the capability and resources to meet these standards.

Staff must be provided with training to develop their customer service skills. The purpose of training is to ensure that all staff:

- understand the organisation's vision, goals, plans, standards and practices related to the delivery of excellent customer service
- understand their own roles and have the necessary skills to deliver excellent service.

The aim of setting standards and providing training is to enable the organisation to deliver products and services to a consistent standard and quality. This should cover both the **tangible goods** – the food customers eat, the wine they drink, the room they sleep in, etc. – and the **intangible goods** – the service, the atmosphere and so on that contribute to the overall customer experience. In the hospitality industry, customer satisfaction is influenced by both the tangible and the intangible goods provided by an organisation. It is very important that hospitality businesses do not neglect the intangible aspects of the customer experience.

Key terms

Customer service – what an organisation does to meet customer expectations and produce customer satisfaction.

Focus group – a form of market research in which a small group of people are invited to a meeting to discuss their views and opinions on an organisation's products and services.

Tangible goods – products you can see and touch, such as food, drink and guest rooms.

Intangible goods – products that cannot be seen or touched, such as advice, friendly service and atmosphere.

Activity: Investigating standards

In pairs, visit a local hospitality operation and ask if it can provide a standard of performance for a customer service task. Share the standard with your class. Discuss the similarities and differences in the standards you have managed to obtain.

Provide value for money

Customer satisfaction is also influenced by the price of an organisation's products and services. Customers expect value for money, even in the most luxurious settings. This does not mean that they expect things to be cheap, but they must feel that the prices they are paying for goods and services are fair. If, for example, some of a hotel's bedrooms are more expensive than others, the reception staff should inform customers of the extra benefits and services that they get for paying a higher price for a room.

Encourage repeat custom

One of the main aims of all hospitality businesses is to maximise sales. Research has shown that customers who are happy spend more, and they are likely to tell their friends and family about their experience. Importantly, they are also likely to visit the organisation again. Good customer service encourages repeat business, and this helps an organisation to increase its sales

Activity: Providing customer service excellence

In groups, discuss how a pub can provide excellent service to its customers.

Characteristics of excellent customer service

To provide customer service excellence, all staff must understand their individual responsibilities. They should:

- be aware of the benefits of providing good customer service
- be motivated enough to want to provide good customer service.

We will now consider some of the factors that underpin excellent customer service.

Attitude and behaviour

It is very important that all staff have a positive attitude if customer service excellence is to be achieved. They need to behave appropriately at all times. If you have a negative attitude in the hospitality industry, it will affect the way you behave and give a poor impression to customers.

Knowledge

To provide customer service excellence, staff must not only meet the required service standards but also have a good knowledge of the products and services of the organisation. Good product and service knowledge will help staff to:

- answer a customer's questions
- suggest products and services that might match a customer's needs.

This will make the organisation appear confident and professional, and will help to build customer loyalty. All this will contribute to increased sales.

Activity: Product knowledge

List the product knowledge that would be expected of a receptionist working in a hotel in the heart of London. Then list the type of local information (such as about public transport and visitor attractions) that a receptionist would be expected to know.

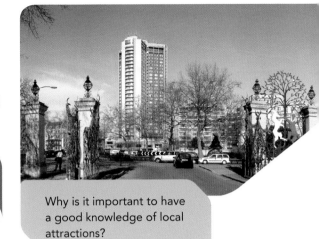

Why is it important to have a good knowledge of local attractions?

Customers generally expect staff to know everything about the organisation they work for, but sometimes a customer may ask a question that surprises you. It may be about the work of another part of the organisation or a new development you do not know about. If this happens, you should always try to give some kind of helpful answer. Sometimes all you can do is suggest someone else that the customer could ask to get the required information.

Quality

All hospitality organisations, no matter how large or small, need to ensure that the quality of their services and products is consistent and reliable. Customers measure quality by how well a product or service meets their needs and expectations. This means, for example, that if a hotel is advertised as family friendly, there should be facilities for children. A service or product is of good quality when it meets customers' needs.

Customers also judge the quality of a hospitality organisation on whether it provides value for money. This applies both to upmarket expensive facilities and to budget operations. The type and level of service obviously varies according to how much the customer is paying. Customers of expensive hospitality organisations will expect higher levels of service and much more interaction with staff than customers of more downmarket and budget facilities. However, every organisation should seek to provide a courteous, reliable and friendly service.

There are many things that influence the quality of hospitality services and products. These include:

- presentation, attitude and behaviour of staff
- availability, cost and value for money
- ability to meet specific needs
- appearance and comfort
- standards of service.

Activity: How do you judge quality?

In groups, discuss how you would judge the quality of a restaurant.

Timing

Organisations must ensure that products and services are provided in a timely fashion. People do not like to wait long to be served. Although customers will not expect to be kept waiting, they will not want to be rushed either. This requires hospitality organisations to perform a bit of a balancing act to get things just right.

However, if customers are likely to face delay or if a service becomes unavailable, the organisation must take some action.

- If there is going to be a delay in service, customers should be informed and advised how long they might have to wait.

- If products and services are not available for any reason, customers should be told as soon as possible.

Cost

Providing excellent customer service requires time and effort. This does not come without a cost. Managers need to ensure they invest in staff training and staff development. They must also provide the correct tools and necessary resources to enable staff to complete their jobs to the required standards.

Meeting specific needs

Customer needs vary – what satisfies one customer may not satisfy another. It is therefore important to find out as much as you can about each customer. In order to find out exactly what a customer wants or expects, you will have to ask questions. You will also have to listen carefully to the answers. You will learn more about communicating with customers in these units, including ways to develop your listening skills.

It is also important to find out if customers have had a good experience. Research has shown that only about half of all customers who are unhappy with some aspect of a service actually complain. The most obvious way to find out if customers are satisfied is to ask them. A hospitality business that does not get feedback from its customers may never know whether it has some unhappy guests, and may not get information it could use to improve its services.

Activity: Compensating the customer

Suppose you are working behind a bar. A customer has queued for a long time at your bar for a particular drink, only to discover that it is not available. What could you do to compensate this customer?

Providing information

Customers often need help when making purchasing decisions. They want information on an organisation's products and services before deciding what they want. If they are staying in a hotel away from home, they may also seek information on the local area. It is important that staff are able to locate information to help them to answer customers' questions. Hospitality organisations often produce handbooks to help staff deal with queries, as well as providing information leaflets for customers.

Working under pressure

The demand for hospitality products and services is not always constant. There can be periods of very low or very high demand. In addition, organisations often have to cope with staff shortages. This can put enormous pressure on the staff. This makes it difficult to provide a consistent level of service.

It is more important than ever to work as a team on occasions when you are short staffed or when there is very high demand. Effective communication is vital, and all staff need to appreciate that other members of the team will be under pressure and are affected in various ways by high levels of demand.

How can you make sure you stay calm under pressure?

Dealing with problems

Customers partly judge customer service on the ability of staff to deal with problems that might arise during their stay or visit. If you deal with a customer's problem efficiently and sympathetically, you will make a very good impression. Problems are an opportunity to show customers that you care about them and that you are willing to go the extra mile to meet their needs.

Benefits of excellent customer service

All businesses value repeat customers. They want customers who will return again and again to the business. Finding new customers is expensive, which is why it is sensible to hang on to the customers you have.

However, all businesses lose customers. Some customers, for whatever reason, do not return. Research in the hospitality industry suggests that 68 per cent of customers are lost because of the attitude of the owner or staff. Only 14 per cent of customers are lost because of dissatisfaction with a product (Feiertag and Hogan, *Lessons from the Field*, 2001).

In hospitality, therefore, service has more impact on customer satisfaction than anything else. So, a key indicator of quality customer service in hospitality is customer loyalty. Loyal customers become repeat purchasers of an organisation's products and services. If customers are consistently satisfied with the service provided, they will be inclined to return.

Good customer service can have a positive influence on the performance of a hospitality business. This is because satisfied customers:

- stay longer and spend more
- buy more expensive products
- often return regularly to the business rather than a competitor
- recommend the business to other people.

Customers also benefit from excellent service. They are likely have a more enjoyable experience and their individual needs are more likely to be met.

Customer types

Customers can be categorised into two broad groups:

- internal customers – those who work for the organisation
- external customers – those who purchase and use the products and services provided by an organisation.

External customers are obviously very important to the organisation. However, internal customers are also important because they rely on getting good service from their colleagues to allow them to meet the needs of external customers.

Internal

All staff in a large organisation such as a hotel – the porters, room attendants, waiting staff, administrators and chefs – have a role to play in providing customer service. They must work as a team and communicate effectively to ensure that the needs of customers are met. A high quality of service to customers can only be consistently achieved by providing good quality internally.

To show how this works, consider this example. A member of the waiting staff cannot lay out a table for a banquet properly if the laundry does not deliver freshly laundered napkins on time. In this case, the waiting staff in the banquet room are internal customers of the laundry service. If the laundry does not provide a good service, it will be eventually reflected in the service offered to the external (paying) customers.

One poorly performing member of a team can affect how the whole team performs and influence what customers think of the organisation. For example, a receptionist who is rude or inattentive can change a customer's impression of the whole business. It can be very difficult for other staff to correct this bad impression.

Activity: A customer database

Make a list of the kind of information that could be included on a customer database for a four-star country house hotel. What can the hotel do with the information it has gathered about its customers?

External customers

Delivering consistently great customer service is difficult. Individual customers will have their own ideas of what constitutes great customer service. To ensure that all customers are happy, a business must meet their individual needs.

To do this efficiently, a business tries to understand of the needs of different groups of customers. For this reason, hospitality organisations place their customers into different **market segments**. In other words, they categorise potential customers into groups of people with similar needs (see Figure 1) and then they aim to provide products and services to meet those needs.

Key term

Market segment – a group of customers with broadly similar needs and expectations.

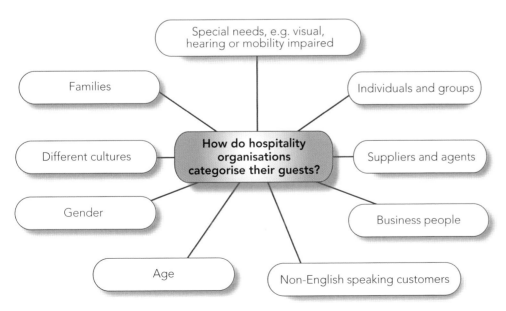

Figure 1: Ways of categorising customers

Activity: Categories of customers

Working in pairs, choose a hospitality business that operates in your area. How do you think this business categorises its customers? List as many ways as you can think of that it could categorise its customers into different groups.

Now let's look at typical ways of categorising customers and at some customer groups that have particular needs.

Existing and new customers

One obvious distinction, as we have discussed above, is between existing customers and new customers. Many organisations monitor the number of existing or returning customers they get. These customers are referred to as **repeat business**. They are very good customers to have, bringing a regular supply of business.

Key term

Repeat business – customers that have previously been guests or clients of the organisation.

- If customers are returning to a hospitality organisation, it is a good sign that they are usually happy with what is being provided.
- Once customers are known to an organisation, it is easier to anticipate what they want. This makes it easier to meet their needs.
- If an organisation gets plenty of repeat business, it is under less pressure to spend money on advertising to attract new customers.
- Word of mouth is a very effective means of advertising. If customers are very satisfied with an organisation's services, they will tell their friends and family who might also become customers.

This does not mean that organisations are not interested in attracting new customers. Of course, they are important too. When new customers visit a hospitality business, it is an opportunity to create a good impression. The aim should always be to convert new customers to regular customers.

It is good practice to keep customer details on a database. Many businesses build up a mailing list of existing customers so that they can post or email details of any new developments or promotional offers. All databases must comply with the law. The Data Protection Act 1998 requires any organisation that holds data about individuals on computerised systems to register with the Information Commissioner's Office. The Data Protection Act gives customers certain rights. These include the right to:

- be informed of where the data is being processed
- be provided with a description of the details being held
- know why the data is being held
- know who has access to it.

Individuals and groups

Many hospitality businesses offer services for groups as well as individual customers. Members of organised groups are often accompanied by a tour guide and group leader, who can help the business look after the group. This can be very useful, especially if the leader or guide knows the group members well.

However, you must remember that each customer in a group or tour party will have individual needs and expectations. When you work in a hospitality setting, you have a responsibility to make sure that these needs are identified and met.

Suppliers and agents

Suppliers and agents are important customers of hospitality organisations. They expect to be treated with courtesy and respect. If they are not treated well, they may think that the business treats all its customers in that way. If this happens, they are likely to advise their friends, family and other clients not to use the organisation.

Business people

Business people expect speedy and efficient service. If they use a hotel regularly, they may expect staff to recognise them and to anticipate their needs. For example, they may expect to be booked into their favourite room or at their favourite table in the restaurant. They will probably want home comforts as well as office facilities to allow them to get their work done. Their needs could include:

- television and DVD player in the bedroom
- phone/fax facilities
- Internet access (ideally wireless).

Non-English speaking customers

Non-English speaking customers expect staff to be able to communicate with them without too much difficulty. This may be tricky if nobody in the organisation speaks the customer's language. If you find yourself having to serve a non-English speaking customer, there are some things you can do to help you to communicate:

- use pictures and hand signs
- speak slowly and clearly
- use the Internet to look up useful phrases.

Making an effort to speak to non-English speaking customers in their own language will create a good impression.

How can you cater for the different needs of people in a group?

Activity: Meeting the needs of non–English speaking customers

Find out how to say the following phrases in French, Mandarin Chinese and Spanish:

Good morning	*Welcome to our hotel*
Good afternoon	*How may I help you?*
Good evening	

Practise using these phrases with your classmates.

> Do you ever find yourself making assumptions about people because of their age?

Age

The age of your customers may affect their needs and expectations. The older generation may prefer a more formal approach to service, but younger customers may find this a bit daunting.

It is wrong to make too many assumptions based on the age of customers. For example, do not assume that older customers are necessarily slow or frail, and do not make the mistake of thinking that teenage customers do not expect to be treated respectfully.

Gender

Whether your customers are male or female may influence their needs but, as with age, you must be careful not to make assumptions.

Many hospitality organisations adapt their products and services to suit the needs of female or male customers. For example, a café that attracts mainly male manual workers may offer basic but filling food that offers good value for money.

Some hotels advertise the fact that they take special care of female customers. They will, for example, make sure that they do not allocate women travelling alone a room on the ground floor which backs on to the car park.

Activity: Meeting the needs of men and women

In small groups, discuss how hospitality organisations could differentiate the products and services offered to male and female customers.

Different cultures

It is important to respect and understand other people's cultures so that you can meet their customer service needs and avoid causing offence. A customer's culture may influence:

- religious practices – days of worship, significance of particular festivals
- social customs – how people are greeted
- dress – the need to cover up
- food and drink – foods that are forbidden, whether drinking alcohol is permitted
- gender – the position of women in society.

Families

Customers with children want to feel that the organisation welcomes children and that they are not seen as 'a bit of a nuisance'. They appreciate facilities such as kids' clubs and play areas that entertain their children. These provide a welcome relief for many parents.

Although it is the adults who are paying for the products and services, the children may well be the ones that influence the purchase so they are worth looking after. Parents will be impressed by extra touches that give the impression that the organisation has thought about the needs of the children. These might include:

- highchairs or booster seats
- children's menus, baby food and smaller portions
- facilities for warming baby food
- activity packs
- books or games.

Special needs

Some customers have special needs. This may be because they:

- have a physical disability, such as being unable to walk or having a hearing or sight impairment
- have special dietary needs or preferences
- are travelling with a baby or small child
- have learning difficulties.

Careful consideration must be given to how to treat customers with special needs. Hospitality staff must look after their needs without causing offence or appearing to be patronising. In this situation, you must not make the customer feel inferior or not worth your time.

Here are some examples of the right way to care for people with special needs.

- If a customer has impaired hearing, you should speak clearly and slowly. Make sure you do not turn your back on the customer. Some people with impaired hearing may only be able to understand what you are saying by lip reading.
- People in wheelchairs need to know about access, lifts and disabled facilities. They may need help moving around the premises.
- If a customer has a speech impediment, such as a stammer, it is important to listen carefully. Repeat any request or order back to the customer to be sure you have understood what they want.

Product knowledge and sales

Selling is an important part of many hospitality jobs. The front office in a hotel sells rooms and other services when customers make reservations, the conference and banqueting department sells meeting rooms, wedding receptions and a whole host of other events, and staff in the bar and restaurant sell food and drink.

Let's consider some of the attributes that are required to sell hospitality services.

Know the product

A characteristic of good customer service is product knowledge. This helps customers to form a good impression of the business. It also helps staff to sell products. It is much easier to make a sale if you know about your employer's products and services.

Activity: What's on the menu?

List the product knowledge needed by a waiter working in a fine dining restaurant.

Give honest advice and answer questions

Customers often seek advice when buying products and services. They expect members of staff to recognise their needs and to provide accurate, honest and knowledgeable responses.

Hospitality staff should be prepared to answer both routine and more unusual questions, and know where to find answers to any question they are not sure about. There are ways to help staff remember or find the information they need. In a restaurant, waiting staff often make notes on the menu about the make-up of dishes. Front office staff often have a manual behind the desk containing all sorts of frequently requested information. However, if you are asked a question and don't know the answer, never just guess – ask a colleague or a manager.

Suggest products

If customers are unsure about what to buy, they will expect staff to suggest suitable products. For example, a customer might want suggestions for a suitable wine to go with a meal, a light dessert to round off a meal, or the best package for a family break. The list of possible requests is endless. When suggesting products, it is very important to make sure you understand the customer's needs and have some idea of their budget. However, it is also an opportunity to sell.

Increase sales

A good salesperson will take any opportunity to increase sales. For example, if a customer is booking a room, the reservation staff should try to sell the best room that would suit the customer's needs and budget. Don't assume that customers always want the cheapest option. With experience, it is possible to judge how much customers are willing to pay for the products and services they are seeking and to sell accordingly.

Organisational procedures

In order to provide high standards of customer service, it is very important to have efficient organisational procedures as well as good administrative systems in place. Let's take a brief look at some of the procedures needed in a hospitality business. We shall cover some of these procedures in more detail later in the book when we consider hospitality front office operations (see pages 370–96).

Checking availability and booking

When a customer makes an enquiry to buy a product or a service, there must be a system for checking availability. So, there needs to be a system for recording the availability of meeting rooms, rooms for private dinners, restaurant tables, hotel guest rooms and other facilities for hire. Increasingly, staff will use computerised reservation systems to see if the product or service is available and to make bookings for customers.

Communicating customer orders

Although it is vital to have systems for recording customer bookings, it is important to understand that administration does not end at this point. There must also be a system for communicating customer information between departments, so that the products and services the customer has ordered can be delivered.

Activity: Communicating information

Identify all the information that will need to be communicated to the kitchen, bar and restaurant to ensure that the correct products and services are delivered to customers staying in a hotel. Visit a local hotel and ask how it communicates this information.

Cancellations

Sometimes, customers change their minds once they have made a booking or they have to change their plans. In these cases, the customers will wish to cancel or amend their bookings. There must be a system of dealing with cancellations and alterations, so that the relevant departments are informed. Most hospitality organisations have a cancellation policy, which will state whether the customer needs to be charged a cancellation fee and, if so, how much this will be.

Activity: Cancellation fees

A party of ten cancels a reservation for a table in a restaurant on a Saturday night a couple of hours before they are due to arrive. Discuss whether the party should be charged a cancellation fee.

Payment

We will look at systems for taking payment later in the book (see pages 393–4). However, it is worth noting here that all the good work in looking after customers is wasted if the hospitality business does not manage to collect the money it is owed.

Complaints

Unfortunately, customers sometimes have cause to complain. Most hospitality establishments have a policy for dealing with complaints as it is absolutely vital that any customer problems are properly resolved. You will get the opportunity to practise your skills in dealing with a customer complaint in Assessment activity 5 on page 106.

Assessment activity 1

You are working as a training officer for Visit London, the official visitor organisation for the capital. You have been asked to prepare customer service training materials for the hospitality industry. These training materials should consist of posters and training guides that can be used by hospitality organisations to train their staff.

1 Prepare a poster that:
- states all the things an organisation must do to ensure it provides excellent customer service **P1**
- identifies the characteristics and benefits of excellent customer service **P2**
- gives two examples of internal customers and two examples of external customers. **P3**

2 Produce an information bulletin describing:
- why staff in the hospitality industry should have good product knowledge **P4**
- how organisational procedures help businesses deliver good customer service. **P5**

3 You need to investigate customer service in two local hospitality organisations. This should not be too similar. For example, one could be a hotel and one might be a café. They could be organisations you know well; perhaps one might be a business in which you have a part-time job or have undertaken work experience.

You need to visit each organisation to talk to a manager or a member of staff about customer service procedures and to observe some customer service at first hand.

Having reviewed their customer service provision, write a report that compares how well each organisation delivers consistent and reliable customer service to their internal and external customers. **M1**

Grading tips

P1 Run through the customer service journey, from the customer's first contact with a hospitality organisation to the last contact, to identify how the organisation can provide excellent customer service.

P2 Ask your friends and family what they consider to be excellent customer service.

P3 Make sure you remember the difference between internal and external customers.

P4 You are not being asked to describe what product knowledge staff should have, but why it is important. Make sure you relate your answers to the overall aims of the hospitality organisation.

P5 Again, you are not being asked to describe organisation procedures in detail, but describe why they are important and how they help businesses deliver good customer service.

M1 You should check with your tutor before starting this work that you have chosen two suitable organisations for this task. You need to identify how each organisation meets the needs of its internal and external customers. Make sure the two businesses have sufficient similarities and differences in their approaches to analyse the effectiveness of their customer service and make valid comparisons. Prepare some questions to ask before you visit each organisation.

PLTS

You will develop your skills as an **independent enquirer** when investigating customer service in two hospitality organisations.

Functional skills

You will use your **ICT** skills to produce your poster and information bulletin. You will develop your **English** skills of reading, speaking and listening in gathering information about customer service.

3.2 Understand the role of the individual in delivering customer service in the hospitality, leisure, travel and tourism industries

So far we have looked at the role of the hospitality organisation in providing excellent customer service and the benefits this brings that organisation. Now we will focus on the role of individual staff members in delivering customer service. We will look at:

- benefits to the individual
- factors in excellent customer service
- personal presentation
- communication
- listening skills.

Benefits to the individual

Good customer service does not just benefit hospitality organisations. It also offers benefits to their staff. Imagine that you are working for a hospitality business that delivers good customer service.

- You can be proud of where you work.
- You can get a buzz out of seeing that the customers are happy.
- It may be easier to reach targets and/or get a bonus.
- It will be a nicer work environment.
- You will receive fewer complaints from customers.

This should provide greater job satisfaction and increase your motivation to do a good job. You are likely to have a good feeling about your job.

In general, staff who are happy at work are less likely to turn up late or take unplanned leave. They will also be less likely to leave and look for another job, which reduces **staff turnover**. The service they provide customers will reflect the fact that they are proud of the organisation they work for.

In this situation, everyone is a winner: staff are happy at work, customers are happy with the level of service provided and the organisation benefits because customers are happy to spend their money and staff turnover is low.

Key term

Staff turnover – the frequency with which members of staff leave an organisation.

? Did you know?

Most hospitality organisations like to keep staff turnover to a minimum. It is expensive to recruit and train new staff. Some employers invest substantial sums in the training and professional development of their staff, and they want to get some benefit by retaining employees for a long period.

Factors in excellent customer service

The attitude and behaviour of staff has an enormous influence on customer service. No matter how nice the food tastes or how comfortable the hotel room is, the whole customer experience can be spoiled if staff are rude, disinterested or uncaring. Staff who are motivated project a good company image and work harder to achieve targets.

Personal presentation

Customers will judge an organisation on the image that its staff present, so it is vital that staff put forward a professional image and follow any guidelines on personal presentation issued by the organisation.

First impressions

You never get another chance to make a first impression. A customer's opinion of you and the organisation you work for will be formed within a few moments of meeting you. If the first impression is a poor one, it will be very difficult to turn this around and to impress the customer. On the other hand, if the first impression is good, customers are more likely to approach the rest of their time with you in a positive state of mind.

Activity: The first impression

You are working in a restaurant. How can you create a good first impression to a group of customers arriving at the restaurant for a Christmas party?

Personal hygiene and appearance

If staff present a positive image, customers will be confident about the whole organisation. To present a positive image, staff must pay attention to their:

- personal hygiene
- appearance.

Staff who are scruffy, untidy and (worst of all) dirty will convey a very poor image of themselves and the organisation they work for. This will not give the customer confidence. Staff who are smart and presentable are already halfway to satisfying customers. Their appearance looks professional. It suggests that they know their job and are ready to do business.

Good personal hygiene is obviously essential in the hospitality industry. You should:

- wash or shower daily
- keep your hair neat, tidy and clean
- keep your fingernails short
- avoid wearing too much make-up or jewellery
- avoid bad habits such as chewing or playing with your hair
- keep your uniform clean and in good repair
- keep all cuts and wounds covered with appropriate, clean and waterproof dressings.

How does your appearance affect customers' impressions of you and your organisation?

Communication

People don't just communicate using speech. When talking to people face to face, they use gestures, poses, movements and facial expressions to help them communicate what they want to say.

It is very important that you are aware of your own **body language** when dealing with customers. You should always make sure that your body language gives a positive and confident image.

Our body language is conveyed through:

- eye contact
- facial expressions
- body posture and movement
- hand gestures
- touching.

Key term

Body language – the gestures, poses, movements and facial expressions that a person uses to communicate. It is sometimes called non-verbal communication.

Body language is also conveyed through the physical distance that is maintained between the people who are communicating.

Body language can convey a powerful message to customers. Suppose you have an appointment at a hotel and, when you go up to the reception desk, the receptionist seems very busy and is on the telephone. If the receptionist does not acknowledge your presence, you will feel ignored and perhaps even angry. On the other hand, if the receptionist smiles at you, you will feel noticed and welcome even though you cannot be attended to immediately. A small gesture can make all the difference.

How is this waiter's behaviour having a negative impact on his customers?

Did you know?

How familiar are you with hospitality jargon?

- 'No-shows' are guests who have made up a booking but who fail to show up.
- 'ETA' is short for estimated time of arrival.
- 'Rack rate' is the full price of a room.

Try not to use slang or jargon when dealing with customers as they may not understand these terms.

The effectiveness of your communication is affected by the tone and pitch of your voice. You need to be aware of how you might come across to customers in a hospitality setting.

- A varied pitch and tone will demonstrate interest in the customer and enthusiasm for your subject. A flat pitch and tone suggests boredom.
- If you do not speak clearly, customers will not be able to understand you and they might become frustrated or dissatisfied with the service.
- Customers must be able to understand what you are saying. This means that you should be careful about the type of language you use.
- Do not use slang or jargon, or specialist terms such as no-show, ETA or rack rate, that customers may not understand.

Listening skills

According to an old saying, you should 'Hear twice before you speak once'. We often listen with 'half an ear' because we are worrying about what to do or say next. Do not be tempted to do that. Listen carefully to what is being said otherwise you may not get a full picture.

In any dealings with customers, listen both to what they are saying and how they are speaking. The way in which they say something – the level, pace and strength of their voice – may give you clues to their feelings.

It is only when we listen carefully to what customers say that we can identify their needs. It is important to:

- ask appropriate questions

- repeat back important information to the customer

- look attentive.

Using sensitive questions may help you understand better how your customer is feeling. There are two main types of questions that you could use when trying to identify and interpret a problem affecting a customer. These are open questions and closed questions.

Open questions are used to get the customer talking. They often begin with 'Who?', 'What?', 'Where?' and 'How?'. They can also take the form of an invitation, such as 'Can you describe the problems you have been having?'

Closed questions are used when you do not want or need the customer to go into detail. These are questions that often invite a simple 'Yes' or 'No' answer. For example, 'Would you like a large, medium or small?' is a closed question because it only needs a one-word answer.

Assessment activity 2
Unit 3 P6 P7 P8 P9 P10 M2 D1 · BTEC

Recent feedback on a travel website suggests that customers have not been entirely happy with customer service provision in your area. Much of the feedback indicates that some staff in the local hospitality industry do not seem to care about customers. They can display a negative attitude in their work.

You are working in the training office of the local tourist board. You have been asked to help rectify this problem by organising a series of training sessions for local organisations.

1   Create a PowerPoint® presentation that describes how individual members of staff can themselves benefit from providing excellent customer service. **P6**

2   Produce a staff handbook that:

- describes the importance of positive attitude, behaviour and motivation in providing excellent customer service **P7**

- describes the importance of personal presentation for staff working in the hospitality industry **P8**

- explains the importance of using appropriate types of communication with customers **P9**

- describes why it is important that staff in the hospitality industry have effective listening skills. **P10**

3 For this task, you should continue your investigations into the two local hospitality organisations that you visited for Assessment activity 1, Task 3.

It is impossible for hospitality businesses to meet the needs of their customers if they do not understand these needs. Analyse how each organisation tries to serve its customers through accurately recognising their needs and finding suitable solutions. **M2**

Evaluate the extent to which each organisation is successful in meeting and exceeding of customer needs and expectations. Suggest ways each organisation might improve its customer service. **D1**

Grading tips

P6 Speak to people working in the hospitality industry to find out what they feel are the benefits to them of providing good customer service.

P7 Speak to family and friends about how the attitude of customer service staff affects their impressions of a hospitality business. Think about your own experiences of customer service.

P8 Observe the personal appearance of hospitality staff in different organisations. Think about the impression that this can give to customers.

P9 Carry out your own experiment. Make enquiries at some hospitality organisations and consider the different ways that the organisations respond to you. What does this say about how communication with customers can create an impression of a hospitality operation?

P10 Try to imagine the consequences if customer service staff do not listen properly to what customers are saying. What problems could it create?

M2 Prepare some questions for each organisation before your visit. Visit travel review websites such as TripAdvisor to see whether any customers have posted messages about the service at these organisations. To find the web address for the TripAdvisor website, go to the Hotlinks for this book (see page ii).

PLTS

You will develop your skills as an **independent enquirer** when investigating customer service in two hospitality organisations.

Functional skills

You will use your **ICT** skills to produce your PowerPoint® presentation and staff handbook. You will develop your **English** skills of reading, speaking and listening to gather information about customer service.

3.3 Understand the importance of customers' needs and expectations in the hospitality, leisure, travel and tourism industries

Having considered the role of the organisation and individual members of staff in delivering good customer service, we will now focus on customers. To deliver good customer service, a hospitality organisation has to deliver what its customers want and to meet their expectations. To do this, we will consider:

- assessing customers' needs and expectations
- meeting customers' needs and expectations
- complaints.

Assessing customers' needs and expectations

Customers have a variety of needs for customer services. Some can be urgent, whereas others are less urgent. The urgency of a particular need will influence the action that is taken and the method of dealing with the problem. For example, a hospitality organisation will want to take immediate action to:

- handle any customer complaints
- tell customers of any change in products and services
- inform other departments of any change in levels of business or customer requirements.

Dealing with these urgent issues will be more important than:

- promoting products and services to customers
- making small talk (chatting) with customers
- telling other departments about things that will be happening in the future.

Activity: Tackling urgent problems

Visit a local hotel and ask about its procedures for dealing with:
- a fire
- a bomb alert
- aggressive visitors
- people who are drunk.

Information

People working in hospitality spend a lot of time giving customers information and advice. This means that, as we have discussed already, it is absolutely vital for staff to have a good level of service and product knowledge.

In order to meet the needs of customers, members of staff need to learn everything they can about their organisation. This will allow them to provide information to customers on the organisation's products and services and it will help them advise customers who are undecided about which options to choose. In addition, staff need to be able to answer a wide range of questions on many other topics. Working in hospitality, you may be asked to:

- recommend a suitable wine to go with a customer's meal
- give information about the local area
- advise guests on holiday about how they could spend their day.

Because customer service is all about understanding the needs of customers, sometimes they will expect you to offer to help without actually asking for assistance. It is wise to observe customers' behaviour. If they look hesitant and unsure, ask how you can help them.

Sometimes customers need help in choosing the product or service that will be most suitable for them. You must learn to ask appropriate questions and listen carefully to the responses, so that you can suggest the most appropriate product and service for the customer.

Activity: A Christmas party

What questions should a party co-ordinator ask someone who is booking a Christmas party for 100 guests to make sure that the event meets their needs and expectations?

Special needs

All customers have individual needs. However, as we saw on page 71, some have additional needs (or special needs) that go beyond the general needs of most customers.

This may be because the customer has a physical disability, such as hearing, sight or mobility impairment. It may be because the customers do not speak English or because they are with children and want to order children's meals and have highchairs around the table. They may be travelling on business, and want to use business equipment and have access to office facilities. Some organisations also recognise that men and women can have different needs and expectations, and they adapt their services and perhaps offer **gender-specific products**.

Key term

Gender-specific products – products for, or associated with, persons of one gender (male or female) to the exclusion of the other.

It is important that customers are given the opportunity to communicate any particular requirements, and staff should also be trained to recognise special needs. Once special needs have been established, these must be communicated to relevant staff so that customers do not have to keep explaining what they require. It is also important to be aware of the costs involved in providing for people with special needs.

Cultural needs

It is very important to respect the cultural needs and practices of customers. For example, some customers may require a special diet for cultural or religious reasons. A hospitality business would not want to cause any offence, and it would expect staff to show that they understand and respect the needs of all its customers.

We live in a multicultural society and a hospitality organisation's staff may come from a variety of cultural backgrounds. This means that an organisation's internal customers may also have cultural needs, and managers and other members of staff should respect their customs. This means respecting the way that they dress (as long as this does not compromise health and safety) and other social differences.

Factors that influence choice

To understand customers' needs and expectations, it is also important to know why they buy particular hospitality products. Many factors influence customers' choice of products and services. Price is one of the strongest influences on buying decisions, but other factors influencing choice include:

- previous experience of the hospitality organisation and its staff
- brand name and company reputation
- recommendation from friends or family
- marketing information
- the particular occasion – customers might choose different venues for a business meal, a celebration or a quick bite to eat while shopping
- special needs – customers might choose particular venues that can meet their dietary or cultural needs.

Activity: A class meal

In groups, discuss where you might go out as a class for a meal. Identify the factors that influence your choice.

Meeting customers' needs and expectations

Before a hospitality organisation can meet its customers' needs, it has to find out what they are. This means finding answers to some important questions.

- What are customers' specific needs and what are their expectations of the organisation?
- What products and services can the organisation provide to meet these needs?

Getting answers requires that staff talk to customers. Organisations should constantly monitor the views of their customers and check whether they are satisfied with the service they are getting. We will look at how organisations can do this on pages 87–92.

Having taken the trouble to find out what customers need, an organisation should respond accordingly. The time spent understanding what customers need is wasted if an organisation does not (or cannot) deliver a service that meets these needs. To ensure that it does, everyone involved in serving guests and dealing with customers must know exactly what they should be achieving, and they should be provided with the resources to enable them to provide a service to the required standards.

Satisfying customers means delivering service that meets their **needs** or **expectations**, whichever is higher. This is the basic principle underpinning customer service. Note that expectations are not always greater than needs. A hotel might have a reputation for bad customer service, and if guests receive very bad service, their expectations would have been met but their needs would not have been satisfied.

However, if an organisation only meets customers' needs, then its customers are likely to go away thinking that the organisation is all right but nothing special. Therefore, more organisations aim to exceed their customers' needs and expectations. By delighting every one of their customers, they hope that customers will return soon.

In short, the best organisations seek to:

- anticipate needs
- respond to these needs
- meet and exceed expectations.

Key terms

Needs – the very basic requirements that customers seek, such as good food, clean toilets and a safe environment. If these basic needs are not met, customers will never be satisfied.

Expectations – what customers are expecting to get. If they have high expectations because of everything they have heard or previously experienced, then these must be met because anything less will leave customers dissatisfied.

Complaints

Although nobody likes to get complaints, they should be seen as an opportunity to improve rather than simply regarded as a bad experience. If something is wrong with the products and services that an organisation is providing, it needs to put it right. If customers do not tell you when they are unhappy with the service, how will you know that they are dissatisfied? If you don't know that something is wrong, how will you be able to put it right?

Unfortunately, when some customers are unhappy, they do not feel able to, or cannot be bothered to, complain. However, they might not return and they may say bad things about the service or the organisation.

Activity: Meeting needs and expectations

Think of an occasion when your expectations were met but your needs were not satisfied. Share it with the rest of the class.

Taking a positive approach

A complaint is an opportunity to improve. Therefore, it is extremely important to deal with complaints in a positive manner. One way to do this is to offer customers some form of compensation.

- If they are eating in a restaurant and their main course has been delayed, the restaurant might offer them a free drink.

- If a guest wants a meal that is not available, the restaurant could offer a more expensive choice on the menu at a discounted price.

- If a customer arrives at a hotel to check in and the room is not ready, the hotel could offer the use of another room to freshen up.

Even if a business does not feel that the customer needs to be compensated, it is important to maintain a positive attitude. Do not be defensive, but try to ensure that the customer feels you are doing all you can to put the problem right.

Activity: The day after the party

It is the day after the Christmas party at the Swan Hotel, a 150-room city-centre property. Four of the room attendants due at work that day have called in sick. The hotel was full the night before and is fully booked for the coming evening.

How can the housekeeper, the room attendants and other members of staff work together to provide the best level of customer service despite being understaffed?

Most organisations have a complaint handling procedure. We will look more closely at complaint handling procedures on page 101.

Assessment activity 3

Your manager has asked you run a training session for the staff at a new hotel in the city. The aim of the session is to ensure the staff understand the importance of meeting customers' needs and expectations. You will also need to address the issue of dealing with customer complaints.

1 Produce a poster that describes:
- what is meant by customer needs and expectations in the hospitality industry (P11)
- the importance of anticipating and responding to customers' needs and expectations (P12)
- the importance of meeting and exceeding customer expectations. (P14)

2 Design an information bulletin describing the factors that influence customers' choice of products and services. (P13)

3 Create an interactive training programme that:
- explains the importance of complaint handling procedures (P16)
- describes the importance of dealing with complaints in a positive manner. (P15)

4 To underpin the training, your manager asks you to write an article for the hotel's staff magazine. The article must analyse ways of meeting customers' needs and expectations. It should outline the strengths and weaknesses of each way of meeting customers' needs. (M3)

Grading tips

(P11) Remember that needs and expectations are different. You must make this clear in your poster. To provide an example, you could describe the typical needs and expectations of customers in any hospitality businesses that you have previously investigated.

(P12) You could continue your poster by focusing on the needs and expectations that you identified for (P11).

(P13) Focus first on factors that influence the choice of organisation (such as which restaurant to eat in) and then consider the factors that influence the choice of purchase at the organisation.

(P14) Reflect on all you have learned about customer service in this unit to show that you understand the importance of meeting and exceeding customer expectations.

(P15) One way of showing the importance of complaint handling is to provide a case study about a bad customer service experience. You should provide two or three questions at the end of the case study so that it could be used as interactive training material. Remember that complaints can be a positive thing.

(P16) Your training programme should investigate how hospitality providers deal with complaints and how seriously they take them. To make it interesting and interactive, you could devise some role plays to show good and bad ways of dealing with customer complaints.

(M3) You should be critical when pointing out the strengths and weaknesses of different ways of meeting customers' needs and expectations.

PLTS

You will develop your skills as an **independent enquirer** when identifying what is meant by customers' needs and expectations in the hospitality industry, and your skills as a **creative thinker** when asking questions when undertaking visits to local hospitality businesses.

Functional skills

You will use **ICT** to produce the work for this assessment. You will develop your **English** skills of reading, speaking and listening to gather information about customer service.

4.1 Be able to monitor and evaluate hospitality businesses' customer service

As we have seen, customer service is a key part of a hospitality business. This means that hospitality businesses need to make regular checks on their customer service. We will now consider how they check their customer service performance. We will look at:

- monitoring customer service
- evaluating customer service
- customer service aims
- making improvements.

Before we do this, try this activity.

Activity: Monitoring customer service

Suppose you have been asked to monitor and evaluate the catering provision at your school or college. Make a list of the ways you could measure the service provided. How could your school or college best monitor the service?

Monitoring customer service

One way of monitoring customer service is to get the opinions and views of customers and staff. This helps organisations provide a more effective customer service. This is important for several reasons.

- To remain competitive, a hospitality business needs to provide a service to its customers that is at least as good as, and preferably better than, its competitors.

- The more that a business knows about its customers' likes and dislikes, the more it can adjust the service so that it suits their tastes and preferences.

- Customers' needs, tastes and preferences can change over time. By getting customer feedback on a regular basis, a business can adapt its products and services to reflect the changing needs and expectations of its customers.

Informal customer feedback

Getting feedback from customers does not have to be a formal process. A member of staff in a hospitality business can learn a great deal from informal contacts with customers. You can find out how customers view the service by speaking to them or observing their reactions.

Remember that it is generally only a minority of customers who make complaints or offer compliments on the service. If they are dissatisfied, most customers simply leave and decide to go somewhere else in future. Therefore, informal feedback from customers may only tell part of the story. However, when you have dealings with customers you can encourage them to pass on comments that relate to your organisation's service. You can do this by asking them questions and checking that they have enjoyed themselves. You should listen to what customers are saying and use their comments to improve the service that you give.

You can gain feedback by chatting to customers. What other informal feedback methods can you think of?

You do not always need direct contact with customers to form an opinion on what they think of the service. In many situations, you can simply observe the reaction of customers to get a feel for their views on your organisation's products and services. In particular, watch out for:

- body language – do customers raise their eyebrows when they see the price, and do any customers walk out without waiting to be served?
- overheard comments – listen out for particularly loud remarks about the products or service
- queues – long queues at checkouts are a major source of customer discontent.

Activity: Reading body language

In pairs, take it in turns to show a feeling through body language rather than words. Try to guess what the other person is feeling.

Questionnaires and comment cards

Although informal feedback is extremely useful, it should not be used as the only means of monitoring customer service. Many hospitality businesses also use formal methods of feedback such as questionnaires and comment cards. These enable a business to:

- measure something specific such as the customers' reaction to a new menu
- determine if customers' needs are being met
- check that standards are being kept
- evaluate written feedback more easily.

Questionnaires and customer comment cards are a common way of getting feedback from customers. Hotels and restaurants have used this type of approach for some time, and other sections of the hospitality industry are making more use of both methods to get feedback.

- Comment cards tend to be short and are useful as a source of instant feedback.
- Questionnaires are often given to customers at the end of their meal or at the end of their visit. Sometimes they are sent to customers after their visit. They are a way of getting more detailed information.

Customers in a restaurant are generally asked to complete comment cards while they are being served or immediately after their meal. Because of this, they are designed to be brief and may only seek a limited range of information.

Questionnaires should be well laid out, easy to complete and reassure customers that any information they give will be treated confidentially. A letter or email sent with a questionnaire can act as an introduction by explaining the purpose of the questionnaire. Some organisations offer an incentive, such as a free gift or entry in a prize draw, to customers that complete and return their questionnaires by a certain date.

Considerable care needs to be given to the phrasing of the questions on comment cards and questionnaires. They should be easy to understand and unambiguous – both the customer and the organisation must have the same understanding of what is being asked.

We introduced the idea of open and closed questions earlier in these units (see page 79). To establish facts, such as whether the service was good, how long it took to be served or the gender of the customer, use closed questions. These require brief answers, such as 'Yes', or can be answered by indicating one or a limited range of answers. If more information is required on a customer's feelings or opinions, the questions can be more open.

Organisations often use rating scales and tick boxes to make questionnaires and comment cards easier to complete. For example, Figure 2 on page 90 shows a comment card that asks five questions that can be answered by tick boxes and then leaves room for customers to make any other comments if they wish.

Customer Feedback Questionnaire

We value your opinion. Please use the questionnaire below to make any comments following your visit.

Quality of food/drink

☐ Very good   ☐ Good   ☐ Average   ☐ Poor   ☐ Very poor

Menu

☐ Very good   ☐ Good   ☐ Average   ☐ Poor   ☐ Very poor

Comfort/ambience

☐ Very good   ☐ Good   ☐ Average   ☐ Poor   ☐ Very poor

Service

☐ Very good   ☐ Good   ☐ Average   ☐ Poor   ☐ Very poor

Value for money

☐ Very good   ☐ Good   ☐ Average   ☐ Poor   ☐ Very poor

Thank you for your feedback

Figure 2: Example of a customer feedback form

Staff feedback

Members of staff can also provide useful feedback. This will be just as valuable when it comes to getting an overall picture of the service that an organisation provides.

By talking to staff and observing how they interact with customers, managers can get feedback on any standards of service that staff find difficult to uphold. Staff should also be encouraged to give their ideas for improving service.

Mystery customers

When you work in hospitality, you will often be urged to put yourself in the place of the customer. **Mystery customers** are paid to do this in practice. Working with a checklist of points to consider, mystery customers behave just like ordinary customers, but they will note the service that they get and provide detailed feedback afterwards. They do not tell members of staff that they are checking on the customer service. This means that hospitality organisations get an anonymous assessment of the service they provide, with feedback from an informed yet impartial source. It is simply another way of getting feedback about the service that your organisation provides. Figure 3 shows one example of the type of feedback that can be provided by a mystery customer.

Key term

Mystery customer – someone who poses as a normal customer but who is paid to give an organisation feedback about its services and products.

Activity: Mystery shopping

Next time you go shopping or to a restaurant, become a mystery customer. You should evaluate the:

- promptness of service
- product knowledge of the staff
- general appearance of the outlet
- availability of products and services
- attitude and behaviour of the staff.

How could the shop or restaurant use your findings?

Seaview Hotel, Brighton: Internal Mystery Visitor Audit

Area: Restaurant (Breakfast)   1 = satisfactory, 0 = unsatisfactory

	Location: Seafront Road, Brighton	
	Customer Satisfaction	Comments
Acknowledgement of guest (30 seconds)	1	
Assistance with seating and satisfaction confirmed	0	No assistance with sitting and no explanation of breakfast offered
Service style explained/order taken	0	
Promptness of breakfast tea/coffee (3 minutes)	1	
Friendliness of staff	1	
Use of name at least once during meal or greeting	0	
Appearance of staff (including name badge)	0	Man who met at front door did not have a name badge
Cleanliness of restaurant	1	
Cleanliness of cutlery and crockery	1	
Satisfaction checked during meal or offer of any replenishments	0	Fresh fruit was missing
Quality of food: taste, temperature and freshness	1	
Tables cleared of plates as required	0	
Bill and payment processed correctly	1	
Customer acknowledged and thanked on departure	1	
Rating (%)	57%	

Figure 3: Example of feedback from a mystery customer

Complaints and compliment letters

Feedback can also come in the form of complaints or unsolicited compliments. If customers take the time and effort to feed back their feelings, an organisation should take notice of what they say. Customers might give their feedback in person or by letter. In either case, the feedback should be acknowledged to let customers know that views are welcome and appreciated.

Customer complaints give the organisation and its staff a chance to put a problem right. The key to customer complaints is to adopt a positive attitude – treat them as an opportunity to improve the reliability and standard of customer service.

Customer compliments are equally useful to the organisation, as they highlight areas where the service meets the needs of the customers providing the feedback. Sometimes these comments are used in publicity and marketing materials. Permission should be sought from customers if their names are to be used in any advertising or marketing material.

Complaints and compliments should always be fed back to any staff who provided the service that was criticised or praised by customers.

Evaluating customer service

Feedback can be collected from customers in several ways. In most customer service situations, it is possible to generate plenty of information from customers. However, collecting feedback is useless unless an organisation can use it properly. When organisations make a decision to collect customer feedback as a basis for updating and improving customer service, they need to be clear about what information they want and what they will do with it. For example, they may want to collect information to:

- make improvements in terms of product quality, reliability or value for money
- evaluate procedures
- monitor job satisfaction.

Many organisations evaluate performance on the basis of quantitative information, such as:

- level of sales
- number of repeat customers
- number of new customers
- level of complaints
- number of compliments received
- staff turnover – that is, how long staff remain with an organisation.

Customer service aims

Customer feedback also helps organisations assess whether their customer service is helping to achieve their overall aims. Generally, the aims of customer service in the hospitality industry are to:

- achieve customer satisfaction
- exceed customer expectations
- meet organisational targets.

It is only through monitoring and evaluation that organisations can assess whether they are meeting these aims.

Making improvements

Seeking the opinions and views of customers helps organisations provide a more effective customer service. Time and money spent gathering customer feedback is wasted if it is not used to make improvements.

Activity: Taking action

Table 1 is an extract from a mystery customer report for Spencer's restaurant. Identify two actions the manager can take with the staff to address these findings.

Service standard	Average score
Food delivered within 15 minutes (target 90%)	75%
Telephone answered within three rings (target 85%)	60%
Smile when greeting customers (target 99%)	100%
Food quality satisfaction (target 99%)	76%

Table 1: Extract from a report by mystery customers

Improvements can generally be made in several areas, including product quality and offering value for money. Feedback can often help to improve the quality of products and services.

- Both formal and informal feedback should indicate any aspects of the service that customers are not happy with.

- Employing mystery customers is an excellent way of gauging the quality of service because they are taking a customer service journey.

Value for money goes hand in hand with customer service excellence.

- The most obvious indication that an organisation is not offering value for money the level of sales. Customers will not buy anything they consider gives poor value for money.

- Informal and formal feedback will also identify individual products or services that customers tend to avoid, and this could be because they do not offer value for money.

Reliabilty

Hospitality organisations want to offer a reliable service. This means that customers know what to expect when they make a visit.

- An excellent indication that customers feel that an organisation is reliable is that they visit it time after time.

- The level of customer complaints is also a good way of measuring problems. A surge in the number of problems could indicate that the service is becoming unreliable.

- Customers are much more inclined to fill out questionnaires or comment cards if they are particularly satisfied or dissatisfied with an aspect of the service.

Activity: What should we ask?

Suggest four questions that you could ask customers to gauge the reliability of service in a city-centre wine bar.

Internal procedures

Many organisations set standards of performance for customer service and train their staff to follow these procedures. Formal and informal feedback will allow you to determine whether procedures are being followed. If they are not being followed, the organisation should make a plan to take corrective action.

Compliance with legal obligations

Compliance with legal obligations is obviously vital, and obtaining customer feedback is an excellent way of checking that this is happening. Even if customers are not aware of their legal obligations, their feedback could identify a failure to comply with the law.

Staff job satisfaction

Formal and informal feedback from staff can show if they are satisfied with their job. Many hospitality organisations regularly survey their staff to check that they are happy in their work.

If staff are involved in the collection of feedback, they will be interested in the results of evaluation exercises and motivated by any changes resulting from their involvement.

Activity: Are staff happy at work?

How can you assess whether staff are satisfied with their job just by observing them?

Assessment activity 4

Unit 4　**P1** **M1** **D1**　BTEC

You have been asked to monitor and evaluate the customer service provision in two hospitality businesses. You must first select two businesses. These could be the two organisations you investigated for the earlier assessment activities in these units or they could be different organisations.

Next, visit these businesses to find out the methods that they use to monitor and evaluate customer service. You need to focus on:

- what information is gathered
- how the information is obtained
- how it is used to improve customer service.

Grading tips

P1 Investigate each organisation before each visit. Prepare some questions to ask the staff about how they monitor customer service and how they use the information gathered to improve customer service.

M1 When determining the strengths and weaknesses of different methods of monitoring customer service, consider factors such as ease of use, the cost of obtaining the information and how easy it would be to analyse the information gathered. Does the information allow the hospitality business to recognise areas for improvement? Is it reliable?

1 Based on your visits and investigations, produce a report identifying the methods of monitoring and evaluating customer service used in the two businesses. **P1**

2 Following your investigations, produce a set of guidelines that analyses the strengths and weaknesses of each method you identified in Task 1. **M1**

3 Produce a further report that evaluates the customer service provision in both hospitality businesses, making suggestions for improvement. **D1**

D1 You could collect information from tourist boards, such as brochures and leaflets, and do some research on the Internet to find out more about the type of service that each business aims to provide. You might be able to find on the Internet some opinions from customers of their provision. You could also do your own mystery customer exercise. The recommendations you suggest can be minor, but all should be realistic and in line with each organisation's customer service policies. You must justify your recommendations by relating them to existing customer service policies, general industry practice or the potential benefit to the business.

 PLTS

You will develop your skills as an **independent enquirer** when you monitor and evaluate customer service provision.

 Functional skills

You will use your **ICT** skills to produce the work for this assessment. You will develop your **English** skills of reading, speaking and listening to gather information about monitoring and evaluating customer service.

4.2 Be able to demonstrate customer service skills in different situations in hospitality

You now have to put what you have been learning into practice by demonstrating your own customer service skills. To do that, you need to consider:

- customer types
- presentation skills
- communication skills
- customers' needs
- interpersonal skills
- common customer service situations.

Customer types

First, you need to remember that each customer is different. However, as we have discussed, customers can be grouped into different categories and customers in each category often have similar needs. Look back at the different types of customers in the hospitality industry (see pages 67–71). You will be given the opportunity to practise your customer service skills on different types of customer.

Customers' needs

We have also considered the different needs of customers, and stated how important it is to meet and exceed customer expectations. Now let's consider some of these ways that this can be achieved.

Value for money

All customers expect to get value for money, but it can be a little difficult to demonstrate this to customers. It is important to price competitively. This does not necessarily mean always undercutting the competition. If a hospitality organisation has the cheapest products and services, it may be sending the message that it does not have confidence in them and they may be of poor quality. A business can show customers that it offers value for money by promoting its goods and services in a positive way and describing their benefits.

Activity: A room with a view

Find a hotel on the Internet and identify how you would promote its most expensive rooms to show that they offer guests value for money.

Accuracy and reliability

Customers expect an organisation to deliver the service that has been promised. It should be consistent and dependable.

- If a response is promised in a certain time, does this always happen?
- Are menu items correctly described?
- Are customer accounts free of error?
- Is the service performed right the first time?
- Are levels of service the same at all times of day?
- Do all members of staff provide service to the required standards?

Information, advice and assistance

By now, you should understand that hospitality staff are often required to give customers information, advice, assistance and guidance. This creates a good impression and it helps organisations to meet their targets. It also helps staff to identify and respond to customers' needs.

Customers often want information on products and services. What information may you need to provide in a hotel?

Activity: Customer assistance

Consider each of these jobs:
- room attendant
- conference and banqueting sales co-ordinator
- concierge
- waiting staff.

For each, list three things that a person doing the job might be asked by a customer seeking information or assistance.

Special needs

It is really important that you are able to deal with any customers that have special needs in a professional manner. For example, you may have to help customers who:

- cannot speak English
- have a learning difficulty or physical impairment
- have special dietary requirements.

Activity: A family day out

Suppose you are working in the reception team at a hotel. A family with two small children is staying at the hotel for the weekend. They have asked you to help them plan a day out in the local area. In pairs, prepare and act out a role play showing how you would assist these guests.

Identifying and dealing with problems

Despite all efforts and care, customers sometimes encounter problems when visiting a hospitality organisation. It is important that any problems are dealt with immediately and that the customer is satisfied with this action.

When you are working in the hospitality industry, some problems may be beyond your control. For example, you may have to deal with a customer who has:

- lost their wallet or handbag
- been taken ill
- had some bad news from home.

Unfortunately, problems will sometimes be caused by your organisation. For example, you may have to deal with a customer who:

- has booked a family room at your hotel and has arrived to find that they have been allocated a twin room
- finds the meal that they have been served in the restaurant too cold or badly prepared
- complains that a member of staff has been rude to them.

Whatever the problem, and regardless of whether your organisation was responsible, each customer needs to be assured that you are taking them seriously. The problem must be dealt with promptly and in a sensitive manner.

Health, safety and security

When customers are on a hospitality organisation's premises, the organisation has a duty of care towards them. Both employers and employees must make sure that the premises are healthy, safe and secure for all customers, members of the public and staff.

Presentation skills

All your contacts and dealings with customers will influence how these customers think about you and your organisation. First impressions are especially important as they set the tone. Let's look in more detail at how you can make a good impression.

It is extremely important to maintain a high standard of personal hygiene and appearance. It creates a good impression for customers, and it reflects well on you and on your employer.

The impressions that customers form of an organisation are based not only on the presentation of the staff but also on the appearance of all work and public areas. If your work area does not look well organised, customers may assume (rightly or wrongly) that you and your organisation are disorganised. Make sure that:

- your work area is neat and tidy
- you have all the equipment and supplies that you need when you first start a shift.

In this way, you will not only make a good impression but you will also be able to offer a better service to guests.

Activity: Creating the right impression

In small groups, prepare a guide on personal hygiene and appearance for waiting staff working in a fine dining restaurant.

Interpersonal skills

Excellent customer service depends on being able to demonstrate a high level of interpersonal skills when dealing with customers. This means that you should be able to:

- get along with customers
- show that you care about them and recognise their needs.

Attitude and behaviour

A positive attitude and appropriate behaviour are essential when dealing with customers. Your attitude should let customers know that you care and that you are trying your best to make their visit a good experience. A negative attitude, such as appearing or being bored and uninterested, will affect how you communicate with customers. They may even think you are being deliberately rude.

First impressions

Many organisations train staff in how to greet guests and in personal presentation skills so that they are able to make a good impression. It is important to remember that customers can arrive at any time, so you always need to be alert and ready to welcome guests. Many organisations have standards for how staff should address customers and how they should respond when taking phone calls.

Greeting customers

Greeting customers is one of the most important duties that you will perform for your organisation because this is when customers' first impressions are formed. Hospitality organisations often have their own performance standards for greeting customers. They will usually expect that customers should be greeted with eye contact and a warm smile.

How can you make sure you make a good impression when customers arrive?

Activity: Meeting and greeting

Two children have been staying in your hotel for over a week. How would you greet them when they come into the lobby?

Respect for customers

The way in which you interact with customers will create an impression of how much you care. Customers will expect you to show them respect by:

- being courteous
- showing an interest in what they are saying
- trying to help them.

Their mood will be influenced by the experiences they have when receiving goods and services. This is great if the experience has been positive, as customers will be happy. It will be more difficult to deal with customers if the experience has not been so good. If customers are not happy with the service being provided, they may become aggressive and rude. If they do, it is important to stay in control and to get assistance if necessary.

Responding to customer behaviour

Customers have differing needs and expectations, and they also behave in different ways. In other words, they display different types of behaviour. For example, they may be nervous, angry, shy, distressed, concerned, excited or happy.

It is important to respond appropriately to customer behaviour. For example, if customers are distressed, find out what is bothering them and try to help them; if they are angry, find a way of calming them down; if they are excited, share their enthusiasm. This is called **empathising** with the customer.

Key term

Empathising – to identify with another person's feelings by emotionally putting yourself in their place.

Activity: Dealing with different customer behaviour

It is a very busy Friday afternoon at the Swan Hotel, with almost 50 guests due to check in. These guests display many types of behaviour. Some show:

- anger
- disappointment
- aggression.
- excitement
- distress

Take each of these behaviours in turn. In pairs, role play how you would respond to customers checking in and displaying this type of behaviour.

Dealing with complaints

It is particularly important to show respect to customers who have cause to complain. Customers are far more aware of their consumer rights nowadays; they know what they should expect from a product or service, and they can be very quick to complain if something is wrong.

When dealing with a complaint, you must remember that the customer is likely to be angry, which might make them impatient, unhappy and sometimes rude.

- Act in an efficient and diplomatic way, or the customer may lose their temper and become even more angry.
- Remain calm and polite no matter how angry the customer gets.
- Remember not to take the customer's anger personally.

It is important to comply with any policy your organisation has on dealing with complaints. This will vary from one business to another. However, generally, you should follow this course of action.

- Acknowledge the customer immediately, and say you are sorry that they are unhappy with the service they have received.
- Listen carefully to the complaint without interrupting. You must let customers finish what they are saying, otherwise you may stop them from fully explaining what is wrong.
- Summarise the complaint by repeating back its main points to the customer. This way you can make sure there is no misunderstanding about the nature of the complaint.
- Explain what action will be taken and how quickly.

Besides keeping customers informed when there is a problem, your other priority is to maintain the highest possible service at all times. This means doing your best to reduce inconvenience to customers while the problem lasts and doing everything to get back to normal service as quickly as possible.

Sometimes this requires you and other team members to be flexible. You might have to agree to do things outside of your normal routine activities. It always requires extra effort from one person, if not the whole team.

Case study: A bad review

TripAdvisor is a free travel guide and research website that assists customers in gathering travel information. Visitors to the website can post reviews on their own experiences (good and bad) of hotels, restaurants, flights and holiday rentals. The website attracts millions of visitors every month.

Many people are influenced by what they read on TripAdvisor. Both leisure and business customers often use the reviews to help them choose hotels, and the first thing that some hotel managers do each day is to check whether there are any new reviews of their establishments on the website.

Some reviews offer constructive feedback whereas many offer praise and recommend the establishment to other guests, but some postings can be very critical. This is one example of a bad review posted by a guest at a hotel.

'We checked into the hotel for a one-night stay. The receptionist, to begin with, was curt but professional. The room was small and very hot, but adequate for one night, until we used the bathroom. The bathroom was very old and the shower was very mouldy, but that wasn't the biggest problem, that was when we tried to fill the wash hand basin and food came back up from the pipes. We spoke to reception who gave us two options, a refund or they would get one of the staff to attempt to unblock the sink. We were not very happy with these offers of help.

'However, our main complaint was the restaurant. We had reserved a table with the receptionist when we checked in, but on arrival no table had been booked. Far from the stylish setting promised on the hotel website, the restaurant resembled a café with a bar. No tablecloths, no candles, flowers, nothing. Adjoining tables were used by people on laptops conducting business, not eating. The waiter first brought us the breakfast menu, it was 8.30 pm! The food was well below expectations. The rotisserie chicken, whilst tasty, came completely on its own and was too big. The dessert took over 30 minutes, and arrived only after we had reminded the staff. When we complained, we were told that there was a new chef and that the staff often laughed at the restaurant description on the website.

Let this be a warning to everyone. Do not stay at this hotel!'

1 Outline the actions you would take if you were a general manager reading this review of your hotel.

2 Identify alternative ways staff could have dealt with each complaint.

3 Explain what this review tells us about the way hospitality organisations describe their goods and services to customers.

4 The receptionist is described as 'curt'. Define this term and identify the impression this manner could give to guests.

5 If you have the opportunity to visit a local hotel during your investigations for these units, find out its policy for dealing with customer complaints.

Communication skills

It is essential to communicate with customers accurately and effectively if you are to meet their needs. You will need to show good listening skills as well as verbal and non-verbal skills. You must also be able to adapt your method of communication to suit different situations.

Voice

The effectiveness of verbal communication is very much influenced by the tone and pitch of your voice. Varying the pitch and tone shows that you are interested in what a customer has to say and are keen to help. A monotonous pitch and tone can demonstrate the opposite and suggest that you are not concerned about what the customer is saying.

Listening

It is important that you listen not only to what customers are saying, but the way they are speaking such as their tone of voice. This will help you to identify how the customer is feeling and it will make it easier for you to respond appropriately.

Body language

It is important to be able to read a customer's body language as this will also help you to understand how the person is feeling. You must also ensure that your own body language gives a positive message to the customer. For example, leaning forward slightly towards the customer conveys that you are paying attention and listening carefully.

Common customer service situations

You will deal with customers in a variety of situations, and you need to be confident dealing with customers face to face, on the telephone, by email and in writing.

Face to face

Communicating face to face has many advantages over other forms of communication. For a start, you can observe body language and get an idea of how the other person is feeling. It is easier to find out exactly what the customer wants because you can have a conversation and gauge the reaction to what you are suggesting. For this reason, it is much easier to build a rapport with customers when you can see them.

When communicating face to face with a guest, you should:

- maintain eye contact
- smile
- practise the art of listening
- try to gauge their mood.

Activity: Communicating with customers

How would you talk to customers who:
- wanted to make a complaint about the food they have been served?
- had just arrived at your hotel after a long and tedious journey?
- had a happy holiday experience?

On the telephone

The only thing that you can use to create an impression when you are on the telephone is your voice. However, it is very important to remember that the impression you make comes both from the words you use and from the pitch and tone of your voice.

Tips for answering the telephone

- Answer the call within three or four rings or apologise for the delay in taking the call.

- Use an appropriate greeting.

- Sound confident and pleasant.

- Smile while you are talking. Your smile will transfer to your voice.

- Speak clearly.

- Ask the caller's name and use it.

- Ask the caller if you can provide any further help before ending the call.

- Thank the caller for the enquiry.

- Do not hang up until the caller has disconnected the line. The caller may have remembered something else they wanted to ask.

Many hotels and hospitality businesses insist that their staff answer the telephone in a standard way. For example, Suzanne, a receptionist at the Swan Hotel, might be expected to answer the phone by saying: 'The Swan Hotel, Bournemouth. Suzanne speaking. How may I help you?'

How can you create a good impression on the telephone?

In writing

Customers can communicate in writing by letter, fax or email. When replying in writing, it is essential that you think very carefully about what you want to communicate. This is because once the communication has been sent, you will have no influence over how the customer may interpret your message and you will have no chance to change its tone. For many potential guests, the written communication they receive will be their first contact with the establishment.

A badly written or typed letter gives a very bad impression, particularly if it contains incorrect spellings or bad grammar. Many customers will equate the standard of letter writing with the service provided by the organisation. You will be expected to follow any conventions used by your organisation. Many establishments have adopted a standard form for **mailshots** and confirmations of bookings.

Email is becoming an increasingly popular method of written communication and it is important that business emails are treated with the same professionalism as letters. For example, it is important to check all emails for spelling or grammatical errors before they are sent. You must also make sure the email sets the right tone; for example, writing in capital letters will give the reader the impression that you are shouting. Finally, always check who you are sending your email to: never click Reply All unless you want everyone to see what you have said.

Key term

Mailshot – promotional material sent out to attract customers.

Urgent or non-urgent

Before sending a message, you need to decide whether the communication is urgent or non-urgent. This will influence the method used. For example, there is little point in sending an email to the chef saying that there has been a last-minute booking for a table of 20. The chef is unlikely to check emails while working in the kitchen.

The urgency of a communication may also influence the pitch and tone of your voice. You might use a loud voice to communicate an instruction to evacuate in the event of a fire alarm, although you will want to adopt a calm and firm tone rather than one that might encourage guests to panic.

Difficult or routine

Most of your communications with customers will be routine. For example, you may take customer orders in the restaurant several times in each sitting. However, communication is sometimes more difficult or complex. You may have to deal with angry, aggressive, drunk, distressed or upset customers.

It is important in these situations to stay calm and try to identify the exact needs of the customer. You may need to seek help from a more senior member of staff. Dealing with this kind of communication requires a basic knowledge of the organisation's policies and procedures. It also requires experience, and it is likely to get easier when you have dealt with similar situations in the past.

Follow safe working practices

No matter how happy customers are with the service you provide, they are unlikely to return to your organisation if they do not feel safe. It is therefore vitally important to follow safe working practices and to abide by any health and safety regulations. This is the responsibility of all employees under the Health and Safety at Work Act 1974.

Assessment activity 5

Unit 4 **P2** **M2** **D2** BTEC

1 In groups of three, develop and role play these three scenarios:
- taking a restaurant booking for a Christmas party consisting of 25 guests
- explaining to a young family on a weekend break what leisure activities they could take part in throughout your area
- dealing with an irate customer who has checked into a room that has not been cleaned.

One person should be the customer and one person the member of staff that deals with the customer. The third member of the group should observe the role play and provide some feedback to the person playing the member of staff. Take it in turns to be the customer, the member of staff and the observer in each scenario. **P2**

2 For this task, you have to show that you are able to look after customers independently and confidently in different situations. This may be something you can do during a work placement or at work if you have a part-time job. Alternatively, your tutor may organise a training day in which you have to serve customers in different situations.

You need to get a witness statement from your supervisor or line manager (if you are doing this at

work) or from your tutor (if you are doing this in a training environment). You should also get direct feedback on your performance. **M2**

3 Bearing in mind the feedback of your peers (in Task 1), and your tutor or supervisor (in Task 2), evaluate your customer service performance. Suggest ways that you could improve your performance. **D2**

Grading tips

P2 Remember to respond to each situation as if it is real. When you are playing the member of staff, make an effort in terms of your personal presentation and appearance.

M2 You must demonstrate that you are competent in providing customer service without direct supervision, and that your body language and manner indicate that you are confident about what you are doing.

D2 Remember to identify your strengths as well as areas for development. Make sure your recommendations for improvement are realistic and achievable.

PLTS

You will develop skills as an **effective participator** and a **self-manager** when demonstrating customer service skills in different customer service situations. You will also show that you are able to be a **reflective learner** when evaluating your own performance.

Functional skills

You will develop **English** skills of speaking and listening when demonstrating your customer service skills.

Claire White
Guest service agent

Claire White has been working as a guest service agent at the Swan Hotel in Cardiff for a year. It is the largest five-star hotel in the city, with 269 newly refurbished bedrooms. It has the biggest banqueting and meeting facilities, with a capacity of up to 500 and an award-winning restaurant.

Her role is to ensure that the hotel provides high levels of guest satisfaction and operational excellence by offering an efficient and personalised service. Claire is often the first point of contact for guests, and it is her responsibility to ensure that it is a good one. She needs to have a professional manner at all times, with an emphasis on hospitality and guest service.

Claire is in charge of the guest relations desk in the hotel lobby, which deals with guest queries, problems and complaints. She has particular responsibility for looking after VIPs, acting as the main point of contact for VIP guests and ensuring hotel departments are fully briefed on their requirements. She checks the guest arrival reports in advance and liaises daily with housekeeping on room allocation for VIP guests. She welcomes VIP guests, escorting them to the executive lounge and their rooms.

Claire loves her job and she has been voted employee of the month three times since she joined the hotel. She says: 'I believe I am an excellent team player and a keen learner. I am adaptable and I have been told I have exceptional interpersonal and communication skills. The job isn't always easy. Some of our guests can be really demanding. We promise them exceptional customer service on our website and we have to deliver this.

'Anyone wanting to work in a similar role should be able to work under pressure, have excellent attention to detail, a high standard of personal presentation and a confident, professional and welcoming personality.'

Before joining the Swan Hotel, Claire worked as a receptionist in an airport hotel for two years, having studied hospitality at college.

Think about it!

- One of Claire's responsibilities is to ensure the other departments in the hotel are fully briefed on the requirements of VIP guests. Identify the specific tasks that she may undertake to ensure this happens.
- Claire often has to deal with very demanding guests. Identify five tips for dealing with demanding guests.

Just checking

1 Define 'customer service'.

2 Who are the internal customers in a hospitality organisation?

3 List four benefits to a hospitality organisation of providing good customer service.

4 Explain why hospitality organisations categorise their customers into market segments.

5 List six words that describe consistent and reliable customer service.

6 Name three ways of collecting customer service feedback.

7 Give three reasons why it is important to gain customer feedback.

8 What is an open question? Give an example of an open question you may ask a customer who is making a booking at a hotel.

9 Describe the process you would follow if a customer complained to you about a meal they had just eaten in the restaurant.

edexcel

Assignment tips

- Ask friends and family about their experiences of customer service to try to better understand customer expectations.

- Take notice of how people behave in restaurants, hotels and other hospitality settings. Observe how customers react to different types of service so that you can improve your understanding of how to meet customers' needs.

- Carry out thorough research for each establishment you investigate for your assignments. It is important to understand the type of service each is offering and to find out what existing customers think of the service provided.

- For one of your assignments you will have to demonstrate your customer service skills. You need to be aware of the image you project and your body language in customer service situations. Ask your friends and family if you have any mannerisms that might upset or distract customers.

5 Planning and running a hospitality event

In this unit you will be involved in planning, organising, running and reviewing a hospitality event. This could be a restaurant service, an open day, a religious celebration, a barbecue, a charity dinner or another event of your choice.

You will need to consider the specific requirements of your customers or clients to ensure that this event meets their needs. You will also need to think about the people and equipment you might need to run the event, as well as the health and safety measures you will need to put in place so that everything runs smoothly. After learning about the purpose and types of promotional material, you will produce marketing material to promote your event.

You will put all you have learned about planning into practice by running the event. To do this, you will work as part of a team. Finally, you will review whether the event was a success using information collected from the people involved, including the members of your team, your tutor and, most importantly, the customers who attended the event.

Learning outcomes

After completing this unit, you should:

1. Know about the planning process for a hospitality event
2. Be able to participate in the organisation of a hospitality event to meet customer requirements
3. Be able to promote a hospitality event
4. Be able to contribute to the running of a hospitality event to meet customer requirements
5. Be able to review the success of a hospitality event.

Assessment and grading criteria

This table shows you what you must do in order to achieve a pass, merit or distinction grade, and where you can find activities in this book to help you.

Unit 5 Planning and running a hospitality event

To achieve a pass grade the evidence must show that you are able to:	To achieve a merit grade the evidence must show that, in addition to the pass criteria, you are able to:	To achieve a distinction grade the evidence must show that, in addition to the pass and merit criteria, you are able to:
P1 describe the planning process for a hospitality event **Assessment activity 1, page 122**	**M1** produce a detailed record of the event planning process, explaining any deviations from the original plan **Assessment activity 2, pages 130–131**	**D1** review the planning and organisation of the event, including own role, and make recommendations on how these could be improved **Assessment activity 2, pages 130–131**
P2 produce a plan for a chosen hospitality event to meet given customer requirements **Assessment activity 2, pages 130–131**		
P3 contribute to the organisation of a chosen hospitality event **Assessment activity 2, pages 130–131**		
P4 produce material suitable for promoting a chosen hospitality event **Assessment activity 3, page 135**	**M2** analyse the impact of using the promotional materials in a chosen event **Assessment activity 3, page 135**	
P5 contribute to the running of a chosen hospitality event **Assessment activity 4, page 140**	**M3** analyse the success of a hospitality event using feedback collected from a variety of sources **Assessment activity 5, page 146**	**D2** make recommendations for improving the success of a hospitality event based on feedback collected from a variety of sources, including the success of the promotional materials used **Assessment activity 5, page 146**
P6 review the hospitality event by designing different methods of collecting feedback **Assessment activity 5, page 146**		

How you will be assessed

You will be assessed by assignments that will be designed and marked by tutors at your centre. You will be assessed on your individual contribution to the planning, organisation, running and evaluation of an event. The evidence that you could provide for your assignments might include:

- detailed plans of your event
- minutes of meetings
- detailed logs of your contribution in the planning process
- witness statements, tutor and customer feedback, and peer observations
- an evaluation of the event.

Katie, 16-year-old learner

I want to work as a wedding planner, organising weddings for the rich and famous! I will probably try to start my career in the events department of a hotel to learn as much as I can about the wedding industry.

I have really enjoyed this unit as we had to arrange our own event. My team organised a fair to raise money for a local charity. It really opened my eyes to how much is involved in making sure that an event is successful. It was really important to plan carefully, to think about things that could go wrong and to make plans to deal with any problems that cropped up. We had to make sure we were aware of health and safety requirements and other legal matters, and we had to be careful to stick to our budget and not spend too much money.

By the day of the charity fair, I really understood the benefits of working as a team, of doing what you say you will do on time, and of communicating effectively. The best thing was that the event was a great success and we raised money for charity.

Over to you
- What events are you interested in organising?
- Have you any previous experience of working in teams?
- If so, what lessons has this taught you about making a success of a project?

5.1 Know about the planning process for a hospitality event

Welcome

An end-of-year party

A rich benefactor has given your class £5000 to organise an end-of-year party. In small groups, decide on a venue, a theme and food and drink for the event. Your ideas should be achievable within the £5000 budget. Present your ideas to the rest of the class and take a vote to see which group came up with the best proposal.

To start your investigation into planning and running hospitality events, you will first look at:

- the planning process
- types of hospitality events.

The planning process

Planning is the process of setting goals and targets, and working out what tasks and activities you will need to complete to meet those targets. It is the most important stage of the event process. Without good planning, the event is unlikely to succeed.

In this section, we will review the factors that influence the planning of a hospitality event and the process you will need to follow to plan your own event.

There are many things to consider when organising an event. They include:

- the nature of the event
- its location
- the target audience
- timing
- resources
- budget
- constraints
- contingency planning
- roles and responsibility
- health and safety requirements.

We will look at each of these considerations in more detail below.

The nature of the event

Before you start the planning process, you must consider the nature of the event. What type of event are you planning to hold, and how many

Activity: Planning a birthday party

Make a list of all the things you should consider when organising a special birthday party, such as an eighteenth or twenty-first birthday party. Think about:

- who you will invite
- where you will hold the party
- what time it will start and finish
- what food and drink you will provide
- who will prepare and serve the food
- what entertainment there will be
- what invitations you will send out
- how much money you will have to spend
- how you will decorate the party room.

What would be the consequences of not planning the party properly? You might end up with no entertainment, with a room that is too small for the number of guests that you have invited or with too few people to serve the food.

people are likely to be attending? This is very important as it will help you to make plans.

- Is it a conference, party, lunch or dinner?
- Why are you holding the event? Is it to celebrate, inform, teach, or reward?
- Will there be entertainment?

Once you have decided on what type of event you are going to run, you can start to organise and plan. It is a good idea at this stage to write a list of all the tasks you have to complete and to set a target date for their completion. You then need to determine who is responsible for each task. Table 1 is an example of the type of format you could use for this purpose.

Target date	Task	Progress
September	Select the event Design the event format Outline planning for the event Set the aims and objectives Confirm the budget Look at suitable venues	
October	Book the venue Identify and allocate roles and responsibilities of the team	

Table 1: Extract from a planning table

Location

A very important stage of the planning process is finding a suitable venue. The venue should be suitable for the type of activities planned and it should be the right size for the number of people expected at the event.

The venue has to be large enough to accommodate everyone, but it is equally important that it is not too big. If you are organising a party for 20 guests but hold it in a room that could accommodate 200 people, your guests may feel uncomfortable and it would be difficult to create a good atmosphere.

You should ask yourself these questions.

- How much does it cost to hire the venue?
- Is it convenient and easy for guests to get to?
- Is there enough parking for guests coming by car?
- Does it have facilities for people with special needs, such as ramps or wide doors for wheelchair users?
- If you are planning to serve a meal, are there facilities for storing and cooking food?

Target audience

The type of event you plan – including the activities, any entertainment, and the food and drink – will depend on who is attending: the target audience. Throughout the planning process it is vital to bear in mind your target audience as the event must meet their needs and expectations.

Activity: How shall we celebrate?

In small groups, discuss what type of event you might hold to:
- raise money for a children's charity
- celebrate the anniversary of the opening of your school or college
- promote a range of new courses at your school or college.

How will you consider the needs of your target audience?

Timing

You will obviously need to schedule a date and time for your event. Here are some of the things to consider.

- Are there any other events happening at the same time?
- Is your chosen venue available when you need it? Some venues are booked up a long time in advance.
- What is the weather likely to be at the proposed time of year?
- Is it an expensive time of year (or day of the week or time of day) to hire your chosen venue?
- What time of day is most likely to suit your target audience?
- How long should the event run for?
- Is public transport available at the time of day you plan to run your event?

In finding a suitable date, you need to make sure that you allow yourself enough time to plan the event. You therefore need to think about the time you will need to plan and organise the event properly. You should allow yourself slightly more time than you think you will need in case you have underestimated the amount of planning involved.

Resources

You will need to make a list of what you need to run your event and to find out the cost of each item. The resources you may need include:

- the venue itself and the cost of its hire
- technical equipment, such as a public address (PA) system
- promotional materials, such as posters and flyers
- stationery, such as invitations
- food and drink (if your team is going to do the catering) or outside catering services
- payment for guest speakers
- transport for guests and participants, such as taxis and minibuses.

It is important when you make your list to think about the cost and availability of each item.

Staffing an event can be a problem because it is sometimes difficult to know how many guests you will have. It is important to get the right balance of staff and guests. Unless you can get volunteers, you will have to pay for staff at your event. If you have too many staff, you will be wasting money and some staff will have little to do. However, not enough staff will result in poor customer service. The right number of staff will give good customer service and meet the needs of the guests.

The planning process here involves not only working out how many staff you need, but also making sure that the right people are doing the right job.

Budget

An event organiser is often given an amount of money to spend on a hospitality event. This is called a **budget**. It is very important that you do not spend more than the budget for your event. There may be one overall budget for the event or separate budgets for different resources.

To make sure there is no overspend on the budget, it is very important to cost out every aspect of the event. It is useful to break the event costs down into different categories, such as:

- food and beverages
- labour (wages, uniforms, meals for staff)
- promotion (advertising and marketing materials)
- entertainment
- equipment
- venue hire.

Carry out some research before ordering any resources for your event in order to get the best possible deal and keep records of all purchases. It is a good idea to appoint someone to look after all purchasing for your event. This person can keep track of everything that is purchased, making sure that spending is in line with the budget.

Activity: What do we need for the party?

You have been asked by the Browns to organise a twenty-first birthday party for their daughter. It has been decided to hold the birthday celebrations in a marquee in the family's back garden. Make a list of all the things you will need to buy for the party.

Constraints

A constraint is something you cannot do because of a limit or difficulty with an objective you have been set. Figure 1 shows some of the common factors that can cause constraints when planning an event. For example, there might be a possible constraint with the location of the event. Some venues do not have the necessary licences for music or entertainment.

It is important to identify possible constraints in the planning stage so that you can think about how you might be able to overcome them.

Contingency planning

Because so many things can go wrong at an event, it is important to have a series of **contingency plans** in place. A contingency plan is usually developed by identifying the things that could go wrong and

Key terms

Budget – the sum of money available to spend on an event or an activity. Separate budgets are often set up for the specific resources needed for an event, such as promotion and administration, food and drink, and equipment.

Contingency plan – a plan devised for a specific situation when things could go wrong.

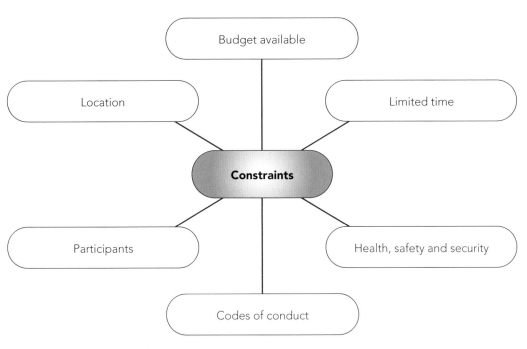

Figure 1: Factors that might cause constraints

developing plans to overcome these problems. For example, if you are planning to hold a barbecue, what will you do if it rains on the day of the event? The contingency plan should describe in detail what to do if a particular problem occurs.

Activity: You can't depend on the British weather

You have been asked to organise a garden party to celebrate the centenary (100th anniversary) of a local school. Although the party is to take place in July, there is still a chance it could rain on the day. Suggest a contingency plan to deal with possibility of rain.

Roles and responsibilities

When planning an event, different members of the organising team will be allocated different jobs and responsibilities so that, by working together, everything gets done. It is important to create a shared and balanced workload. Each member of the team should be given a role they feel comfortable with and that is within their capabilities.

Once roles have been allocated, you should not assume that the work will progress smoothly. Event organisers meet regularly to check on the progress of the plans and to resolve any problems that may arise.

Your team is likely to hold several progress meetings when organising your event. To make sure that these are productive, you should consider the following guidelines for running successful meetings.

- Consider carefully what the purpose of the meeting is.
- Set out clear and precise objectives for the meeting.
- Set out a formal agenda (schedule) outlining exactly what you will be talking about in the meeting and in what order.
- Keep a written record of what was said and what follow-up actions were agreed. These records are called **minutes**.
- Set a date for the next meeting if necessary.

Health and safety requirements

The health and safety of everyone involved in the event – organisers, staff and participants – is of prime importance. It is important for organisers to identify any potential health and safety **risks** as early as possible.

One way to do this is to complete a risk assessment. By carrying out a risk assessment at the planning stage, you can look at possible **hazards** and put in place controls to avoid them or minimise their effect. A hazard is anything that can cause harm by way of injury, hurt or damage.

You need to be aware of possible hazards within hospitality so that you can protect yourself and your customers. A good way of reducing hazards is to have a responsible employee complete a regular check for potential hazards, such as blocked fire escapes or unhygienic toilets. Immediate action can be taken to deal with any hazards found during these checks.

Key terms

Minutes – a written record of a meeting. Minutes are usually sent to everybody present at the meeting, setting out what each person agreed to do at the meeting.

Risk – the chance of something causing damage or harm.

Hazard – something that has the potential to cause damage or harm.

Did you know?

The Health and Safety Executive suggests that organisations follow five steps when completing a risk assessment.

Step 1 Identify the hazards

Step 2 Decide who might be harmed and how

Step 3 Evaluate the risks and decide on the precautions to be taken

Step 4 Record the findings and implement the precautions

Step 5 Review the assessment on a regular basis and update if necessary

Activity: Identifying hazards

Working in small groups, identify the potential hazards that could pose a risk to guests and staff at a summer barbecue held for 100 guests on a beach. When each group has completed this task, share your lists and discuss your ideas with the rest of the class.

Types of hospitality events

In the assignments you will be set for this unit, you will need to organise, promote and run a hospitality event. So, you will need to choose an event to organise. The list of possible events is endless. Hospitality functions could be:

- promotional events to highlight a good cause or an issue
- business events to promote a product or a range of services
- social events.

These groupings are just a guide as some events can belong to more than one category. For example, lunches or dinners could be promotional or business events.

Let's review some of the types of the event you might consider organising for this unit.

Open evenings

An open evening or open day is usually held to attract more customers to a venue or organisation. For example, an open evening might be held by:

- a college to attract new students
- a leisure club to attract new members
- a restaurant to attract new customers.

Visitors are usually given a tour of the premises. They will expect to meet staff from the venue who will explain the services that can be offered. There may also be an opportunity to sample the facilities, services or food the venue can offer.

As the open evening is all about attracting new customers, it is essential that visitors have a favourable experience and that they are impressed with what they see.

Activity: An open day at a leisure centre

In small groups, make a list of activities that your local leisure centre could offer if it decides to hold an open day.

Governors' reception

Many charitable and not-for-profit organisations are controlled by a board of governors. The governors are responsible for ensuring the effective management and development of the organisation. Every school, college, university and hospital has a board of governors, which meets regularly. Occasionally, an organisation will host a reception for its governors. This is an opportunity for the governors to meet socially and for the organisation to thank them for their help – many governors work on a voluntary and unpaid basis. Usually food and drink are served, and part of the evening is set aside for speeches.

Party

Parties can take many forms. They are intended primarily for celebration and are organised for many reasons. They take many forms and can be quite different:

- wedding receptions – anything from a buffet in a local pub to a formal sit-down meal followed by dancing in a large hotel
- birthdays or anniversaries – perhaps a children's party with an entertainer or magician
- religious festivals – these might need special food or decorations.

Case study: The Haywood Hotel

The Haywood Hotel was named South-East Wedding Venue of the Year 2010 at a ceremony in Brighton.

Receiving the award, Andrew Baker, the Haywood's general manager, said: 'Every wedding is unique at the Haywood. We want to make sure each wedding is perfect. We only host one wedding a day, so our customers are guaranteed a personal service throughout. With more than a thousand weddings behind us, we can advise on any aspect of the occasion to help create a truly memorable day for the bride and groom.'

Now in its fourth year, the South-East Wedding Venue award is a celebration of the wedding venues that offer the best possible service to couples planning their big day. All votes are cast either online or by post by brides and grooms themselves, with the winners chosen from the shortlist of nominees by a panel of industry professionals.

Awarding the prize, Taz Brown said: 'The Haywood Hotel is one of the most popular wedding venues in the area, and it has an absolutely excellent reputation. It is licensed for civil wedding ceremonies and civil partnerships, which means that couples can actually marry on the premises. Famous for its award-winning cuisine, we chose the Haywood Hotel because we believe it turns the bride and groom's wedding dreams into reality.'

The hotel has a professional and dedicated team, experienced in all aspects of wedding arrangement and procedure. Its wedding package includes:

- red carpet on arrival
- complimentary glass of champagne on arrival for the bride and groom

- a wedding supervisor acting as master of ceremonies throughout the day
- a dedicated wedding and special occasions co-ordinator to help with the planning process
- personalised menu cards and printed table plans.
- mouth-watering menus carefully compiled by the executive chef
- use of hotel's facilities and grounds for photography
- supervision of the special day by a member of the hotel's management team
- private lounge and bar facilities for guests throughout the day
- changing room on the morning of the wedding
- a dedicated toastmaster throughout the day
- exclusive room rates for wedding guests
- complimentary menu tasting for the bride and groom.

1 Why do you think the Haywood Hotel has made a decision to only host one wedding a day, even though it could easily accommodate two wedding parties and make more money as a result?

2 The general manager believes that each wedding is unique. State three things that the hotel could do to ensure it provides a unique experience for each wedding party.

3 To turn the bride and groom's 'dreams into reality', it is absolutely vital that nothing goes wrong on the day. With this in mind, many venues use checklists to help with planning. Design your own checklist for the Haywood Hotel.

When planning a party, the most important thing to consider is how to create the right event to suit your guests. For example, you will need to consider the ages and the likes and dislikes of your guests. This will help you decide whether to have:

- a formal sit-down meal or a buffet
- a disco or a string quartet
- party games or no planned entertainment.

A barbecue is a very popular type of party in the summer. People like to be outdoors when it is warm (providing it is not raining). Many organisations, businesses and clubs, such as Scouts and Guides, hold barbecues so that their members can get together and have fun.

The main considerations for anyone holding a barbecue are that:

- there is enough barbecue equipment to cook the amount of food needed
- the organisers have a thorough knowledge of how long everything takes to cook so that food is ready on time and does not pose a health risk
- there is a contingency plan in case it rains.

Activity: A Christmas party

Discuss the difficulties you may have in deciding on the type of Christmas party to hold for your class at school or college.

Charity fundraisers

Organising an event can be a great way to raise money for charity. If you are involved in a fundraiser, such as a sporting event, picnic, fashion show or meal, you will be taking part in a worthwhile activity that can bring you a lot of personal satisfaction.

When organising a charity event, you need to:

- consider the target market
- decide how the money will be raised, such as through ticket sales, a raffle or an auction
- see whether the charity you are supporting will supply publicity material for the event
- make it clear to your guests what proportion of the money they are spending is being donated to the chosen charity.

If you are planning to hold an auction or raffle at your event, see if local companies will support your charitable cause by donating prizes.

Activity: Charitable causes

Working in small groups, conduct a brainstorm to identify a range of charities that you could support by putting on an event. Record the results on a large sheet of paper. Choose the five most popular charities and think of a suitable event you could put on for each one.

Themed lunch or dinner

You can make a charitable lunch or dinner much more interesting and fun by adding a theme. There are many different ways that you can theme an event. For example, it could be based around:

- a historical period
- the food and culture of different nations
- a film or television programme
- a season
- particular foods, such as organic products, chocolate or local produce
- a sporting event.

The main considerations in all cases are choosing the right food, drink, decorations and staff uniforms to reflect the theme.

Activity: Choosing a theme

Choose a theme for a Year 11 Prom. List all the things you might need to make the theme work.

Assessment activity 1

Unit 5 **P1** **BTEC**

Your group has been asked to organise a talent show in a local junior school. The performers in the show will all be from Year 6. There are 50 children in Year 6. The show will be performed in front of the whole school the day before it breaks up for the Christmas holidays.

Outline the planning process that you will need to follow to organise the event. **P1**

Grading tip

P1 Make sure you think about all aspects of organising the event in your plan. You need to show that you have considered the nature of the event, the target audience, where and when to hold the event, budget, the resources that you will need, the roles and responsibilities of the organising team, and health and safety considerations.

PLTS

When you are considering the planning process, you will develop your skills as an **independent enquirer**, showing that you are able to support conclusions using reasoned arguments and evidence.

Functional skills

You will develop your **English** skills in speaking, listening and communication when gathering information for this task and in writing when presenting your work in an appropriate format.

5.2 Be able to participate in the organisation of a hospitality event to meet customer requirements

The assessment for this unit requires you to plan, organise, run and evaluate an event of your own. This section will help you to plan your own event so that all the necessary jobs are carried out on time and you can keep track of your progress. We shall look at:

- customer requirements
- resources
- participation of team members
- contingencies.

Customer requirements

The requirements of guests or customers will vary enormously according to the type of event that you are running. It is the organiser's responsibility in the planning stage to ensure that the customers' needs are clearly identified and that the event is structured to meet those needs.

Every event should have a purpose. Once the purpose has been established, the organisers can begin to plan. One of the first stages of planning an event is to set out the objectives of the event. Objectives state what the organisation aims to achieve, how success will be measured and the timescales for achievement. Examples of objectives could include:

- to celebrate student successes this term by holding a party for all students by the end of term
- to raise £500 for a given charity by the end of the year.

When setting objectives, try to write SMART objectives. SMART is short for specific, measurable, achievable, realistic and time bound.

- **S**pecific – the objective has to be written so that everyone involved in meeting it understands what they need to do. For example, the objective 'to raise money' is not specific as it does not tell people how much money they need to raise. Make sure your objectives have defined targets.
- **M**easurable – you need to be able to work out to what an extent an objective is being met. For example, if your event is a college open evening to recruit students to a particular course, your objective should state how many people you want to recruit. In this way, after the event you will be able to measure the extent to which you have succeeded in meeting this objective.

- **A**chievable – do not be tempted to be too ambitious by setting yourself targets that are almost impossible to achieve. If it becomes obvious that you cannot achieve your objectives, the event team will become demotivated and disheartened.
- **R**ealistic – make sure you can provide the resources needed to meet your objectives. You may need staff, equipment, money and premises.
- **T**ime-bound – an objective should contain a date or a time by which it will be achieved. You need to state when you intend to achieve your objectives.

Activity: Customer requirements and objectives

Once you have chosen an event to organise, make sure you are clear about your target audience. What are the requirements? Write an objective (or objectives) for your event. Makes sure that these are SMART objectives.

Resources

It takes resources to run any event, and it is the responsibility of the events team to organise these resources. You must make sure that the resources meet the needs of the guests and do not cost too much money. Resources include:

- physical items, such as the venue and equipment
- financial resources – a budget for the event
- human resources – staff to run the event.

Physical resources

One of the most important physical resources is the venue for the event. Before you make a decision about hiring a room, you should visit possible venues to make sure they meet your needs. Take a list of the information you need to find out and the questions you need to ask. When visiting a possible venue:

- ask to see the room(s) you will be using
- check the public areas, the access to the building and the parking arrangements
- try to get a feel for whether the venue staff are friendly and welcoming
- find out how much the venue will cost to hire and what will be included in the price, such as any furniture you might need
- check that the venue has the correct licenses and insurance for your event. You will probably need to ask your tutor about these.

Once you have decided on a venue, you will need to make a formal booking. At this stage you will be entering into a contract, so you must make sure that you understand exactly what you are committing yourself to.

Activity: Venue checklist

Draw up a checklist to use when visiting premises to see if they might be potential venues for your event.

Every event needs a variety of equipment and materials, such as:

- stationery for advertising
- catering equipment to prepare and serve food and drink
- audiovisual equipment for presentations
- prizes for raffles or items for auctions
- decorations to suit a theme.

It is essential to identify exactly what you need, how to get any required equipment or materials and how much this will cost. The equipment you need will obviously depend on the type of event, but you must consider:

- how easy it is to get
- how much it costs
- how easy it is to use.

You do not always have to buy or hire equipment. Find out what equipment is already available at the venue. See what you can borrow. You may be surprised at how willing local businesses are to support or sponsor your event, particularly if it is in aid of a good cause. They might also be prepared to provide food, drink, prizes or decorations.

Transport

It is also important to consider transport.

- How will the customers or guests get to your venue?
- How will you transport your equipment?

It may add to the costs considerably if you have to hire taxis or minibuses. You therefore need to check bus and train routes, and the availability of parking at the venue.

How can you encourage local businesses to support your event?

Food and drink

You must decide what kind of food and drink is best suited to your event. Think carefully about how to present food to your guests. There are several options, including a fork buffet, a finger buffet and a sit-down meal. There are many questions to consider.

- How much money do you have to spend?

- What are your customers' preferences?

- What equipment is available at the venue for catering?

- What skills do you have as a team?

- Will the venue provide the food and drink, or will your team have to sort out the catering? Note that some venues will not let event organisers bring their own food and drink.

- How much time will the guests have for eating and drinking?

- Is the venue licensed to serve alcohol?

- Are there any food safety regulations to be considered?

- Will you have to cater for any special dietary requirements? Some guests may have allergies or dietary restrictions for cultural or religious reasons.

- Are there any seasonal or regional factors that could influence your menu? For example, consider what produce is in season. Are there any popular food items from the region or location of the event that might look good on the menu?

Activity: A shopping list

Make a list of the physical resources you will need for your event. Shop around for good deals.

Financial resources

In the early stages of planning, you should establish how much money you have to spend on the event. You could try to find some kind of sponsorship for the event to help you raise more money.

You need to create and stick to a budget. You should draw up the budget by first working out what you will need to spend to make the event a success. Remember to keep a check on what you are spending so that you do not go over this budget. It is essential to keep all receipts and invoices relating to the event.

Shop around to make sure you are getting a good deal when buying or hiring equipment and materials. However, the cheapest price may not be the best deal – you want to consider quality as well as a low price.

Activity: Please can you help?

Suppose you plan to hold a raffle at your event to raise money for a charitable cause. Write a letter that could be sent to local businesses asking them to donate prizes for the raffle.

How can you ensure your hospitality event is profitable?

Human resources

The success of an event will partly depend on having enough trained and competent staff to greet and serve customers and to provide a level of service that meets their needs and expectations. You will need to work out:

- what jobs need to be undertaken
- what skills are needed for those jobs
- how many people you will need to do this work.

You may need staff to prepare and serve the food and drink. You may need staff for administration on the day of the event, including meeting and directing guests. You may also need people to provide any planned entertainment.

You need to keep a strict watch on staff costs. Some jobs can be filled by members of your team and other volunteers. However, you may have to hire staff for the event to perform specialist tasks and to give you enough people to look after the number of guests that you are expecting.

Before the event you need to draw up a staff schedule. Everyone involved should know what they are doing and who their points of contact are in the lead-up to and during the event. Keeping staff informed is very important to the success of the event.

Participation of team members

Every member of the event-organising team should have a role. Individual roles will come with specific responsibilities. Examples of the different roles and responsibilities are:

- co-ordination – to organise other members of the team
- marketing – to advertise and promote the event
- finance – to keep control of the budget and to monitor and record spending
- administration – to deal with correspondence and keep paperwork in order
- food and beverages – to be responsible for catering
- health and safety – to make sure all relevant legislation is followed.

Activity: Choose your role

Using the list at the bottom of page 127, choose roles for each member of your event team and list the responsibilities that go with each role. Bear in mind the individual skills of your team when allocating roles.

Teamwork

A team approach is essential if the event is to be a success. It is important to make the best use of the various skills of team members. When a team is working well, all its members are clear about what they are trying to achieve.

How can good teamwork contribute to a successful event?

Meetings and communication

It is important to hold regular meetings to:

- monitor progress
- evaluate each person's input
- make changes to plans if necessary.

When organising an event, you should schedule a series of meetings and put the dates (and where they are to be held) in your diaries. Make sure the whole team knows:

- what the meetings are for
- when they are taking place
- where they are taking place.

Customers and potential guests also need to be kept informed about the event. We will look at ways to promote a hospitality event later in this unit (pages 132–135).

Activity: What are the risks?

Complete a risk assessment for your event. Make sure you consider any relevant legislation and explain how you will take this into account.

Health and safety

It is clearly important to ensure the health and safety of your guests as well as any staff working at the event. Remember that you must:

- identify the risks posed by all parts of your event
- have a plan to minimise those risks and deal with problems if they occur.

Check the legal requirements. There may be legislation related to what you are doing covering areas such as:

- insurance
- food safety
- fire regulations.

Contingencies

A plan is a guide. It sets out a sequence of tasks and activities to be completed. However, it is not set in stone and it will need to be monitored and changed as necessary. Your planning may be going well, but you must always be prepared for unforeseen situations. Therefore, as well as planning what you need to do to run a successful event, you must also make plans for what you will do if something goes wrong. These are called contingency plans.

You will need to think about things such as:

- what to do if it rains during an outdoor event such as a barbecue or fête
- coping with any accidents or emergencies
- last-minute changes to the numbers of people attending
- coping with any staff shortages
- what to do if you cannot get hold of certain equipment.

It is important to have written contingency plans in place for each part of your event so that you are ready to deal with any problems that arise. Make sure that everyone knows the contingency plans.

Weather

If you are holding an outdoor event, such as a barbecue, you must decide what to do if it rains. Ideally, you would want to provide some arrangement so that the event can go ahead and your guests can keep dry. If you have to postpone the event, think about ways of letting people know as soon as possible what has happened.

How can you make your event a success even if the weather is bad?

Accidents

Your risk assessment should have identified the accidents that are most likely to occur and the measures that should be put in place to prevent these occurrences.

Unfortunately, accidents cannot be completely prevented. They do still happen despite safeguards. You will therefore need to appoint someone responsible for first aid. If there is an accident, you should make sure that one of your team writes down what happens. You may need to interview the witnesses. This will enable the cause of the accident to be investigated.

Make sure everyone knows what to do in the case of fire and that necessary equipment is available.

Changes in numbers

If the number of guests changes at the last moment, you may need to alter your plans. You may not be able to run the activities you had planned.

Staff shortages

A staff member may be ill or absent for other reasons on the day of the event. If this is the case, you may need to reallocate their duties. It is a good idea to have two or three volunteers to call on in case of staff shortages.

Lack of equipment

You should arrange for equipment to arrive in good time for the event. If it is delayed for any reason, make sure you have the telephone numbers of the suppliers with you so that you can find out what has happened.

 Activity: How well are you prepared?

What contingency plans have you made for your event? Who needs to know what they are?

Assessment activity 2

Unit 5 **BTEC**

As a group, decide on the event you will run for this unit. You must present an outline of your plans to your tutor. Your objective is to convince your tutor that you are capable of organising the event. If you are successful, your tutor will become your client, and you will need to keep in constant contact with him or her to make certain that your plans are acceptable and appropriate for the event you have proposed.

1 You should first produce an itinerary for the event, including your target market, details of the venue and its reasons for suitability, and a brief outline of the activities that you will run.

Produce a set of objectives for the event. These should relate to client and organisational outcomes and quality standards. They should be SMART objectives. You must show how your team intends to meet these objectives.

Decide on the tasks that you will need to undertake to run the event and develop a suitable staff structure to carry out the tasks effectively. Draw up a timetable, detailing the date by which each task should be completed.

Compile a budget forecast for the event. This should include details of all expenses (such as room hire, food and beverages, administration, staffing costs) and any revenue (from ticket sales, donations, sale of goods).

Identify the types of promotional activities you could carry out to promote the event. In addition, describe the tools you might use to help you evaluate the event. **P2**

2 Once your plan has been approved by your tutor, put it into operation by organising your event as a team. Keep a record of your progress, detailing how the work was carried out (including who actually did what). This should include details of any work to:

- comply with health and safety requirements
- arrange provisions of suitable equipment, food and beverages
- organise the marketing of the event
- communicate effectively with suppliers, team members and guests
- make contractual arrangements
- negotiate the provision of goods and services. **P3**

3 Explain the process you used, as a group, to plan the event. Describe the contingencies that you put in place to deal with any deviations from your original plan. **M1**

4 Evaluate the strengths and weaknesses of the overall planning process of your team. Also evaluate your own role in contributing to the planning process.

Make realistic recommendations as to how things could have been changed to improve the planning process. **D1**

Grading tips

P2 Ensure you are able to show your individual contribution to the work and that you have clearly stated how you will meet your objectives.

P2 Show evidence of your contribution to the organisation of your event throughout the planning stage. This could be done through a diary, blog, video or audio log, but you should also collect any relevant tangible evidence such as a menu you planned or a poster you designed. Your tutor may provide additional evidence on your contribution through observation sheets.

M1 You must show how your team monitored progress against the original plan. Explain any changes, deviations or problems encountered during the planning process.

D1 Make sure you evaluate the strengths and weaknesses of the planning and organisation of the event, rather than the event itself. Strengths might include good teamwork and keeping to deadlines, and weaknesses might include arguments within the team and noting that some group members did not fully contribute.

 PLTS

Coming up with ideas for your event and with effective plans to make it work will develop your skills as a **creative thinker**, especially as you generate ideas and explore possibilities to ensure the event is successful. This activity involves a lot of teamwork and this will give you the opportunity to develop your skills as a **team worker** as you collaborate with your team members to achieve your objectives.

 Functional skills

You will develop your **English** skills in speaking, listening and communication when gathering information for this assessment activity and in writing when presenting your work in an appropriate format. There will be an opportunity to develop your discussion skills as you develop your plan as a group. You will develop your **maths** skills in preparing a budget and working out costs.

5.3 Be able to promote a hospitality event

Now let's focus on how you tell potential guests and customers about your event. We will consider:

- the purpose of promotion
- promoting an event.

The purpose of promotion

Once you have defined the target audience, set objectives and got your plan under way, you need to communicate details of the event to your customers. The purpose of promoting an event is to make people aware of it and to inform them about it.

Informing customers

It is important to give customers detailed and clear information about the event. When deciding on the message you want to give out, think about:

- what you want to say
- to whom you want to say it.

Anyone attending the event will need to know:

- the date and time of the event
- where it will take place (details of the venue)
- how much it costs – this could include the ticket price, plus any extra charges for activities or refreshments
- what food and drink will be available
- the purpose of the event – to have fun, to raise money for charity or to celebrate
- what will be happening at the event – any theme, entertainment or activities.

This information could be given to the target customers in stages. For example, the date, time, location and theme of the event could appear on a poster or in an advertisement announcing that the event is going to happen. Further details, such as the food available and itinerary, could be communicated by means of an information or delegate pack given out at the event itself.

Raising awareness

In order to raise awareness, you need to consider these questions.

- Does the promotional literature present the image you are trying to project to the target customer group?
- Have advertisements been placed where the target customer groups will see them?

- Does the promotional material give a clear message about the purpose of the event? For example, if you are planning a fundraising event, make it clear why you are fundraising and which organisation you are supporting.
- Is there enough information about the event within the material to allow people to decide if they want to take part or attend?

Promoting an event

The purpose of promoting an event is to publicise the function and make it appealing to your target audience. You need to consider several factors, such as:

- advertising – will you need to advertise to inform customers about the event?
- timing – when should you begin promoting the event and when should you stop any promotion?
- cost – how much can you afford to spend on promotion?

The trick is to adapt your promotional material to appeal to your target market. Some events may not require much promotion. If you are organising a birthday party or an end-of-year celebration, you may just need to send invitations or text messages to friends and colleagues.

Making good use of resources

The timing of a promotional campaign is very important. You need to decide when to start promoting the event and you should produce a time frame for each promotional activity. If you start to promote too early, people may lose interest or may have forgotten about it by the day of the event. If you leave it too late, they may have already arranged to do something else.

As with other aspects of event planning, you should set a budget to cover promotional costs. The amount of money you have to spend will have a bearing on what method of promotion you can use. For example, you could not afford television advertising on a small budget.

How you advertise your event will depend on your budget, the type of event, the venue and the target audience. However, all promotional material must be effective to attract customers. Promotional material should ideally have an immediate impact. It should be designed so that target customers can quickly see your main message. Most people do not expect to read too many words before finding the point of an advertisement. One way to design good promotional campaigns is to use the **AIDA** model. AIDA stands for attention, interest, desire, action.

- **A**ttention – the promotional material must be placed where it is likely to be seen by the target audience for your event and it must attract the attention of the reader. This might be achieved through the colours, images or words used in the material.

Key term

AIDA – short for attention, interest, desire, action. The AIDA model provides a reliable template for the design of marketing material.

- **I**nterest – once you have got the attention of people in the target audience, the material must create interest in the event. Try to encourage readers to find out more.

- **D**esire – the promotional material must make readers want to come along. You need to make potential customers or guests feel that the event is too good to miss.

- **A**ction – if you have been successful in getting people to want to come to your event, you need to let them know what to do next. How do they book or make a reservation? Provide clear information about what they should do, such as 'tickets are on sale now at the main reception'.

The methods of promotion are also important. For example, you might decide to:

- put an advert in a local paper
- design posters to place around your school or college
- post flyers through letterboxes of the houses in your neighbourhood.

Activity: How effective is this poster?

Look at this poster for a masked ball. Analyse how the organisers have used each element of the AIDA model in the poster. Do you think it will be successful in attracting attention, interest, desire and action? Can you suggest ways that it could be improved? Compare your findings with others in your group.

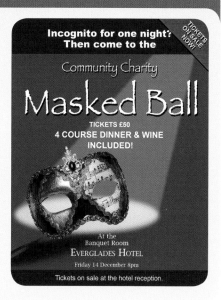

The promotional materials and methods that you use will depend on the target customer group, the message you are trying to communicate and the available budget. Advertising in national newspapers and on national television or radio is very expensive, but some local radio and television stations might mention your event for free if you give them a **press release**. This is a document produced by organisations to provide the media with a public interest story or information about their events, products and services. It is usually written in the form of a newspaper story. If your event aims to raise money for charity, it is more likely to interest the local media.

Key term

Press release – information sent by businesses to media organisations (newspapers, radio stations, television channels) about their products and services, forthcoming events and other developments of possible interest.

As you are likely to have a very tight budget, you could also use social networking sites such as Twitter and Facebook as well as your college or school intranet at no cost at all. You may be able to use other free services, such as:

- your local council website
- local radio stations, which often have regular 'what's on' bulletins
- listings websites, such as those that list family events, leisure activities or local events
- the 'what's on' section in local newspapers.

Activity: Fantasy Land Drama School

A local drama school, Fantasy Land Drama School, has asked you to design a campaign to promote a drama workshop. Prospective students will be invited to spend a day at the school to get a taste of the kind of things drama students do. The budget is small. The school wants to know the best promotional method to use. Make some suggestions and design some promotional material for them.

Assessment activity 3

Unit 5  BTEC

1. Plan the promotional campaign for your chosen event. Provide:
   - a time frame for the campaign
   - details of costs
   - a copy of promotional materials. **P4**

2. Put your plan into practice. After the campaign, produce a short report that analyses its impact. Did it help you to get enough customers? Were your target audience aware that your event was happening? **M2**

Grading tips

P4 Carry out some research before deciding on a promotional campaign and designing your materials. Find out how some other event organisers have promoted their events. Remember that your budget may be a

constraint on what you can do, and ensure you have the technical expertise to make your ideas come alive.

M2 You must devise a way of monitoring the effectiveness of your campaign.

PLTS

Designing a promotional campaign and promotional materials will develop your skills as a **creative thinker** as you generate ideas to ensure the campaign is a success.

Functional skills

You will use your **ICT** skills to design promotional materials and your **English** skills when writing the text for these materials.

5.4 Be able to contribute to the running of a hospitality event to meet customer requirements

So far we have considered how to plan, organise and promote a hospitality event. Now let's look at what needs to be done on the day itself by considering:

- setting up
- work during an event
- clearing up.

Setting up

It is vital that the organising team sets up the event properly because it will save a lot of work when the event is actually running. Walk through your event before any of the guests arrive and make sure you brief your team well. In particular, you need to check:

- signs
- rooms
- food and drink service areas
- equipment.

Why is it important to make sure everything is set up correctly before an event?

Signs

It is really off-putting for customers and guests to arrive at an event only to find that they have no idea where to go. Make sure that there are adequate signs to guide guests to:

- meeting rooms
- toilets
- the restaurant or refreshment service area.

Rooms

The rooms that are being used for the event should be fully prepared so that they are ready for use before guests arrive. The furniture should be laid out with the customers' comfort in mind.

- Is there enough room for customers and staff to move around comfortably?
- Are there enough seats?
- If customers will be expected to write during the event, are there tables?
- Does the decor reflect the theme of the event?
- Is there adequate ventilation and lighting?

Food and drink service areas

Make sure you have done as much as possible to prepare for the event with regard to the service of food and drink. The preparation of the refreshment areas is called **mise-en-place** (preparation for service). Mise-en-place entails:

- making a plan for the event staff to show where they will be working
- going over the menu with staff
- ensuring that all the equipment needed for food service is available
- checking that all the glasses, crockery and cutlery are clean.

Equipment

You should be confident that you have all the equipment you need because this will have been organised during the planning stage. However, you may be getting equipment from many different sources, and when you are busy it is easy to forget things. It is therefore useful to prepare a checklist of what you will need on the day of your event. This will include equipment for:

- entertainment
- food and drink service, including crockery, cutlery and glasses.

At least one member of the event team should be responsible for ensuring that there are enough glasses, crockery and cutlery for the event, that they are clean and that they are where they should be.

Key term

Mise-en-place – a French phrase meaning, literally, 'putting in place'. The phrase is used in hospitality and catering to mean everything being in place.

Activity: What do we need?

List the mise-en-place that would need to be completed to prepare for a finger buffet for 100 guests. Design an equipment checklist for your event.

Work during an event

Everyone should know what their duties are on the day of the event. However, you still need to consider how you can make sure things run smoothly at this stage. One of the keys to the success of any event is effective communication. It is very important for the whole team to communicate with each other throughout the event.

Let's look at some of the contributions that will be needed from staff and team members during an event.

Food and drink service

If you have completed your mise-en-place and the event team know their responsibilities, the service of food and drinks should be relatively trouble free. You will learn about the general principles of food and drink service in Unit 8. However, when catering for an event there are some special issues to consider.

- It may be necessary to announce to the customers that the food and drinks are about to be served.

- If you are providing a buffet for large numbers, then guests should be sent through to the buffet in small groups to avoid long queues.

- Communication with the chef is vital as the food service may have to be delayed for speeches and other activities.

Meeting customer requests

It is a good idea to get as much information as possible about your customers before the event. You will want early notice of any special requests, such as special diets. However, it is highly likely that some guests will make individual requests during the event. For example; they might

- not like the food or drink being served

- need a piece of equipment that you have not anticipated

- want you to call them a taxi.

Even though these requests may come at a time when you are very busy, you must remember that customer satisfaction is vital if your event is to be a success.

Responding to the unexpected

Your contingency planning should help you cope with unexpected situations. However, *planning* for the unexpected and *dealing* with the unexpected are two different things. If something unexpected does happen, it is vital that you stay calm and do not let the customers know that something has gone wrong.

Activity: Expecting the unexpected

Identify how you would deal with each of these unexpected occurrences.
- Some items of food that you ordered have not been delivered.
- A member of the team phones in sick on the day of the event.
- A party of 10 want to amend their booking and now want a table for 15 guests.
- One of the ovens breaks in the middle of food service.
- You run out of the vegetarian option.

Clearing up

Clearing up or tidying away is likely to be the last thing that you want to do once your event is over, but it is an important part of running your event successfully. You should give this the same attention as all the other tasks that you complete. Once you have finished clearing up, remember to thank your team and everyone who made a contribution to the event.

Waste disposal

The hygienic and safe disposal of waste is vital. If you are hiring a venue for your event, check out the procedure for disposing of waste with one of the venue staff. If your event is likely to generate a lot of litter, it might be wise to clear up as you go.

Glasses, crockery and cutlery

The person in your team with overall responsibility for this area should make sure that all these items are washed up. All glasses, crockery and cutlery should be counted and returned to where they came from. You will need to report any breakages or missing items.

Surplus food and drink

If you have catered for your event yourself, it may be your responsibility to deal with any leftover food and drink. Although it may be tempting to take the food home, you must ensure that you have considered whether it is safe to do so. If food is to be returned to your college or school kitchen, you must make sure that you follow all relevant food hygiene regulations.

Rooms, signs and equipment

If you are using a school, college or someone's home for your event, you must ensure that all rooms and outside areas are left in a clean and tidy state. If you have hired a venue, it is a good idea to check who is responsible for cleaning and tidying the rooms you have used.

- Equipment must be put away carefully and returned to the correct place. You must also make sure it is stored securely.

- Signs put up specially for the event should be taken down.

- Rooms should be tidied and vacuumed.

Assessment activity 4 Unit 5   **BTEC**

Participate in the running of your event. Describe what roles and tasks you undertook at the event.

Grading tip

 You must produce evidence that you have contributed towards the running of the event. This can be in the form of your own written descriptions of what you did, as well as witness statements and observation sheets from your tutor and others involved in the event, which showed that you have been involved in all stages of the event, including the clearing up.

 PLTS

You will have the opportunity to develop your skills as a **team worker** in running the event with your peers. You will also develop skills as **self-manager** as you prioritise your time, work to deadlines and show flexibility to ensure the event is a success.

 Functional skills

If you produce a written description of your event and the role you played, you will be practising your **English** skills in writing.

5.5 Be able to review the success of a hospitality event

Once your guests have left and you have finished the clearing up, you will want to ask whether the event was a success. To do that, you need to consider ways of:

- reviewing an event
- measuring success.

Reviewing an event

When an event is over, it is necessary to review its success. This usually means determining to what extent the objectives have been met.

Although the review mainly comes after the event, you need to decide how to review your event during the planning stage. This is one of the reasons why it is important to set SMART objectives (see pages 123–24). How can you measure if the event has been successful if you have not decided beforehand what will make it a success?

The way in which you will review the success of the event also needs to be identified. This should include feedback given by people involved in the event, such as customers, staff and other members of the organising team.

One of the best ways to make sure you have learned something from planning, organising and running an event is to evaluate your own performance. This can be a difficult process because you need to be very honest with yourself.

Sources of feedback

There are several possible sources of feedback on your event. These include your:

- team
- tutor
- customers or guests.

You and your team are obviously in a very good position to review the success of the event – both as individuals and as a team. Here are some of the questions that need answering if you are to learn from your experiences.

- Which objectives were met?
- Why were they met?
- How were they met?
- Who was responsible for meeting them?

- Which objectives were not met?
- Why were they not met?

In order to answer these questions, you need to be honest and fair. Make sure that you allow everyone involved in the team to give their opinions.

Activity: How will you judge?

As a team, decide how you are going to evaluate your performance. Draw up a form that you could use to assess your performance.

Your tutor will also be in an excellent position to review your event. He or she will know what you are hoping to achieve and will be reviewing your progress throughout the planning process.

Despite the fact that the success of the event can only be reviewed once it is over, it is wise to keep your tutor informed of decisions you are making throughout the planning process. This is because he or she will be able to make sure that you are on target to meet your objectives. You should agree some dates with your tutor when you can meet to review the progress of your event.

Your tutor will have set criteria to use when reviewing the success of the event and your performance as a team. However, you might like to produce your own feedback form that your tutor could use.

Your customers or guests are probably the most important source of feedback. This is because you have run the event for them. If you do not give guests the opportunity to feed back their opinions, you will never really know if they were happy, satisfied or dissatisfied with your event.

Customer feedback can be formal or informal. You can get informal feedback simply by asking the customer if they have had a good time or by observing their behaviour.

Formal feedback can be gathered by a variety of means, such as questionnaires, comment cards and telephone surveys. Formal feedback should always be recorded, whether it comes from the customer, your tutor or you.

Activity: Gathering feedback

As a group, discuss the advantages and disadvantages of gathering formal and informal customer feedback.

Questionnaires

One of the most common ways of gathering customer feedback is by using questionnaires. These could be sent out as part of a marketing follow-up or handed out at the end of the event. They should be designed to obtain:

- factual information that can be turned into statistics
- the opinions and feelings of the customers.

Figure 2 shows a feedback questionnaire given out at a hospitality training event.

Feedback Questionnaire

Event/Course Title:
National Association of Hotel Concierges Forum 2011

Trainer/Host:
Mary Rees

Date:
21 April 2011

Venue:
Conference Room

We are always trying to improve the forum, events and courses we offer and would value your feedback to help us identify any improvements.

Please mark in the appropriate boxes your view of each of the following statements. Any additional comments would be welcome.

Question	Strongly agree	Agree	Neither agree nor disagree	Disagree	Strongly disagree
1. The event was relevant to my needs	☐	☐	☐	☐	☐
2. I found the forum interesting	☐	☐	☐	☐	☐
3. The presentation was informative and applicable to my needs	☐	☐	☐	☐	☐
4. The hospitality and catering presentation was appropriate	☐	☐	☐	☐	☐
6. The event was the correct length	☐	☐	☐	☐	☐
7. The event was the correct pace	☐	☐	☐	☐	☐
8. The room was comfortable (e.g. lighting, temperature, surroundings)	☐	☐	☐	☐	☐
9. The facilities were accessible and purposeful (e.g. car park, toilet facilities, lift)	☐	☐	☐	☐	☐
10. I enjoyed the forum and would recommend it to others	☐	☐	☐	☐	☐

Comments: Please include any topics and/or future course you would like to hear about at the next forum

....

Figure 2: Example of customer feedback questionnaire

You should always explain the purpose of questionnaires to customers. For example, if you are handing out forms to customers at the end of your event, you might say: 'We would like to thank you for attending our event and we hope that you have had an enjoyable evening. To help us in the organisation of future events, please complete this form and return it to one of the event team before you leave.'

Comment cards are also a very popular way of gaining feedback from customers in the hospitality industry. They are short questionnaires, often placed with products purchased at a hotel or between the salt and pepper pots at a restaurant.

Other feedback documentation

As you will be assessed on your participation in organising and running an event, your performance may be watched by your tutor and other observers. They will produce witness statements and observation records that can be added to the other evidence you produce in your assignments. As these observers are able to comment on your participation in the event, some of their written comments may be passed to you, and these should be used to help you review your performance.

Measuring success

Once you have gathered feedback, you can start evaluating the responses to see if the event you organised has been a success. There are four sets of criteria against which you can assess the success of your event:

- against customer expectations
- against objectives
- against budget
- against your original plans.

Against customer expectations

We have stressed that it is vitally important that you consider the needs of your target audience (your customers or guests) when planning, organising and running your event. Throughout the planning process, you will have considered your customers when deciding on every aspect of the event, such as its location, the food and drink, the time it starts and finishes, and the entertainment.

Having put all this effort into considering the needs of customers, it is obviously essential to make sure you have met them. You need to discover their views to see what you have done well and what you could have improved on.

Against objectives

You should have also learned how important it is to set measurable objectives for your event. Once the event is over, you should see whether you have met these objectives. You can determine your successes and identify what could be done better next time.

Having reviewed your objectives, you can consider whether you:

- charged the right price
- targeted the right market
- included the right activities

- promoted your event effectively
- served suitable food and drink
- held the event in the right venue and at the right time
- made the right amount of profit or raised the sum of money you wanted for your charity.

Answering these questions honestly will help you to learn from the experience. You should recognise what you have done well and congratulate yourself. You should also recognise the things that did not go so well and think about how you could improve them next time.

How can you and your team recognise your successes and improve your weaker areas?

Against budget

It is all very well to pat each other on the back if your customers are happy and you feel that you have met your objectives. However, before you start celebrating your success, you must make sure that you have not spent too much money.

In the planning stage of your event you should have determined how much money you had to spend (your budget). You should have decided how you were going to spend your budget. It is too late to review your spending once the event is over. This is something you should have done throughout the planning process at team meetings.

However, at the end of the event, you can review whether your event generated any income. Your budget might have been worked out on the basis that your event would generate some money through:

- ticket sales
- food and drink sales
- raffle tickets
- customers paying for activities and competitions.

If you planned to generate some money from the event, then at the end of the event you need to add up the money you raised and set it against the money you spent in putting on the event to see if you made any profit.

Against your original plans

When you first started to plan for your event, you should have written a list of tasks that you needed to do, with target dates for their completion. However, for many reasons, you may have needed to make changes to your plans.

It is perfectly acceptable to make changes, but you should account for any deviations from your original plans. You will need to review why the changes were made.

- Were you too ambitious, setting your sights too high?
- Did some members of the team not pull their weight?

- Did you discover that some things cost more than you thought?
- Did you find that you were not selling enough tickets?

There are many reasons why your plans might have needed to be changed. The important thing to consider is whether the changes were as a result of weaknesses in your team's work or whether they were caused by events beyond your control.

If changes were made because of shortcomings in your original plans, do not feel too downhearted. Instead, you should congratulate yourself on recognising those weaknesses and discuss how you might overcome them if you were to run an event again.

Activity: What happened to the profit?

In your groups, suggest reasons why an event might make less profit than was forecast in the project plan.

Assessment activity 5
Unit 5 **P6** **M3** **D2** **BTEC**

1 Design and use at least three different methods to collect feedback that can be used to review your event. **P6**

2 Use the feedback you have gathered to analyse the success of your event. **M3**

3 Make recommendations for improving your event based on the feedback you have collected. You should include ways of improving your promotional materials and the methods you used to publicise your event. **D2**

Grading tips

P6 Get a tutor to check the methods you are proposing to use before you approach customers or others. This should ensure that each method can be understood easily and that it will give you the information you need.

M3 Make sure you analyse the success of your event against your original objectives.

D2 Make sure your recommendations are achievable and that they do not require additional resources that you would not be able to provide or afford in the future. Remember to be fair and honest.

PLTS

When you reflect on your own and your team's performance, you will develop your skills as a **reflective learner**.

Functional skills

If you design a questionnaire to use to gather feedback, you will be using your **English** skills in writing. As you analyse your results, you will use your **English** skills in reading.

Patrick Matthews
Assistant conference and banqueting manager

Patrick Matthews graduated from university with a BA (Hons) degree in events management. He is now working in an independently owned country house hotel in the Yorkshire Dales. The hotel has 80 bedrooms, leisure facilities, a multi-rosette awarded restaurant, two bars and nine conference and banqueting rooms. He has recently been promoted to assistant conference and banqueting manager.

His duties include team training and development, setting the rota, wage and stock control, upselling, development of the customer service experience, liaison with the sales team, attending departmental meetings and hands-on running of events.

The best part of the job is that it is a glamorous world, and there is no scope for boredom. Patrick meets all types of people and gets great satisfaction from making events go smoothly. The worst part of the job is that sometimes he just cannot anticipate what might go wrong – and when it does, he finds it difficult to think on his feet and to lead his team in sorting the problem out.

At a recent wedding reception he felt completely overwhelmed by the problems he encountered and even considered handing in his notice. The wedding party arrived late and the chef became very angry because he was worried about the food being spoiled, two waitresses had a big argument and refused to work together for the rest of the evening, and the DJ turned up an hour late!

However, despite its ups and downs, he loves the job, and he is very enthusiastic whenever he is invited to a careers event to talk to some hospitality students about his role.

Think about it!

- How would you have handled the wedding reception when things started to go wrong?
- Suggest some contingencies that the hotel could have in place for a wedding party arriving late or the DJ or other entertainment not being ready on time.
- One of Patrick's duties is upselling. Find out what this means. Give some examples of upselling in the context of conference and banqueting services.

Just checking

1   List four things you must consider when choosing a venue for an event.

2   What is a contingency plan?

3   Why is it important to set objectives for your event?

4   Identify three risks of holding a summer barbecue for a group of college students.

5   What does AIDA stand for?

6   Identify three ways of promoting your event.

7   What is mise-en-place?

8   Identify three ways of reviewing your event.

9   Name two ways you can show you participated effectively in the planning, organisation and running of your event.

Assignment tips

- To prepare for your assignments, in which you will have to take part in organising and running your own event, investigate the planning of some hospitality events, such as a school summer fête or a wedding.

- Visits to local hotels and function suites could give a valuable insight into the planning involved in organising conferences or other events such as weddings and company dinner dances.

- Research the ways that hospitality organisations promote their own events. Do they advertise in the local or national press? What other promotional activities do they use? This will help you learn how best to promote your own event. However, you will not be able to copy everything professional organisations do to promote their events as they will have much bigger budgets. You need to be creative and innovative. Think, for example, whether you could use social networking sites to promote your event.

- You will have to work as a team when you are organising and running your event. You need to be a team player. Stick to any timetable you have agreed. Be prepared to listen to the opinions of other members of your team and to offer your own opinion, even if you think it may not be important.

6 Healthier food and special diets

There is a lively interest in healthy lifestyles, with programmes on television and articles in the press on healthy eating. Few could have missed the debate started by chef Jamie Oliver's programmes about school dinners.

People in the hospitality industry can make a positive contribution to the health of others by adopting best practice in menu planning and the preparation, cooking and serving of food. Hospitality organisations have a responsibility to their customers, and people working in hospitality should know the current nutritional guidelines and understand the influence the industry can have on the lifestyles of others.

This unit looks at the principles of a balanced diet, including food choices and eating patterns. You will also explore why some individuals have special dietary needs and learn how to cater for these needs.

Learning outcomes

After completing this unit, you should:

1 Understand the principle of balanced diets

2 Understand how to plan and provide special diets.

Assessment and grading criteria

This table shows you what you must do in order to achieve a pass, merit or distinction grade, and where you can find activities in this book to help you.

Unit 6 Healthier food and special diets

To achieve a pass grade the evidence must show that you are able to:	To achieve a merit grade the evidence must show that, in addition to the pass criteria, you are able to:	To achieve a distinction grade the evidence must show that, in addition to the pass and merit criteria, you are able to:
P1 outline current government nutritional guidelines for a healthy diet **Assessment activity 1, page 156**	**M1** compare the positive and negative influences on healthy lifestyles **Assessment activity 2, page 166**	
P2 state the sources of essential nutrients **Assessment activity 1, page 156**		
P3 describe the impact of diet on health **Assessment activity 2, page 166**		
P4 describe catering practices that help maintain the nutritional value of food **Assessment activity 1, page 156**		
P5 outline the main features of special diets **Assessment activity 3, page 178**	**M2** design a healthy eating menu for a selected client group **Assessment activity 4, page 180**	**D1** assess the menu you have designed in relation to the specific needs of your client group **Assessment activity 4, page 180**
P6 describe the impact of special diets on health **Assessment activity 3, page 178**		
P7 describe catering practices to be considered when planning and providing meals for those on special diets **Assessment activity 4, page 180**		

How you will be assessed

You will be assessed by assignments that will be designed and marked by tutors at your centre. The evidence that you could provide for your assignments might include:

- presentations
- reports
- menus
- demonstrations such as completing tables.

Michael, 16-year-old trainee chef

This unit was really interesting because I had to think about what people eat and why they make different food choices. I think eating a healthy diet is becoming very important nowadays.

I work as a trainee chef. More and more of our customers are expecting chefs to know how to prepare and cook food in a more healthy way. So this unit was also helpful for me to understand how to cook and prepare healthy food.

At first I found it quite difficult to find out which foods have the best nutrients, but with practice I now know exactly where to look for information on foods that contain calcium or other nutrients. I also found it fun writing my own menu for restaurant customers and explaining in a presentation how I was going to make the dishes healthier.

I now think about what I am eating when I am choosing food from a menu for myself. I like to choose a healthy starter and main course, so that I can have a less healthy sweet. I am more keen than ever to pursue a career in hospitality. I really want to work as a head chef in a busy kitchen. I know at first I will have to work as a trainee chef and improve my skills to get promotion.

Over to you

- Think about the typical foods you eat. Which ones are healthy?
- Discuss with your friends and family which foods you eat that are less healthy.

6.1 Understand the principle of balanced diets

What are the government's suggestions?

In small groups, think about any information about healthy diet that you have seen or heard recently. This could be something you have seen on television or heard on the radio; anything you have got from newspapers, magazines, billboards and leaflets in supermarkets or health centres; or any other source.

Make a short list of all the healthy diet advice that you can find from these sources of information. Discuss how much of this advice affects what you normally eat.

In the first section of this unit, we will look at:

- developing a healthy lifestyle
- positive influences on a healthy lifestyle
- negative influences on a healthy lifestyle.

Developing a healthy lifestyle

To start, let's consider how paying attention to our diet and the nutritional value of what we eat can improve our health.

Diet

As you may have found when looking for information about healthy diets, there is a huge amount of published advice. However, there are three basic rules for a good diet:

- eat a variety of foods
- eat the right amount to maintain a healthy weight
- eat regular meals.

Eating a variety of foods should give us all the nutrition that our bodies need. As we will see when we discuss nutrition, there are five main food groups (see page 155). We should try to eat some foods from each of these groups.

Eating too much of any one food is not healthy. We all know carrots are good for us, but a diet of only carrots would leave us lacking in other nutrients that we need to be healthy. Foods sometimes need to be eaten together for the body to be able to use them effectively. This is why it is good to eat a variety of foods.

As well as eating a variety of foods, we should eat the right amount of food to maintain a healthy weight. If we eat more **calories** than we spend in effort, the extra ones are stored in the body as fat. We all need to be aware of the healthy weight range for our height. Figure 1 shows a chart that can be used to check whether someone is underweight or overweight.

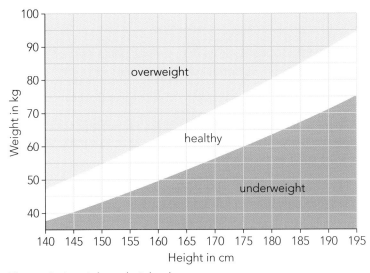

Figure 1: A weight-to-height chart

There is growing concern about the numbers of people who are overweight in the UK; according to the 2009 Health Survey for England, 22 per cent of men and 24 per cent of women are now classed as clinically **obese**. There is a national debate about this so-called obesity explosion and the problems it may cause for the National Health Service (NHS).

Key terms

Calorie – a unit of energy in food.

Obese – so overweight that it is dangerous to your health.

Activity: Check your own weight

Use Figure 1 to check your weight. Are you underweight, overweight or a healthy weight? Do you think should you consider changing your diet? If so, how?

Another way to maintain a healthy lifestyle is to eat regular meals. If we eat regularly, we are more likely to think about what we are eating and its content. Our energy levels will also be more constant during the day.

Regular meals mean:

- eating enough food three or four times a day for the stomach to feel comfortable
- not missing breakfast, not snacking during the day and not having a huge evening meal.

Government nutritional guidelines

The government is aware that it is important to have a good diet from childhood. The School Food Trust was set up to introduce dietary standards in primary and secondary schools. This involves schools using menus that are nutritionally balanced.

The Food Standards Agency (FSA) also issues healthy eating advice. It recommends that all healthy individuals should consume a diet that contains:

- plenty of starchy foods such as rice, bread, pasta and potatoes (choosing wholegrain varieties when possible)
- plenty of fruit and vegetables, with at least five portions of a variety of fruit and vegetables a day
- moderate amounts of protein-rich foods such as meat, fish, eggs and alternatives such as nuts and pulses
- moderate amounts of milk and dairy, choosing reduced-fat versions or eating smaller amounts of full-fat versions or eating them less often
- less saturated fat, salt and sugar.

Nutrition

Our bodies need to gain a certain amount of nutrients or nourishment from our diets. These nutrients fall into different classes. The amount we need depends on factors such as age, gender, state of health and how active we are.

Each class of nutrient gives the body what it needs to perform certain functions. Table 1 shows the main classes of nutrients and their uses in the body.

Class	Description	Main use in the body
Carbohydrates	There are two groups of carbohydrates: sugars and starches (complex carbohydrates)	A major source of energy
Fibre	There are two types of fibre: soluble and insoluble. Fibre is also known as NSP (non-starchy polysaccharides)	Helps the body digest and absorb food
Fats	There are two main types of fats: saturated and unsaturated	Gives the body energy, prevents heat loss and aids the absorption of fat-soluble vitamins
Proteins	Made from chains of amino acids	Essential for the growth, repair and replacement of body tissue
Vitamins	There are two types of vitamin: fat-soluble vitamins (A, D, E, K) and water-soluble vitamins (B, C)	Essential for the release of energy from foods, fighting infection, the formation of new cells and promoting healthy bones and teeth
Minerals	These are part of the body's structure	Helps regulate body fluids
Water	Water is not strictly a nutrient but it is an essential part of any diet	Essential for the body to function

Table 1: Nutrients and their uses in the body

Table 2 shows the five major food groups and the nutrients contained in some of the typical foods in each group.

Food group	Typical foods in the group	Main nutrients
Bread, cereals and potatoes	Bread, pasta, couscous, rice, oats, polenta, wholegrains, breakfast cereals, yams, potatoes, sweet potatoes	Complex carbohydrates, dietary fibre, calcium, iron, B vitamins
Fruit and vegetables	Fresh, frozen and canned fruit and vegetables, dried fruit, fruit juices	Vitamins C and K, B vitamins, calcium, magnesium, potassium, dietary fibre
Dairy foods (not butter or cream)	Milk, cheese, yoghurt, fromage frais	Protein, fats, vitamins A and D, B vitamins, calcium, magnesium
Protein foods: a) meat and poultry b) fish c) eggs, pulses and nuts	a) Salami, bacon, sausages b) Fresh, frozen and canned fish c) Fresh, canned or dried beans, chickpeas, lentils	Protein, fats, complex carbohydrates, B vitamins, vitamin D (eggs), vitamin E, iron, zinc, magnesium
Fats and sugary foods	Butter, lard, margarine, ghee, other spreading fats, cream, chips, oil-based dressings and mayonnaise, pastry, biscuits, cakes, chocolate, fried foods, ice cream, jam, sugar, sweets, pickles, soft drinks	Fats, sugar, vitamins A, E and D

Table 2: Major food groups and their sources

Activity: A food diary

Keep a food diary for a week. Write down what and when you eat and drink each day. Do you eat a variety of foods on a regular basis? Do you eat a lot of snacks? Discuss this in your group.

Review your diary and consider these points.

- What is your diet lacking?
- What are you eating too much of?
- How might your diet affect your health and lifestyle?
- How might your diet affect you in the future?

Catering practices that help maintain the nutritional value of food

When preparing and cooking food in the hospitality industry, it is important to use healthy cooking methods and good ingredients to ensure that the dishes you serve to customers have a high nutritional value.

Examples of healthy eating cooking methods are:

- steaming – food such as vegetables can be cooked in steam so that nutrients are not boiled away in water
- baking – in the oven without fat

- stir-frying – vegetables, meat, fish and chicken can be cut into strips and cooked quickly using very little oil
- roasting – in the oven with a minimum of fat added
- braising – a method of slow cooking meat with a little liquid
- grilling – a quick method of cooking where fat can drain away
- poaching – using a minimum of liquid and with no fat added for fish and fruit
- boiling – in water.

Methods of cooking which are not healthy involve the following:

- using too much extra fat in the cooking method
- overcooking vegetables and fruit, thereby destroying vitamins
- using large amounts of water that will remove water-soluble vitamins.

? Did you know?

Minced meat from supermarkets is now sold with labels that give the fat content, but it is more difficult to know how much fat is in mince when buying large amounts wholesale. All visible fat on meat should be removed before cooking.

Activity: Healthy alternative foods

Foods with high fat, high sugar or high salt content can be unhealthy. In groups, make a visit to the supermarket and make a list of the healthy alternatives that you can find on the shelves.

Assessment activity 1

Unit 6 **BTEC**

You have recently started work as the catering manager in a school canteen. It is important that all your staff understand the importance of a healthy diet for the young people who eat there. They should always know the basic facts about nutrition.

1 Produce a poster setting out the government nutritional guidelines for a healthy diet. The poster should be designed to be put on the wall in the kitchen so that the staff are always aware of the guidelines. **P1**

2 Produce a wall chart listing the essential nutrients and some of the foodstuffs that are good sources of these nutrients. **P2**

3 Prepare and give a short presentation explaining at least five measures that can be taken to keep or improve the nutritional value of meals when preparing and cooking food. This will help staff in the canteen produce food that promotes healthy lifestyles. **P4**

Grading tips

P1 Make sure you outline all the government guidelines and cover all aspects of maintaining a healthy diet.

P2 Remember to include all the essential nutrients. Make sure that the foodstuffs you name are good sources of the nutrients – you will need to make comparisons with other foods to do this.

P4 You must cover at least five measures or changes that the staff could adopt to maintain the nutritional value of food.

PLTS

Researching current government nutritional guidelines for a healthy diet and investigating the nutritional values of different foods will develop your skills as an **independent enquirer**. Remember that a good independent enquirer will not restrict research to just one website; they might use a range of websites, books and other publications. While you are making a presentation, you are developing yourself as an **effective participator**.

Functional skills

You will use your **ICT** skills when researching the government guidelines and sources of nutrients, and when you are preparing the poster and wall chart. You will be using your **English** skills when describing the measures that could be taken to promote healthy lifestyles.

Exercise and fitness

A healthy lifestyle is not only about diet and nutrition, the role played by exercise in keeping us fit is important as well. Staying physically fit is a vital part of a healthy lifestyle. It is recommended that we all do 30 minutes of exercise three times a week.

The type of exercise you take should be:

- load-bearing, where weight should be on your limbs – this includes hiking, jogging and dancing
- aerobic, which is sustained for a long period such as 50 minutes and is moderately intense – examples of aerobic exercise include running, swimming and cycling.

Whether we want to become healthier, lose weight or gain weight, exercise is an important part of a healthy lifestyle and has many benefits for the body. For many people, exercise is also an enjoyable and social activity.

Exercise should be enjoyable. Do you enjoy exercising?

Activity: How much do you exercise?

How much do you exercise each day, or each week? In your group, discuss how much and what sort of exercise you do each week. How do your exercise levels compare with recommendations? Discuss ways that different people could fit exercise into their daily lives.

Exercise has many benefits.

- It can help us feel better and healthier, and it boosts our immune system.
- It keeps bones strong and helps prevent bone thinning as we get older. We start to lose bone mass from the age of 20.
- It tones our muscles and improves blood circulation, body systems and body shape.
- It prevents us from putting on weight by balancing calorie intake and expenditure.
- It can boost our energy; as we breathe deeply we push more energy round the body.
- It can enhance our mood; there is a feelgood factor after exercise.
- It can help to relieve stress.

Did you know?

'Aerobic' literally means requiring or depending on the presence of oxygen for life. Aerobic exercise is designed to stimulate the circulation of oxygen through the blood.

Lifestyle choices

People make their own lifestyle choices, but these choices are often based on positive or negative influences.

- Positive influences include a balanced diet, fitness and exercise levels, social awareness campaigns and government health initiatives.
- Negative influences include smoking, drinking, inactivity, medical problems, eating disorders, fad diets and media advertising.

Let's look at these in turn in some more detail.

Positive influences on a healthy lifestyle

There are many positive influences that affect our ability to have a healthy lifestyle. It is important to know what these influences are and their possible effects on people. The positive influences we will look at here are:

- a balanced diet
- image and social awareness
- social integration
- mental and physical fitness
- personal hygiene
- government initiatives.

A balanced diet

One of the most important ways to maintain a healthy lifestyle is to have a balanced diet. We have a balanced diet when we eat a mix of foods that supply us with the nutrients we need in the correct proportions to maintain our health.

Mental and physical fitness

Mental and physical fitness are closely linked. Both are important for a healthy lifestyle. A good way to see how healthy you are is to calculate your body mass index (BMI). This is a method of measuring body fat based on weight and height.

To calculate your BMI, divide your weight in kilograms by your height in metres squared. For example, let's calculate the BMI of someone 1.7 m tall and weighing 70 kg.

$$BMI = \frac{weight}{height^2}$$

$$BMI = \frac{70}{1.7^2} = \frac{70}{1.7 \times 1.7} = \frac{70}{2.89} = 24.2$$

Table 3 shows how you can use your BMI to check whether you are the right weight for your height.

BMI	Status
below 18.5	underweight
18.5–25	healthy weight
25–30	overweight
over 30	obese

Table 3: What does your BMI mean?

So, using the table, we can see that the person in our example with a BMI of 24.2 is a healthy weight. BMI is only a general guide. Allowance has to be made for someone with a lot of muscle because muscle is heavier than fat. It should also be noted that BMI is a guide for adults only. It should not be used to check whether children are the right weight.

As people have become more concerned about their weight and general health, fitness classes have become increasingly popular and more common. There are a wide variety of classes to suit all tastes and age groups. These are offered by leisure centres, youth groups, private companies, gyms and adult education centres. These include:

- gym classes for babies and toddlers
- classes in homes for the elderly
- fitness dance classes
- aerobics and step classes
- yoga and Pilates for all levels
- swimming classes.

There are fitness classes to suit all ages, tastes and abilities. What fitness classes are available in your area?

Activity: Fitness classes

Investigate how many different fitness classes there are in your local area and share the information with the group. Are any focused on a particular age group? Did you find any for elderly people or children?

Image and social awareness

With so much emphasis on diet, health, image and exercise in the media, healthy lifestyles are now becoming much more desirable. For example, most people now see smoking as antisocial and a bad habit. The image that people have of themselves can be positively influenced in a variety of ways.

- Self-esteem – we need to have positive self-esteem by feeling good about ourselves from both a physical and a mental perspective. This will be helped and continually boosted by living a healthy lifestyle.
- Body image – this has become increasingly important for young and old of both sexes. To look good, we need to keep ourselves in good shape and be aware of our body image.
- Peer pressure – most people are influenced by how others see them. Some people like to look like others in their age group so that they feel part of the group and not left out.
- Advertising – glamorous images of slim, fit and healthy looking people of all ages are often shown in adverts throughout the media. These images give the message that this is a desirable way to look. We are also given ideas of how to attain this body image. Adverts use models of different ages and sizes to show what we can aspire to.

Why do some television adverts use models to create an ideal to which we can aspire?

Weight-watching clubs are very big business in the UK, with most areas likely to have at least one club. They can have a positive effect as they encourage people not only to lose weight but also to live healthier lifestyles by suggesting exercise regimes. The clubs use positive images of people who have lost weight to advertise themselves. They also use peer pressure from other members in a positive way to keep everyone on track and to try to develop a social atmosphere.

Their diets work by trying to retrain people's eating habits through various methods, such as counting points or calories. Whatever dietary method is used, they are based on eating less but more healthily. The regimes include lots of fruit, vegetables and water in the diet.

Personal hygiene

Much information is given in the media on how to keep ourselves, our clothes and our homes clean. Television programmes and articles in newspapers and magazines all give a positive image of cleanliness, and they try to show us how to reach these goals with regard to cleanliness in our lives.

Social integration

Social integration is very important as most people like to feel a part of the society in which they live. All the media pressure for healthy lifestyles has an effect in making more people adopt a healthy lifestyle so that they continue to be socially acceptable.

Government initiatives

Over the past few years, the government has encouraged people to adopt a healthy lifestyle. The government and its agencies such as the Food Standards Agency (FSA) have made recommendations and offered initiatives.

Tips for eating well

- Base meals on starchy foods.
- Eat lots of fruit and vegetables.
- Eat more fish.
- Cut down on fats (especially saturated) and sugar.
- Eat no more than 6 g of salt per day.
- Keep active and try to be a healthy weight.
- Drink lots of water.
- Always eat breakfast.

In summary, the key points to remember are that a healthy lifestyle includes a diet with a variety of foods eaten on a regular basis, which maintains weight within a healthy range and ensures we eat all the necessary nutrients. You also need to take enough exercise and make correct lifestyle choices, such as not smoking and drinking alcohol only in moderation.

Negative influences on a healthy lifestyle

Although there are many positive influences to help us achieve a healthy lifestyle, there are also many negative influences that need to be overcome. We will look at:

- smoking
- alcohol
- drugs
- inactivity
- medical problems
- fad diets
- low self-esteem
- time pressure
- peer pressure
- media advertising
- isolation
- income.

Smoking is increasingly seen as antisocial. What new anti-smoking measures have been introduced recently?

Smoking

Smoking is a risk factor in illnesses such as cancer, asthma, and heart and lung disease. It can also cause red eyes and dry, wrinkled skin. This can make smokers look older than they actually are. Smoking makes the body less efficient at absorbing nutrients such as vitamins and minerals, so a smoker needs to eat more food in order to get the necessary amounts. However, as smoking also depresses the appetite, a smoker is actually likely to eat fewer nutrients. Smoking is a danger to the health of smokers themselves and to anyone who breathes in the smoke (passive smoking).

A law banning smoking in enclosed public spaces came into force in England on 1 July 2007, following similar bans in other parts of the UK.

Alcohol

It is recommended that we drink alcohol only in moderation. It can help reduce stress and blood pressure, and a daily glass of wine is often recommended to the elderly. While a little may be good for you, too much can cause major problems. One unit of alcohol is considered to be a small glass of wine, a pub measure of spirits or half a pint of standard-strength beer or lager.

One negative effect of drinking alcohol is to lower a person's self-control, perhaps leading to another drink and then another. Drinking alcohol, if done in moderation, is considered acceptable by most groups in society. However, too many alcoholic drinks can cause terrible effects.

* Too much alcohol can gradually destroy the liver.

* It can make people behave very badly, getting into fights, being sick and taking up ambulance, police and hospital time.

* Alcohol can contribute to weight increase. There are many calories in alcohol that do not have any nutritional value. These are called 'empty calories'.

* Alcohol is an addictive drug. Someone who regularly drinks too much can become dependent on alcohol. Many alcoholics lose control of their lives, and they risk losing their jobs and their families.

Did you know?

The Health Education Authority (HEA) guidelines for over-18s are:

* no more than 21 units of alcohol per week for women

* no more than 28 units of alcohol per week for men

* a couple of alcohol-free days a week.

Activity: Smoking and drinking

In groups, discuss what you think the effects of drinking and smoking are on the body and people's behaviour.

Drugs

Many drugs have a negative affect on health, so it is always a good idea to steer clear of them unless you are advised to take a drug to treat a medical condition. Some drugs are marketed as helping you to become more healthy looking. For example, slimming pills are supposed to help you lose weight. These act as appetite suppressants so that you do not feel like eating, or they are designed to prevent the digestion of fats. However, slimming pills do not help you lead a healthy lifestyle. Because they do nothing to change bad habits, they do not help towards achieving a healthy lifestyle.

Inactivity

If you sit on the couch all the time and do nothing, you will become a 'couch potato'. Because couch potatoes take no exercise, they can develop many mental and physical problems. The problems associated with inactivity include:

- weight gain (getting fat)
- laziness
- inefficiency – the brain does not work as efficiently as it might
- poor self-esteem
- poor body image
- depression.

Eventually, other health problems associated with lack of exercise can also occur.

Medical problems

Obesity is one of the medical problems that negatively influences lifestyle. People who are obese can find it very difficult to maintain a healthy lifestyle, exercise and lose weight. They therefore keep adding to their weight.

Other medical problems associated with an unhealthy lifestyle are eating disorders such as anorexia and bulimia. Anorexia is a condition where people starve themselves by eating far too little food, although they may think they are eating healthily and may see themselves as too fat. Bulimia is when a person binge eats (consumes a lot of food in a short time) and then makes themselves sick to get rid of the food so as not to gain weight.

Disorders such as anorexia or bulimia can often be the result of low self-esteem, peer pressure, or media pressure.

Fad diets

The people and companies that promote fad diets claim that the diets can help achieve massive weight loss, often in a very short time. They all 'work' because they involve starving the body, and so they can show rapid results in the short term. They are sold by adverts, often in magazines, which make claims such as 'lose 18 lb in 4 days' or 'lose 4 kg every 11 days'.

Examples of fad diets are:

- some very low-carbohydrate diets
- the grapefruit, the banana, the three-day, the cabbage soup, and the bread and butter diets.

Fad diets are not recommended because the body tends to shut down and protect itself, so it begins to starve. As soon as you start to eat normally, the weight goes on again. These diets do not encourage people to live a healthy lifestyle and they create nutritional problems by excluding many essential foods.

Low self-esteem

When people are suffering from low self-esteem, they may find it difficult to exercise or watch their weight. They may prefer to sit on a couch and comfort eat foods with little nutritional value such as chocolate or go on a fad diet to try to achieve massive weight loss quickly. Low self-esteem can also lead to a person developing anorexia or bulimia.

Time pressure

Most people have busy lifestyles. They may spend a lot of time at work or travelling, or they may work shifts. There is pressure on their time, and sometimes convenience and processed foods seem a good alternative to preparing and cooking fresh food. You will learn more about these types of food in Unit 8.

You may have noticed how people often eat in the street and when on public transport, buying food from booths at the station or shops in the high street. These foods often contain large amounts of fat, sugar and salt – all foods that we should eat in very small quantities. Convenience and fast foods are often expensive, they come in packaging that is often thrown away, generating litter, and the smells can annoy others if eaten on buses or trains.

Peer pressure

Has someone ever said to you: 'Just have one, it won't hurt', 'Have another to finish the plate' or 'I'm having one, why not join me'? In this way, a friend or a member of your family might encourage you to have a cake, an ice cream, a drink, a burger or more chips with your meal. Peer pressure can be very difficult to withstand, especially as nobody wants to be seen as a killjoy. However, peer presure can have a negative influence on your choices.

Media advertising

We have looked at the positive influences of the media, but advertising can also have a negative impact. Think of all the examples of skinny young men and women in advertisements. Many are very underweight

Did you know?

'Grazing' on the move – in the street or on public transport – leads to unhealthy food choices, is expensive and generates litter. In addition, the food portions are getting larger than we need.

– particularly the size 0 models. They can influence the way that people want to look or make some people unhappy with their appearance. This can lead to much unhappiness and dissatisfaction. More seriously, some young people have taken dieting to extremes to achieve a very thin look, making themselves ill in the process, and a few have even died.

There has been a shift in what is regarded as the acceptable size for portions of food sold by restaurants. Customers like to see value for money, so some restaurants now advertise the size of the meat portion in a meal or print this information on their menus. A portion of meat may now be as much as 340–450 g (12–16 oz), whereas not so long ago it used to be 170 g (6 oz).

Foods are marketed to children by using cartoon or other television characters in advertising. These foods are often high in fat, sugar and salt. Even after all the debate about obesity in children, some breakfast cereals containing as much as 30 per cent sugar are still being marketed. This type of marketing relies on the 'pester power' of children in the supermarket.

Much negative or misleading advertising that encouraged unhealthy habits has now been stopped. For example, it is no longer permitted to run adverts linking smoking and drinking with sport or other healthy activities.

Do you think the media can have a negative impact on people's eating habits?

Isolation

Many more people, both young and old, now live on their own compared with a generation ago. These people often do not eat properly for a variety of reasons.

- Sometimes older people living on their own find it difficult to get to the shops.
- People on their own may think it is not worth cooking for one.
- Many pre-packaged portions of fresh meat and fish in supermarkets are for two people.

Even members of a family living in the same house can lead separate lives for much of the time – watching television in a bedroom, playing computer games, etc. Frequently, meals are taken in front of the television, in bedrooms or at a games console, and not as a family group sitting round a table. This can lead to snack meals and little exercise.

Income

Research has shown that people on a low income tend to spend less on fresh food and use convenience foods. They are more likely to purchase the cheapest brands of food, which may have lower nutritional values and contain more additives than more expensive brands. People on low incomes may also have less money to spend on exercising in leisure and fitness centres.

Activity: Eating habits

How often do you sit at a table and eat a group meal? Why is a group meal important? Discuss in small groups why people today do not eat as a group as often as they used to.

Assessment activity 2

Unit 6 P3 M1

You are working as a chef in the staff dining room of a local newspaper. The editor wants to run an article about the impact of a healthy diet and has asked you to help him by producing some notes on the subject.

1 Describe how diet affects health. Include lifestyle factors like diet, nutrition, exercise, alcohol and smoking. P3

2 You should also compare two negative and two positive influences on healthy lifestyles. M1

Grading tips

P3 You should describe how health is affected by all the lifestyle factors.

M1 The comparison of the negative and positive influences should include your judgements about how important each influence is compared to the others.

PLTS

When you are comparing the negative and positive influences on healthy lifestyles, you are extending your skills as a **creative thinker**.

Functional skills

You will use your **English** skills when describing the concept of healthy lifestyle and the positive and negative factors that influence a healthy lifestyle.

6.2 Understand how to plan and provide special diets

Now let's consider how you can help promote a healthy lifestyle when working in the hospitality industry. In this section, we will look at:

- positive contributions to a healthier lifestyle
- constraints in catering for a healthier lifestyle
- benefits of change
- features of a healthy menu
- recommendations for healthy eating
- factors to consider when planning a menu.

Positive contributions to a healthier lifestyle

There are several ways in which the hospitality industry can make a positive contribution to healthier lifestyles.

Menu design

A healthy menu can have a positive influence on the lifestyle of your customers. It should incorporate a good balance of fruit and vegetables and other ingredients with high nutritional content, and the use of healthy cooking and food preparation techniques. We will look further at the features of a healthy menu on pages 171–73.

Green issues

With growing awareness of green issues such as carbon footprints and sustainability (making sure that stocks do not run out), there has been pressure on different parts of the hospitality industry, including school meal providers and pubs, to source ingredients locally and to support local farmers and growers. Many outlets that have adopted this approach use it as a marketing tool.

The advantages of using locally grown food are that:

- the premises of farmers and producers can be visited to check for cleanliness
- caterers can build good relationships with food producers
- checks can be made on whether humane methods of food production are used
- caterers can reduce their carbon footprint as their food supplies will not need to be transported large distances.

There is also increasing use of **organic** produce in the hospitality industry. To be called organic, food production has to meet certain criteria, such as being grown in a natural way without the aid of chemicals.

By using organic and locally produced foods, the hospitality industry can check whether its ingredients have been produced in a healthy and humane manner. Many people consider that it is important to use only humanely produced animal products. This is because they feel that the food would be healthier if the animals are treated well and they prefer to eat food that has been produced without causing cruelty to animals.

Key term

Organic – foods produced without the use of chemicals such as pesticides in farming.

Activity: Local produce

Working in groups, can you identify foods that are produced locally to where you live? Produce a list to display in class.

Catering for specialist diets

Hospitality businesses will appeal more to their customers if they can provide meal options for those with special diets, including options for people who are vegetarian or have an allergy. More information on specialist diets is given on pages 177–78.

Showing nutritional values

Menus can show the nutritional value of dishes, thereby allowing customers to make an educated choice about what to eat. The nutritional value can be shown in a number of ways.

- A traffic light system can be used, similar to the one adopted by supermarkets.
- In a hospital, the menus show the type of special diet that each dish is appropriate for.
- On many menus a large V is put beside a dish to indicate its suitability for vegetarians.
- At a health farm or local leisure centre, the menu may show the actual calorie value of a portion.

Staff training

Staff training can make a big contribution to promoting healthy lifestyles. Catering staff who come into contact with customers at mealtimes can have an influence on what gets eaten. Staff can be trained to:

- be aware of the role diet plays in a healthy lifestyle
- be aware of special dietary needs
- advise on the nutritional content of foods, including warning if a dish may contain too much fat, sugar or salt
- serve a 'normal' portion
- suggest what might accompany a main course
- serve children's portions
- look out for food left on the plate to see what is uneaten
- make the food look appetising
- observe whether a customer has difficulty eating
- cook and keep hot or cold meals so that they do not lose their nutritional content.

Pricing and promotions

Healthy dishes should be priced so that they are not more expensive than less healthy dishes. When promoting foods, hospitality businesses could offer a deal that combines two healthy dishes. They could use the promotion to educate their customers by emphasising the nutritional value of the dishes.

Constraints in catering for a healthier lifestyle

It is not always possible for a business to do everything it might wish to promote a healthier lifestyle because of various constraints.

Financial constraints

Financial constraints are more significant for some parts of the hospitality industry than others. For example, a large chain hotel will usually have more to spend on catering than a small guest house. Parts of the hospitality industry more likely to suffer financial constraints include:

- hospitals
- school meal services
- catering in care and residential homes
- catering in prisons
- contract catering for people at work.

When food has to be supplied on a limited budget, a menu may have to be planned around cheaper ingredients and dishes. Locally produced foods, organic foods and humanely reared meat products can be more expensive than other food stuffs. Budget constraints:

- can deter caterers from making a positive contribution to healthier lifestyles, although this may not always stop them using local or organic produce
- may affect the total number of dishes which can be produced for the menu
- may limit the number of healthy options available on the menu
- may not allow for staff training.

When a menu is large and includes complicated dishes, the cost of producing those dishes is high. It may be cheaper to provide a shorter menu with simpler dishes and cut down on the number of chefs needed to prepare and cook them.

Customer lifestyles and trends

Another constraint on the hospitality industry's ability to positively contribute to healthy lifestyles is customer preference. Hospitality businesses have to cater for the tastes and lifestyles of their customers. Despite all the publicity about obesity and its possible causes, many people are still unaware of – or choose to ignore – health initiatives and guidelines, such as the 'five a day' campaign. Chips, chocolate and sugary fizzy drinks sell very easily, and it is difficult for people to change their lifestyle habits.

Case study: A junk food rebellion

In one school in Yorkshire, mothers launched a protest against a new healthy eating regime. The school had stopped students leaving the school at lunchtime, when some bought food from takeways and convenience stores, and introduced a healthy menu for school dinners.

In retaliation, the mothers took food orders from the students at break time and then bought chips, hamburgers and other fast-food meals to deliver through the fence surrounding the school at lunchtime.

The school had the best intentions in trying to improve the diets of its students, but the parents and children preferred other food.

1 Do you think the school was right to try to improve the diets of its students by stopping them going out at lunchtimes?

2 Are there better ways to encourage school students to eat healthier meals during the school day?

Customers have different expectations and requirements. Caterers have to take these into account when planning menus, but they can still produce healthier menus. If many customers like chips, it would be possible to put low fat chips on the menu, which would be a healthier choice.

Benefits of change

There are many benefits of changing menus and practices in the hospitality industry to promote a healthier lifestyles.

Bigger client base

Healthier menus may attract more clients or customers. A caterer with a reputation for producing healthy menus for schools with freshly cooked ingredients may receive contracts from other schools as well as other businesses and organisations. It may also serve more meals in each place in which it operates.

Happier staff and lower costs

One way to promote a healthier lifestyle is to provide staff with the right training and skills. This is likely to have various benefits. Staff will feel more motivated and will want to produce new, healthier dishes. Better-trained staff, with improved skills, are also quicker and more efficient, and this will mean that the business may have lower employment costs.

Cost reduction

Changing to a healthier menu can reduce the amount a caterer spends on food. For example, it would be more healthy to serve smaller portions of some desserts, which would reduce food costs.

Recognition

One benefit of changing the menu to encourage healthy eating is that the outlet might gain some recognition in the form of awards given to

Why are well-trained staff likely to be happier and more helpful?

various parts of the industry. Here are some examples of the awards that are made each year:

- Local Authority Caterer's Association (LACA) School Chef of the Year – for school meals
- Soil Association Organic Food Awards
- Healthy Living Awards (Scotland).

Features of a healthy menu

What should be considered when planning a healthy menu? Let's look at how to plan a healthy menu for people with different dietary needs.

Government guidelines

There is plenty of advice available about what should feature in a healthy menu and what contributes to a healthy lifestyle. Much of this advice comes from websites and free publications, and these are a big help to caterers. Suggestions for menus, recipes, brochures and posters are available to download when needed. Some useful websites can be found by going to the hotlinks for this book (see page ii), and include those for the Department for Education and Channel 4.

A major source of advice comes from government guidelines and initiatives. For example, the Food Standards Agency (FSA) currently advises:

- trimming the fat off meat
- choosing low-fat varieties of dairy and other products
- increasing your intake of starchy foods instead of fatty ones
- eating fewer sugary foods
- increasing your intake of a variety of fruit and vegetables.

Portions of fruit and vegetables

It is important to include enough portions of fruit and vegetables for a healthy menu. We need to do this because eating a variety of these foods gives us plenty of vitamins and minerals such as folic acid, vitamin C and potassium. In addition, fruit and vegetables:

- are a good source of fibre and antioxidants
- are generally low-fat, low-calorie foods which fill us up and help keep weight off
- help to reduce the risk of heart disease and some cancers.

Lean meat

Lean meat is a healthy ingredient which should feature on most healthy menus, but it should be eaten in moderation. It provides the diet with protein, B vitamins, iron and zinc. Lean meats include:

- chicken and turkey without their skin
- lean mince
- pork without its fat and crackling.

Water intake

The human body is made up of 60 per cent water and this needs to be topped up daily to keep us healthy. We can survive for quite a long time without food, but we can only live for a few days without water.

Water is lost all the time from the body through the kidneys and the skin when we sweat, but it is lost more quickly when we are sick. A guide to tell whether you are dehydrated (lacking water) is to check your urine. This should be a pale straw colour – dark-coloured urine is a sign of dehydration, which can be very serious.

The Food Standards Agency recommends that adults drink 6–8 glasses of water daily.

 Did you know?

Our bodies need water to flush out waste products through the skin and kidneys; keep hair, skin and organs healthy; help digestion; and to help fibre swell to prevent constipation.

 Activity: How healthy is your diet?

How much water do you drink daily? Do not include fizzy drinks, tea or coffee. If not enough, perhaps you could carry a small bottle around.

Fat intake

It is fat that gives many foods their flavour, but excess fat has been linked to many health problems such as obesity, heart disease and cancer. However, fat is an essential part of our diets as it carries the fat-soluble vitamins A, D, E and K. The problem is that many people eat too much of the wrong type of fat. All fats are high in energy-giving calories (9 calories per gram), but as it is easy to eat a large amount of hidden fat it can contribute to a weight problem.

Did you know?

There are three different types of fat.

- Saturated fat is hard at room temperature and is found in meat, meat products, dairy products and coconut oil. Eating a lot of this will increase the risk of heart disease.

- Polyunsaturated fat is liquid at room temperature and found in cooking oils such as grapeseed, safflower, sunflower and corn oils, and oily fish such as salmon, trout, sardines and herring. Omega-3 fatty acids are also found in this type of fat, and these can help prevent heart disease and reduce the symptoms of joint problems.

- Mono-unsaturated fat is liquid at room temperature and found in olives, groundnut oil, nuts and avocados.

Mono- and polyunsaturated fats are healthier than saturated fats. Do you know why this is?

Salt intake

Many of the foods we eat contain salt, but pre-prepared and convenience foods can add much more to our daily consumption than freshly prepared dishes. The recommended daily amount of salt for adults is 6 g (about one teaspoon). Babies should have no more than 1 g a day, and salt should never be added to a baby's food.

A label on food might state that it contains 0.5 g of sodium per serving, but this can be misleading. To find the amount of salt in the serving, you need to multiply the amount of sodium by 2.5. So, a serving with 0.5 g of sodium contains 1.25 g of salt – about one-fifth of the recommended daily intake.

Low calorie ingredients

Some foods are available in low-calorie versions. These foods are often also low-fat versions of the original foods. Examples include skimmed or semi-skimmed milk, low-fat yoghurts, sugar-free desserts (flavoured with sweeteners) and many ready-made meals from supermarkets.

Recommendations for healthy eating

Let's look at some more guidelines and information that you can use to help you plan menus.

Five a day

Most people have heard of the government campaign to eat five portions of fruit and vegetables each day. A portion of fruit or vegetables is about 80 g (3 oz).

It is important to know what counts as part of your five a day.

- As well as fresh fruit and vegetables, canned (in juice rather than syrup), frozen and dried fruit and vegetables all count.
- One portion of dried fruit is similar to the amount you would eat if the produce was fresh. For example, three dried apricots or a handful of sultanas (dried grapes) is one portion.
- Fruit or vegetable juice (100% juice) only count as one portion, regardless of how much is consumed. The recommended portion is one medium glass (150 ml) of 100% juice.
- Potatoes do not count as one of the five a day as they are a 'starchy' food.
- Fruit and vegetables added to foods such as pasta sauces, soups and puddings can contribute to your five a day.
- Pulses such as lentils, beans and chickpeas can only count as one of the five a day as they do not have the same mix of nutrients as other vegetables.

Activity: Improving your diet

In groups, discuss how many portions of fruit and vegetables you eat on a typical day. Consider how this part of your diet could be improved.

Case study: Improving school meals

Jenny Allsop is the new catering manager at a primary school. At Jenny's school, some children have breakfast and lunch, as well as mid-morning and afternoon snacks, provided for them at school. Their parents then pick them up from an after-school club.

Parents have become aware of the five a day campaign and are concerned how little fruit and vegetables their children eat. Once they get home

from school in the evening the children are tired and not inclined to eat much.

Jenny has been approached by some parents to discuss how more fruit and vegetables could be introduced into the meals the children have at school.

What ideas do you have which could help Jenny manage this problem?

Balance of healthy eating

We have a balanced diet when we eat a variety of foods to supply us with necessary nutrients in the correct proportions to maintain our health. We do not necessarily need to have three carefully planned meals a day, but should have at least one. This should help to provide a balanced diet over a week.

Food pyramid

A food pyramid (see Figure 2) can help you produce a balanced diet, as it clearly shows how much of each food group we should eat.

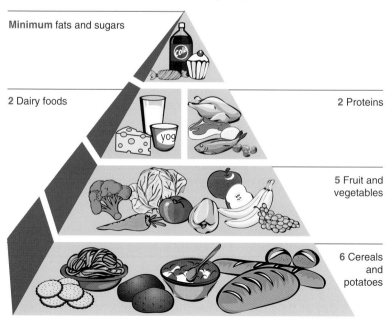

Figure 2: A food pyramid

Labelling

Labelling on food packaging is very useful when trying to follow recommendations for healthy eating. Labels give the nutritional content of packaged foods. They can be complicated to understand, so the Food Standards Agency (FSA) has produced a set of guidelines. There is a system of 'traffic light labelling' for packaged foods that shows whether the product is low (green), medium (orange) or high (red) in fats, saturated fats, sugar and salt.

Recommended daily allowances (RDA)

We have already explained the recommended servings of the different food groups, together with recommended limits on the amount of salt and fat in the diet. Table 4 will help you plan a healthy menu containing the right number of calories.

Age	Male	Female
4–6 months	690	645
4–6	1715	1545
15–18	2755	2110
19–50	2550	1940
65–74	2330	1900
over 75	2100	1810

Table 4: Examples of recommended calorie intakes

Factors to consider when planning a menu

Many different factors need to be considered when planning a menu that contributes to a healthy lifestyle. These include:

- customer age groups
- culture and lifestyle diets
- available skills
- costs.
- special dietary needs
- availability of ingredients
- time

Customer age groups

This section looks at the nutritional needs that people have at different stages of their lives: first as children, then as teenagers, then adults and, finally, when they are elderly.

Children learn their eating patterns from their parents, developing tastes and habits such as sitting at the table. There are several key things to consider when planning meals for children.

- They need the same variety of food in their diet as adults but in smaller amounts.
- Their bodies are growing so bodybuilding foods with calcium and vitamin D are essential.

- Regular small meals to keep blood sugar levels steady are important.
- Avoid processed foods, especially those with additives such as colourings which may lead to hyperactivity.
- Most importantly, use fresh foods.

Activity: A menu for a child for the day

Anya is a six-year-old girl that you are going to look after for the day. She will need feeding a healthy diet that includes breakfast, lunch, dinner and two snacks. Work in groups to produce a menu for Anya's day with you.

There is something special about teenagers. Their bodies are still growing, and they put on a spurt of growth in their teenage years when hormones really kick in and their bodies start to develop into adulthood. Hormonal activity can also affect hair and skin, with spots appearing.

According to statistics issued by the Food Standards Agency:

- 42 per cent of teenagers usually skip breakfast
- almost 50 per cent have fizzy drinks every day
- around 10 per cent eat fast food at least once per day
- 83 per cent are not eating the recommended five portions of fruit and vegetables.

Many teenagers have big appetites and need lots of energy, which should come from starchy carbohydrates not fats and sugars. Teenagers should eat plenty of fruit and vegetables, lots of dairy products and plenty of protein. They should eat breakfast, preferably fortified cereal, semi-skimmed milk and fruit juice.

It is important that adults look after themselves so they will be healthy as they move into the elderly age group. A healthy plan for adults includes:

- watching weight levels – being neither overwright nor underweight
- eating a balanced diet to provide sufficient nutrition
- not eating too much of the wrong foods
- drinking alcohol in moderation.

Activity: Check menus

With the help of your tutor, obtain examples of menus from local institutions. For example, you may be able to obtain menus from hospitals, schools and colleges.

Comment on whether the menus are suitable for a healthy lifestyle. Are they suitable for teenagers and adults? Do they need to be adapted for the elderly or children?

Someone's age does not tell us too much about health and activity. A 35-year-old person may be very inactive, whereas some early morning swimming clubs have people in their nineties as active members.

Our bodies change as we age, and thought has to be given to how the elderly can be kept healthy. Some may be in homes or hospitals where all of their food and nutrition is supplied. However, studies show that there are levels of malnutrition in some homes and hospitals.

These are some points to consider when planning menus for the elderly.

- The bodies of the elderly are slowing down so they need fewer calories, but the level of nutrition has to be kept up.

- They may need vitamin D to help prevent bone loss (osteoporosis), especially as they may not go outdoors so much. Vitamin D is made by the effect of the sun on the body.

- Small portions of attractively served fresh foods are needed.

- Some elderly people have difficulty swallowing.

- One-dish meals can be easy to eat and can include a variety of foods.

- Attention should be paid to the inclusion of zinc in the diet.

Special dietary needs

People have special dietary needs for different reasons. These may be medical, cultural or by choice. The one thing these people have in common is the need for a healthy diet.

People with medical conditions might require special diets, such as low-fat, low-sugar, low-calorie or high-fibre diets. Three relatively common medical conditions that have dietary implications are diabetes, allergies and food intolerance.

- Diabetes – this is a medical condition where an increased amount of sugar is found in the blood. The blood sugar level has to be balanced, either by diet or by medication, depending on the type and seriousness of the diabetes.

- Allergies – a person with a food allergy can become ill even from a tiny amount of the food that causes the allergy. This can lead to the person going into **anaphylactic shock** and requiring immediate treatment. Many people are allergic to nuts.

- Food intolerance – some people's bodies react badly to certain foods, which can make them very unwell. For example, some people have an intolerance to gluten (found in wheat, rye, oats and barley) and others to dairy products. Serious gluten intolerance is known as coeliac disease. A doctor can carry out tests to find out which foods are making someone unwell.

Key term

Anaphylactic shock – a life-threatening reaction to an allergy, often caused because the windpipe swells and the person cannot breathe.

Culture and lifestyle diets

Many people follow particular diets for cultural or religious reasons or because it suits their lifestyle. Vegetarians do not eat meat, poultry or fish. Vegans do not use or eat any animal products.

People who have a kosher diet:

- follow Jewish food laws
- only eat meat killed by a specialist
- only eat animals with split hooves and that chew the cud
- do not eat blood products or pork
- store, cook and eat meat and dairy products separately.

People who have a halal diet:

- follow Muslim food laws
- only eat animals slaughtered by having their throat cut and blood drained
- do not eat blood products or pork.

Assessment activity 3

Unit 6 BTEC

You are working as the catering manager in a school canteen. Your school has to deal with several people who have special diets.

1 Describe to your staff the features of three special diets in a short presentation. **P5**

2 Continue your presentation by describing how special diets affect health. **P6**

Grading tips

P5 You must describe three diets in such a way that the staff will be able to produce suitable food for a person on each of these diets.

P6 Remember to comment on how each special diet can affect a person's health, considering any bad aspects as well as positive benefits.

 PLTS

Describing the impact of special diets on health will develop your skills as an **independent enquirer**. Giving the presentation will develop skills as an **effective participator**.

 Functional skills

You will use your **ICT** skills when preparing the presentation on special diets.

Availability of ingredients

Supermarkets stock ingredients and food from all over the world. Fresh, chilled, frozen, tinned and bottled foods are brought in by air, road or ship and quickly distributed to suppliers. Foods now available out of season in the UK include:

- lamb – shipped chilled or frozen from New Zealand
- fresh fruit and vegetables flown in from many parts of the world.

Activity: Seasonal foods

Visit a supermarket and look at the selection of fruit, vegetables and meat. See how many examples you can find that have been imported to fill a seasonal gap.

The availability of so many ingredients means caterers have a huge choice of dishes they can put on the menu. This should allow them to cater for everyone's taste and need.

Available skills

An important factor in planning a menu is the skill of the chef and the kitchen team. The skills they need to have include:

- knowledge of food – to be able to recognise what a **commodity** is, and know its taste and nutritional values
- food preparation and cookery skills
- literacy and numeracy skills for designing and costing a menu.

This may seem obvious, but one problem faced by the school meals service is that people without these skills have replaced fully trained chefs and cooks. There is now a move to provide cookery skills training for school meal staff.

Key term

Commodity – an item of food. For example, milk is a commodity.

Time

Another factor to consider is how long you have to prepare and cook a meal. Normal working hours may not leave enough time for some foods to be prepared and cooked. In these cases preparation can be done on the previous day, but not in a five-day operation when the kitchen is closed over a weekend.

Costs

The cost factor influences every caterer's decision when menu planning, but costing may serve different purposes depending on the setting.

- In an upmarket and expensive restaurant, the dishes need to be costed to decide whether they can be produced without the price becoming too high.
- In a school, hospital or old people's home, the dishes are costed to see whether they fit the budget.
- In any profit-making business, products must be able to sell and make the required amount of profit.

Cost should not prevent healthy menus being designed, but will lead caterers to choose dishes that fit the budget.

Assessment activity 4

Unit 6 P7 M2 D1 BTEC

You are the manager in a healthy eating restaurant and you have just employed a new member of kitchen staff. The restaurant has a reputation for serving customers who have special diets and you need your new staff member to understand what needs to be taken into account when planning and providing meals for customers with special diets.

1 Describe catering practices that need to be taken into account. **P7**

2 Design a new healthy menu for vegetarian customers. Include as many seasonal, locally produced commodities as possible. Your menu should contain at least three starters, three main courses and three sweets. **M2**

3 Having completed your menu, assess how this will meet the needs of a vegetarian following a healthy diet. **D1**

Grading tips

P7 Remember you should include what you will take into account when planning and providing the food. Think about the needs of each special diet you covered in Assessment activity 3.

M2 Have a look at menus from other establishments to get ideas – there are many menus on the Internet.

D1 You should consider whether all of the food groups are included in the menu in sufficient amounts to maintain the customer's health.

PLTS

When you are describing the catering practices that need to be taken into account, you are developing as an **effective participator**. When you are designing and assessing your menu, you will be developing yourself as a **creative thinker**.

Functional skills

You will use your **ICT** skills when producing your menu.

John Desai
Hospital caterer

John Desai has worked as a chef in a hospital for five years. Most of his work involves planning and preparing three meals a day for approximately 600 patients on the hospital wards. There is an extra challenge as John has to keep to a very tight budget.

As in every hospital, there are many patients with special dietary needs. John needs to cater for vegetarians, diabetics, people with religious dietary requirements and people with special diets as a result of a serious health problem. These include low-cholesterol, gluten-free or lactose-free diets. John never knows a patient's dietary requirements until they arrive in the hospital, so he has to be prepared to meet these needs at short notice.

Patients do not usually know in advance that they will be staying in hospital (unlike hotel guests) and their dietary needs are particularly important because they cannot leave the hospital to eat out. This is John's main daily challenge: ensuring he can provide foods that meet the dietary requirements and nutritional needs of every patient. He also has to ensure that the whole team knows how to prepare special meals.

The most enjoyable thing about John's job is that he does not know from one day to the next exactly what he will have to cook. He has to use his knowledge of nutrition to ensure that the menus he plans and cooks are suitable for the patients' diets.

Think about it!

- How would you deal with patients with different dietary needs? What information would you need to have available?

- Can you think of a range of other special diets that John might have to deal with?

Just checking

1 Give six benefits of taking exercise.

2 What are the five food groups?

3 How many portions of fruit and vegetables should be eaten daily? Give two examples of a portion.

4 Give three reasons not to drink alcohol.

5 Explain five healthy cooking methods and find two recipes using each method.

6 What is essential to life but not a nutrient?

7 What should be the maximum amount of salt intake daily for an adult?

8 What should be features of a children's healthy menu?

9 Why are teenagers special in terms of their dietary needs?

10 Give ways in which the hospitality industry can contribute to healthy lifestyles.

edexcel

Assignment tips

- Studying Unit 8 will help you when you are thinking about healthier cookery and preparation methods.

- Do not forget to include a reference to the recommended intake of alcohol in your work as well as the amounts of food you should eat when you are asked about eating guidelines.

- You need to compare at least two positive and two negative influences on a healthy lifestyle. Try to pick influences that are opposites as these are easier to contrast.

- You will be required to design a three-course healthy eating menu as part of your assignments. It would be a good idea for you to find menus from similar establishments to help you. For example, if you chose a pub menu, find some pub menus on the Internet as a basis for you to work on.

- You will have to assess the menu that you have planned. When you are doing this, you need to think about what are its good points and what are its less good points, and write the results of your thoughts.

7 Applying workplace skills

A wide range of skills is required of those working in customer-focused, hospitality-related businesses. You must have good interpersonal skills and the ability to work as part of a team. You must be able to deliver a high level of customer service, and have in-depth knowledge of all the products and services offered by the business for which you work. You must also have the ability to maintain these skills when working under pressure.

In this unit you will learn how to identify the skills you presently have and how to develop other employability skills you might need to be able to work effectively. You will investigate the different job roles and career opportunities available in the hospitality and related industries, and start the process of applying for these, including the completion of application forms and CVs.

Learning outcomes

After completing this unit, you should:

1 Be able to maintain personal presentation
2 Be able to work effectively with customers and colleagues
3 Be able to prepare for a job application
4 Be able to produce a plan to develop skills.

Assessment and grading criteria

This table shows you what you must do in order to achieve a pass, merit or distinction grade, and where you can find activities in this book to help you.

Unit 7 Applying workplace skills

To achieve a pass grade the evidence must show that you are able to:		To achieve a merit grade the evidence must show that, in addition to the pass criteria, you are able to:	To achieve a distinction grade the evidence must show that, in addition to the pass and merit criteria, you are able to:
P1 maintain personal professional appearance **Assessment activity 2, page 196**	**P2** demonstrate a positive and professional approach in your working condition **Assessment activity 2, page 196**	**M1** explain the impact of personal presentation on customer perception **Assessment activity 1, page 194**	
P3 explain what is considered to be professional presentation of oneself **Assessment activity 1, page 194**	**P4** describe the reasons for maintaining professional presentation and the effect this has on the organisation **Assessment activity 1, page 194**		
P5 explain the skills required to maintain the work area **Assessment activity 1, page 194**			
P6 demonstrate a positive attitude and behaviour with customers and colleagues **Assessment activity 2, page 196**	**P7** demonstrate use of correct procedures and good practice in dealing with customers and colleagues **Assessment activity 2, page 196**	**M2** explain the impact of excellent and poor customer service on business success **Assessment activity 1, page 194**	
P8 communicate effectively to identify and provide support to customers and colleagues to solve problems should they arise **Assessment activity 2, page 196**	**P9** demonstrate working with others to achieve targets **Assessment activity 2, page 196**		
P10 describe the skills required to work effectively with customers and colleagues to provide a quality service or product **Assessment activity 1, page 194**	**P11** describe how to identify and solve customer and colleague problems and complaints should they arise **Assessment activity 1, page 194**		
P12 list the key stages in working to meet team targets **Assessment activity 1, page 194**			
P13 state the purpose of a curriculum vitae and the information to be included **Assessment activity 2, page 196**	**P14** explain the purpose of a covering letter and its importance **Assessment activity 3, page 212**	**M3** compare sources of job and career information in terms of their suitability for the employer and the potential applicant **Assessment activity 3, page 212**	**D1** analyse effectiveness of own performance in all aspects of the job application process and recommend improvements **Assessment activity 4, pages 212–13**
P15 state the importance of professional presentation and quality of content of the curriculum vitae and covering letter **Assessment activity 3, page 212**	**P16** list the preparations that should be made for an interview **Assessment activity 3, page 212**		
P17 explain the importance of evaluating an interview **Assessment activity 3, page 212**	**P18** produce a curriculum vitae and covering letter **Assessment activity 4, pages 212–13**		
P19 demonstrate a variety of interview skills **Assessment activity 4, pages 212–13**			

Unit 7 Applying workplace skills

To achieve a pass grade the evidence must show that you are able to:		To achieve a merit grade the evidence must show that, in addition to the pass criteria, you are able to:	To achieve a distinction grade the evidence must show that, in addition to the pass and merit criteria, you are able to:
P20 evaluate current skills against job aims **Assessment activity 5, page 222**	**P21** identify an opportunity to develop a skill **Assessment activity 5, page 222**	**M4** explain the skills and personal attributes necessary for selected job roles in hospitality-related industries **Assessment activity 5, page 222**	
P22 set and work towards a target **Assessment activity 5, page 222**	**P23** keep a record of skills development **Assessment activity 5, page 222**		
P24 describe the purpose of a personal development plan **Assessment activity 5, page 222**	**P25** describe how development plans are produced **Assessment activity 5, page 222**		
P26 explain the importance of feedback **Assessment activity 5, page 222**			

How you will be assessed

You will be assessed by assignments that will be designed and marked by tutors at your centre. These assignments are designed to allow you to show your understanding of the unit outcomes. The evidence that you provide for your assignments could be in the form of:

- presentations
- role plays
- practical tasks
- mock job interviews
- written work.

Harry, 17-year-old learner

I didn't really consider a career in hospitality until I went to an open evening at my local college. I didn't know what I wanted to do so I went to see what was on offer. I was really surprised by the subjects covered in the BTEC Level 2 in Hospitality. I have always been an outgoing and social person, and the idea of having a career that could take me anywhere in the world sounded really good.

I found Unit 7 particularly interesting, especially the role plays. We have learnt how important customer service is to a business and what skills are needed to provide excellent service.

I also liked taking part in the interviews and I feel more prepared for when I start looking for a job. The teamworking task was more difficult, as you have to get all of the team to work together, but we did manage to meet the deadline and I was pleased with our presentation. Practice and preparation are the key to this unit.

Over to you

- Do you think you will find it difficult to work as part of a team and meet deadlines?
- Have you thought about things you could do to make yourself stand out from other applicants when you apply for a job?
- Have you thought about doing some volunteer work or getting involved in clubs and sports teams? This might show future employers that you can get on well with other people.

7.1 Be able to maintain personal presentation

Welcome

Why are first impressions so important?

As a group, discuss why you think first impressions are important when you:

- talk to a customer
- meet a colleague for the first time
- go to an interview.

This section covers:

- personal presentation
- professional approaches to work.

Personal presentation

All staff working in hospitality are likely to have some contact with customers. It is important that staff display a professional attitude and create the right impression. Earlier in this book, we covered personal presentation (see pages 76–77) and presentation skills (see pages 98–99). We will summarise the main points here, but it may be useful to look back at this material.

First impressions

You will never get another chance to make a first impression. A customer's opinion of you and the organisation you work for will be formed within a few moments of meeting you. If you make a poor impression on a customer, it will be very difficult to turn this around and impress them. On the other hand, if their first impression is good, they are likely to approach the rest of their time with you in a positive state of mind.

Customers will be confident about your whole organisation if they are presented with a positive image of you. Presentation skills relate to:

- personal hygiene and appearance
- work areas and equipment.

Staff who are slovenly, scruffy, untidy or (worst of all) dirty will convey a negative image of themselves and the organisation they work for. This will not give the customer confidence. Staff who are smart and presentable are already halfway to satisfying customers. Their appearance says: 'I am a professional. I know my job and I am ready to do business.'

Activity: Impressions

- What kind of first impression would be created by a member of waiting staff in a restaurant who had nose and tongue piercings? Do you think this is acceptable?
- You are working on reception and a guest asks to borrow a pen, but you cannot find one. What impression will that give?
- How do you feel when a member of staff ignores you when you walk into a café? What kind of impression does this create?

Personal hygiene and appearance

Good personal hygiene is obviously essential in the hospitality industry. You should:

- wash or shower daily
- keep your hair neat, tidy and clean
- keep your fingernails short
- avoid wearing too much make-up or jewellery
- avoid bad habits such as chewing or playing with your hair
- keep your uniform clean and in good repair
- keep all cuts and wounds covered with appropriate, clean and waterproof dressings.

Activity: Uniforms

In pairs, design a uniform for a member of the reception staff and a member of the housekeeping staff for a major hotel group.

What are the benefits of requiring staff to wear a uniform?

Work areas and equipment

The first impression that customers get of an organisation is formed not only by the presentation of the staff but also by the presentation of their work area. If your work area does not look well organised, customers may assume that you and your organisation are not organised either. Make sure that:

- your work area is neat and tidy
- you have all the equipment and supplies that you need when you first start a shift so that the service you offer guests is not hindered.

Professional approaches to work

In Units 3 and 4 we examined why providing excellent customer service is so important for any business. Every member of staff has a responsibility to ensure that the service they provide is of the highest standard – this includes having a positive and professional approach to your job. You will get a lot more satisfaction from your job if you are happy and friendly than if you are bad tempered and miserable. You need to do your job to the best of your ability all day and every day.

7.2 Be able to work effectively with customers and colleagues

This section covers:

- customer types
- interpersonal skills
- coping with different situations.
- important job skills
- communication skills

Customer types

Customers can be categorised in various ways.

- You can categorise customers as existing clients (those who have used the business before) or new customers (those who are using it for the first time).
- You can also distinguish between external customers (those who purchase the products and services provided by an organisation) and internal customers (other members of staff who use the services provided by colleagues to do their work).

We covered the different types of customer served by the hospitality industry earlier in this book (see pages 66–71). Remember that hospitality staff need to be confident in dealing with:

- individuals and groups
- business people
- non-English speaking customers
- customers of different ages
- customers of different cultures
- families
- customers with special needs.

Important job skills

Whatever the level of your job, there are certain skills you need to have in order to be successful. We will look at some of these skills here.

Customer service skills

Many jobs in the hospitality industry are customer facing. To serve customers professionally, you will need:

- good communication and listening skills
- the ability to work under pressure
- the ability to work as part of a team
- problem-solving and complaint-handling skills
- product and organisational knowledge
- commitment to the organisation.

Teamwork skills

Most jobs in the hospitality industry will involve teamwork. There are very few jobs where you would be working totally on your own.

So, what does teamwork mean? A group of people who are working to achieve the same goal can be classed as a team.

- You may be part of a chef's brigade whose goal is to ensure that all meals are ready on time.
- You may be part of a team of retail assistants whose goal is to make the most sales.

Activity: Teamwork

Think about a time when you were part of a team – this could be a sports team, a work team or a team at school or college. Consider the skills that you needed to make the team successful. Make a list of these skills.

Discuss your list with a group and compile one list of the key skills needed to make a successful team. Make sure you have your own copy of the final list.

A team of people should be united – members should realise that their goals cannot be achieved without the help and support of the other team members.

Problem–solving skills

You will encounter problems in most jobs that you do. The following skills will help you to solve these problems:

- patience
- listening skills to enable you to fully understand the problem
- good product knowledge
- flexibility – in order to solve a problem, you may have to change the way in which you work.

Communication skills

Effective communication is one of the key success factors of any business. To communicate effectively, you need good listening skills so that you can focus on what the other person is saying. You also need to speak clearly at the right pace and tone – not too quickly or too slowly and not too loudly or too quietly.

Communication is not only about speaking; you will also communicate in writing – by letter, email or fax. We also communicate non-verbally through body language, which can often be a good indication of what a person is feeling. For example, you can tell if somebody is happy, sad or angry just by looking at their face – a person's eyes and mouth usually give the game away.

Interpersonal skills

To be able to work effectively with customers and colleagues, you will need to demonstrate strong interpersonal skills. We will go through some of these skills here.

Attitude and behaviour

A positive attitude and appropriate behaviour are essential when dealing with colleagues and customers. Your attitude should let others know that you care and that you are trying your best. A negative attitude will affect how you communicate with the customer and they may even think you are being rude deliberately.

No matter how delicious the food tastes or how comfortable the hotel room is, the whole customer experience can be spoiled if staff are rude, uninterested or uncaring.

Greeting customers

Greeting customers is one of the most important duties that you will perform for your organisation because it is where the customers' first impressions are formed.

Hospitality organisations often have their own performance standards for greeting customers. They will usually mention that the customer should be greeted with eye contact and a warm smile.

Respect for customers

The way in which you interact with customers will give an impression of how much you care. Customers will expect you to show them respect by:

- being **courteous**
- showing an interest in what they are saying
- trying to help them by dealing with their problems.

Key term

Courteous – polite and well mannered.

Activity: Greeting customers

In a small group, decide how you would greet each of the following types of customer:

- a young child aged about 7 or 8
- a customer who has a hearing difficulty
- an elderly couple
- a family group
- a customer with mobility difficulties.

Dealing with complaints

It is particularly important to show respect to customers who have cause to complain. Customers are far more conscious nowadays of what they can expect from a product or service and they can be very quick to complain if there is something wrong.

When dealing with a complaint, you should:

- remember that the customer is likely to be angry, which might make them impatient, unhappy and sometimes rude
- act in an efficient and diplomatic way or the customer may become very impatient with you
- remain calm and polite no matter how angry the customer gets
- remember not to take the customer's anger personally.

It is important to comply with the complaints policy of your organisation. This may vary from one business to another, but you should usually follow the course of action outlined below.

- Acknowledge the customer immediately and say you are sorry that they are unhappy with the service they have received.
- Listen carefully to their complaint without interrupting. You must let the customer finish what they are saying, otherwise you may stop them from fully explaining what is wrong.
- Summarise the complaint by repeating back its main points to the customer. In this way you can make sure that you fully understand the nature of the complaint.
- Explain what action will be taken and how quickly.

Besides keeping customers informed when there is a problem, your other priority is to maintain the highest possible service at all times. This means doing your best to:

- reduce inconvenience to customers while the problem lasts
- get back to normal service as quickly as possible.

This may require you and other team members to be flexible and agree to do things outside your normal routine activities. Problem solving will almost always require extra effort from one person, if not from the whole team.

Personal attributes

Many of the functions carried out in hospitality require staff to have a particular set of **personal attributes** if they are to be carried out successfully. Your personal attributes are the qualities that you bring to your job. They include such things as:

- patience, tact and diplomacy
- being a good team player
- honesty
- initiative
- self-motivation.

It is important to have all of these qualities if you are working in hospitality or related industries.

If you have patience, tact and diplomacy, you will be able to show sensitivity when dealing with other people. These qualities are essential if you are solving problems or handling complaints.

The ability to work well in a team is essential for the hospitality industry. Being a team player does not come naturally to everyone as some prefer people to work independently. However, most jobs in the service industries need team players.

> ## Key term
>
> **Personal attributes** – an individual's personality, qualities and characteristics.

Activity: Working with others

Imagine that you work in a retail outlet. It is Christmas time and late-night shopping has started. You are coming into work for the late shift starting at 4 pm. The colleague you are taking over from tells you that the float in the till is accurate. You have a busy evening, taking lots of money. When you come to cash up you cannot get your takings to balance. Eventually you realise that the float was in fact incorrect – it was down by £20. Discuss with your group how this would make you feel and how it would affect teamwork.

Honesty is essential if you are going to have long-term success in your job. You will not make a very good employee if you are dishonest.

The *Oxford English Dictionary* defines initiative as 'the power or opportunity to act before others do'. If you show initiative, you will be anticipating customers' needs and demands – thinking about them even before they have. Initiative is also very useful when solving problems.

If you can solve a customer's problem quickly and efficiently, without having to go and ask somebody else for advice, your customer will be very happy.

Motivation is the reason, desire or enthusiasm to do something. Often, we feel motivated by a reward or by praise. This is called extrinsic motivation. For example, an extrinsically motivated person might carry out a job well because they have been promised a pay rise. In contrast, intrinsically motivated people are motivated by their own desire to achieve. This means they want to do well in a job purely for their own sense of achievement. If you are intrinsically motivated, you will be self-motivated. This is a very positive attribute from an employer's point of view because self-motivated employees:

- do not always have to be asked before carrying out tasks

- work to a high standard

- have lots of energy

- turn up to work on time (or even early)

- have good personal presentation skills

- usually do more than what is required of them in their job.

If you are self-motivated, you are likely to progress more quickly in your career than someone who is motivated purely by external rewards.

The importance of customer service

Service has more impact on customer satisfaction than anything else. Good customer service can positively influence the performance of your business. This is because satisfied customers:

- stay longer and spend more

- buy more expensive products

- visit your organisation more often

- use your organisation, rather than a competitor's

- tell other people to visit your organisation.

The customer will benefit as they are likely to have a more enjoyable experience and their individual needs are more likely to be met.

Another benefit to the organisation is that staff will be more efficient and less likely to leave. Good customer service also offers benefits to staff.

- There will probably be fewer complaints.

- You can be proud of the organisation you work for.

- You can get a buzz out of seeing that the customers are happy.

- It may be easier to reach targets and/or get a bonus.

- Your working environment will be more pleasant.

Activity: Wrong again

Discuss the likely consequences if a hotel porter regularly delivers luggage to the wrong rooms.

Assessment activity 1

Unit 7 P3 P4 P5 P10 P11 P12 M1 M2 BTEC

You work for a hotel chain and a school has asked you to deliver a short presentation and produce an information sheet to help prepare Year 10 students for part-time jobs. You will be expected to provide handouts with your presentation and to make your fact sheet as interesting as possible.

Your presentation needs to:

- explain what is considered to be personal professional presentation P3
- describe the reasons for maintaining professional presentation and the effect this has on a business, including its importance for employees and customers P4
- explain the impact of personal presentation on customer perception M1

- describe the skills required to work effectively with customers and colleagues to provide a quality service or product P10
- explain the impact of excellent and poor customer service on business success so the students are fully aware of how their behaviour at work can impact on the business. M2

Your information sheet should:

- provide details of the skills needed to maintain the work area P5
- describe how to identify and solve customer and colleague problems and complaints should they arise P11
- list the key stages in working to meet team targets P12

Grading tips

When you prepare a presentation, you need to keep the information on your slides to a minimum: they should include key words only. This will make your slides easier to read and it will give you room to add pictures or graphics to make the presentation more interesting. If you have a lot to say, put this information on the notes pages or in handouts, not on your slides – your audience will get bored if you simply read from the slides. You should practise your presentation so that you can remember the information on your notes pages and use the key words on the slides to remind you what you need to say.

P3 P4 M1 You need to focus on the importance of personal professional presentation and explain why it is important for businesses. You also need to explain why the personal professional presentation of staff affects customers' views of a business.

P10 M2 You should think about the skills needed to provide excellent customer service and

what happens when staff do not provide this. Consider how the behaviour of staff affects the levels of customer service provided.

P5 Your information sheet should be fun and interesting as it is aimed at Year 10 students. You could use pictures to show good and bad practices for maintaining a work area and the possible impacts of these practices.

P11 You could create a flow chart to describe how to identify and solve problems or complaints. You should add a description of the process in order to meet the grading requirements.

P12 You will need to do some research or think about a situation when you worked as part of a team. This could have been when you were on work experience at a hospitality business or while you were working with a hospitality business. You should list the key stages you followed in order to meet team targets.

PLTS

As you carry out independent research and manage your time to prepare your presentation, you will be developing your skills as a **self-manager**.

Functional skills

You will need to bring together suitable information to prepare your presentation. This will require you to demonstrate **ICT** skills in developing, presenting and communicating information. As you give your presentation, you will practise your **English** skills in speaking.

Communication skills

Accurate and effective communication with customers and colleagues is essential if you are to meet their needs and work effectively. You will need to show good listening skills as well as verbal and non-verbal skills. You must also be able to adapt your method of communication to suit different situations.

Look back at the material on communication skills on pages 102–103. Make sure, in particular, that you know how to use:

- body language
- tone, pitch and pace of voice
- appropriate language
- listening skills.

Coping with different situations

Working in hospitality, you are likely to be faced with many different situations. This means that you will need to be able to deal with customers, colleagues and supervisors appropriately. It is important that you assess each situation and choose the most appropriate method of communication. The choice could depend on:

- who you are communicating with
- the message you are communicating
- the mood of the person you are communicating with.

You will need to be confident in face-to-face communications, on the telephone and when communicating in writing (by letter, email or fax). You must be able to distinguish between urgent and non-urgent situations, and between difficult and routine problems. Look back at the advice on communication in different situations on pages 103–105.

Assessment activity 2

In this activity you will be given a series of scenarios to role play. You will be expected to respond as if the situations are real and as you would if employed in a hospitality organisation.

You will be assessed on your ability to:

- maintain a personal professional appearance **P1**
- show a positive and professional approach to work **P2**
- show a positive attitude and behaviour with customers and colleagues **P6**
- use correct procedures in dealing with customers and colleagues **P7**
- communicate effectively **P8**
- solve problems in a hospitality context **P8**
- work in a team to achieve targets. **P9**

Scenario 1

You are working as a receptionist at a three-star hotel on the late shift, 3 pm to 11 pm. Two guests arrive to check-in at 6.30 pm. Ask the guests to fill in the guest detail form, give them their key and direct them to their room on the third floor.

Scenario 2

You are working at a seaside B&B over the summer. An elderly couple come to stay. They are not happy with their room – they requested a ground floor room and they have been given a room on the second floor. It overlooks the car park and the pub over the road, so it is noisy at night. You did not check them in and you cannot change their room without the manager. Deal with the situation by talking to the guests initially, and then ask the manager to resolve the room issue.

Scenario 3

You are assistant events manager at Mead Castle, a hotel located on the Cornish coast and surrounded by beautiful gardens with a wood and lake. There are 12 guest bedrooms: 11 doubles and 1 large single. Four double rooms have four-poster beds. Catering is provided by the hotel's own restaurant team.

You have an appointment with Molly Dow and Clive Dupont, who wish to have their wedding at the castle. Molly's parents, Mr and Mrs Dow, and Clive's mother, Ms Bridget Kelman, are with them. You need to talk through the menu options and help them select the most suitable package. Several of their friends are vegetarians and a number of children will be coming to the wedding, so they want to talk to the chef to design a menu to suit everyone's needs.

Scenario 4

You are a marketing assistant at a nightclub called Moon. You and four other members of the marketing team have been asked to investigate the events and promotions at other nightclubs in the UK before coming up with two different ideas for events that could be held at Moon. You need to design posters to promote these events and then present your ideas to the marketing manager. Your tutor will take the role of marketing manager.

You have four weeks to do the research and develop your ideas before the presentation. Start by preparing an action plan setting out targets for meeting the deadline. As part of your presentation, hand out your action plan and any notes on whether your team stuck to the plan or had to change it as the project developed.

Grading tips

You must perform in the role plays as if you are actually doing the job set out in the scenario. Your tutor will make an audio recording, take photographs or video the role plays as well as providing an observation record, which will assess your performance. You will be judged, in part, on your personal appearance and your attitude and behaviour.

This means that you need to dress appropriately for each role play. You cannot just read from a script: you need to show that you are doing the job set out in the scenario. You will need to interact with the customers to ensure you can meet their needs.

Tables 1 and 2 show the type of outline action plan and notes you might provide for the planning element of Scenario 4.

Action	Key dates
Assignment handed out	Wednesday 3 Nov
First meeting	Wednesday 3 Nov
Research completed by	Wednesday 10 Nov
Ideas decided by	Friday 12 Nov
Presentation finished by	Monday 22 Nov
Posters finished by	Thursday 25 Nov
Decide how we will dress	Friday 26 Nov
Run through presentation	Friday 26 Nov
Print out notes pages	Monday 29 Nov
Final practice	Tuesday 30 Nov
Presentation date	Wednesday 1 Dec at 10.00 am

Table 1: Example of an action plan

Date	Action	Decisions	When by	Completed
Wed 3 Nov	Decide on group leader. Research what's going on locally	We have decided that Kyle will be our team leader. Me (Lenny) – visit Bath and see what promotions are advertised around town. Jasmine – go to the library and look at the local papers for adverts about events. Kyle – research on the Internet to see what local nightclubs are advertising on their websites. Katya – research on the Internet to see what events are being advertised by nightclubs in big cities such as Glasgow, Leeds and Nottingham.	Wed 10 Nov	Yes
Wed 10 Nov	Review information and decide what ideas we think we could use for our presentation	We have decided to look at the information in pairs over the next few days and meet on Friday with some ideas	Fri 12 Nov	Jasmine off sick, but Kyle told us what she thought were good ideas

Table 2: Example of progress notes

PLTS

Demonstrating a professional approach and a positive attitude will help you to develop your skills as a **self-manager**. Working through Scenario 4 will allow you to develop as a **team worker**.

Functional skills

As you take part in the role-play activities, you will develop your **English** skills in speaking and listening. If you use the Internet to carry out research or prepare presentation materials for Scenario 4, you will be able to develop your **ICT** skills.

7.3 Be able to prepare for a job application

In this section of the unit we look at what is involved in applying for a job, including the documentation you will need to complete to show your prospective employer why you think you have the skills required and tips which will help you during a job interview.

This section covers:

- documents
- interview and selection methods
- preparation for interview
- interview skills
- sources of job information
- sources of careers advice
- suitability of different sources of information
- hospitality-related industries.

Documents

Various documents form part of the job application process, including:

- CVs
- covering letters (letters of application)
- application forms
- letters of acceptance or decline.

These documents may be your only chance to make a good impression on an employer, so it is essential that you get them right.

CVs

CV is short for curriculum vitae, which translates to 'course of life'. A CV should provide a potential employer with a brief account of your education and experience so far. Your CV is an opportunity for you to market yourself to prospective employers.

CVs should provide the following information:

- your name
- your address
- a contact telephone number
- your email address
- schools attended

Grace Minshull	12 FINLEY CLOSE, UPPER ABBOTTS, CAMBS, CB3 8UJ

Personal details	Date of birth: 1 January 1993 Home tel: 01243 987345 Mobile: 07344 586234 Email: graceminshull@net.com
Personal profile	• I have a lot of experience of customer service and have good people skills. • I gained valuable knowledge of the hospitality industry from my part-time job in a hotel restaurant and waiting at events and weddings. • I have a clear understanding of the importance of providing excellent customer service at all times. • I am hard working, reliable, loyal and dedicated.
Experience	April 2009 – Sept 2010 The Bennett Hotel Upper Abbotts, Cambs _Part-time waiting staff and weekend receptionist_ I worked in the restaurant, taking orders, serving and clearing. I re-laid tables for the next service. I had to ensure that all drinks orders were put on the customer's bill. At the weekend I worked the Saturday morning and Sunday evening shifts with the head receptionist, helping with guests checking in and out. I had to offer additional services such as newspapers, restaurant bookings and spa treatment bookings, and give guests information about the hotel. Jan 2008 – Sept 2010 Gordon Events Chesterton, Cambs _Waiting staff_ My role involved serving food at events – weddings, corporate dinners, luncheons and balls/dances. This could be buffet/canapés or silver service. June 2009 – Sept 2010 Red Cross Chesterton, Cambs _Volunteer with Red Cross Projects_ I trained as a peer educator to deliver first aid, humanitarian education and HIV awareness sessions.
Education	Sept 2004 – June 2009 KCD High School Upper Abbotts, Cambs GCSEs: English, Maths, Science, Geography, Art, History Sept 2009 – June 2010 Robinson College Chesterton, Cambs BTEC Level 2 in Hospitality
Interests	Swimming, cycling and computer games
Referees	Amrit Singh, Head of Hospitality Department, Robinson College, Chesterton, Cambs, CA1 4RF Tel: 01356 893432, ext 333. Email: ASingh@robinsoncollege.ac.uk Florence Rian, General Manager, The Bennett Hotel, Upper Abbotts, Cambs, CA3 9PL Tel: 01243 980443 Email: Rianflorence@bennetthotel.com

Figure 1: Sample CV

- qualifications

- employment history

- personal skills and abilities

- interests/hobbies

- any special skills, such as a full, clean, driving licence

- referees.

A CV should be no longer than two sides of A4 paper. It should be word-processed so that it can be amended and updated easily. Your CV should follow a logical order – use headings to group information sensibly. Highlight your headings so that they stand out – use bold, italics, underlining or indenting. Figure 1 on page 199 shows a sample CV.

Covering letters (letters of application)

When you apply for a job, it is likely that you will be asked either to send a CV with a letter of application or to complete an application form with or without a letter of application. Like your CV, a letter of application is an opportunity to create a good impression.

Letters of application generally have a standard structure:

- put your address and contact details on the right-hand side of the letter at the top of the page

- put the date, then the name of the person the letter is going to, with a job title and the business address, on the left-hand side of the letter and below your address and contact details

- start the letter with Dear and the name of the person you are writing to, leaving out the initial or first name (e.g. Dear Mr Jones not Dear Mr John Jones)

- if you do not know the name of the person, start the letter with Dear Sir or Madam

- put a header line setting out the job title and reference you are applying for

- in the main part of the letter, say why you are applying for the job and why you think you can do the job

- sign off the letter with Yours sincerely (if you know the name of the person the letter is going to) or Yours faithfully (if you do not know the person's name).

The covering letter gives you a chance to introduce yourself and explain why you think you would be suitable for the job you have applied for. A sample letter of application is shown in Figure 2.

Grace Minshull

12 Finley Close
Upper Abbotts
Cambs
CB3 8UJ

Home tel: 01243 987345
Mobile: 07344 586234
Email: graceminshull@net.com

10 September 2010

Mrs B Dow
Head of HR
The Grand Hotel Group
12–16 Grand Avenue
Aberdeen
Scotland
AE3 8GH

Dear Mrs Low

Re: Full-time live-in receptionist – The Grand Hotel. Job ref IH555

Please find enclosed a copy of my CV. As you can see, I have just completed a BTEC Level 2 in Hospitality and I am now looking for my first full-time job.

From the job description, the job of receptionist at the Grand Hotel sounds challenging and exciting. I have worked on reception before, so I know that you need to keep calm when it is busy, always be polite and helpful, and talk to the guests to make them feel welcome.

I have excellent customer service skills and I can work well in a team as well as being able to use my own initiative. I am keen to do well and I enjoy learning on the job. One of the things I enjoy most about working in the hospitality industry is having the opportunity to meet new people and I get great satisfaction from doing a good job.

I feel that I have the skills and experience required to be an excellent receptionist at the Grand Hotel and I look forward to hearing from you.

Yours sincerely

G. Minshull

Grace Minshull

Figure 2: Sample letter of application

Application forms

Some employers prefer you to apply for a job by completing their application form rather than sending in your CV. This allows them to get the information they want from you. The application form may ask for information that would not normally be found on a CV. Some employers ask that the application forms are handwritten as this gives them an opportunity to assess the applicant's level of handwriting.

As with the CV and letter of application, an application form needs to be completed with care and thought. If this is what the employer has requested, this will be their first impression of you.

Tips for completing application forms

- Always try to have two copies, so you have one you can practise on.
- Read through the whole form before you start, so you know exactly what information is expected.
- Follow the instructions carefully; some may ask for the forms to be filled in using black ink, capital letters and so on.
- Make sure you answer the questions asked specifically and clearly.
- To avoid spelling mistakes, ask someone to check your form.
- Do not leave out any sections; if you feel that they do not apply to you, put N/A (not applicable) in the box.
- Always provide honest answers.
- Once accurately completed, take a copy for your own records.

Activity: Application forms

Have a look at the websites of some hospitality organisations and find some examples of job application forms. Choose two examples, and have a go at completing them. Once completed, swap your forms with someone in your class to check for any spelling errors.

Letters of acceptance or decline

Once you have applied for a job and had an interview, you will be informed either verbally or in writing whether you have been successful. Successful applicants will be expected to put in writing their decision to accept or decline (turn down) the position. This is an important stage in the application process as it formalises your decision. In most cases, if you have applied for a job, you probably want it, so if you receive a job offer it is likely that you will be writing a letter of acceptance. However, if your circumstances have changed since applying for the job and you are no longer able to accept the new position, you will need to turn down the offer.

Like all of the documents mentioned above, your letter needs to look professional. The format of the letter will be the same as the letter of application, but obviously the content will differ.

- It is important that the letter is sent promptly.

- In the letter, be clear about whether you are accepting or declining the position.

- If you are declining the position, notify the organisation immediately so they can re-advertise or offer the job to another applicant.

Interview and selection methods

Employers will use different interview and selection methods and they will probably inform you of this before you actually attend an interview. The different methods employers may use are shown in Figure 3.

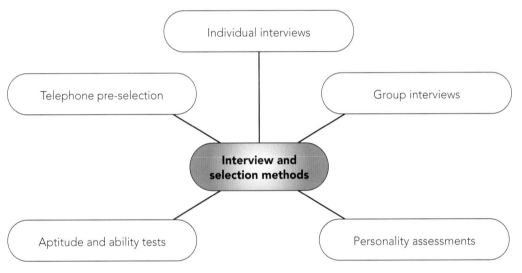

Figure 3: Interview and selection methods

Telephone pre-selection

This type of selection method can be used at several points during the recruitment process.

- As part of the screening process – some employers may use this method to give the applicant a chance to make an early verbal impression on the employer. Be aware that, at this stage, the call may be unannounced.

- As part of the interview process – in this case, the call will be pre-arranged at a time convenient to employer and applicant. If you are applying for a job overseas, it may not be practical to have a face-to-face interview, so a telephone interview is more appropriate.

- As part of an ability test – particularly if the job you have applied for is in sales and marketing.

Tips for telephone interviews

- If possible, ensure the call is on a landline rather than a mobile.

- Choose a quiet place to take the call, where there will be no distractions.

- If you know the time of the call, make sure you answer the phone in a professional manner.

- Be prepared for the call – have all relevant information available (your CV, information on the company and so on), plus pen and paper.

- Stand up or sit up straight – your voice will sound louder and more assertive than if you are slouching or lying down.

Face-to-face interviews

These are the most common method and you may have already experienced them. If you are invited to attend an interview, it is likely to involve the following process.

- You will be invited to the prospective employer's business premises.

- You will need to announce your arrival to a secretary or receptionist, who will inform your interviewer of your arrival.

- The interview will take place in the employer's office or in a meeting room.

- The layout of the room traditionally will be the interviewer(s) seated behind a desk with a chair for the interviewee (you) to sit in front.

- There could be more than one interviewer (a panel) and there is likely to be a person making notes.

- At the beginning of the interview, you will be introduced to all those present and their role in the interview will be explained.

- After formal introductions, the interview will start and questions will be asked.

A group interview will follow a similar sequence, but part of the interview process may involve a group activity.

Preparation for interview

Preparation for an interview is essential. You are unlikely to be successful at an interview if you do not plan carefully for it.

Company knowledge

Your preparation needs to include research into the company to which you are applying. Often, the first question an interviewer will ask is why you want to work for the company. Technology makes this research easy as most companies now have their own websites giving information about the business. If this is not the case, it would be a good idea to ring the company before the interview and either ask some questions or ask for information on the company to be sent to you.

Knowledge of the job

Be absolutely clear about the job you are applying for and what it involves. If you have been sent the job description, refresh your memory before the interview. This will also help you to think of any relevant questions you may wish to ask at the interview.

Dress code and personal appearance

Decide what you are going to wear before the day of the interview. You must dress appropriately. This will usually mean wearing a suit – either trousers and jacket or skirt and jacket with an appropriate top or shirt and tie.

Hair needs to be clean and tidy, as do hands and nails. Only a minimal amount of make-up, aftershave or perfume should be worn.

What should you consider when dressing for an interview?

Activity: Dress code and personal appearance

Look at the photo on the right. Identify the positive and negative aspects of each person's dress code and personal appearance for a job interview.

Attitude and behaviour

Interviewers like to see interviewees who:

- are confident
- can speak clearly and knowledgeably
- can answer questions thoughtfully.

Being over-confident is seen as negative, as is being under-confident. With careful planning, you should be able to walk into the interview with confidence. Take the interview seriously; it is not a time to tell jokes and be silly. Your behaviour needs to be professional from the moment you enter the building until the moment you leave.

Interview skills

You have planned ahead for your interview; the next and final stage is actually attending the interview. The following activity will improve your understanding of good interview practice.

Activity: Skills and behaviour

Study the lists of interview skills and actions or behaviours that you could display in an interview situation. Match the actions to the appropriate interview skills.

Then discuss with others in your group why you feel the skills listed are important for a successful interview.

Interview skills

body language	social skills	personal skills	active listening
presentation techniques	responding to questions	asking questions	

Actions

sit up straight

be honest

use the right tone of voice – not too soft or too loud

do not interrupt

do not chew

turn your mobile phone off

be succinct (short, to the point)

use clear visual aids

confirm understanding using gestures, such as nodding

think before you answer

answer fully

be polite

knock before entering the interview room

speak clearly

maintain good eye contact

have a firm handshake

maintain an open posture, do not cross arms or legs

dress appropriately

professional PowerPoint® slides – points not paragraphs

ask open questions

sit down when asked

avoid nervous habits such as tapping a pen

be sensible – no telling jokes

ask relevant and appropriate questions

wait until a question is asked before giving an answer

Responding to and answering questions

Being prepared for an interview will help you to perform better. It is worth thinking about questions you may be asked and how you could respond.

Activity: Answering questions

Working in a small team, compile a list of questions you think you might be asked at a job interview for a junior position in a hospitality business. Compare your list with another team's and make a note of questions that are not on your list.

Individually, select five questions and write down how you would answer each question. Then review your responses with others to see if you can improve your answers.

An interview is not just about an employer seeing if you are suitable for the job. It is also about you seeing if the job is right for you. During an interview, you will be asked whether you have any questions to ask. You need to have thought of things you want to know about the employer and the job. Some of your questions may be answered during the interview, so it may be useful to have a list of questions ready beforehand so you can tick off the ones that have already been answered and focus on asking the remaining questions at the end of the interview. It is never a good idea to start with a question about pay or holidays. You could consider asking about training opportunities or development within the organisation or you could confirm any details of the job role of which you are unsure.

Activity: Asking appropriate questions

As a group, discuss the kinds of questions you might ask during an interview.

Interview evaluation

It is useful to evaluate your performance after an interview. The point is not to make yourself feel bad about the mistakes you may have made during the interview, but to reflect and see if you can improve your technique.

After any interview, ask yourself the following questions.

- How well did I present myself?
- How well did I respond to all questions?
- Had I prepared enough for the interview?
- Were there questions that I was not expecting and had not prepared for?
- How could I do better next time?

You may not get an interview for the first job you apply for, you may not get the first job you are interviewed for and you may not want the job you are offered. Recruitment is about getting the right person for the job and sometimes it is as much about skills as personality. The important thing is not to give up and to make sure that you are happy with the job you accept.

Remember:

- planning for an interview is essential; without planning you will reduce your chances of success
- for any type of interview, you must plan well, dress smartly and have good personal and social skills
- do not turn up late, tell jokes, look scruffy, lie or talk too much but (do not say too little).

Sources of job information

When you start to look for a job, you may wonder where to begin. You may already have a part-time job which had been advertised in the window of a local business, or you may have just gone inside and asked if there were any jobs available. Both of these methods are classed as sources of job information, but there are more sources available, such as:

- newspapers
- trade magazines, such as *Caterer and Hotelkeeper*
- company websites
- employment agencies.

 Activity: Sources of job information

In pairs, find two jobs using each of the sources listed above. The jobs must be hospitality related.

Sources of careers advice

Sometimes, it is helpful to talk to someone to get some advice. Three useful sources of career advice are Connexions, people from the industry and your tutors.

Connexions is an organisation specifically set up to help and advise young people between the ages of 13 and 19 who are trying to decide where they want to be in life.

- Connexions offices are scattered across the UK and you should have one local to you. They have up-to-date details of all the educational courses available. They advertise local job vacancies and there is also a dedicated Connexions website which lists job vacancies.

- You can arrange a private one-to-one meeting with a Connexions adviser who will help you to realise what you would like to do in the next stage of your life. The adviser can also help you to identify what jobs would most suit you.

People from industry may visit your school or college to discuss the jobs available to you in their businesses. Some industries have open events where people are invited to visit the employer's premises to learn about the different job opportunities available in that company.

Your tutor or the careers adviser at your college or school will also be a valuable source of advice, and they are probably the most logical people to contact first. They may be able to offer you more specific advice because they will know you well, including your likes, dislikes and strengths.

Suitability of different sources of information

Not only is there a great deal of choice in terms of the number of jobs available, you can also get a wide variety of advice. Table 3 looks at the suitability, advantages and disadvantages of each source of information.

Source	Advantages	Disadvantages
Newspapers	Up to date and reliable Many newspapers are available in libraries	May not have many jobs suited to young people Not free Can be expensive to place advertisements, so many employers use other sources
Trade magazines	Up to date and reliable Only advertise jobs relevant to the specific industry covered by the magazine Advertise local and overseas jobs	Can be expensive to buy Not easily accessible Can be expensive to place advertisements, so many employers use other sources
Company websites	Can often apply online Job adverts are free to view Accessible to anyone with Internet access	Can be out-of-date Job choice may be limited Only jobs in the company are advertised
Employment agencies	Lots of agencies available Access to agencies on the Internet	Some may not be reliable and up to date Some ask for personal information before you can log on to job pages of the site
Connexions	Lots of choice, up to date and reliable, and a free service Opportunity to meet with an adviser Accessible via the Internet and the high street Aimed specifically at the 13–19 age group	Service may be reduced because of cuts in public spending
Industry sources	Specific jobs for that industry Up to date and reliable Jobs to suit different people and ages May be able to visit and experience the actual workplace Good for employers as they can invite people to their premises at minimal cost	Can be difficult to access
Tutors and school or college sources	Reliable, trustworthy, specific to you Easy access and free If you have put your tutor down as a reference, employers may make contact Employers may ask tutors if they can advertise job vacancies on the school/college noticeboard, and usually this is free of charge	

Table 3: Advantages and disadvantages of sources of information

The information in the table clearly shows that there are numerous sources you can draw on when you are ready to enter the job market. Your task is to make sure you use the sources which are right for you.

Hospitality-related industries

The hospitality industry is huge, and in any city or town you will find a mix of hotels, restaurants and bars. However, in addition to these businesses, there are others that are closely related to the hospitality industry which employ people with similar skill sets to those who work in hospitality businesses. Hospitality-related industries include:

- retail
- sport and leisure
- travel and tourism.

Retail

By walking along your local high street, you will find a variety of different retail outlets. Some may be part of big chains, such as Marks and Spencer, Debenhams, Gap, New Look and Next, whereas others will be smaller independent shops owned by one person or a small number of people.

Are there many small, independent shops in your area?

Sport and leisure

It is likely that within your local or surrounding area there will be a large health club, for example one which belongs to a chain like Fitness First, David Lloyd or Cannons. Alternatively, you may have a smaller independent local gym. The large health clubs are usually open to members and guests only and offer a vast range of facilities, including:

- gyms
- studios for exercise classes
- swimming pools
- solariums
- beauty treatment rooms
- restaurants and bars.

Alongside these large private health clubs there will also be council-led leisure centres and sports clubs. These last two will offer a range of facilities for the general public to use. Unlike private clubs, council-led centres allow both members and non-members to use the facilities.

Travel and tourism

The third related industry comes under the umbrella of travel and tourism. Examples include:

- travel agents such as Thomas Cook and First Choice
- airlines such as Ryanair and easyJet
- online tour companies
- caravan parks and campsites
- tourist information centres
- cruise lines and ferry operators such as P&O Ferries, Norfolkline and Condor Ferries
- local attractions, places of interest and theme parks.

Activity: Which category?

In groups, take one of the industries mentioned above and draw up a list of businesses which fall into each category. Share your findings with your group. Now compile a list of the similarities and differences between these industries.

Looking at your list, identify how each of the businesses works with the hospitality industry. For example, airlines such as easyJet transport people to and from destinations. These people need hotels to stay in and restaurants and bars to eat and drink in while they are away.

From your own lists and the information above, you should see the huge number of different businesses which fall into the category of hospitality-related industries.

Assessment activity 3

1 You work for Hampton Recruitment, a specialist hospitality recruitment agency. You have been asked to help prepare members of the team to carry out first interviews of applicants to several positions. Second interviews will be held by the employer. You have been asked to produce a booklet that:

a) states the purpose of a curriculum vitae and sets out the information to be included in a CV P13

b) explains the purpose and importance of a covering letter P14

c) states the importance of professional presentation and quality of content in a CV and covering letter P15

d) lists the preparations that should be made for an interview P16

e) explains the importance of evaluating an interview. P17

2 Produce a table that compares three sources of job and career information in terms of their suitability for the employer and the potential applicant. Your table should have both negative and positive features from the employer's point of view and the potential applicant's point of view. Based on your research, state which you think is the best source to use. M3

Grading tips

P13 P14 P15 P16 P17 Make your booklet as informative as possible. Think about the layout and the design so you can fit all of the required information into it. You could use bullet points when listing the information to be included in a CV and the preparations that should be made for an interview. This will make the information easier to see and understand.

M3 When you complete your table on the three job sources, remember to state which (in your opinion) is the best source.

Assessment activity 4

A stunning four-star hotel in Exeter is looking for a reception manager to join and lead its reception team. The individual who takes on this exciting position will have previous experience in a hotel or hospitality environment including reception and reservations. As well as looking after the guests, the reception manager will support the senior hotel management with the day-to-day running of the hotel. Figure 4 shows an advert for the position and Figure 5 shows an application form that the recruitment agency has prepared for this position.

1 Make an application for this job. Photocopy the application form and then complete it. Produce a curriculum vitae suitable for someone applying for the reception manager's job and write a suitable covering letter. P18

2 You will be given a telephone pre-selection interview. You will be asked about why you have applied for the job, your previous experience, and why you think you would be good at the job. Your tutor will act as the interviewer.

You will then be invited to attend a group interview and an individual interview. At the group interview you will be asked to complete a group task, to give an opportunity to demonstrate your skills. For example, you could be asked to design a poster for the reception area to tell guests about a special 2-for-1 offer for spa treatments.

You will then have an individual interview where you will be given the opportunity to tell the interviewer more about yourself and to ask questions. You will be interviewed by your tutor and/or other learners.

You will be asked more specific questions about why you think you are suited to the job. For example, you may be given some scenario-type questions, such as: Can you give an example of a time when you had to deal with an angry customer? How did you resolve the problem? How would you deal with a lost child who arrived in the reception area in tears?

You could also be asked questions about your skills and your views, such as: What are the most important qualities for a hotel receptionist? What are your main strengths? What will you bring to this job? **P19**

3 After your interview, you will need to produce a report that analyses the effectiveness of your own performance in all aspects of the job application process and which recommends improvements. **D1**

Grading tips

P18 When you fill in the application form and complete your CV and covering letter, get someone to check the documents to make sure there are no mistakes. Mistakes when applying for a job could result in you not being asked for an interview.

P19 Practice is the key to success in an interview. You need to make sure that you know what is involved in the job role and think about how good you would be at each main task. Dress appropriately as first impressions really do count.

Reception Manager

Exeter
£17,000

A FOUR-STAR HOTEL
Location: *Exeter, Devon*

Salary:	£17,000
Date posted:	01/10/2011
Employer type:	Hotel
Company:	Hampton Recruitment
Contact:	Amy Hampton
Ref:	Caterer/PCAT16600
Job ID:	48394105/at

As reception manager, you will receive a salary of £17,000 as well as tips and meals on duty. The hours are straight shifts, and you will work 5 days in 7, including evenings and weekends.

This is a great opportunity to work in a fantastic establishment so apply now with CV or call Amy Hampton on 01988 666666.

Figure 4: Job advert

PLTS

When you think about the importance of professional presentation and the quality of the content of the CV and covering letter, you will be using your skills as a **reflective learner**.

Functional skills

You will develop your **ICT** skills when you prepare your CV as you will enter, develop and format information independently to suit its meaning and purpose including text and tables. During your interview, you will have a chance to develop your **English** skills in speaking and listening.

Hampton Recruitment

Specialists in Hospitality Recruitment

Helping to get the right fit

Job title	Job reference number

Personal information

Please enter all relevant personal information in the fields below.

Title: Mr/Mrs/Ms/Miss/other:	
First name:	Last name:
Address:	Postcode:
Email address:	Home telephone number:
Mobile telephone number:	Work number:
National Insurance number:	Date of birth:
Where did you hear about this job vacancy?	

Questionnaire

Please answer the following questions as accurately as possible.

1 How much experience have you had working in a sales environment?

Less than a year ☐   1–2 years ☐   2–5 years ☐   Over 5 years ☐

2 Please indicate which of the following you are competent at using.

Microsoft Word ☐   Email ☐   Microsoft Excel ☐   Microsoft PowerPoint ☐

3 Indicate the property management systems that you have experience with.

Fidelio ☐   Opera ☐   Lanmark ☐   Maxial ☐

H.I.S. ☐   Other ☐

I have no experience with any computerised property management system ☐

4 Do you have the required work visas and/or residency in the UK?

Yes ☐   No ☐

Work experience				
List your work experience below, starting with your most recent placement:				
Job title	Name and address of employer	Dates	Main duties	Reason for leaving

Education				
List the most recent first:				
Institution	Subjects	Level	Grade	Year achieved

Personal statement

Please provide any relevant information, based on the job description, to support your application.

_____

_____

_____

_____

Please use additional sheets if required.

Figure 5: Application form for Assessment activity 4

7.4 Be able to produce a plan to develop skills

We have looked at the skills required for working in hospitality and its related industries. This section of the unit focuses on you, the skills that you already have and the skills that you may need to develop on entering the world of work. It covers:

- employability skills
- matching skills
- job roles
- career opportunities.

Employability skills

Employability skills are the different types of skills and experience that an employer is looking for when trying to fill a job vacancy.

Vocational skills

Employers are usually looking for someone who has some experience of the relevant type of work, for example bar work.

Personal skills

These include attributes and qualities such as motivation, enthusiasm and personal appearance. Look back at the material on job requirements on pages 24–27 to remind yourself of the personal qualities that are expected of staff working in the hospitality industry.

Qualifications

Most jobs will require the job holder to have certain qualifications. These will be stated in the job specification and might include:

- GCSEs
- BTECs and NVQs
- A levels
- degrees and other university qualifications
- apprenticeships.

The level of job that you go for, whether operational or management, will determine the level of qualification and experience required. For example, if you apply for a management job, the employer is likely to expect you to have a degree or HND and management experience.

Courses and training

Along with a qualification, some employers will want you to have attended certain courses. For example, if you apply for a job in a kitchen, the employer might want you to have attended a basic food hygiene course. Other courses or training relevant to hospitality-related industries are basic health and safety, first aid and the control of substances hazardous to health (COSHH).

Experience

Some employers will recognise that, if you are applying for the job straight from school or college, you may not have any actual experience. In this case, if you have had any work experience while at school or college then the skills you have learned will certainly make you more employable.

Matching skills

When you start to look for a job, you need to carry out a matching exercise to see if you have the skills that an employer is looking for.

Reviewing vocational and personal skills

By making a list of the skills you would need in order to apply for a particular job, you are taking the first step towards identifying your strengths and areas for development.

Activity: Matching skills to specifications

Using the resources available to you (for example, the Internet or newspapers), identify two jobs that you could realistically apply for. Look carefully at the job specification and see if the employability skills you currently have match those on the job specification.

By carrying out this activity, you will have identified some gaps between the skills you currently have and the skills an employer will want you to have. You have therefore started to review your own vocational and personal skills.

Identifying skill development requirements

A checklist can be used to identify your strengths (the skills you have and are good at) and the areas where you require some development. Produce a table like Table 4 on the following page, including any other relevant vocational and personal skills you do, or do not, have.

Strengths	Development areas
Good timekeeper	Limited knowledge of food hygiene
Good personal presentation	No till experience
Enthusiastic	No vocational experience
Self-motivated	No experience of complaints handling
Good written communication	

Table 4: Example of skill development check list

Activity: Assess your own strengths and areas for development

Have a go at assessing your strengths and areas for development. You may want to get feedback from your tutor, friends, family, part-time employers and so on – people who will tell you honestly what they think your strengths and areas for development are.

Personal development plans

After identifying your skill development areas, you should be ready to complete a personal development plan. A personal development plan is an exercise in which you list:

- all the areas of development you need to address
- when you will address these areas
- how you will address these areas
- whether it will cost you any money.

An example of a personal development plan is shown in Table 5. This example is for a 16-year-old school-leaver wishing to have a career as a receptionist in a health club.

Development need	How the need will be met	Time frame	Cost
To learn ICT skills: email, Microsoft Excel and Word	Computer course, evening classes	6 weeks, 1 evening per week	£50
Reception experience	NVQ Level 2, part-time at local college	1 year	Free
Till experience	In my part-time job – will move on to working on the till	2 months	Free
Health and safety awareness	Health and safety course at local college	1 day	£60 as part of NVQ programme
Complaints handling	Covered in NVQ 2 Reception and on work experience	1 year	Free as part of NVQ programme

Table 5: Example of a personal development plan

Activity: Your own personal development plan

Draw up your own personal development plan in line with one of the jobs that you found earlier. Use the strengths and development areas checklist as a basis for your personal development plan. Having completed the plan, show it to your tutor, who will give you feedback and help you address your identified skill needs.

By carrying out this exercise:

• you are identifying the gaps you have in terms of employability skills

• you are planning how to address these gaps.

Once you have addressed these gaps, you will be far more employable.

Your development plan can travel with you as you progress through your career. You will remove areas from it as skills gaps are met, and you will add to it as you discover new areas for development. Remember, we all continue to learn and develop new skills throughout our lives.

Job roles

We looked at the different job roles in the hospitality industry, including chef, waiter, bar person, receptionist and room service attendant, on pages 22–24. Each of the hospitality-related industries – retail, sport and leisure, travel and tourism – also has several job roles and career paths. The main ones are shown in Figures 6, 7 and 8.

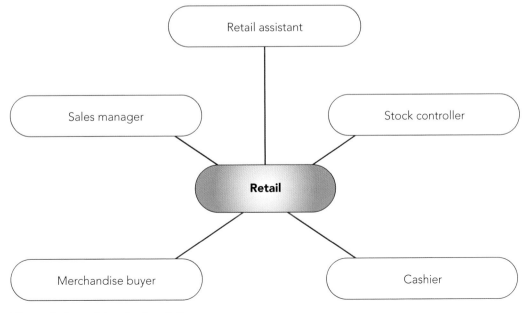

Figure 6: Some job roles in retail

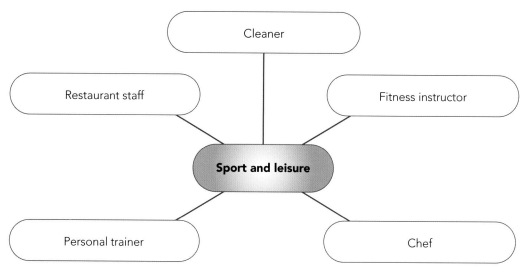

Figure 7: Some job roles in sport and leisure

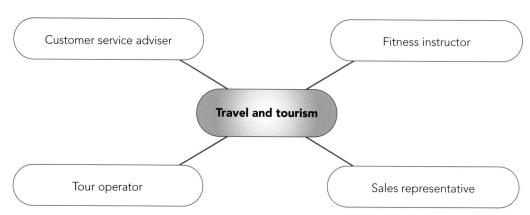

Figure 8: Some job roles in travel and tourism

Activity: Job roles

Working in groups, choose one of the diagrams in Figures 6, 7 or 8 and try to add as many job roles to it as you can. Once everyone has finished, come back together and feed back, noting where the overlaps are between the different industries.

Contracts

We looked at job contracts on pages 22–23. To recap, a contract may be:

- **full-time** – these are for people who work five or more days a week.
- **part-time** – this type of contract is for people who work less than a full working week. Someone working on a part-time basis may, for example, work three days a week. Part-time contracts will specify the number of days or the total number of hours to be worked each week.

- **permanent** – these are issued for any job offered on a permanent basis. This means that the job holder becomes a permanent member of staff. Most full-time and part-time contracts are permanent contracts.

- **temporary** – these are issued when a job role will only exist for a fixed period of time. For example, a temporary contract would be issued to someone working as maternity cover. The job is only available while the person normally in that job is on maternity leave.

- **seasonal** – the hospitality industry employs many staff on a seasonal basis to provide cover for extremely busy periods. Many students work for the hospitality industry on a seasonal basis in their Christmas, Easter and summer holidays.

- **live-in** – this type of contract is common in large hotels that provide accommodation for their staff. Staff on live-in contracts will have some deductions from their pay for the accommodation, and they will be given instructions on how the accommodation is to be looked after and other house rules.

- **freelance** – these are issued to people who are self-employed. For example, a hospitality business may commission a freelance person to provide some staff training. The contract will state the fee for the work, how long the work is expected to take, the number of employees to be trained and the location of the training.

Note that some staff who work in an organisation may be employed by another company. For example, contract catering companies provide services to organisations like hospitals that need to provide meals to patients and staff. Staff working in these restaurants and kitchens are employed by the contract caterers not the hospital, so their contract is drawn up by the contract catering company. The contract catering company would also have to sign a contract with the organisation receiving the catering service.

The job and type of contract you choose will undoubtedly have an effect on your lifestyle. As you get older, your lifestyle will change: you may get married, have children or buy a house.

Career opportunities

During your working life you are likely to progress up the career ladder. There are three clear levels that you may progress through.

- **Operational** – many people start at this level when they enter the world of work. If, for example, you wanted a job as head receptionist in a hotel, you would probably start off as a receptionist.

- **Supervisory** – in time, you may be promoted to a supervisory role. A job at this level in hospitality would be a reception shift manager. At this level you would have additional responsibilities such as being in charge of staff training and liaising with Housekeeping as to which rooms need to be made up or cleaned.

- **Managerial** – the next promotion could be into management. A job at this level could be a general manager of a hotel, who would be responsible for all aspects of the running of the hotel.

Assessment activity 5

Unit 7   BTEC

This assignment will give you an opportunity to look at your current skills and your skills development so you can prepare and work towards getting the job of your dreams.

1 Assess your own personal and professional skills. Using Figure 4 on page 213 and one other hospitality-related job that interests you, match your current skills with the job aims. Complete the skills audit in Table 6 (pages 223–24). **P20**

Then explain the specific skills and personal attributes required for these two job roles. This can be either a written report or a presentation. **M4**

2 Identify an opportunity to develop a skill. What other activities could you do over the next six months that will help you to develop your skills? **P21**

3 Create an action plan to enable you to develop the skills identified in your skills audit (Task 1). Table 7 on page 224 contains a template that you can use in drawing up your action plan. Your plan must cover a minimum period of six weeks and you must set targets for the skills development identified in Task 2.

You must then follow this plan. Make sure that you keep on top of your action plan and carry out the skills development tasks and actions you have listed. Your tutor may suggest ways of completing your skills development by working on other assignments or units in this course. **P22 P23**

4 Write a report about the purpose of a personal development plan. Your report should describe how personal development plans are produced. It should also explain the importance of feedback in the skills development process. **P24 P25 P26**

Grading tips

P20 P21 P22 P23 M4 You need to think very carefully about the skills you have and the skills you will need. It is worth asking your tutor for feedback so you can get a range of views. Some of the skills you need to work on will need little practice (using PowerPoint®, for example), whereas others will take much more time and experience (for example, giving a presentation to a large group or talking to people you do not know). Once you have decided which skills you need to work on, talk to your tutor about ways to develop these skills. Set yourself some targets, so you have deadlines to work to. For example, you could arrange to give a presentation about the hospitality industry to another year group or to students taking other courses. Alternatively, you could offer to help at an open evening and talk to prospective students and their parents about your course.

 PLTS

Setting and working towards a target will help you develop your skills as a **reflective learner**.

 Functional skills

If you use the Internet to research jobs for Task 1, you will be developing your **ICT** skills as you select and use a variety of sources of information independently for a complex task. When producing your report for Task 4, you will be developing your **English** tasks in writing.

Written communication	I have this	Like to improve
Being able to express yourself clearly in writing		
Thinking through in advance what you want to say		
Gathering, analysing and arranging information in a logical sequence		
Developing your argument in a logical way		
Being able to condense information/produce concise summary notes		
Adapting your writing style for different audiences		
Avoiding jargon		

Verbal communication	I have this	Like to improve
Expressing your ideas clearly and confidently in speech		
Listening carefully to what others are saying		
Being able to clarify and summarise what others are communicating		
Helping others to define their problems without interrupting		
Being sensitive to body language as well as verbal information		
Making the right impression by making effective use of dress, conduct and speech		
Keeping business telephone calls to the point		
Thinking up an interesting way to put across your message to groups		
Successfully building a rapport with your audience when speaking to groups		

Flexibility	I have this	Like to improve
Adapting successfully to changing situations and environments		
Keeping calm in the face of difficulties		
Planning ahead, but having alternative options in case things go wrong		
Thinking quickly to respond to sudden changes in circumstances		
Persisting in the face of unexpected difficulties		

Persuading	I have this	Like to improve
Being able to convince others, to discuss and reach agreement		
Putting your points across in a reasoned way		
Emphasising the positive aspects of your argument		
Understanding the needs of the person you are dealing with		
Handling objections to your arguments		
Making concessions to reach an agreement		
Using tact and diplomacy		

Teamwork	I have this	Like to improve
Working confidently within a group		
Working co-operatively towards a common goal		
Contributing your own ideas effectively in a group		
Listening to others' opinions		
Taking a share of the responsibility		
Being assertive rather than passive or aggressive		
Accepting and learning from constructive criticism		

Leadership	I have this	Like to improve
Being able to motivate and direct others		
Taking the initiative		
Organising and motivating others		
Making decisions and seeing them through		
Taking a positive attitude to failure persevering when things are not working out		
Accepting responsibility for mistakes/wrong decisions		
Being flexible and prepared to adapt goals in the light of changing situations		

Planning and organising	I have this	Like to improve
Being able to plan activities and carry them through effectively		
Setting objectives which are achievable		
Managing your time effectively/using action planning skills		

	I have this	Like to improve
Setting priorities – most important/most urgent		
Identifying the steps needed to achieve your goals		
Being able to work effectively when under pressure		
Completing work to a deadline		
Investigating, analysing and problem solving	**I have this**	**Like to improve**
Gathering information systematically to establish facts and principles		
Clarifying the nature of a problem before deciding action		
Collecting, collating, classifying and summarising data systematically		
Analysing the factors involved in a problem and being able to identify the key ones		
Recognising inconsistencies in reasoning		
Using creativity/initiative in the generation of alternative solutions to a problem		
Differentiating between practical and impractical solutions		
Numeracy	**I have this**	**Like to improve**
Being able to carry out arithmetic operations/understand data		
Multiplying and dividing accurately		
Calculating percentages		
Using a calculator		
Reading and interpreting graphs and tables		
Using statistics		
Planning and organising your personal finances effectively		
Managing a limited budget		
Computing skills	**I have this**	**Like to improve**
Word-processing skills		
Using databases (e.g. Access)		
Using spreadsheets (e.g. Excel)		
Using the Internet and email		
Designing web pages		
Programming skills		
Developing professionalism	**I have this**	**Like to improve**
Accepting responsibility for your views and actions		
Showing the ability to work under your own direction and initiative		
Making choices based on your own judgement		
Paying care and attention to quality in all your work		
Taking the opportunity to learn new skills		
Developing the drive and enthusiasm to achieve your goals		

Table 6: Skills audit form

Skills needed	Date to be completed	Tick when completed
1		
2		
3		
4		
Things I need to do	**Date to be completed**	**Tick when completed**
1		
2		
3		
4		
5		

Table 7: Template for action plan for skills development

Nasreen Singh
Guest service agent

Nasreen had always wanted to own and manage her own pub in the country, with a great restaurant and a few luxury bedrooms with en-suite bathrooms. When she had completed her BTEC Level 3 National in Hospitality, she knew for sure that she wanted a career that involved dealing with people and providing them with a fantastic experience. Nasreen went on to university to study a BTEC Level 5 HND Diploma in Hospitality Management.

While at university, Nasreen took a part-time job working in a busy bar in the local town. This really gave her the chance to practise her customer service and bar management skills. Now that Nasreen has successfully completed her HND she is not sure where to start her career path. She knows what she wants to do eventually, but she is not sure how to develop the skills to enable her to make this dream come true.

Think about it!

- Provide Nasreen with some career guidance. Outline what jobs would suit her qualifications and help her start to develop the skills she needs to run her own pub.
- What application procedures will Nasreen have to go through in order to apply for the jobs you have identified?
- What agencies and websites could she use to look for jobs in the areas you have identified?
- Do you think there are any other courses or qualifications that Nasreen could obtain to support her future application for the jobs you have identified?

Just checking

1 Why are first impressions so important?

2 Name the various categories of customers.

3 List four personal attributes, explaining why they are important to employers.

4 How should you prepare for an interview?

5 List three sources of job information, explaining the suitability of each source.

6 List the three main hospitality-related industries and, for each, give two examples of businesses that fall into these categories.

7 What are employability skills?

8 Why is it important for you to be able to match your own skills with the required employability skills?

9 What are the benefits of having a personal development plan?

edexcel

Assignment tips

- Your personal presentation can have a significant impact on customer perceptions. Make sure you maintain a positive and professional approach in all areas of your work.

- Make sure you understand the impact of excellent and poor customer service, and the effect this can have on a business. Consider situations in which you have been particularly satisfied or dissatisfied with the customer service you have received, and work out how you can improve your own practice.

- Your curriculum vitae must be an honest representation of your skills, qualifications and experience. Try to find examples of good and poor CVs and remember that the design and layout are as important as the content.

- When researching different job roles, look at hospitality websites as well as recruitment websites. Make sure you consider job opportunities in a wide range of outlets – do not limit yourself to one particular area (e.g. hotels).

- Prepare thoroughly for your interview tasks. Make sure you have matched your skills against the job description and that you know what the job involves. Carry out some practice interviews before your final assessment and ask for feedback from your tutor or other people helping you.

- Once you have completed your interviews, you need to analyse your performance and write a report. Ask for feedback from your interviewer, make a note of what went well or badly, and work out what you need to improve on for next time.

- When completing a skills audit and producing your personal action plan, be realistic about the skills you can develop over 6 weeks and seek advice from your tutor. Remember to put the plan into action and keep track of which tasks you have completed.

8 Prepare, cook and finish food

Most people have eaten a meal in a café, restaurant, hotel or bistro. There has been a huge increase in the numbers of people eating out and customers are becoming more adventurous in their choices. People working in the hospitality industry need the knowledge and skills to use a variety of food preparation and cooking methods, and should be able to work with a range of food items.

Processes should be followed to ensure that ingredients are purchased in the right quantities, with the desired quality and at the right cost. It is also important to charge the right price for the dishes. This is key for the success of a hospitality business.

This unit enables you to develop some basic culinary skills. You will develop your understanding of how to buy food and how to cost basic recipes for a hospitality business. You will look at how food can be presented and you will critically evaluate dishes to improve their quality.

This is a practical unit. You need to be very organised to work in a kitchen, and you will be required to plan what you are going to do before your lessons. You will also be required to demonstrate that you can clear down all work areas and equipment at the end of a session and store any remaining food safely for future use.

Learning outcomes

After completing this unit, you should:

1 Know the basic principles of food preparation
2 Know the basic principles for cooking food
3 Know the basic principles of finishing food
4 Know how to clear down work areas and equipment and store food at end of production.

Assessment and grading criteria

This table shows you what you must do in order to achieve a pass, merit or distinction grade, and where you can find activities in this book to help you.

Unit 8 Prepare, cook and finish food

To achieve a pass grade the evidence must show that you are able to:		To achieve a merit grade the evidence must show that, in addition to the pass criteria, you are able to:	To achieve a distinction grade the evidence must show that, in addition to the pass and merit criteria, you are able to:
P1 list appropriate tools and equipment for preparing food commodities **Assessment activity 1, pages 247–48**	**P2** describe the importance of quality when preparing food commodities **Assessment activity 1, pages 247–48**	**M1** demonstrate the purchasing cycle through the completion of relevant purchasing documents **Assessment activity 1, pages 247–48**	**D1** assess how the purchasing cycle and documents improve the control of food purchases **Assessment activity 1, pages 247–48**
P3 describe the importance of checking that commodities meet requirements **Assessment activity 1, pags 247–48**	**P4** describe the importance of reporting problems with commodities **Assessment activity 1, pages 247–48**		
P5 describe the importance of correct storage of prepared food **Assessment activity 1, pages 247–48**			
P6 identify different cooking methods used for a range of dishes **Assessment activity 2, page 260**	**P7** state appropriate methods for cooking food **Assessment activity 2, page 260**	**M2** demonstrate appropriate use of techniques in the preparation, cooking and presentation of dishes on different occasions with limited tutor support **Assessment activity 4, page 264**	**D2** reflect on how the dishes are prepared, cooked and presented and make recommendations for improvement **Assessment activity 4, page 264**
P8 state key features of healthier foods **Assessment activity 2, page 260**	**P9** describe the importance of providing healthy eating options **Assessment activity 2, page 260**		
P10 describe the importance of holding cooked food correctly **Assessment activity 2, page 260**			
P11 describe the importance of finishing dishes for service **Assessment activity 3, page 263**	**P12** state the importance of using appropriate food garnishes **Assessment activity 3, page 263**	**M3** accurately use calculations to justify realistic selling prices **Assessment activity 5, page 271**	
P13 describe the importance of checking that dishes meet requirements for colour, consistency and flavour **Assessment activity 3, page 263**			
P14 describe the correct procedures for clearing down **Assessment activity 6, page 276**	**P15** identify food suitable for re-use or disposal **Assessment activity 6, page 276**	**M4** effectively clear down area in accordance with food hygiene regulations **Assessment activity 6, page 276**	

How you will be assessed

You will be assessed by assignments that will be designed and marked by tutors in your centre. The type of evidence that you will be asked to present when you carry out an assignment could be in the form of:

- a written report
- preparing and cooking dishes in a kitchen
- a tutor observation record of your practical work
- completed dish-costing sheets showing calculations of the selling prices of menu items and dishes.

Jack, 18-year-old learner

This unit helped me appreciate how well organised I will need to be when I work in a kitchen cooking and when I'm serving food to customers. It has helped me realise the importance of good time-keeping skills, having a smart personal appearance and having good knowledge of food hygiene.

I like to be busy when I am studying as I get bored easily. I liked this unit because there was a lot to do, and it was good that I could have a say in the dishes that I cooked for some of my assignment work.

There is plenty of practical work as well as written assignments, so I could use all of my skills to get a good grade. However, I realise that I need to show good skills in all aspects of the unit, including calculations and the written assignments. Working with food is very skilful and you need to know what you are doing.

I would like to have a career in the hospitality industry where I can use my practical skills as well as all the knowledge I have gained studying the theory. Eventually, I would like to be a catering manager running my own operation, so I am going to take a BTEC National after this course to get skills in supervision and to increase my knowledge of the hospitality industry.

Over to you

- Do you like to work in a busy environment?
- Are you good at solving problems?
- Do you enjoy being part of a team?
- Think of a really good meal that you have eaten recently. Why was it so good?

8.1 Know the basic principles of food preparation

Welcome

A lunch club

You have been set a challenge to run a lunch club once a week at your school or college to raise money for charity. Customers will be outside visitors and about 30 are expected to come each week. What dishes would you have on the menu? Where would you go to buy or source ingredients for the menu items? How would you safely store any leftover ingredients from one week to the next?

In the first section of this unit, we will look at:

- basic foods
- preparing food
- tools and equipment
- storage methods
- purchasing food
- documents used in the purchasing cycle.

Basic foods

Let's start by looking at the basic foods and ingredients held in most kitchens.

Meat

Meat is the edible flesh and organs of animals and birds. It is rich in protein – a bodybuilding food.

- Meat is the general term for beef and veal from cows, lamb and mutton from sheep, and pork from pigs. These are all domestic animals reared especially for eating.
- Game describes meat from wild animals and birds that are eaten, such as venison (from deer) and pheasant.
- Offal is the term used to describe the edible internal organs of animals, such as liver and kidney.
- Poultry is the term used to describe meat from domesticated birds reared for eating, such as chickens and turkeys.

Fish

Fish are an excellent source of protein. Fish come from several sources:

- saltwater fish, such as cod, haddock and tuna, come from the sea
- freshwater fish, such as trout and bream, come from rivers and lakes

- farmed fish, such as some salmon, trout and bass, are grown in large tanks of salt or fresh water
- shellfish, such as lobsters, crabs, prawns, oysters, mussels and scallops, are saltwater creatures that are either harvested from natural resources in tidal mudflats or estuaries or sourced from shellfish farms.

Farmed fish are a good alternative to wild fish, as some species have been over-fished in the wild and are now in danger of extinction. There are many newer varieties of fish to try, which helps conserve the stocks of endangered fish.

Vegetables

These are plants grown to be eaten. Vegetables are very rich in vitamins and minerals, and so they are important parts of the daily diet. They can be classified by the part of the plant they come from.

Part of the plant	Examples of vegetables
Root	Carrots, turnips
Tuber	Potatoes
Bulb	Onions, garlic
Stem	Celery, asparagus
Leaf	Cabbage, spinach
Flower	Cauliflower, broccoli
Pod and seed	Peas, green beans
Vegetable fruit	Cucumber, tomato, aubergine (eggplant), squash

Table 1: Vegetable classifications

Activity: Vegetable tasting

As a class, obtain eight different vegetables that some members of the group may not have eaten before.

Prepare the vegetables for tasting. Many vegetables can be eaten raw, so they may not need cooking. Try each vegetable. Make notes of the names, where they come from and comment on how they taste.

Fruit

Fruit is the fleshy seed container of a plant. Fruits are an essential part of a good diet and are classified into five main groups:

- soft fruits – strawberries and raspberries
- stone fruits – plums and peaches
- hard fruits – apples and pears
- citrus fruits – lemons and oranges
- tropical fruits – bananas and pineapples.

Do you recognise all of these fruits?

Pasta

Pasta is a traditional food associated with Italy. It is made from durum wheat, a strong variety that is high in a soluble protein called gluten. Other ingredients are water, eggs and olive oil. There are two main type of pasta:

- dried pasta, which can be bought in a large variety of shapes and sizes
- fresh pasta, also available in many sizes and shapes, and may produce a better quality product when cooked than dried varieties.

Pasta is served with a wide variety of sauces, many of which can be purchased in a convenience form ready to cook.

Rice

Rice is a grain. It is cereal crop that is obtained from a variety of cultivated grass. Rice is the main food crop for half the world's population. The main nutritional ingredient in rice is carbohydrate – it is food to fill you up.

- Short -grain rice is used for making sweet rice puddings and risotto dishes. An example of this type of rice is arborio.
- Long-grain rice is served to accompany curries and other savoury dishes. An example of this type of rice is basmati.

Most of the rice eaten in the UK is white rice. Wholemeal varieties are also available that contain more fibre or roughage than white varieties, and are considered to be more healthy.

Eggs and dairy

Eggs are regarded as dairy produce from a catering perspective. Hens' eggs are most commonly used in cooking, but eggs from ducks, geese and quails are also available.

Dairy is the general term for milk and the products produced from milk, such as cream, butter, cheese and yoghurt. Milk generally comes from cows but goats' milk is growing in popularity as many people are developing allergies to cows' milk and its products.

Pulses

Pulses are peas, beans and lentils. They are known as legumes. They are high in protein and dietary fibre, and are widely used in Asian and vegetarian cookery.

Meat alternatives

Soya beans are used to produce a bean curd called tofu, which is either bland or lightly smoked, and textured vegetable protein (TVP). This is the name given to soya mince chunks. It is used in the same way as minced beef or lamb.

Quorn is a low-fat, high-protein food. It has a mild flavour and can be used instead of chicken or minced meat.

Nuts, which contain high amounts of protein, can also be used instead of meat in some vegetarian dishes.

Importance of quality

Before preparing all basic commodities and foods, chefs must carefully check the produce for quality. Many food labels contain a written specification, and this can be used to ensure that the kitchen is receiving the products with the right quality.

It is also necessary to check that any food brought into the kitchen is free from any contamination. Check that vegetables and fruits do not have any insect, animal or bird damage, and that fresh fish and meat smells fresh and has not started to go off.

If food is of poor quality, it usually means that a kitchen will produce a lot of waste as much will need to be thrown away. This can reduce the profit that the business makes. Always buy the best quality produce that can be afforded.

Activity: Checking for quality

Discuss all the points that chefs should consider when checking the quality of fresh fish, fresh vegetables and fresh eggs before they start to use them.

Preparing food

Preparing food prior to cooking is a technical activity that requires care and attention from staff in the kitchen.

Weighing and measuring food

Chefs need to understand basic weights and measures so that they can follow the instructions given in **recipes** successfully. Food is expensive to buy, and chefs need to weigh and measure ingredients accurately. If they do not, food will get wasted and money lost.

Recipes can be written using either metric measurements or imperial measurements. It is more common to use metric measurements, but you will still find many recipes that use imperial units. It is very important not to mix metric and imperial measures when following recipes – use one or the other.

Key term

Recipe – a set of instructions on how to make a food dish. Recipes specify the ingredients, the amounts to be used, and the preparation and cooking methods.

Metric	Imperial
Weight	
kilogram (kg) = 1000 g	pound (lb) = 16 oz
gram (g)	ounce (oz)
Capacity	
litre (l) = 100 cl = 1000 ml	gallon = 8 pints
centilitre (cl) = 10 ml	quart = 2 pints
millilitre (ml)	pint = 20 fluid ounces (fl oz)
Freezing point/boiling point of water	
Celsius (°C)	**Fahrenheit (°F)**
0°C/100°C	32°F/212°F

Table 2: Useful weights and measures

Oven temperatures are shown in either degrees Celsius (°C) or Fahrenheit (°F). Table 3 below shows a comparison chart that you can use to convert from one to another. If you are using a fan-assisted oven, you will have to make a further adjustment because these ovens are more efficient and therefore should be set at lower temperatures than ovens that are not fan assisted.

Celsius (°C)	Fahrenheit (°F)	Gas mark
120	250	$\frac{1}{2}$ (very low)
140	275	1 (low)
150	300	2
170	325	3 (moderate)
180	350	4
190	375	5
200	400	6
220	425	7 (hot)
230	450	8
260	500	9 (very hot)

Table 3: Oven temperatures

Food preparation techniques

Before food can be cooked, it often needs to undergo some preparation. For some foods, this can be quite a basic task. For example, when making salads or sandwiches the ingredients only need to be washed and cut. For more complex dishes, such as a fruit crumble, the preparation can be more involved and you may need to grate, peel, chop or dice food items before cooking can take place.

You need to know the basic preparation techniques used in the kitchen. Chefs need to select the correct tools and equipment for each task so that they can be efficient, work in a safe manner and not waste food. As a general rule the larger the job, the larger the tool.

Technique	Equipment	Function
Peeling	7.5 cm small cook's knife or vegetable peeler	To remove outer skin or layers from fruit and vegetables such as potatoes and apples
Chopping	Large cook's knife, hand-held chopper or food processor	To cut large food items into smaller pieces for cooking, when used as an ingredient in a recipe or for eating
Dicing	Large cook's knife	To cut raw or cooked food items into large or small cubes when used in dishes such as fruit salad and soups
Grating	Hand grater or food processor	To reduce the density of foods such as cheese and carrots when used as toppings on pizzas and salads
Creaming	Wooden spoon, hand or bench food mixer, or food processor	To incorporate air into fat and sugar as part of the cooking process, as in sponge cakes
Rubbing in	Usually done by hand	To incorporate fat and flour together in baking, as for a crumble topping
Folding	Metal spoon	To combine ingredients in a gentle way so there is no reduction in volume or lightness, as in sponge cakes
Beating	Wooden spoon, hand or bench food mixer, or food processor	To incorporate air into fat and sugar as part of the cooking process, as in sponge cakes
Stirring	Wooden spoon, spatula or electric mixer	To blend solid or liquid ingredients
Mixing	Wooden spoon, spatula, metal spoon or electric mixer	To blend solid or liquid ingredients
Seasoning	Salt, pepper mills, garlic crusher, mustard pot	To improve the flavour of foods

Table 4: Techniques and equipment

Activity: Food preparation

Identify some basic foods that need to be prepared prior to cooking. Look through recipe books to help you get going. For each technique, try to find two foods that can be prepared using that method.

Preparation of raw foods can be a time-consuming activity. Foods can be purchased for cooking with most if not all of the preparation already done by the supplier or producer. This has become very popular, and a huge range of completely prepared items is now available for use in the catering industry. These are sometimes referred to as **convenience foods**.

Key term

Convenience foods – bought foods that have already been prepared and/or cooked.

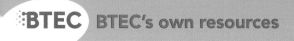

Selecting and using appropriate equipment

All equipment used in the preparation of food must be clean, safe and in good working order. We will review the range of equipment and utensils used in a typical kitchen below. What is actually needed depends on the food being cooked, and this is influenced by the style and size of the menu.

Safety and hygiene

Attention to safety and hygiene is vital in food preparation. Raw food can easily become contaminated with germs and bacteria during preparation. This can cause food poisoning. Food that is waiting to be cooked or that is to be eaten raw must be stored in accordance with the food hygiene regulations. It is important that prepared foods are stored correctly and protected against possible contamination that could make them dangerous to eat.

Food that is delivered to the kitchen by suppliers must be carefully checked by chefs to ensure that it is fresh and safe to bring into the kitchen.

- Check the smell – everything must smell fresh.

- Look for insect or bird damage on fruit and vegetables.

- Inspect all packaging, such as containers, packets, jars, bottles and boxes. Packaging must not be damaged. If it is, the food inside could have been damaged or contaminated, and it might be unsafe to prepare and eat.

- Check any use-by dates on the packaging. To ensure compliance, food that is out of date must be thrown away.

Activity: Food hygiene

Research the food hygiene regulations. Describe the rules chefs are required to follow by law when preparing food in a kitchen.

As well as paying attention to food hygiene, you must also consider safety in the kitchen. When using preparation equipment, such as mixers, peelers and choppers, always follow the manufacturer's instructions. Make sure the power is turned off before changing tools and attachments. It is also safer to take the plug out of the socket when cleaning electrical equipment after use. This helps prevent accidents by ensuring that the item cannot be accidentally turned on.

Activity: Food hygiene

In groups, discuss some of the safety issues that need to be considered by chefs when preparing food in a kitchen. What equipment in the kitchen is the most dangerous to use? Why is this?

Tools and equipment

Let's review the equipment used in a typical kitchen.

Small-scale equipment

Small-scale equipment includes:

- knives
- lemon zester
- garlic crusher
- kitchen scissors.
- potato peeler and apple corer
- round scoops for cutting fruit
- poultry secateurs (strong scissors)

Most chefs have their own knives; they are the tools of the trade. They are expensive to buy and are always looked after very carefully. Knives can be made of:

- carbon steel with wooden handles – these can be difficult to keep clean
- stainless steel with plastic handles – this combination makes them easy to keep clean and hygienic
- stainless steel including the handles – these are easy to keep clean and well maintained.

Chopping boards are available in many sizes and colours. Today the trend is for them to be made in strong plastic so that they may be easily washed and sterilised. Some are colour-coded to stop cross-contamination – each food type has its own colour board so that germs do not spread from one food to another or from cooked food to raw or uncooked food.

Many chefs prefer to use traditional wooden chopping boards. These, however, are more difficult to keep clean and free of bacteria.

Large-scale equipment

There are many mechanical devices that can be used in the kitchen to help with food preparation. They can reduce the time it takes to complete repetitive and boring tasks. The use of mechanical devices also:

- enables staff to be used more effectively
- contributes to reducing kitchen costs
- produces a better-quality finished product.

Are you familiar with these items of small-scale equipment?

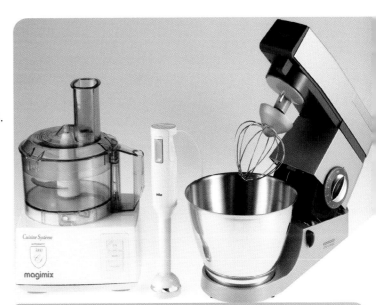

How can large mechanical devices help reduce preparation time?

237

Large-scale equipment	Definiton
Oven	Equipment for cooking food, which can be fuelled by gas, electricity, oil or solid fuel. Used for most cookery methods.
Steamer	Equipment for steaming foods such as fish, vegetables and some puddings. Considered a healthy way to cook foods.
Microwave oven	An electric oven using high-frequency power to cook food or heat liquids very quickly. Metal cannot be used in microwaves.
Rice cooker	A slow electric cooker that is used to cook rice by steaming. Useful where large quantities of rice are required.
Bratt pan	A large versatile item of equipment that can be used to cook food by shallow and deep frying, stewing, braising and boiling.
Flare grill	A grill heated from below. Used for cooking steaks. The bars give a characteristic stripped appearance to grilled meats.
Salamander	A type of grill heated from above, usually fuelled by gas. For cooking food such as steaks, vegetables and breakfast items.
Bains-marie	A shallow open bath or well-shaped appliance that uses water for keeping food hot at service times without burning items.
Griddle	A solid metal plate heated from beneath which is used for cooking hamburgers, eggs, bacon and meat.
Deep-fat fryer	An appliance for frying food. Items are completely immersed in oil. A very dangerous method if not well managed.
Hot smoking oven	A special oven used to smoke fish and meats. Wood chips are burnt to give a smoky flavour to food.
Pasta machine	A hand-operated machine for rolling out pasta into different shapes and sizes.
Electric mixer	Hand held, bench top or floor standing. Used for mixing pastry and cakes, making mayonnaise, and beating cream and egg whites. Can also be used to chop and mince meat and vegetables.
Liquidiser/blender	A high-speed electrical machine for chopping, blending and puréeing foods. It can be dangerous to blend hot food.
Food processor	An electrical machine with sharp blades and cutters for mixing, chopping, slicing.
Slicer	Manually and electrically operated machines for slicing meats and bread. Can be dangerous if not used correctly.
Mould	Made from metal, rubber, glass or china for giving fancy shapes to pâtés, terrines, jellies, ice creams, mousses and custard-based sweets. Used also to help give accurate portions.

Table 5: Large-scale kitchen equipment

Kitchen equipment can be dangerous if not used properly by trained staff. Some equipment such as meat slicers should not be used by anyone under 18 years of age. Before you use a new piece of equipment, make sure that you have received appropriate training and that you know the proper methods for using the equipment and any necessary safety requirements.

Activity: Kitchen equipment

Visit the kitchen at your school or college. Identify all the items of equipment used for food preparation. Has the kitchen all the equipment needed to prepare food using the preparation techniques listed earlier in this unit?

Storage methods

All food on the premises of a catering business must be stored properly. If food is not stored in the correct manner, it can spoil (go off) and become contaminated. The business will have to throw the food away, which is a waste of money, or it risks making its customers ill by using food that is not fit for consumption.

The temperature at which food is stored influences how quickly it starts to spoil. Food spoilage is caused by micro-organisms and bacteria that are naturally present in the air and in food items. Micro-organisms spoil the colour, texture, flavour and nutritional value of foods.

Most food items used in a catering business are perishable. They have a very short life before they start to lose quality or become unusable and unfit to eat. For this reason, many foods are preserved – by chilling, freezing or other processes – to keep them for use at a later time. Preserved foods are widely used in catering today.

Fresh food

Fresh foods are just that – 'fresh'. Suppliers and producers may have simply prepared the food for sale by washing and packaging, but otherwise the food comes straight from the producer without any preservation process or cooking.

Fresh food will not keep for a very long time before the quality starts to reduce. Fresh food is therefore normally bought on a daily basis, as it is not possible to keep it for long periods. It should be stored at room temperature or placed in a cool room out of direct sunlight or extreme cold.

Chilled food

Foods are chilled to slow down the rate of spoilage. Chilled foods are delivered, stored and kept at temperatures just above freezing. They are stored between 1°C and 8°C (36°F and 45°F) in specially designed cabinets or refrigerators.

Do you know how to store chilled foods safely?

Why should you never re-freeze frozen foods once they have thawed?

Chilled foods are usually safe to eat and keep their quality for up to four days (96 hours) if correctly stored. The damage caused by micro-organisms is slowed down but not completely stopped. Foods that have not been eaten within the four-day period should be thrown away, as they may contain a build-up of harmful bacteria.

Food manufacturers and producers often print guidelines on the packaging of some chilled foods. These guidelines include use-by dates, correct handling and storage procedures, and serving advice. These guidelines must be followed. By following the advice on storage procedures, some chilled foods may have a slightly longer shelf life than four days.

Frozen food

Foods are frozen to stop the growth of micro-organisms. The normal storage temperature of frozen foods is −18°C (0°F) or below. No bacteria can grow at this temperature. Freezing food does not kill any bacteria that may be present when the item is frozen, and therefore careful handling is still necessary. When frozen food is thawed the bacteria will begin to grow again, so the food must be eaten or used within a short time or thrown away.

Pre-cooked food

Pre-cooked foods are available in either multiple or single portions. These foods need careful handling and storing. They can be a source of bacterial food poisoning as the foods are not cooked again after purchase.

Dry goods

Dry goods is the collective term used in catering for all the food items that are usually called groceries in the home. These foods are called dry because much of their moisture has been removed during the preservation or manufacturing process. Dry goods should be stored in cool, dry conditions such as a larder or storeroom.

Typical dry goods in the kitchen include tea, coffee, flour, sugar, pasta, rice, biscuits and breakfast cereals. Some fruits used in baking, such as sultanas, raisins and currants, are usually bought in dried form. They are known as dried fruit.

Tinned and bottled goods

Before the invention of refrigeration and freezers, many foods were bottled or tinned. These methods of food preservation are still used today. A very wide range of foods is available in either tinned or bottled form, especially products sourced from overseas. Foods preserved this way have a long shelf life – that is, they can be stored for a long time after buying.

Some foods preserve very well in tins, such as pulses, tuna fish, salmon and tropical fruit, and ingredients for Indian or Chinese dishes such as coconut milk and water chestnuts. Bottled items include pickles, sauces, vinegars and other condiments for cooking, and fruits such as blackcurrants and plums.

Some foods do not preserve well in tins and bottles. For example, when carrots are tinned the heating process damages their texture and reduces their vitamin content.

Purchasing food

Purchasing is the technical term used in catering for buying. Purchasing food for a catering business is a very skilful job that requires a great deal of experience and good knowledge of food and **commodities** (raw products).

In most catering businesses, it is usually very difficult to predict exactly how many customers are going to require meals each day. Many catering outlets do not require that customers book in advance – they just arrive unannounced. There are many factors that affect the number of customers that come into a catering outlet, including the:

- weather
- time of day
- season of the year
- location of the business.

A catering business needs to have thought-out arrangements for buying food so that what is needed in the kitchen is always available, either in stock or ready for delivery.

Hospitality businesses, such as cafés, restaurants, hotels and contract caterers, buy food or commodities from suppliers daily, weekly or monthly, depending on the style, size and location of the business and on the type of food that is being purchased. For example, fresh fruit and vegetables may be bought on a daily basis, whereas frozen foods might be purchased once a week and dry goods, such as tea and coffee, only once a month.

Suppliers

A hospitality business will always seek good suppliers. Suppliers should:

- be able to supply what is wanted at a price that is acceptable
- know their products
- be able to supply the products when the caterer needs them
- have a good trading reputation
- use correct storage and delivery procedures.

There are many types of supplier that can supply food to a catering business. Choosing the right suppliers needs care and consideration. Most catering businesses buy from several suppliers. Their choice will depend on:

- what is being bought
- the size of the catering business – a small owner-managed café may have different suppliers to a large national restaurant chain
- the amount of food being purchased.

Key terms

Purchasing – another word for buying. Purchasing is the term usually used in catering and the hospitality industry.

Commodities – raw food products before any preparation or cooking.

Choosing suppliers

There are several key decisions to make in choosing suppliers. First, a business needs to decide whether to buy from wholesalers or retailers.

Wholesalers will only supply to recognised businesses and not to individuals, as they are not open to the public. They usually specialise in one basic type of food such as meat, fish or fruit and vegetables, and they will only supply in large quantities. The advantages of using a wholesaler are that:

- the items that caterers want are usually in stock
- the prices charged are very competitive
- there is a wide choice
- deliveries can be made direct to caterers at a specified time.

The shops in the high street and shopping malls in every city and town are known as retailers. They supply to the general public. Supermarkets are retailers, for example. They buy goods in large quantities that are then repackaged and sold to shoppers in smaller amounts. The advantage of using a retailer is that items are available in relatively small quantities, and this is helpful if a caterer is worried about buying too much stock. Retail shops have long opening hours, and they are open when other types of supplier are closed. The disadvantage of buying from retailers is that they are usually the most expensive option – most food can be sourced more cheaply from elsewhere.

Activity: Advantages of retailers

Think of a retail shop that you use on a regular basis. Write down all the reasons why you use this retailer. Discuss your reasons with the rest of the group.

Another factor in choosing suppliers is whether they are national or local.

National suppliers can supply customers throughout the country. They are usually very large companies. Some can supply everything a catering business will need in one weekly delivery; others may provide one main product such as meat or dry goods (groceries). National companies usually require that each delivery should have a minimum financial value. It is also necessary to set up formal accounts, and possibly sign a contract (a legal agreement). This can create a lot of paperwork, particularly for a small business.

Local suppliers are based in the same area as the businesses they supply. The attraction of using local suppliers for a catering business is that the delivery arrangements can be much more flexible as journey distances are small. The caterer can even visit the supplier to see how the food is produced. Many restaurants and hotels advertise the fact that they serve locally sourced products and regional specialities, which will be purchased from local suppliers. This is a good way of increasing business, and offers customers something.

Specialist suppliers tend to be small, independent businesses that concentrate on one or only a few product items. They can be very knowledgeable about the products they supply. They can supply products such as regional cheeses and smoked meats that may be difficult to source anywhere else. Specialist suppliers may actually produce or manufacture the items themselves.

A final option for caterers are two special types of wholesale suppliers: markets, and cash and carry warehouses.

There are several local and national wholesale markets that specialise in a particular product. For example, in London there is Smithfield market for meat and New Covent Garden market for fruit, vegetables and flowers. These markets help to set the wholesale rates for different food products. They issue market lists or price lists, usually on a weekly basis.

Have you ever bought food from a specialist supplier?

- Buying in markets may not be very convenient, as they tend to open very early in the mornings.

- Buyers need to have good knowledge of the products they are buying.

- Buyers also have to manage transport arrangements, as markets tend not to have delivery services.

- However, there are some good bargains to be found in markets and the quality can be very high.

A cash and carry is a large warehouse where chefs and caterers go in person to buy goods and products to stock up the kitchen. Only a registered business can use a cash and carry, as they do not serve the general public.

- There is a cash and carry in most towns and areas.

- They hold a large product range, including meat, fruit and vegetables, frozen foods and groceries.

- Products are often available in a variety of package sizes, from small to very large.

- It is possible to buy everything for a catering business.

It is usual to pay for purchases after going round the cash and carry – just as a customer would at a supermarket – and then transport everything back to the workplace. This can be hard work if buying in bulk, and it also requires a large vehicle. However, a cash and carry is a popular option for many small catering businesses. It is flexible and creates little paperwork, and shopping can be done at a quiet time.

What might you buy from a cash and carry warehouse?

Activity: A visit to a catering supplier

As a group, try to arrange a visit to a large catering supplier. This needs to be done with your tutor.

During your visit, investigate:
- how goods and food are handled
- the equipment used in the store or warehouse
- the storage facilities
- the packaging of food and goods
- the range of food supplied
- how food is delivered to customers
- the paperwork involved
- how customers are contacted.

Checking that commodities meet requirements

It is important to check that all purchases meet the specific requirements of the catering business. If items do not meet requirements or the necessary quality standards:

- customers might complain about the poor quality

- profits might fall because more food has to be thrown away

- some dishes may become unavailable because the ingredients have gone off.

Take as an example beef steaks. If the meat is supplied with too much fat, this has to be trimmed off by chefs. However, the supplier is still charging for the meat by weight. So, the establishment is buying fat to throw away. This is profit in the waste bin.

Reporting problems with commodities

If there are any quality problems with any purchased food and commodities, these will need to be reported to supervisors and managers as soon as they become apparent. It may be necessary to return items to suppliers and request a replacement or refund. Most hospitality businesses have strict requirements for the quality of the food and commodities that they purchase. A **specification** can be used to help determine whether the food meets the required quality.

Documents used in the purchasing cycle

An important part of a chef's work is to monitor the food stored in a kitchen and to control what food is purchased. Effective management of purchases means that:

Key terms

Specification – a document that describes exactly what is required. For a catering business, a specification is about quality of food and commodities purchased.

- only food that is needed is bought
- wastage (unused food that has to be thrown away) is kept to a minimum.

The **purchasing cycle** is the system used in a catering business to place, receive and pay for orders of food and other goods from outside suppliers.

As buying involves spending large amounts of money as well as possibly entering into legal agreements with suppliers, it is important that strict procedures are used. These should be supported by formal paperwork. This applies even in the smallest catering operation, such as a snack bar or a seaside bed and breakfast (B&B).

To illustrate how business documents are used, let's consider how the ingredients for vegetable crumble might be purchased and tracked through the system. This is a dish offered at the Anchor, a small bistro in the West Country.

First, the quantities of each ingredient needed for the dish should be calculated by the chef at the Anchor. These will be based on a forecast of how many portions of the dish will need to be prepared in the forthcoming period (say, a week or a fortnight). Then, the chef needs to check whether these ingredients are in stock in sufficient quantities or whether new supplies will need to be purchased.

Internal requisition

If there are sufficient quantities of each ingredient in stock, then the kitchen just needs to get the ingredients from the stores. In large establishments, there will be a formal procedure for obtaining food and commodities from the stores. Items should not be issued without the correct documents. An **internal requisition** will have to be signed by the head chef and sent to the stores. A copy of the requisition will be sent back with the items. The cost may also be put on the returned requisition form to show the kitchen. This is part of internal cost control.

Purchase orders

If the items are not in stock, an order will need to be placed with suppliers. As the dish is a vegetable crumble, most of the ingredients can be sourced from the greengrocer or the bistro's fruit and vegetable supplier, the Fruit Bowl.

A **purchase order** will be completed showing how much of each item is needed, together with the required delivery day. The order will be completed in duplicate (two copies) and either telephoned, sent or given to the supplier.

One copy will be kept by the Anchor. Orders made by phone must be confirmed in writing using a purchase order, which is sent to the supplier.

Key terms

Purchasing cycle – a system used in catering to place, receive and pay for orders of food and other goods from outside suppliers.

Internal requisition – a document that is completed by a chef or kitchen staff to obtain food from the stores.

Purchase order – a document sent to a supplier to order goods and services. It shows how much of each item is needed and the required delivery date.

Key terms

Delivery note – a document sent by a supplier to show what is being delivered and the amount of each item being supplied.

Returns note – a note sent by a customer when returning goods to a supplier because they are faulty, of poor quality or had not been ordered.

Credit note – a note given to cover the value of faulty goods. The customer will not be charged for these goods.

Invoice – a bill for goods received.

Statement of account – a document prepared each month by a supplier, showing items bought and the money owed by a customer.

Delivery notes

When the Fruit Bowl (the supplier in this case) delivers the order of vegetables to the Anchor, it is accompanied by a **delivery note**. This is a note prepared by the supplier to accompany the delivery of an order to a customer. It shows what items are being delivered and in what amounts. This should match exactly what was ordered on the purchase order. Staff at the Anchor will check the actual food delivered against the delivery note for quantity and quality.

Returns notes

Suppose, in this case, the carrots were of such a poor quality that they could not be used by the bistro. They would be refused and sent back to the supplier. The Anchor would complete a **returns note** detailing the item that is not being accepted and stating the quantity that is being returned.

Credit notes

When the Fruit Bowl receives back the poor quality carrots, it will send the Anchor a **credit note** to cover the value of these supplies. The bistro will not be charged for the carrots. Credit notes are the only documents used in the purchasing process that are printed in red; this is so they stand out.

Invoices

An **invoice** is a bill for goods received. The supplier will make out an invoice and send it to the customer. This is done for each separate purchase order the supplier receives, and each invoice will detail the goods that have been delivered and the price charged for those goods.

So, the invoice sent by the Fruit Bowl will detail the amount now owed by the Anchor for the delivery of vegetables. The bistro must keep all the invoices it receives from its suppliers, and use them to check that it only pays for food that has actually been delivered. It will usually pay the invoices at the end of each month.

Statement of account

A **statement of account** is prepared at the end of each month by the supplier. This shows the transactions that have taken place during the month, as well as the the total amount owed at the end of the month. If any credit notes have been issued during the month, the value of these will be deducted from the total amount owed. So, a statement of account is a summary of all the invoices and credit notes issued to a customer in the previous month.

Normal practice in a commercial catering business is to pay invoices at the end of each month, rather than make a payment every time a delivery takes place. Payment is usually by cheque, not cash.

Large companies can also make payments electronically using the BACS banking system. This is a very secure system because it allows payments to be made without sending cheques or cash through the post to suppliers. It is also a very quick way of making payments because the payment goes directly into the supplier's bank account.

Case study: Tomato soup and crispy croutons

This is a recipe for tomato soup and crispy croutons. It makes enough for four people.

Ingredients for the soup
Olive oil, 50 ml
Onion, 100 g
Flour, 25 g
Fresh ripe tomatoes, 1.5 kg
Tomato purée, 25 g
Vegetable stock, 1.25 litres
Salt and pepper
Brown sugar, 1 tsp (optional)
Vinegar, 1 tsp (optional)

Ingredients for the croutons
Bread, two slices
Olive oil, 50 ml

Method for the soup
Gently heat the olive oil in a pan, add the onion and fry without colouring. When the onion is cooked, mix in the flour and cook to a sandy texture.

Wash and chop the tomatoes and add to the pan, gently cooking with a lid on for 5 minutes. Then remove from the heat and add the tomato purée, stir and return to the heat.

Make the stock by using good quality vegetarian stock cubes and follow the manufacturer's instructions. Add the stock and bring to the boil.

Season lightly with salt and pepper. Simmer for approximately 1 hour.

Remove from the heat and liquidise using either a hand-held or bench-type liquidiser. Put through a strainer if a smooth soup is desired, or leave with the 'bits' in for a more healthy country style. Pour back into a clean saucepan and bring back to the boil.

Test for seasoning and add more salt and pepper if needed. If you want a slightly sweet and sour flavour, a little brown sugar and vinegar can be added to the soup.

Method for the croutons
Cut the crusts off the bread and dice into small cubes.

Add the olive oil to a frying pan and heat. When the oil is hot, place the bread in the pan and fry to golden brown, stirring all the time with a pallete knife to stop the croutons from sticking to the pan and burning.

When cooked, drain on a piece of kitchen paper and sprinkle on the soup as its being served.

★ ★ ★

You are organising a snack lunch for 35 people at school or college. You are going to serve this tomato soup with croutons. Write out a purchase order to cover the food needed to prepare enough soup for all your guests.

Assessment activity 1

Unit 8 P1 P2 P3 P4 P5 M1 D1 BTEC

The Anchor is a 40-cover good quality bistro in the West Country. It is situated in a large coastal town that attracts a wide variety of visitors all the year round. The bistro changes the menu three times a year to reflect the seasons and changing preferences of its customers.

The head chef is new to the bistro and has many ideas to implement. She has been working with the owners to expand the range of suppliers to better reflect the quality of food they want to serve.

1 Chef has requested that you check to see if the kitchen has got sufficient tools and equipment to prepare and cook the dishes she has designed for the new menu.

Select any three dishes suitable for a lunchtime main course. Make a list of the tools and equipment needed to prepare and make these dishes. P1

2 Provide some written guidance to the kitchen team on how the bistro should purchase and store its food commodities to ensure that it complies with best practice. Produce a leaflet or poster that:

- sets out how kitchen staff can ensure quality when preparing food commodities **P2**
- describes the importance of checking that food commodities meet the kitchen's requirements **P3**
- explains why the kitchen team should report any problems with the quality of commodities that have been delivered **P4**
- describes how to correctly store commodities and prepare food in the kitchen. **P5**

3 The owners of the Anchor want to update the bistro's purchasing procedures. Demonstrate the purchasing cycle by showing the paperwork that would need to be completed and received in sourcing the ingredients for the dishes you looked at in Task 1. **M1**

4 Produce a written report assessing how a restaurant could improve the control of its food purchases by adopting a purchasing cycle and by keeping the relevant documents. Relate your report to the Anchor. **D1**

Grading tips

P1 State the dishes you have chosen for this task. Make sure you list the equipment and identify the tools you will need to prepare different types of commodities.

P2 For this task, you could produce a checklist for chefs to use in the kitchen that sets out the points they must look for to maintain quality.

P3 In this section of your leaflet or poster, you must take into account any relevant laws and regulations.

P4 You could produce another checklist here that sets out the procedures that chefs must follow for reporting any problems they may find with the quality of the food in the kitchen.

P5 You must describe the correct storage methods for a range of typical foods and commodities that would be used by the bistro. A table would be a good way of presenting the required information.

M1 You need to complete all the documents that would be used from the start to the finish of the purchasing cycle. You will need to design some simple documents for this purpose. You could customise these for use by the Anchor.

Another way of producing the required evidence would be to show that you have prepared the necessary documentation in a catering setting. Your tutor may be able to arrange for you to work in your school or college catering service so you can demonstrate your competence in completing purchasing documentation.

D1 You need to provide written evidence to show how the use of the purchasing cycle documents can improve the control of food purchases in the bistro, and how this helps the owners to make more effective use of their financial resources.

PLTS

You will be developing skills as an **independent enquirer** when identifying the equipment needed to prepare some dishes, as a **creative thinker** when working on your checklists, and as a **self-manager** when completing the documents for the purchasing cycle.

Functional skills

You will develop your **English** skills when constructing your answers. By using correct grammar and good sentence construction, you will show you can apply these skills to a real situation.

8.2 Know the basic principles for cooking food

So far, the focus in this unit has been on preparation and kitchen management. Now we will consider the cooking process itself by looking at:

- cooking methods
- choosing ingredients
- planning and working methods.

Cooking methods

Many foods cannot be eaten raw, so cooking is essential. Food is cooked to:

- develop, improve and/or alter its flavour
- improve its digestibility and allow the nutrients it contains to be more easily absorbed by the human body
- destroy any harmful bacteria and micro-organisms that could damage health
- improve its appearance
- extend the life of some **perishable** items.

When we cook food by applying heat, changes take place in the structure, texture and taste of the ingredients. These changes are affected by:

- the way that the heat is applied to the food
- the length of time that the heat is applied
- the temperature the food is cooked at.

A wide range of cooking methods are used in catering today. Let's review the main methods and techniques.

Boiling, simmering, steaming and poaching

These are all methods that involve cooking foods in a liquid (usually water) or water vapour.

Boiling involves submerging food in water and cooking it at 100°C – the boiling point of water. Wherever possible, the cooking water should be retained rather than thrown away as it contains water-soluble nutrients such as vitamins. The water can then be used in the preparation of other foods, such as making gravy.

Simmering is similar to boiling but the food is cooked at a slightly lower temperature. The food is first placed in the boiling liquid and then brought back to the boil. The heat is reduced so that the liquid is only

How many ways of cooking fish can you think of?

boiling very gently – this is known as simmering. Simmering is preferable to boiling as there is less shrinkage and evaporation of the liquid, and the texture and colour of foods being cooked are not damaged.

In steaming, the food is cooked by the heat given out by steam (water vapour) as it condenses. Steaming can be done in saucepan-like containers or specially made high-pressure steamers that cook foods very quickly. The steam may come directly into contact with the food or with the container holding the food. Steaming is a highly favoured method of cooking as much of the nutritional content of the food is retained in cooking.

Poaching involves cooking food in a liquid below 100°C. Frequently, the liquid is brought to the boil before the food is added, and then the food is held at a simmering temperature – that is 90°C – until cooked. Alternatively, both the liquid and the product can be brought slowly to the required simmering temperature and then held at that temperature. Foods cooked this way are often tender, juicy and full of flavour.

Grilling

When food items are grilled, they are cooked by placing the item either under the heat source, above the heat source or a combination of both, such as when you make toast in an electric toaster. Food items cooked in this way need to be good quality and tender. It is a suitable way of cooking small amounts. Care needs to be taken not to grill food for too long. Foods that are overcooked when grilled have a tendency to dry out and they can become unpalatable very quickly.

Barbecuing is a type of grilling where the food is basted (coated) with a sauce or marinade prior to cooking. The smoke created by the barbecue adds flavour to the food.

Frying

Deep frying is a method of cooking food by immersing it in pre-heated fat or oil. Deep-fried items are often dipped in batter or breadcrumbs to protect them from the heat. This allows some of the nutritional content of the food to be sealed in. Deep-fried food has a high energy content because it absorbs some of the fat in the pan in the cooking process. However, foods cooked this way, such as as chips, are very popular.

Shallow frying is the fast cooking of small, delicate food items in a small amount of pre-heated oil or fat in a shallow pan or on a metal griddle plate. Foods cooked this way need to be of good quality.

Roasting and baking

These are two methods of cooking food in an oven, although food can also be roasted on a spit.

Roasting involves cooking food in the dry heat of an oven or on a spit. Oil or fat is added to keep the foods moist and give them a crisp outer coating. High temperatures are used, which gives foods the characteristic dryness. Sunday roasts of beef, chicken or turkey with roast potatoes are pub favourites. Roasted vegetables are also very popular.

Baking involves placing food in greased pans or on trays and then cooking them in an oven at a controlled temperature. The cooked products can look similar to fried foods, but because they absorb no fat while being cooked the energy content of the food is lower and therefore baking is considered a healthier way of cooking.

Stewing

Stewing is the slow and prolonged cooking of small pieces of meat, poultry or game in a small amount of liquid, often with added flavourings such as vegetables and herbs, in a covered container. The cooking liquid forms part of the finished dish. Casseroling is a similar method of cookery. An example of food cooked this way is beef and vegetable stew with savoury dumplings.

Microwaving

Food placed in a microwave is cooked by the high-frequency power waves generated from a magnetron contained in the oven. The waves, which are similar to a television signal, disturb the molecules within the food, causing friction and therefore heat. This is done at very high speed. Metal objects cannot be placed in a conventional microwave oven. Some combination ovens have a forced air and microwave facility. Some foods cooked in this way still look raw when they are fully cooked. Food can also be burnt and overcooked when cooked for too long in a microwave.

Activity: Cookery methods

For each cookery method listed above, identify three foods or dishes that could be cooked by that method.

Seasoning

Many foods are seasoned during cooking to improve and bring out their flavour. Traditional seasonings are:

- salt – table salt or sea salt
- pepper – ground white or black pepper
- mustard – English (hot) or French (mild)
- garlic – fresh cloves or garlic purée.

Chefs use many other seasonings in their cooking. This is partly because many dishes from around the world are popular today, and chefs need to use a wider range of seasonings to create these meals. So, for example, it has become much more common to use the following seasonings:

Do you use many seasonings in your cooking?

- soy sauce, ginger and chilli peppers
- commercially made seasonings such as Worcestershire and tabasco sauces.

There are other ways of seasoning food, including the use of marinades and artificial additives.

Marinades are mixtures of oils, vinegars and spices used to soften and flavour foods prior to cooking. Foods are soaked in marinades for long enough to absorb the flavours. Some foods that are marinated are fish, meat and chicken, often before grilling.

Some commercial seasonings may contain lots of artificial (manmade and chemical) additives. For example, some foods contain monosodium glutamate (MSG), which is used to enhance flavours in Chinese cookery. There are many people who do not wish their foods to contain these additives as they have been linked to health problems.

Foods are seasoned:

- during preparation before cooking takes place, such as putting salt and black pepper on a steak before grilling or using a marinade
- while cooking is taking place, such as putting garlic into a soup
- after cooking but just before serving, such as sprinkling fried chips with salt.

Care should be taken not to over-season food when cooking. Too much seasoning can spoil the taste of food and make it unpleasant to eat. Remember, it is better to add more seasoning towards the end of cooking than to add too much at the beginning, as it is impossible to remove seasoning once it has been added to the dish.

Tasting

Tasting is an important process in cooking. It takes time and experience to learn the skill of tasting. Chefs taste the dishes they are cooking to ensure that the:

- food is fully cooked
- flavours have been developed and the dish tastes as it should
- level of seasoning is correct
- texture and consistency of the food is right.

For example, chefs wills regularly taste soups and foods that have been cooked in sauces to ensure that they are not too thin or too thick.

Timing

Good timing is essential when cooking, and chefs need access to an accurate clock. All recipes give guidelines for preparation and cooking times. These can be very precise and you should keep to the timings given.

It can be useful to prepare a time plan to help sequence the tasks needed to prepare a meal and to map out how long individual tasks will take. With experience, time plans can be done in your head, but this might take many years of practice. Until then, write them down. Table 6 shows a time plan for preparing a lunch of roast chicken, roast potatoes and vegetables.

Sequence	Task	Time	Notes
1	Turn oven on to gas mark 7 (electric 220°C)	10.30 am	
2	Wash and peel potatoes, and leave in water	10.30 am	
3	Season chicken and place in roasting dish	10.45 am	If frozen chickens are being used, make sure they are fully defrosted before cooking
4	Put potatoes in oven	11.00 am	
5	Put chicken in oven	11.15 am	
6	Prepare vegetables	11.20 am	Do not do this too early or vitamins will be lost
7	Check potatoes	11.30 am	
8	Turn chicken over	11.45 am	Be careful not to splash yourself with hot fat
9	Put pan with water on stove for vegetables	11.55 am	
10	Cook vegetables	12.00 noon	
11	Check chicken and potatoes	12.05 pm	
12	Serve meal	12.10 pm	

Table 6: Example time plan

Here are some ideas to help you write time plans.

- Do not be too ambitious with your timings. Allow for many tasks to take longer to prepare and cook than you initially expect. You will get faster as you get more kitchen experience.

- Dishes with long cooking times need to be cooked first and should be started as soon as possible.

- Dishes with short cooking times should be prepared and cooked last.

- It may be possible to prepare some dishes in advance and keep them chilled until required for use.

- Some dishes, such as omelettes, fried foods and grilled steaks, can only be cooked when they are needed, as they become unpalatable very quickly if left standing in the kitchen.

- Some smaller tasks do not need a fixed place in the schedule. Tasks such as grating cheese for use in a cheesy bake or chopping parsley to garnish a vegetable crumble can be done when time allows and the prepared food can be kept ready for later use.

Using appropriate equipment

A variety of equipment can be used when cooking. Generally, the more expensive the equipment, the better it is in terms of quality. Cheap, light pots and pans produced from thin metal will not conduct (spread) heat evenly, but will develop hotspots that can cause food to burn and stick. They will also damage easily – handles fall off and lids do not fit – so they have quite a short useable life. Heavy, thick-based pots conduct heat more evenly and produce the best results in cooking.

Traditionally, cooking pots and pans were made from copper as this metal is the best conductor of heat. However, copper pots are very expensive and they are difficult to keep clean and serviceable. Today, most cooking pots and pans are made from stainless steel or aluminium.

Good-quality pans are more efficient and last longer. Why is this?

Safety and hygiene

Cooking can be dangerous and proper training is needed before using the tools and equipment in a kitchen. Chefs need to be taught how to turn equipment on and off, not only to prevent accidents but to conserve fuel and reduce running costs. Deep-fat frying is a particularly dangerous cooking method as the fat can catch fire, and this can cause major kitchen fires if not properly managed.

Great care is also needed when taking hot food out of ovens and from under grills. Chefs can burn themselves and others around them. They must wear the correct protective uniform and use equipment such as thick oven cloths to reduce the risk of injury.

A kitchen must be cleaned at the end of each session to ensure that there is no waste food left on equipment, kitchen surfaces or inside ovens. Spillages must be cleaned off so that they do not burn next time the equipment is used, as these can cause smoke to accumulate in the kitchen. Cooking oils and fat in fryers must be changed regularly. Old oil and fat can be dangerous as it can easily catch fire.

Choosing ingredients

One of the key tasks of a chef is to choose the ingredients and dishes that will prove popular with customers.

Fresh food

Many customers want to eat fresh foods in season. This reflects a more general consumer trend for wanting less food packaging, fewer preservatives and more environmentally responsible business practices. In catering, this means that some consumers want to see fewer food miles – the distances travelled by food between the producer and the final consumer – to reduce transport pollution.

- Examples of fresh foods include fruit, vegetables, bread, cakes and potatoes.
- Fresh foods are usually those in season. This means they have just been picked or harvested at the end of the growing period. At this time, the quality is very good.
- The nutritional value of fresh foods can be very high.
- Many fresh foods have not been prepared in any way. For this reason, it is usually cheaper for caterers to buy fresh food rather than processed foods or other alternatives.

Chilled foods

Some chilled foods are simply fresh foods stored at a lower temperature to help maintain quality and hygiene. Some chilled foods have been totally prepared and just require cooking or simple reheating.

- There is a wide range of high-quality chilled foods. Examples include meat, fish, fruit juices, yoghurt, cheese and cream, as well as a wide range of ready-made meals such as Chinese and Indian dishes and pizzas.
- Chilled foods are very convenient to use.
- Chilled foods can be much more expensive than fresh foods, as the suppliers or producers have done much of the preparation. The costs of packaging can also push up the price.

Frozen foods

Frozen food may be stored for some months. The lower the temperature, the longer the storage time, although there may be some loss of quality. Almost all foods, both cooked and raw, may be frozen.

- There is a very wide range of frozen food to buy. It is available all through the year – there are no seasons.
- Examples of frozen foods include meat, fish, vegetables, fruit, bread, cakes, pastries and puddings, as well as complete meals.
- The quality of frozen food can be very good.
- The nutritional value of some frozen foods such as vegetables is as good if not better than their fresh equivalent.
- Frozen foods can be expensive to buy, as preparation and packaging costs are included in the price. However, as the foods are ready prepared, there is no wastage.

How often do you buy pre-cooked foods?

Pre-cooked foods

Some foods have been cooked by the producer or supplier so that they are ready to serve and eat, and require little or no further preparation by the caterer.

- Examples of pre-cooked foods include delicatessen meats such as salami, roast beef, meat pies, pasties, samosas, whole roast chickens, poached fish such as salmon, patés and salads.
- These foods can be expensive to buy as all the preparation and cooking has already been done by the producer.

Activity: What is your preference?

What kind of food do you prefer eat: fresh, frozen, chilled or ready prepared? Why is this?

In developing menus and preparing dishes, you should attempt to produce balanced meals with healthy ingredients.

Key features of healthy foods

There is a lot of interest today in having a healthy lifestyle. Eating foods which are considered to be healthy can contribute to people's healthy lifestyles and therefore better health. From a food perspective, good health generally involves a diet based on low-fat grain products, legumes (pulses, such as beans, peas and lentils), fruit and vegetables, with moderate amounts of lean meat and dairy products.

Healthy foods are those that are:

- low in saturated fat
- low in refined sugar
- low in salt
- high in fibre or roughage
- generally fresh and not in a convenience form
- without preservatives, artificial colourings and flavourings or other chemical additives.

However, although people should pay attention to the nutritional content of the food that they eat, it tends to be the quantity of food consumed that causes problems. Over-eating combined with an unhealthy lifestyle, which includes a lack of exercise, contributes to obesity and other potential health problems. Eating less fat, eating fish two or three times a week, and eating fresh fruit and vegetables each day are the main recommendations for good health.

Look back at the tables in Unit 6 on the nutrients in food (page 154) and the five food groups (page 155). Healthier foods are those that, when taken in combination, provide the balance of nutrients that people need.

Providing healthy eating options

When chefs are planning and designing menus, they must make sure that some of the dishes they provide comply with the guidelines for healthy eating. On menus, these dishes are usually highlighted by a special symbol or a different style of writing, so customers can quickly identify them. It is also usual to state why the dish is part of a healthy option, for example, by stating the number of calories per portion or by saying that it is a low-fat or low-sugar option. These dishes can be very popular.

It is important to remember that many customers cannot eat a 'normal' diet, as they may be suffering from medical problems such as diabetes or high blood pressure which will require them to avoid certain foods. Alternatively, they may simply wish to lose weight and will be looking for healthier options.

Keeping hot food correctly

In some catering operations, hot dishes are prepared in advance so that they are ready to serve to diners as they arrive. These meals must be kept hot so that there is no possibility of any bacterial growth occuring between the food being cooked and it being served to customers. It is a legal requirement to keep hot food that is going to be served to customers at 63°C or above to stop bacterial growth.

Planning and working methods

Cooking is a highly organised activity. Good forward planning is the key to success. When starting to cook a meal, you will need to think about:

- the number of people that are being catered for
- the budget available
- the dishes to be cooked
- how the food is going to be purchased
- who is going to do the cooking
- whether there is enough correct equipment to cook and serve the food
- the time the meal is needed.

Timing

Being able to plan the times of your practical work is important, as the cooking of food needs to be sequenced with the time that it is to be served. It takes practice to get timing right, but it is always better to have dishes ready slightly before they are needed rather than too late. Extra time can always be given to presentation if the food is early.

How can you make your working environment as safe as possible?

Working methods

Being able to plan your work will help you to be efficient and to manage your time effectively. People working in kitchens need to work safely as well as efficiently. Kitchens are dangerous places where accidents can happen with misuse of tools and equipment.

It is important to be well organised and to pay attention to hygiene, health and safety.

- Work surfaces should be clear of unnecessary equipment.
- Store food away correctly and always off the floor.
- Wash equipment and tools, and put them away immediately after use.
- Be aware of others working around you.
- Understand emergency procedures.

Quality

There are several factors that can be used to judge the quality of a dish. These include its appearance and colour, its texture and taste, and the portion size.

- **Appearance** – does the dish look clean, fresh, appetising and appealing or tired and stale? Has the dish been prepared with care or just thrown together?
- **Colour** – overcooking damages the colour of food. The food looks washed out or even burnt. Undercooked food can look bland and unappetising, and it can be unsafe to eat. Gauging the colour of food is part of the skill of a chef.
- **Texture** – overcooking food affects its texture. Some foods, like meat, become tough; others, such as pasta and vegetables, become sloppy and slimy. Undercooking also affects the texture of food, leaving many dishes too hard to eat and unpalatable. Generally, the more food is cooked or kept hot, the more moisture is lost. Dried-up foods have little appeal.
- **Taste** – customers like tasty food that is well seasoned. However, if a dish has too many strong flavours, people may find it difficult to eat as it can be confusing on the palate. A well-balanced dish should use the minimum number of ingredients to achieve the required results. Do not forget that many customers will alter the seasoning by adding extra salt and pepper at the table.
- **Portion size** – getting the portion size right is a skilful task. If the portions are too small, customers will think that they are getting poor value for money and they could still be hungry at the end of the meal. These customers may not return. If the portions are too large, there will be 'plate waste' – that is, many customers will leave some of the food. This means that food is thrown out and the caterer is wasting money on food that is not eaten.

To maintain quality, follow recipes carefully, use a time plan and give thought to the presentation of the food on the plate. We will consider dish presentation later in this unit (see pages 260–64).

Activity: Individual taste

Do you think customers should add extra seasoning to meals? This might spoil the food. Shouldn't chefs make the dishes just right to eat from a taste perspective? Discuss this with your group.

Think of a meal you have eaten that you did not enjoy. Why was this? How could the quality of this meal have been improved?

Getting feedback

You need to be able to review your food preparation and cooking critically, and to come up with suggestions on how you could improve the quality of your work in the future. This will help to improve standards and, of course, it will be appreciated by your customers.

When cooking food for other people, you should seek their views on how it looks and tastes. This is called customer feedback, and successful companies take this feedback very seriously. A good rule for business success is to give customers what they want, not what you *think* they want.

Customers can help with quality control, and they can have ideas on how a dish or meal can be improved. Listen to customers and watch what they leave on their plates. They have a different perspective to chefs and can provide helpful criticism, such as:

- there was too much food, and they could not eat it all
- there was not enough to eat and they are still hungry
- the food was cold
- there was too much seasoning.

Feedback can be obtained in several ways. People working in catering often have face-to-face contact with customers. Simply asking guests if they are enjoying the food gives instant feedback. More formal and structured information can be obtained by using printed questionnaires or comment cards. Some businesses hire trained staff, possibly from a market research organisation, to formally interview some customers. If you are cooking for your tutor or other people you know, seek their feedback on the dishes you have prepared.

Why is it a good idea to ask for customer feedback?

Assessment activity 2

Unit 8 **P6 P7 P8 P9 P10** · BTEC

The chef at the Anchor wants to make some big changes to the menu at the bistro. She wants to improve the quality of the food and would like the bistro to be winning awards for the quality of its food in the next two years. She also wants to serve food that reflects current trends; the menu at the moment is a bit old fashioned.

1 Identify six dishes that could go on the new menu. Choose two starters and four main courses. These dishes should each have a different main food item. Identify the appropriate cooking methods that should be used for each dish. **P6 P7**

2 Write a brief report for the chef on healthy food. This should set out the key features of healthier foods. You should also describe why it is important that the bistro provides healthy eating options on its menu. **P8 P9**

3 Describe the importance of storing and holding any cooked food correctly before it is served to customers. **P10**

Grading tips

P6 You will need to submit your menu ideas in writing. One way of doing this would be to produce recipe cards. Your dishes should use several different methods of cooking.

P7 You need to set out the methods you will use to cook each dish. These could be presented in the form of a table, as this is a good way of giving a considerable amount of information in a clear manner.

P10 You must identify the legal minimum temperatures at which cooked food must be stored, as well as the risks that occur when cooked food is not stored correctly.

 PLTS

You will be developing skills as an **independent enquirer** and **creative thinker** when designing your dishes.

 Functional skills

You will develop your **English** skills when you write your report. If you complete your report on a computer, you will develop your **ICT** skills.

8.3 Know the basic principles of finishing food

An important part of cooking is the presentation of the meal on the plate. We are now going to look at how to present dishes professionally, as well as how to cost and price dishes, another key task for chefs working in catering businesses. So, this section covers:

- presentation of dishes
- calculating costs
- setting prices.

Presentation of dishes

Good presentation of food is an important part of the meal experience. Customers 'eat with their eyes'. If the food looks unattractive on the plate, customers will quickly turn off and begin to look for faults in the catering.

Presentation of food is an art. The best chefs and caterers show individuality, flair and imagination in the presentation of their food, and display creative talent.

Here are some basic rules that you should follow to achieve good presentation.

- All food must look clean and fresh.
- The serving dishes, plates and serving equipment must complement the food. They should be the right size and shape.
- All food must be served at the right temperature. Hot food must be served hot, that is above 63°C (145°F). Cold food must be served cold – below 8°C (46°F).

Why is good presentation so important?

Equipment

Food should be very attractively presented on plates by the kitchen staff. This applies to both silver and plate service. However, a plate service allows chefs to organise complex garnishes and layouts on the plates in the kitchen before they are in front of customers at the table. Some restaurants combine silver and plate service to achieve good presentation. They organise the main part of the dish on the plate in the kitchen so that they can produce a high quality presentation, and then waiting staff add the vegetables or other side dishes at the table from serving dishes.

Plates come in many interesting shapes, designs, sizes, patterns and colours. A caterer has a huge choice. They range from plain white to handmade bone china with complex gold-leaf designs. Highly colourful plates can distract from rather than complement the food that is being served, and plain white china is considered a very good background for most foods. The plates should reflect the style and quality of the food, as well as the character of the establishment.

Ovenproof dishes enable food to be cooked in the container in which it is served to customers. Indeed, customers might even eat their meals from these dishes. Not only does this save washing up, but these dishes keep the food hot and make it easier for kitchen staff to achieve good portion control as one dish is the size of a portion. The use of individual ovenproof dishes also enables quick service to be achieved, as the food does not need to be portioned by serving staff.

The choice of serving dishes also can add to customer satisfaction and to their appreciation of meals. When choosing what dishes to use, take into account the quality, shape and size of the equipment. Some dishes come with lids that will help to keep food hot. This is useful when customers sit some way from the kitchen, such as on an outside terrace or patio.

Activity: Choosing the right equipment

Obtain some catalogues or brochures from suppliers of china, crockery and restaurant serving equipment. Choose some suitable plates and serving dishes for a bistro such as the Anchor. Why did you make your choices?

Placing food attractively

The appeal of cooked food can be lost when it is not attractively placed on plates and in serving containers. The shape, size and quantity of the meal will determine how food is arranged. Plates must be the right size. A plate should hold the meal well within the rim, otherwise the dish will look cramped and carelessly prepared, and food could spill on to tablecloths and clothing.

Garnishes

Garnishes are used to make the finished dish appear more appetising. They must be edible and should contribute to the food or dish by adding form, colour and texture. They should complement the food and lift the presentation but not distract from the main part of the dish.

Most garnishes are made of fresh fruit and vegetables. The range and variety are endless. Some examples of garnishes include:

- lemon wedges, usually served with fish
- oranges, lemons and limes sliced with the skin scored to make a cartwheel effect
- slices of scored cucumber cut into strips
- gherkins and olives cut into attractive shapes
- parsley in small 'picks' or finely chopped
- radishes cut into roses
- celery and spring onion twirls.

How can you use garnishes to improve the appearance of dishes?

Finishing dishes for service

To finish a dish for service, chefs check the temperature, consistency, portion size and taste of the dishes, and make sure that any garnish or decoration has been added. They do this before dishes leave the hotplate or service area. Accompaniments such as sauces will also be checked to ensure that the correct ones are served with the dish.

The aim of finishing dishes is to ensure that customers get the food in the best possible condition and that dishes match menu descriptions. In other words, finishing is a form of quality control done by the kitchen staff. Customers will be satisfied if dishes are finished properly.

Safety and hygiene

A final consideration in presentation and bringing the finished meals to customers is safety and hygiene.

To prevent accidents, kitchen staff should not place too much food on serving trays or plates. This is especially important if the dish comes with gravy or sauces that can easily run off the plate. By not overloading plates and serving dishes, you can avoid situations in which food gets spilt on to the clothes of serving staff or customers.

If serving dishes are very hot, service cloths must be used to prevent waiting staff burning their hands. It is good practice to warn colleagues and customers that dishes are very hot before they touch them.

Chefs and service staff must ensure that all service equipment is completely clean. All plates and dishes should be properly washed so that they are free from food from previous use.

Assessment activity 3

Unit 8 **P11** **P12** **P13** BTEC

The Anchor, like all hospitality businesses, needs to make a profit. Good profits will follow if the bistro serves food that is imaginatively cooked, attractively presented and well served.

Write some guidelines for a new commis chef who is due to start in the kitchen, setting out the basic principles of presentation. Your guidelines should include notes on the importance of:

- finishing dishes for service and an outline of how dishes should be presented **P11**
- using the appropriate garnishes agreed by the chef and the kitchen team **P12**
- checking that dishes meet requirements and a description of how each dish should be checked for colour, consistency and flavour. **P13**

Grading tips

P11 Make sure you include factors such as meeting timescales for serving customers and using the correct serving dishes.

P12 You will need to consider factors such as customer satisfaction and the improvement to eating quality.

P13 It will be necessary to suggest ways of checking for colour, texture, taste and flavour, and seasoning.

PLTS

You will develop your skills as a **creative thinker** when writing your guidelines for a new commis chef, and as a **reflective learner** when identifying how dishes should be presented.

Functional skills

Writing the guidelines will develop your **English** skills.

Assessment activity 4

Unit 8 **M2** **D2** BTEC

This is a practical activity in which you will demonstrate your skills in preparing, cooking and presenting food.

1 You will need to prepare and cook some dishes on at least three occasions. You could cook the dishes that you have suggested in Assessment activity 2 for the new menu at the Anchor. Cook at least three of the dishes and present them as they should be served in the bistro. **M2**

2 When you have cooked these three dishes, review your work. How could you improve on the quality of the dishes or your own performance next time you are in the kitchen? You should reflect on the dishes that you have cooked and presented, and make recommendations as to how they could be improved from a quality perspective. **D2**

Grading tips

M2 Photographs are a good way of providing evidence for your practical cookery work. You should label each photo with the unit number, what you have photographed and your name and centre number.

D2 Your evidence here could be in the form of a written review that first sets out how you prepared, cooked and presented your chosen dishes. Then you should reflect on the final results and make recommendations on how you could improve the quality of the finished dishes if you cooked them again. You could ask your tutor and other members of your group to take part in a taste panel. Get them to complete a comment card that identifies their views on the taste, texture and appearance of the dishes you have cooked.

PLTS

You will need to be a **self-manager** when planning and organising your practical cookery work and when working in the kitchen to produce your dishes. You will be a **reflective learner** when reflecting on how your dishes were cooked and making recommendations for improvements to the preparation, cooking and presentation of dishes.

Functional skills

You will develop your **English** skills as you complete your review.

Calculating costs

An essential part of a chef's role is to monitor the costs of the products and raw materials that are purchased by a catering business to produce meals for its customers. The profitability of a business depends in part on good purchasing decisions, and that requires a good knowledge of the cost of basic ingredients. The price of many food items can fluctuate considerably. This means that the prices can go up or down quite sharply, often on a daily or weekly basis or according to the season of year or factors that may affect food production such as unusual weather conditions. These fluctuations need to be taken into consideration when planning menus or setting the prices to charge customers.

Activity: Buying decisions

Do you buy things just because they are very cheap or on special offer? If so, do you always need them? In groups, discuss the factors that may influence the purchasing decisions of a catering business.

Ingredients are the foods that go into dishes. Prices can change on a daily or weekly basis, particularly for fresh foods such as fruit, vegetables, fish and meat. Chefs need to check prices regularly. Price increases will need to be taken into account in menu planning and in the prices that get charged to customers to ensure that a catering business can meet its profit targets. Note that just as the price of basic foods can go down as well as up, a catering business can also bring down the prices of its dishes to try to attract more customers.

Portions

A portion or serving is the amount of food that a customer will be given when ordering a standard meal. For example:

- desserts such as apple pie or gateau will be served by the slice
- side orders such as fried chips might be served by volume
- a main ingredient such as steak might be served by the weight of the raw steak before grilling.

Therefore, when calculating the cost of a portion, it is necessary to know both the cost of the ingredients of that meal and the size of a portion or serving.

In practice, it is not always easy to serve portions that are exactly the same size. However, it is important to realise the implications of being too generous or too mean when serving a portion. One of the dishes on the menu at the Anchor is tuna fish pizza. A recipe for this dish is given in the next section. The bistro charges £5.50 a portion for this dish. The chefs make up the pizzas in batches that contain ten portions. This means that the sales return from one batch should be £55 as it has ten servings. However, if the kitchen staff give servings that are too generous, only nine portions might be obtained from one batch and the bistro will lose £5.50 in income. This is a common problem in catering.

On the other hand, however, it can upset customers if a restaurant serves too small a portion. Customers may leave still feeling hungry and they are unlikely to think that they have had good value for money. They may not return. Remember, however, that not everybody has the same size appetite. Judging how much to serve each customer comes with experience.

Recipes

A recipe is a set of instructions for making a food dish. It lists the weights or amounts of all the ingredients needed. We have already shown one recipe in this unit, for tomato soup with crispy croutons (see page 247), and the case study below shows the recipe for tuna fish pizza, one of the dishes served at the Anchor.

Case study: Tuna fish pizza

This is a recipe for tuna fish pizza. It is for four portions or servings.

Ingredients for the plain pizza dough
Plain white flour, 200 g
Salt, pinch
Fresh yeast, 10 g
Water or milk at room temperature, 140 ml
Olive oil, 15 ml

Ingredients for the standard topping
Olive oil, 10 ml
Chopped onion, 25 g
Crushed garlic, 1 medium clove
Oregano, pinch
Basil, pinch
Chopped tomatoes, 150 g
Tomato purée, 5 g

Extra ingredients for the tuna fish topping
Tinned tuna fish, 100 g
Sliced mozzarella cheese, 50 g
Stoned and halved black olives, 50 g

Method
Mix together the flour and salt. Break down the yeast with some of the liquid, and add it to the flour. Then add the remaining liquid and oil, and mix to form a smooth, pliable dough.

Cover the dough with a clean tea towel and leave to rest at room temperature for 15 minutes. Then divide into two pieces and mould into two balls.

Roll out the balls of dough into thin rounds. Place on lightly greased baking trays.

Add the prepared toppings (see below), leaving a small, clear border around the edge of the pizza. Allow to stand (dry prove) for 30–40 minutes.

Bake at 225°C or gas mark 7 for about 15–20 minutes until cooked.

Preparing the basic topping
Sweat the onions and garlic in the oil until soft. Add the oregano and basil, and continue cooking for 2 minutes. Add the tomatoes and tomato purée, and slowly simmer to make a thick sauce. Check seasoning and place on top of pizza bases.

Preparing the tuna fish topping
Flake the tuna fish and spread over the tomato topping. Add the cheese and olives evenly over the topping.

Recipes should be followed quite closely. However, flair and imagination play an important part in catering, and so it is quite common for chefs to make variations to basic recipes. From a business point of view, these variations should not change the basic costs of a dish or the planned profit it should generate. Most outlets want their dishes to taste and look the same every time they are produced. Regular customers may have a favourite dish, and they will want it always to taste the same.

Standard recipes are used to help manage food production by stating:

- the name and quantity of all ingredients
- the method of production and service instructions
- the expected yield (how many servings).

This allows a restaurant to work out the ingredients needed for different numbers of portions. For example, Table 7 shows the ingredients needed for making 4, 10 and 25 portions of tuna fish pizza respectively. Note that amounts given for the ingredients in a recipe are an approximation only, so it is acceptable to round up or round down a little when multiplying up to get the required ingredients for making a larger number of portions.

	4 portions	10 portions	25 portions
Plain pizza dough			
Plain white flour	200 g	500 g	1250 g
Salt	1 pinch	$\frac{1}{2}$ tsp	1 tsp
Fresh yeast	10 g	25 g	65 g
Water or milk	140 ml	350 ml	875 ml
Olive oil	15 ml	37.5 ml	95 ml
Standard topping			
Olive oil	10 ml	25 ml	65 ml
Chopped onion	25 g	65 g	155 g
Crushed garlic	1 clove	2 cloves	6 cloves
Oregano	1 pinch	$\frac{1}{2}$ tsp	1 tsp
Basil	1 pinch	$\frac{1}{2}$ tsp	1 tsp
Chopped tomatoes	150 g	375 g	950 g
Tomato purée	5 g	12 g	30 g
Tuna fish topping			
Tinned tuna fish	100 g	250 g	650 g
Sliced mozzarella cheese	50 g	125 g	300 g
Stoned and halved black olives	50 g	125 g	300 g

Table 7: Ingredients for tuna fish pizza

Costs of meals

Once the ingredients of a dish are known, the basic production (or food) costs for the dish can be calculated. This is done by multiplying the unit price of each ingredient by the amount of that ingredient that needs to be used in making the dish. For example, if butter costs 90 p per 100 g and the dish requires 200 g of butter, then the cost of the butter in the dish would be £1.80 (2 x £0.90).

Chefs use a dish-costing sheet to help calculate the costs of each portion or batch of a particular dish. (A batch may contain several portions.) To do this, they need to know the price that their outlets get charged for ingredients. Good sources of information on food prices for caterers include trade journals, magazines, suppliers' price lists and catalogues. Regular checks need to be made on costs of ingredients by reviewing invoices and price lists from suppliers.

Table 8 shows a dish-costing sheet for tuna fish pizza. The costs reflect the prices for the ingredients in November 2010. It has been assumed that water rather than milk will be used in making the pizza dough.

	4 portions	Cost
Plain pizza dough		
Plain white flour	200 g	13 p
Salt	1 pinch	1 p
Fresh yeast	10 g	21 p
Water	140 ml	–
Olive oil	15 ml	7 p
Standard topping		
Olive oil	10 ml	5 p
Chopped onion	25 g	4 p
Crushed garlic	1 clove	5 p
Oregano	1 pinch	0.5 p
Basil	1 pinch	0.5 p
Chopped tomatoes	150 g	92 p
Tomato puree	5 g	3 p
Tuna fish topping		
Tinned tuna fish	100 g	72 p
Sliced mozzarella cheese	50 g	40 p
Stoned and halved black olives	50 g	40 p
	Total	**£3.04**

Table 8: Dish-costing sheet

Activity: Food costs for a tuna fish pizza

Use the dish costing table, to work out the cost of the ingredients of one portion of tuna fish pizza. What is a cost of a portion of standard pizza – that is a pizza without the special tuna fish topping?.

Any catering business must be able to calculate what it costs to produce meals for its customers. Dish costing provides a way of calculating the costs of the food, and this can be used to help set the prices charged to customers. However, food is only one of the costs incurred in running a catering business. A business needs to take into account its full production costs, including:

- food – all food purchases, including any food that is not used but has to be thrown away
- labour – wages, holiday pay, overtime and pension contributions for all staff
- overheads – gas, water, electricity, rent, rates, advertising, insurance and telephone charges.

This information will be used to set the prices for an outlet's standard menus, as well as to cost and price any specials or one-off functions.

The menu is made up of many dishes set out in the order in which food is eaten – beginning with starters and ending with puddings. Each dish will need to be individually costed and priced. With some set menus, customers can eat a complete meal of several courses for one price. Here, expensive dishes need to be balanced with more economical ones. This gives a balance so that customers are offered a good choice but the business can still make a profit.

Functions such as weddings have special menus. These will be designed and costed in advance so that some indicative prices can be given to any customers making enquiries. They are similar to set menus, with customers charged an inclusive price per guest for the meal. The type and time of the function and the number of courses that are to be served will influence the food on the menu and the price charged per guest.

What factors influence the cost of special menus for functions?

Setting prices

The price charged for dishes has to be fixed at a level that will:

- make a profit
- cover all the costs
- be acceptable to customers.

If there are several similar outlets in the same location, consideration needs to be given to the prices being charged by competitors. If one establishment charges more for the same dishes or the same type of food, it may lose out to its competitors as many customers compare prices before they make a choice of where to eat. However, it would be unwise to undercut rivals by too much over a long period as this may cut into **profits** and even result in the outlet making a loss.

Gross profit

Gross profit is the money left after the production costs are taken away from the revenue generated by a business activity. It is sometimes known as kitchen profit in the catering business. Gross profit is usually expressed as a percentage of **sales**, and this is sometimes known as the gross profit margin. Many hospitality businesses would look to make a 60 per cent gross profit on overall food and drink sales, with some items making a considerably higher gross profit. Chefs are often given gross profit targets to make each month.

Profit margins

A business will determine how much gross profit it needs to make each month to pay all its bills (including staff wages) and to still have money left over (its final profit). Not all dishes make the same level of gross profit. Some items can be sold at a high gross profit. Soup is a good example, as it is a tasty and popular dish that can be made for quite a low cost. Other items may only make a small contribution to gross profit. Generally, a business will set a target for the gross profit (or the gross profit margin) it wants to make each month.

Let's see how a business might establish a price for a dish. We will use tuna fish pizza as an example. Once the cost of all ingredients has been identified, then the required gross profit level can be added and the selling price calculated.

According to the dish-costing sheet on page 268, the food cost of four portions of tuna fish pizza is £3.04. Suppose the bistro wants a gross profit margin of 40 per cent. The selling price can be calculated using the formula:

$$\text{selling price} = \frac{\text{food cost}}{\text{gross profit margin}} \times 100$$

So, in this case:

$$\text{selling price} = \frac{3.04}{40} \times 100 = £7.60$$

However, we must make two adjustments. First, we must find the price for one portion. The price of £7.60 is for four portions, so we must divide this by four to find the cost of one portion: this is £1.90.

Second, we must add VAT. Food sold in restaurants for consumption on the premises attracts VAT. The VAT rate (as at 4 January 2011) is 20%, so for the pizza the VAT amount is 38p ($1.9 \times 20\% = 0.38$). We can calculate the final price of a portion of tuna fish pizza as follows:

price including VAT = 1.9 + 0.38 = 2.28

So, the price on the menu should be £2.28.

This basic method can be used to work out any selling price.

Kitchen percentage

The kitchen percentage is another figure used in catering businesses to help manage costs. It expresses the food cost as a percentage of the menu price. It can be calculated using the formula:

$$\text{kitchen percentage} = \frac{\text{food cost}}{\text{menu price}} \times 100$$

So, for a portion of tuna fish pizza:

$$\text{kitchen percentage} = \frac{0.76}{2.28} \times 100 = 33.3\%$$

Fixing the price of menu items is a very important task. If prices are set too high, customers may go elsewhere. If prices are set too low, they may not cover the costs of production. Note that customers can also be put off if the prices are too low, because they might think that the food or the cooking is of poor quality.

Assessment activity 5
Unit 8 **M3** **BTEC**

The Anchor needs to cost all its dishes on the new menu accurately to ensure that it achieves the desired profit margins.

Cost three dishes on the new menu and calculate the menu prices for one portion of each dish. Use three of the dishes you selected for the new menu as part of Assessment activity 2.

You will need to find detailed recipes for these three dishes. Scale each recipe to provide enough portions for one person, for 16 people and for 36 people. Research the prices of the ingredients, so that you can find the food cost for a portion of each dish.

Calculate the menu prices for one portion of each dish. Produce three prices using gross profit margins

of 45 per cent, 60 per cent and 75 per cent. Use your calculations to justify the price. **M3**

Grading tip

 Use costing sheets to work out the food costs, and submit your costing sheets as part of your evidence. You will also need to provide a written statement to explain what you have done. For example, explain how you got prices for each ingredient in your dishes and set out clearly how you calculated the final menu price for each dish.

 PLTS

When costing and calculating selling prices for the dishes you have chosen, you will be demonstrating skills as an **independent enquirer**.

 Functional skills

You will use your **maths** skills when costing dishes and calculating selling prices.

8.4 Know how to clear down work areas and equipment and store food at end of production

At the end of any sitting or cooking session, the kitchen staff need to clear up properly. This section covers:

- clearing down work areas
- correct handling of food waste.

Clearing down work areas

It is really important to clear down preparation, cooking and service areas at the end of a production session. This helps to prevent the spread of bacteria as well as limiting the potential for cross-contamination. This occurs when bacteria are spread between food, preparation surfaces and kitchen equipment. Cross-contamination is one of the most common causes of food poisoning. By clearing down effectively, you also help to make the kitchen and ancillary areas a pleasant environment for you or your colleagues when you start the next shift.

All kitchen tables and ancillary preparation areas should be wiped down with clean cloths and sanitiser. Ensure that no waste food remains on any surface.

Cutlery must be put away. It should be dry and free from waste food. Ensure that items are stored in the correct manner. Implements with sharp ends and blades, such as knives and forks, should be stored so that they do not cause someone an injury when they open the cutlery drawer. It is good practice to polish the cutlery with a clean cloth when putting it away so that there are no nasty smears.

Crockery can be quite heavy to handle, so it must not be stacked up too high on shelves and in cupboards. Check for any chips and cracks in crockery, which can hold bacteria and cause food poisoning. Items that are damaged like this must not be used again.

Glasses can be very easily damaged when they are being washed up and put away. It is important to check that they are not chipped or cracked, as these can cause nasty accidents when they are next used. Glasses are normally stored in racks, where they can hang up, or placed upside down on shelves near to the service points.

It is important to work as a team when clearing down work areas at the end of a busy shift. If you have finished your tasks, you should see if others need your help. It is also essential that all team members work safely to prevent accidents. Accidents can occur, especially when equipment and furniture are being moved or rearranged at the end of a service or a special function.

Tips for effective clearing down

- Use hot water with an approved detergent for cleaning.

- Ensure that any cleaning cloths are fit for purpose. They must be clean and smell fresh. They should not be soiled with any old food.

- Use different cloths for each area to reduce the risk of cross-contamination by germs and bacteria. It is a good idea to have separate cloths for raw food areas and for cooked food areas. These can be different colours to ensure staff use the correct ones.

- One of the most hygienic ways of cleaning a food area is to use disposable kitchen towels. They must be thrown away when dirty.

- All equipment that has been used must be thoroughly cleaned before being stored. When cleaning and storing kitchen equipment, always follow the manufacturers' instructions. Never put dirty equipment back into storage.

- Use an approved sanitiser or disinfectant on work surfaces and equipment to help reduce any bacteria that may be present.

- Make sure that the cleaning equipment including any cloths are cleaned and sanitised ready for use next time.

- Make sure that you wash and dry your hands at the end of the session.

Why is it so important to leave everything clean and tidy at the end of a shift?

Leftover food and ingredients

It can be very dangerous to keep leftovers for use another time unless special care and attention is paid to what food is kept and how it is stored. Anything that is to be kept at the end of the cooking or production period must be correctly stored to prevent the food going off.

Any food kept at the end of a session must be wrapped correctly by placing it in foil, cling film or food containers with tight-fitting lids. This not only protects the food from being contaminated, it also helps to stop strong smells from items such as onions, fresh fish or cheese from affecting other foods and making the fridge or freezer smell bad. When food is placed in storage for re-use, it must be clearly labelled. The label should state with what the food is, the date it went into storage and the use-by date.

Deciding what food or ingredients can be kept and re-used is a skilled job. It is usually done by the supervisor, head chef or kitchen managers. Chefs should always be asked what could be kept. This will help reduce the risk of cross-contamination and food poisoning. Some foods, such as raw and cooked shellfish and cooked rice, must not be kept because they go off very quickly and will be dangerous to eat.

Any foods that are to be kept for re-use must be stored in accordance with any legal requirements. These are set out in the food hygiene regulations. Chefs must know and comply with these regulations.

Activity: Keeping food for re-use

Investigate two hospitality businesses that serve food. Find out what foods they keep to re-use the next day and what foods they must throw away. How do they throw food away? What containers do they use to keep food waste and where are they located?

Then obtain a copy of the current food hygiene regulations. Look up the requirements for storing leftovers and food for re-use. Make some notes on these requirements.

Correct handling of food waste

Good chefs work in a clean and tidy manner, and they do not allow food waste to build up where they are working. It is impossible to keep untidy areas clean and free from harmful bacteria.

Food waste, also known as kitchen waste, is food that is going to be thrown out rather than eaten or kept for re-use. Food waste includes:

- vegetable trimmings and peelings
- plate scrapings

- spoiled food, including any that has been badly handled, stored or cooked and would be unpleasant or even dangerous to eat

- food that has gone past its use-by date and may be unsafe to eat.

All food waste must be placed in containers with lids. Foot-operated bins are best, as food can be thrown away without having to touch the lid of the bin. This reduces the risk of hands being contaminated by bacteria in the waste or on the lid. These containers must be made from materials that can be easily cleaned and disinfected. Metal is an ideal material. These bins must not be allowed to get too full. They should be emptied on a regular basis, otherwise the waste food may attract pests and vermin. Harmful bacteria can also start to build up.

Kitchen staff must remove food waste and any other rubbish such as packaging from rooms where food is prepared and cooked as quickly as possible.

If you have a chance to visit a restaurant kitchen as part of your studies, make sure you look at their waste disposal systems.

There is a legal requirement to dispose of all waste in a hygienic and environmentally friendly way. Outside the kitchen, there must be an area where food bins can be emptied and the waste can be left for collection by the local council or an approved contractor. Items such as vegetable peelings and fruit skins can be used for composting. However, cooked food should not be put in composters as this can attract vermin such as birds, mice and rats.

Activity: Disposing of food waste

Investigate how your school or college disposes of its food waste. What legal requirements must be followed?

When you visit a hotel or restaurant as part of your studies, ask how the establishment disposes of its kitchen waste.

Assessment activity 6

There has been an inspection of the kitchen at the Anchor by an environmental health officer from the local council. Although most things were judged good and in compliance with regulations, the inspector highlighted two issues that need to be addressed quickly before they become major problems.

It is clear that the team of chefs has not been clearing down the kitchen properly at the end of each shift. There are also issues with the way the bistro has been choosing which food to keep for re-use and which needs to be thrown away as it is past its best.

1 Make a list of the cleaning tasks that need to be carried out by the kitchen team at the end of each session. Describe the procedures that they need to follow to ensure that the kitchen is left clean and safe. **P14**

2 List a range of foods that cannot be kept for re-use at the end of a service. What foods would be safe to use again? **P15**

3 Finally, you must demonstrate your practical skills by clearing down a work area in which you have been preparing and cooking food. You must do this effectively and in accordance with food hygiene regulations. **M4**

Grading tips

P14 You could make a list of all the tasks that need to be carried out and then describe what would need to be done to complete these tasks successfully.

P15 It is important to remember that some food does not keep for long periods after it has been cooked. You could also think from a customer's perspective for this outcome. What food would you like to eat the next day?

M4 This could be demonstrated after you have cooked some of your dishes in the kitchen. Your tutor – or a supervisor if you are doing this in the workplace – will produce a witness testimony to confirm that you have completed the clearing down to the required standard.

PLTS

When describing the procedures that the kitchen team have to complete and identifying food for re-use, you will demonstrate skills as an **independent enquirer**. You will have to show skills as a **self-manager** when completing the clearing down of a work area to comply with food hygiene regulations.

Functional skills

You will be developing your **English** skills when you are listing the foods that cannot be stored and compiling the list of cleaning tasks.

James Holden
Restaurant head chef

James has been the head chef at the Lobster Pot restaurant for three years now. The Lobster Pot is a very good quality 80 cover restaurant in the south-west of England, which is popular both with local clientele and with tourists. The kitchen has just been refurbished, and the restaurant owners have invested heavily in an outside terrace so that customers can make the most of the good weather.

Because of the excellent standard of the food and the high quality of the service provided, the restaurant has just been awarded its first Michelin star. The kitchen and restaurant teams now have to maintain their standards and increase turnover to pay for the improvements that have been made to the restaurant. This is an exciting time for the Lobster Pot.

James' role is to manage the kitchen, designing and agreeing the menus with the managers and owners, ordering food commodities, and supervising staff to ensure they maintain appropriate standards of conduct, hygiene and appearance. He manages the quality of dishes being cooked, ensures the kitchen achieves the correct profit levels, and makes sure money is not wasted due to bad management of foodstuffs and commodities. James is also responsible for the selection and training of new staff, which he enjoys.

James likes working at the Lobster Pot but as head chef, he finds himself doing much less cooking than he would like. He has good managerial and financial skills, as well as being able to cook, and he is aiming to buy his own restaurant in about 18 months' time. He hopes that with a smaller restaurant kitchen to manage, he will be able to concentrate on the cooking and his partner will be able to run the front of house side of things and do some of the paperwork.

Think about it!

- **What skills does a good head chef have to have?**

- **If you want to manage your own small hospitality business, what will you have to think about and organise? Draw up a list of everything that needs to be considered.**

- **How can chefs prevent food wastage?**

Just checking

1 List the main reasons for choosing a supplier.

2 Why is food dangerous to eat when it starts to go off?

3 Name the business documents used in the purchasing cycle.

4 List six items of equipment that can help with portion control.

5 List the techniques used in the kitchen for food preparation.

6 What happens when food is overcooked?

7 List the main cooking methods.

8 What is the reason for using seasonings in cooking?

9 List some rules for the good presentation of food.

10 How should chefs clear down their work areas at the end of a shift?

11 How should food waste be stored correctly in a kitchen?

Assignment tips

- Make sure your chef's uniform is always clean and well ironed before you attend a practical cookery class. Do not be late for practical classes; you need to develop and demonstrate kitchen discipline.

- The Internet is a good source for information, but do not cut and paste information direct from this source; your answers must be in your own words. In your written assignment work, check your sentences and spelling and ensure that you answer the question in full.

- Some good preparation for both your written and practical assignments is to read recipe and cookery books. This helps to increase your knowledge of food and gives you ideas for the presentation of dishes. Television cookery programmes can also give you some good ideas for dishes. This will help your practical skills as well as increasing your knowledge of food commodities.

- Another way to expand your knowledge is to visit well-stocked supermarkets and specialist food shops to look at the wide range of food on offer. They sometimes have free publications such as recipe cards, healthy eating guidance and ideas for using new foods such as unusual fruits and vegetables. You might be able to use this information in your assignments.

9 Contemporary world food

Every region of the world has its own style of food. This is partly because of variations in climate, conditions for growing crops, and proximity to the coast for fresh fish. It is also because of cultural factors, such as ways of preserving meats, religious considerations and cooking methods. However, with much greater ease of access to an exciting and vibrant range of foods, it is now possible to create fascinating, flavoursome and enticing dishes from around the world.

This unit will allow you to develop your knowledge and understanding of contemporary world food. You will investigate the origins of some worldwide dishes and will learn about the foods and ingredients that are combined to create these meals. You will also have an opportunity to develop practical cooking skills so that you can prepare and cook some contemporary world food dishes.

As this involves practical work in the kitchen, you must understand the basic requirements for hygienic and safe working within a kitchen environment. You will also learn about some of the specialist kitchen equipment you will need for the dishes you will be preparing and cooking.

Learning outcomes

After completing this unit, you should:

1   Know the equipment, food items and methods used to prepare and cook different contemporary world dishes
2   Know the styles of food and dishes that are prepared and cooked around the world
3   Be able to prepare, cook and present contemporary world dishes
4   Be able to review dishes.

Assessment and grading criteria

This table shows you what you must do in order to achieve a pass, merit or distinction grade, and where you can find activities in this book to help you.

To achieve a pass grade the evidence must show that you are able to:	To achieve a merit grade the evidence must show that, in addition to the pass criteria, you are able to:	To achieve a distinction grade the evidence must show that, in addition to the pass and merit criteria, you are able to:
P1 describe equipment, food items and methods used to prepare and cook different contemporary world dishes **Assessment activity 1, page 288**	**M1** compare equipment, food items and methods used to prepare and cook different contemporary world dishes and styles of food **Assessment activity 1 page 288**	
P2 describe styles of food and dishes that are prepared and cooked around the world **Assessment activity 2 page 293**		
P3 prepare, cook and present contemporary world dishes in a safe and hygienic manner with some tutor support **Assessment activity 3 page 296**	**M2** demonstrate appropriate use of methods in the preparation, cooking and presentation of contemporary world dishes with limited tutor support **Assessment activity 3 page 296**	**D1** demonstrate professional, independent and creative working methods in the preparation, cooking and presentation of contemporary world dishes **Assessment activity 3 page 296**
P4 review dishes you have prepared, cooked and presented **Assessment activity 4 page 300**		**D2** reflect on how the dishes are prepared, cooked and presented and make recommendations for improvement **Assessment activity 4 page 300**

How you will be assessed

You will be assessed by assignments that will be designed and marked by tutors at your centre. The assignments are designed to allow you to show your understanding of the unit learning outcomes. The evidence that you provide for your assignments could be in the form of:

- presentations
- case studies
- practical tasks
- written work.

Ash, 15-year-old catering student

This unit allowed me to try out different styles of cooking from around the world. Many of the ingredients and the equipment were new to me. It was good to be able to try something new each week.

I really enjoyed researching and cooking the dishes. It gave me a really good understanding of how people in other countries cook and the ingredients that they use. I now understand why they use certain cooking methods and equipment, and how this affects the food in each dish.

I also enjoyed tasting the food cooked by other people in the class and letting them taste the food I had prepared. I got some really good feedback on my dishes and I am now much better at reviewing my own cooking so that I know how to make improvements.

Over to you

- What might be challenging about cooking foods from around the world?
- What countries do you most want to learn about?
- Which dishes are you most looking forward to cooking?

9.1 Know the equipment, food items and methods used to prepare and cook different contemporary world dishes

Welcome

What contemporary world dishes do you like?

List foods or meals you enjoy eating that are based on cooking from other countries.

Write down which country you think each dish comes from. What do you like about each dish? Is it the flavours, the texture, the appearance or something else?

In small groups, share your lists and compare your favourites. How many different countries feature in your lists?

Researching foods, dishes and cooking methods from around the world can be fascinating. You can learn about the origins of dishes and the ways in which they are made. To start our investigation, we will consider:

- cooking equipment
- food
- preparation, cooking and food storage methods
- contemporary world dishes.

Cooking equipment

A typical kitchen contains many different items of equipment. This is true for home kitchens and those in commercial operations such as restaurants and cafés. However, standard kitchen equipment can vary quite a lot from country to country to suit the particular cooking methods that are used in each region.

The methods of cooking can vary due to the:

- typical ingredients used
- easiest ways of cooking those ingredients
- types of fuel available
- availability of materials to produce cooking equipment.

Table 1 looks at some of the equipment that can be found in a kitchen. Some items may be familiar to you already and you may have the opportunity to use other items during this unit.

Equipment	Description
Ovens	Ovens heat food through convection.
Steamers	Food is placed above boiling water, which produces steam that cooks the food.
Microwave ovens	Electromagnetic waves produced in the microwave oven cook the food.
Chinese burner wok cookers	Woks are used above heat or a flame. They can be used to cook foods very quickly by stir frying.
Rice cookers	A rice cooker is a contained way of steaming rice.
Bratt pans	Bratt pans are suitable for cooking large volumes of food in a variety of ways. They are perfect for braising, sealing, shallow frying and general cooking.
Flare grills	Flare grills are an arrangement of metal bars or a casting with a heat source placed below.
Salamanders	A salamander is a type of grill commonly used to toast, melt or brown foods.
Bain-marie	A bain-marie is a water bath used to cook foods slowly. It can also be used to keep sauces and food hot.
Griddles	A griddle is usually a flat piece of metal that is heated from below to enable cooking on the surface.
Tandoor ovens	A clay oven which is heated with burning timber or charcoal. Food is placed on long skewers above the heat.
Deep-fat fryers	Deep-fat fryers are filled with oil and foods are placed in the fat.
Hot smoking ovens	Hot smoking ovens cook and flavour foods using burning plant materials as fuel.
Pasta machines	Pasta machines allow cooks to produce flat sheets of pasta which can be shaped or cut to make different types of pasta.
Knives	Knives are sharp cutting implements used for preparation of food.
Chopping boards	Chopping boards are used to prepare and cut foods. Commercial chopping boards are colour co-ordinated to prevent cross-contamination.
Mixers	Mixers are appliances that mix and combine ingredients quickly. They are usually powered by electricity.
Bamboo steamers	Steamers made from bamboo which cook food using the heat from steam.
Blenders	Blenders are electrical appliances that cut food so finely that it becomes almost liquid.
Food processors	Food processors can chop, blend and mix foods. They are electrical appliances.
Moulds	Moulds are used to shape food products into consistent sizes and shapes. They are most commonly used to produce desserts such as jellies.

Table 1: Kitchen equipment

Activity: Specialist food equipment

Can you identify the countries that each of these items of equipment originates from?

- tandoor oven
- wok
- pasta machine
- bain-marie.

Carry out some research to find a dish that could be prepared using each of these items of equipment.

Food

The typical food ingredients and commodities used in cooking vary from country to country. Countries around the world have staple foods which are native to the country and can be grown in abundance. These foods are high in carbohydrate and often starchy. For example, rice is part of many Asian dishes, providing bulk to a meal and energy in the form of carbohydrate. In Africa, and in many other parts of the world where the climate is warmer, maize-based products (including many types of flat breads) are staple foods. Western staple foods are often wheat-based, such as pasta and bread. Potatoes are also important in the Western diet as they are bulky and filling, with a high carbohydrate content.

Do you know the staple foods of different countries and regions of the world?

Protein

Proteins are body-building foods. The main sources of protein are meat, fish, dairy produce and beans. The types of meat available in a country will often depend on the animals native to that country – those which thrive in the country's climate and have available food to eat.

Fish are usually the main protein source for coastal areas or regions around larger lakes. Dairy produce (usually derived from livestock) is also a source of protein, but this is secondary to the meat produced from animals.

Beans, especially soya beans, provide alternative sources of protein and can be used as meat substitutes. There are also dairy substitutes, such as soya milk. Many people around the world are vegetarians, either as a result of their beliefs or because there is a local lack of meat products. Vegetarians can eat many sources of protein, such as bean curds, textured vegetable proteins and tofu.

Carbohydrates

Some carbohydrates, such as cereals, pasta and bread, are rich in complex carbohydrate starches. There are also simple carbohydrates, such as sugar. Carbohydrates provide your body with energy. They are bulky so, as well as providing energy for your body, they can make you feel full after a meal.

Many countries' traditional staple foods accompany other foods to produce a balanced diet. Sources of carbohydrate vary from region to region according to the climate and local growing conditions.

As the world becomes more globalised, it is increasingly easy to obtain a wide range of foods anywhere in the world. With the greater availability of these ingredients, it is much easier to produce different regional dishes.

Activity: Staple foods

Fill in the first column of the table below with examples of staple foods. In the other columns, write down a country that has the food as a staple part of its cuisine and an example of a dish which uses the staple food as an integral ingredient. An example has been provided for you.

Staple food	Country	Dish
Pasta	Italy	Lasagne

Fruits and vegetables

Fruits and vegetables are an important part of a balanced diet, as we discussed in Unit 6. They provide fibre and vitamins, and they can change the flavours, texture, aroma and appearance of dishes. The types of vegetables and fruits produced in an area will be influenced by the climatic (including any seasonal variations) and soil conditions.

The use of vegetables and fruits within the typical dishes of a country used to depend on what was available locally, and how well these foods combined with the staple foods and sources of protein in that country or region. However, this is changing as many more fruits and vegetables are now available in all countries throughout the year. There are two main reasons for this. First, societies have developed ways of controlling climatic and growing conditions, which allows them to extend the growing seasons. Second, there is the infrastructure to transport perishable goods across the world very quickly.

Other commodities

There are many different food commodities that accompany the main sources of protein, staple foods, fruits and vegetables. These include spices and other seasonings, sugars, fats and confectionery products. A huge number of ingredients are now available to cooks and many of these are sourced from around the world.

Preparation, cooking and food storage methods

Many aspects of food preparation, cooking and storage have been covered in Unit 8. Some aspects will vary from country to country, but many are similar.

Preparation

Did you know?

French terms are commonly used to describe styles of presenting food. For instance, a dish served 'au naturel' is natural or pure, unseasoned, and usually cooked as little as possible.

The preparation of foods involves getting food commodities ready to cook or ready to eat if they do not require cooking. Preparation methods include peeling and chopping vegetables and salad produce. Peeling removes the skin or peel, usually to improve the taste, texture or appearance of a food. Chopping involves cutting up foods, either to decrease the cooking time or for presentation reasons. French cuisine has led the way in naming and giving terms for different styles of presentation.

Meat often needs to be prepared before cooking. Cooks may remove the fat or bones from meat and cut it into specific pieces or 'cuts' to improve the cooking and to provide pieces of meat with particular properties (such as specific fat content, texture or taste). African cookery often uses meat on the bone and many traditional dishes use larger pieces of meat. These may be cooked over a direct heat source (such as an open fire) or stewed slowly in a liquid base.

Marinades – flavoured or seasoned liquids used to coat meat – are often used before cooking. These generally add flavour or change the texture of a food. Marinades are often used in Asian and Indian cookery.

Cooking

Cooking methods vary tremendously throughout the world. However, all cooking involves applying heat to food in some form. This changes the properties of the food in different ways: to make it taste better, to make it edible or to make it easier to consume. You can apply heat in various ways, such as dry heat by oven baking or 'wet' heat by steaming. Smoking is a good example of a way in which you can add flavour during cooking: the heat of the smoke cooks the food while giving it a smoked flavour.

The cooking method that is used will depend on the equipment available and the produce that is being cooked. The cooking time and the amount of heat that is applied can also vary, and this changes the properties of the food being cooked. For example, in Chinese cooking, food is often cooked very quickly at a high temperature, usually in a wok, so that it remains firm in texture. Slow cooking and braising produce very tender foods, as heating over a longer period of time breaks foods down and softens them. Traditional French cookery often uses wine as a liquid in which to cook meats slowly, which also has the effect of tenderising the meat. Russian cookery often involves stewing and stove cooking; for example, **borsch** is a traditional Russian dish which is cooked slowly for one to two hours. **Stroganoff**, another traditional Russian dish, is pan cooked on a stove using soured cream.

Key terms

Borsch – a soup made of beetroot or tomato, popular in many Eastern and Central European countries

Stroganoff – a Russian dish of sautéed beef, usually fillet, in a sauce made with soured cream. Can also be made with other meats such as pork or chicken, or with mushroom

Storage

It is very important to store food properly, to work safely in the kitchen and to dispose of all food waste correctly. For more information on storage methods for different types of food, see pages 239–241.

When food is stored, it is essential that products are dated, so that cooks do not use foods that have gone past their use-by dates. If food products remain on the shelves or in storage beyond these dates, they are not safe to consume and must be thrown away. A system of putting dates on food should also be applied to any cooked products that are being kept for re-use. By using 'day dots' or a form for dating items made in the kitchen, staff will always be able to keep track of the dates on which foods were produced.

Stock rotation helps to reduce wastage by ensuring that the products that need to be used first are stored at the front of the storage area. This means that they are selected by chefs and used in the correct order.

The physical storage of large, heavy items needs to be done carefully, as lifting and handling heavy items can cause injury. There is also a risk of heavy items falling and injuring people working nearby. Heavy items should be stored at a low level and smaller objects should be stored at a higher level but not so high that they cannot be easily reached by kitchen staff.

Contemporary world dishes

Contemporary world dishes often provide a twist or variation on traditional dishes. Chefs do this by introducing new elements that alter or enhance the dish to give a more modern outcome. This can be achieved by taking the original recipe and altering ingredients, cooking methods or presentation of the dish. A contemporary feel can be achieved by mixing or combining styles of cooking. Combining styles or varieties of cooking in the same dish is sometimes called fusion cooking.

Globalisation has meant that many chefs have a much greater knowledge of food products, dishes and cooking styles from around the world. The availability of fresh, good quality ingredients allows the production of exciting dishes that are pleasing to all the senses. It has also led to traditional dishes being changed to suit the tastes of the country for which they are being recreated. A prime example of this is British curry dishes, which are often very different to traditional Indian curries. Many curries cooked in Britain are sweeter than those cooked in India and are combined with sauces to a greater degree than in traditional Indian cookery.

Assessment activity 1

Unit 9 **P1 M1**

You are on a work placement in a hotel restaurant. You have been asked by your general manager to prepare a presentation for the chefs and waiting staff about contemporary world cookery. It is hoped that this will encourage the staff to develop new menu ideas.

1 Describe the equipment that would be used to prepare four dishes from around the world. Each of the dishes you choose should be prepared in a different style. For each dish, you must be able to describe the equipment that will be needed, the ingredients and the method of cooking. **P1**

2 Compare the equipment, food items and methods used to prepare and cook these four dishes. This will involve making comparisons of how the food cooks and the effects on the food products. Compare the health aspects of the various cooking methods used, the speed of cooking and the different sensory outcomes of the food. **M1**

Grading tip

P1 You should practise your presentation before delivering it to your tutor. You can just talk or you can produce some slides to support the presentation. However, you should produce notes for your presentation that contain descriptions of the equipment, ingredients and cooking methods for four dishes from different countries around the world. In order to prepare for this task, you could read cookery books, watch television cookery programmes or practise preparing the dishes for yourself.

 PLTS

Researching equipment, food items and methods used to prepare and cook different contemporary world dishes will help you to develop your skills as an **independent enquirer**.

 Functional skills

Researching the different dishes for this activity will allow you to practise your **English** skills in reading and using information from a variety of sources. As you give your presentation to your tutor, you will be using your **English** skills in speaking.

9.2 Know the styles of food and dishes that are prepared and cooked around the world

A cooking style is the method or approach taken to produce a dish. There are many different styles of cooking throughout the world. These vary between countries and there may also be regional differences within countries. For example, consider Chinese cooking. Cantonese cookery is one regional style that uses particular spices and the dishes are often characterised by sweetness. Szechuan cookery is another regional style, which differs greatly from Cantonese cookery; Szechuan food is hot and spicy.

Activity: Where do the dishes come from?

Mark the following dishes on the world map below according to their place of origin. If you do not know where a dish comes from, do some research to find out.

Curry	Szechuan chicken	Fajita
Fondue	Irish stew	Chow mein
Carbonara	Borsch	Paella

289

Case study: Curry

Curry is associated mainly with South Asian cooking, especially Indian cooking. The word 'curry' is derived from the Tamil word *kari,* which translates roughly to gravy or sauce. Curry in all its varieties has become a truly global dish and can be found in most countries around the world in different forms.

The various regions of India have different styles of cooking, and many Indian regional specialities are now common in the UK. Regional dishes can be identified through their names and the cooking styles used. Many Indian restaurants in the UK try to give a brief history of each dish in the menu.

Research some specific curry dishes and try to find the origins of each dish.

Did you know?

Many cookery terms come from French cuisine. For example, if meat or fish is cooked 'en papillote', it is wrapped in parchment paper during cooking so that it is steamed in its own juices. The paper keeps in the moisture of the food, and is usually opened at the table for maximum effect and aroma.

Key terms

Haggis – a traditional Scottish pudding of sheep offal, oatmeal and seasoning, cooked in the casing of a sheep's intestine

Sautéing – cooking food over a high heat in a small amount of oil or clarified butter

Tortilla – a flatbread made from corn or wheat; also refers to a Spanish-style omelette

European cuisine

European cuisine is a collective term for the cookery styles of countries in Europe.

French cuisine is very influential. Many cookery terms and names of equipment come from French cuisine, and these terms are now used in kitchens worldwide. France is a great wine-producing country and wine features in a lot of French cookery. Long, slow cooking is traditional, often with the addition of wine, creating tender dishes full of flavour. Fresh salads use local produce and provide full flavours and vibrant colours. Some traditional dishes include coq au vin, cassoulet, salade Niçoise, ratatouille and quiche Lorraine. French patisserie (pastries and cakes) is well known and the basis is usually Genoese (puff or choux pastry) with rich fillings and soft icings.

Pasta and pizza are dishes that are associated with Italian cookery. Pasta provides carbohydrate in the diet. In Italian cooking, pasta will be accompanied by vegetables and meat, and a variety of sauces. Tomatoes often feature in Italian dishes and sauces, along with olives, garlic and other regional produce. Italian cookery is often wrongly imagined to be based on pasta. In Britain, we eat large versions of these dishes as a main course whereas, in Italy, it is the tradition to serve a small pasta dish as a starter, followed by a meat or fish dish as a main course. Cheeses are often a feature of Italian cookery, most commonly parmesan, mozzarella and ricotta.

England is known for dishes such as roast dinners, and Scotland is known for its **haggis**. Roasting and boiling are traditional ways of cooking in the UK and other countries in northern Europe. However, the UK is a multicultural society and foods from around the world are now commonly used in cooking. More contemporary styles of cooking in the UK use cooking methods and ingredients from around the world.

Southern European cookery uses very fresh ingredients which are cooked quickly by **sautéing** or served fresh in salads. Tapas is a meal served in Spain that consists of a variety of foods often like starters, with small plates of fresh or cooked food. Tapas can be served as a main meal with a larger quantity of dishes. Paella is one of the best known Spanish dishes, the main ingredients being fish and shellfish which are abundant on the Spanish coast; the other ingredients vary from region to region. Paella is traditionally cooked in a two-handled, shallow iron pan from which it takes its name.

Latin American cuisine

Latin American cuisine refers to the foods and cooking styles common to many of the countries and cultures in Latin America. Latin America is a very diverse geographical region, and the cuisines vary from country to country. Foods typical of Latin America are maize-based products, such as **tortillas** and **tamales**, and various **salsas**, **guacamole**, **chimichurri** and **pebre**. Latin American cuisine can be quite spicy and has a distinct association with chillies and hot food. Foods are often cooked by being sautéed or **braised** with aromatic spices. Latin American cuisine is often based on sauces of tomatoes with roasted bell peppers, garlic, onions and herbs.

Mediterranean cuisine

Mediterranean cookery is a healthy cuisine made from local produce. The red meats used in Mediterranean cookery tend to be goat and mutton due to the terrain of the area. These are often tough meats which need to be cooked slowly so they are tender enough to eat. Fish dishes are also common due to the availability of fresh fish from the Mediterranean sea, as well as imported fish. Olive oil is prominent in Mediterranean cookery as olives are produced in large quantities in the region. Garlic and tomatoes are also very commonly associated with Mediterranean cookery. Grilling is a common method of cooking for meats and fish. A Portuguese traditional dish is grilled sardines; sardines are plentiful and easy to catch and the most common method in Portugal is to grill them whole.

African cuisine

Central African cookery is very starchy and spicy. The main crops grown in the region are widely used in cooking, including **plantain**, **cassava**, **okra** and chillis. There are many types of meats available in Central Africa, including chicken and beef, with some rarer alternatives such as antelope and other bush meat. **Ugali** and **fufu** are eaten in Central African cookery.

South African cuisine is traditionally meat-based, as many farmers raise sheep, goats and cattle. South African dishes include **braai**, maize-based breads and milk products. Some of the crops used in South African cookery include leafy greens, cabbage and pumpkin beans. These ingredients often form the basis of meat stews.

What type of cuisine is this?

Key terms

Tamales – a Latin American dish made of a starchy dough called masa, which is steamed or boiled in a leaf wrapper, and can be filled with meat or vegetables

Salsa – a spicy sauce, usually tomato based

Guacamole – a dip made with avocado

Chimichurri – a South American sauce or marinade which consists of parsley, garlic, lemon juice, onion, olive oil, thyme and oregano.

Pebre – a sauce that consists of olive oil, hot chillies, parsley, oregano and wine vinegar.

Braising – a cooking method that involves searing meat at a high temperature and then finishing in a covered pot of liquid.

Plantain – a banana-like fruit that is used for cooking

Cassava – a root vegetable that looks like a sweet potato but has a chalk-white or yellowish flesh

Okra – a long green vegetable, also known as 'Lady's fingers'

Ugali – maize flour ground down and boiled to a porridge or dough.

Fufu – paste made by grinding down starchy edible roots.

Braai – meat barbequed over a flame.

West African foods are similar to those of Central Africa. They are starchy and spicy. Couscous, cassava and yams often feature in West African cookery. Palm oil is often used in cooking that mixes meats and fish. Cooking methods vary between roasting, baking, boiling and frying.

Pacific cuisine

There are many countries in the Pacific region, and many types of cooking based on the wide range of available ingredients and the different culinary influences on this region. North-west Pacific cooking has a focus on fresh ingredients. Fish are plentiful in the region. Salmon is a common dish, and smoked fish and shellfish are also commonly used in cooking. Game meats such as elk and moose would have traditionally provided a great deal of meat for native people.

United States cuisine

Cooking in the United States is often associated with frying and red meats. Typical foods include beef burgers, steaks and fries, but there is much more to be found in American cookery. There have been many different influences on the foods cooked and available in the United States as each group of settlers and immigrants has introduced ideas based on the cooking in their home countries. Larger cities often have areas where food from different cultures is readily available in supermarkets and restaurants. These areas often have a high population density of people from those cultures.

Chinese cuisine

The main staple food in southern Chinese cookery is rice, which is commonly steamed. Traditional Chinese cuisine is eaten with chopsticks and therefore the food produced is often in small pieces. The wheat-producing northern Chinese region uses staple foods of noodles, dumplings and breads in its cookery.

Cantonese cuisine originated in southern China and uses a variety of different meats, such as beef, pork and chicken (including items such as chicken feet). The main cooking methods in Cantonese cookery are stir frying and steaming. Cantonese cookery tends to use only a limited amount of spices so as not to overwhelm the flavours of dishes, which can also be quite sweet.

Szechuan cuisine is a style originating in the south-western region of China. Szechuan cooking uses more spices, including hot chillies and a lot of garlic and ginger. Szechuan peppers are also a key feature of this style of cookery and offer a very different and specific flavour. The main methods of cooking, once again, are stir frying, steaming and braising. One of the most popular and well-known Szechuan dishes in the UK is kung pao chicken, a fairly sweet dish with a strong aroma and flavour of ginger.

PLTS

When working independently to research your menu, you will be developing your skills as an **independent enquirer**.

Functional skills

As you carry out your research, you will be using your **ICT** skills in finding and selecting information from a variety of sources. When producing your menu card, you will need to use your **English** skills in writing.

9.3 Be able to prepare, cook and present contemporary world dishes

The practical work in this unit involves the preparation, cooking and presentation of contemporary world dishes. This should be a really exciting opportunity for you to create some interesting and inspiring dishes. There are many restaurants that produce contemporary world dishes and these could be a good source for your inspiration. Looking at their menus could help you get ideas for the dishes you choose to cook.

This section covers:

- food preparation
- cooking methods
- presenting dishes
- safety and hygiene.

Food preparation

Food preparation involves many tasks, including weighing, measuring, peeling and cutting food commodities. Preparation is essentially similar in all styles of cuisine, but the ingredients and equipment used, and the environment in which it is carried out, can differ.

Activity: Cutting and chopping ingredients

Think of some safe practices and give examples with regards to cutting and chopping ingredients. Consider hygiene as well as health and safety.

Cooking methods

There are many methods of cooking and producing foods, from oven baking, steaming, boiling, grilling and frying to barbequing and microwaving (see pages 249–251 for more information). All cooking methods work by applying heat in varying temperatures and humidity, using various cooking agents and fuels to produce this heat.

Methods of cooking vary from country to country, and depend to an extent on the availability of equipment and resources. Some of the more contemporary methods of cooking world cuisine include frying food using woks or steaming ingredients in bamboo steamers as in Chinese cooking, using flare grills or barbeques to cook meat or cooking in clay ovens and tagines.

Many styles of cooking are very complex. For example, Indian cooking requires great skills and involves so many aspects that you would need to conduct a lot of research to learn all the techniques. Spices are an essential part of Indian cooking. They are often roasted to bring out their flavour. Some spices are roasted in the oven whole (that is, without chopping or cutting) and then ground after they are cooked. Indian cooking often uses ghee. This is clarified butter, and it gives a nutty taste and complements the spices well. The ground or whole roasted spices are dropped into the ghee when it is hot. Meat is often marinated to enhance its flavour. This sometimes involves cutting gashes into the surface and rubbing in spiced yoghurt. The meat then takes in the flavours of the spice.

Chinese and Szechuan cooking in a Western style often relies on very fast frying in woks. Woks are heated to a high temperature before ingredients are added. The woks are usually heated by a direct flame on a gas burner. Dim sum, which are parcels in dough, are steamed traditionally but a Western or contemporary approach is to produce parcels in filo pastry which are oven baked.

How can barbecuing affect the flavour of food?

Presenting dishes

Dishes need to be well presented on plates or serving dishes that complement the food and ensure that it looks appealing to the diners. Placing the food neatly, without leaving drips or smears on the plate, gives a clean look to the dish. By placing food neatly, you can also define and show colour contrasts and the shape and form of the meal.

Garnishes (see pge 262) add to the overall attractiveness of a dish, and can provide additional colour and shape. Specialist equipment can sometimes be used for preparing garnishes, such as small cutting tools that can produce specific cuts or shapes in foods. Garnishes are made to suit the dish that they accompany and can vary across the world. Simple garnishes can be made from colourful pieces of salad such as red cabbage and tomatoes, contrasted with other colours such as green cucumber. These salad-based garnishes are very common.

Nouvelle cuisine, a French style of cooking, is very minimalist in quantity of food used but aims at stunning presentation, arranging the various elements of the dish in such a way as to make it look spectacular. Sauces are also used creatively in nouvelle cuisine, with contrasting coloured sauces applied to the plate before the various components of the dish are added.

More rustic dishes, such as Italian baked dishes like lasagne, are often served with a salad-based garnish, which enhances the colour of the dish using fresh coloured peppers, tomatoes and a variety of salad leaves. Many Italian pasta-based dishes present well without garnishes and are simply plated, making the most of the vibrant colours in the sauces.

Western or more contemporary Chinese cookery is often presented with complex accompanying garnishes, such as carrots or radishes cut into flowers and ornate shapes created from a variety of edible ingredients. These styles of garnish have been created for the Western table rather than being traditional Chinese methods of presentation.

In many contemporary dishes, the components are stacked to provide height. Alternatively, the components may be kept very separate, styled and shaped. Using contrasts in colours and textures also gives a contemporary feel to a dish.

Safety and hygiene

In your practical work, you will have to adopt safe working practices and follow hygienic methods of food production. For more information about safety and hygiene, refer back to pages 236–237.

When you are producing dishes, ensure that all food you purchase is in good condition. It should be fresh and of good quality, and should not be past its use-by date. The food you produce must be stored at the correct temperature, whether hot or cold. If you are reheating food, it must be heated to the correct temperature before serving. All food that you produce must be clearly labelled and dated before being stored in a fridge.

Personal hygiene

You must ensure that you follow good practice and maintain your own personal hygiene. Bacteria is present on humans at all times, so you should wash regularly and keep your body and work clothing clean. You should reduce hand-to-mouth contact and wash your hands after going to the toilet. You should also wash your hands after preparing meat or fish and before touching or working on other food products.

If you are unwell, you should report this to your supervisor or the person in charge of the kitchen. People who are ill can spread disease through coughing, sneezing or touching food items. If you are unwell and pose a risk of spreading disease, you should not be working in the kitchen.

Hazard Analysis and Critical Control Points (HACCP)

The HACCP process examines each step or stage in the production of a meal or an individual ingredient. The examination of each stage can highlight areas where there is a potential risk. Kitchen staff can then take steps to minimise or eliminate the risk.

To introduce HACCP, you need to produce a flow diagram of the process including all the stages. Risks or issues can then be identified and measures to eliminate or minimise these risks can be introduced. Kitchen staff can then follow the diagram and be informed about what to do at each stage.

Assessment activity 3

Unit 9   P3 M2 D1   BTEC

This is a practical activity. You must prepare, cook and present three different contemporary world dishes. You could choose to cook three of the dishes you suggested for Assessment activity 2 or you could choose different dishes. P3 M2 D1

Grading tips

Plan and practise your cooking in advance to make sure you have a good idea of how equipment and cooking ingredients should be used for your dishes. You will be observed as you produce your dishes and assessed on how well you can prepare, cook and present these dishes.

P3 Record how each dish was produced as you go along, giving details of the equipment used, preparation methods, cooking methods, safety and hygiene issues and presentation methods.

M2 You will need to demonstrate appropriate methods in your cooking and presentation with limited tutor support.

D1 You must be able to show that you can work both independently and creatively when producing your dishes.

PLTS

You will show your ability as a **self-manager** by demonstrating high standards and creativity in the preparation, cooking and presentation of contemporary world dishes.

9.4 Be able to review dishes

Being able to review your own work is really important. You will only know if the dishes you create are of the required quality by reviewing your work. This will also help you to understand what you might do to improve the dishes next time you decide to cook the recipes.

Your dishes will also be reviewed by others, such as the people eating your food (for example, customers in a restaurant or other learners in your class), as well as by managers, restaurant owners and waiting staff. They will give comments on your dishes which will help you to understand how they could be improved or whether they are just right.

When you are reviewing your dishes, try to be critical about your own performance in a positive way; a self-evaluative approach should allow you to find room for improvement. This is an essential part of advancing your own cooking skills. There are various things you need to check, including:

- preparation and cooking
- quality
- feedback from other people.

When reviewing your food, remember to consider your customers' tastes as well as your own.

Preparation and cooking

By reviewing how you prepared and cooked a dish, you can learn how to improve your performance as a chef. This should be an informative and positive process. Try to list what you did to achieve the final dish and what you could have done differently.

For example, did you use the correct ingredients, tools and equipment? Was your work environment clean and hygienic? When preparing and cooking food, you need to ensure that you comply with all health and hygiene regulations.

Preparation includes the basic cleaning of ingredients, and the weighing, cutting, chopping, shaping and forming that needs to take place before cooking. It is essential that preparation takes place at the correct time before cooking. If your food needs to be marinated, which is common in many Asian dishes, this must have been done at the right time so that the food has absorbed the flavours in the marinade before you start cooking.

Planning

Planning is essential to ensure that preparation and cooking take place in an effective manner and produce a quality outcome. Planning for the production of a dish requires careful thought. Initially, you will need to investigate the availability of ingredients. You need to find out where you are going to buy your ingredients and how much they will cost.

You will need to plan how you are going to make the dish and compile a method for its production. You will need to check that the necessary equipment will be available when required. You could produce a timeline for preparing and cooking your dish, starting from the purchase of your food products and working through to completion.

Timing

One of your main challenges will be to co-ordinate many tasks at the same time. This might involve preparing and processing food items to create one dish or producing numerous dishes at the same time. When you review your work, you must explore possible ways of improving your timings if necessary.

Cooking times need to reflect the dish being prepared and customer preferences. For example, people have different preferences about how steak should be cooked. Steak can be served rare, medium or well done. Steak dishes can be returned to the kitchen by customers if they are undercooked or overcooked.

Some recipes give very precise timings so that dishes can be cooked correctly. This is especially the case for any dishes that are cooked in the oven or thickened on the hob. Fresh pasta needs to be cooked very quickly as it can easily overcook and become too soft.

Timings need to take into account the time required to serve a dish. If food is left waiting on a counter once it is cooked, then the quality can deteriorate very quickly. It can also become too cold to serve or, in the case of chilled or frozen food, it can become too warm and melt. It is also important that adequate time is allowed between courses. Guests need time to eat their starters and rest a little before receiving their main courses. This means that you will need to leave time to cook the main courses without leaving guests waiting too long for this part of the meal.

Working methods

The working methods that you follow will depend on the kitchen environment in which you are working. For example, the number of kitchen staff available has an influence on working methods. The chef can allocate areas of the preparation and cooking to different staff. However, all methods must follow health and safety and hygiene practices.

Generally, working in a methodical manner and cleaning up as you go ensures a good outcome. This will help you to produce the best quality food safely and hygienically in the least amount of time. It should involve using the minimal amount of energy and effort. This does not mean you should be lazy, but you should work as efficiently as possible and plan well.

Quality

When you are reviewing your dishes, you need to assess their quality. Quality depends on several factors, including the quality and freshness of ingredients. You need to consider how the ingredients are produced; for example, are they organic or GM-free (without genetically modified ingredients)? Many people believe that organic and GM-free produce tastes better than foods which are non-organic or which contain GM ingredients. The region from which fruit and vegetables are sourced and the soil types in which they are grown can also make a difference. The way that cattle are raised and fed affects the quality of the meat, and the breed of animal may also affect taste and texture.

The quality of cooking obviously affects the final dish – foods can be overcooked, undercooked or cooked using the wrong method. It is important to know the correct cooking method and the timings for the dish you are preparing. If you are going to use cooking methods that you have not tried previously, you must do some research and practice before you prepare a meal for other diners.

When you are reviewing your dish, you need to have a series of criteria on which to base the review. The main criteria used to assess food are **sensory qualities**. The main sensory qualities are taste, texture, aroma and appearance. These criteria can be graded numerically on a scale from good to poor, for example; this can give an overall numerical grading of a dish. Another way of presenting an assessment is to use a star diagram. Figure 1 shows an example of a star diagram assessment of a dish.

Key term

Sensory qualities – taste, texture, aroma and appearance.

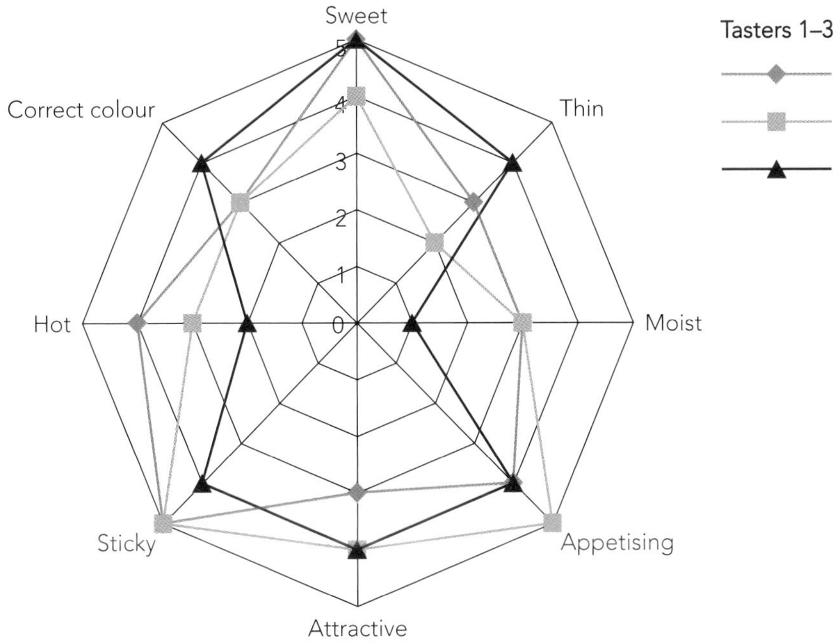

Figure 1: Star diagram showing an assessment of the sensory qualities of a dish

Feedback from other people

Feedback from other people is very important as it will help you to understand how you can improve your cooking and allow you to find out when things are working really well.

Many food critics will comment on the sensory qualities of a dish, discussing whether it has the appropriate combinations of ingredients and whether it is served at the right temperature and with the right accompaniments. Critics also give their views on the style of cooking. You should ask anybody commenting on your food to be honest but to offer practical advice.

Assessment activity 4

Unit 9 **P4** **D2**

Review the three dishes you produced for Assessment activity 3. Produce a written review. **P4** **D2**

Grading tips

P4 Make sure that you review all three dishes that you cooked. When you are reviewing your dishes, make comments on all aspects of the dishes including the taste, texture, aroma and appearance of the food.

D2 You will need to be reflective about the food and make practical recommendations for improvements to the dishes. Think about what went well and what you could have improved during the cooking.

PLTS

By reflecting on how the dishes are prepared, cooked and presented and making recommendations for improvement, you will show that you are a **reflective learner** and an **effective participator**.

Functional skills

In order to produce a written review, you will need to use your **English** skills in writing.

Markus Berg
Trainee chef

I work in the kitchen of a popular and busy city-centre restaurant. The local area is a thriving multicultural community. The menu has a wide selection of dishes based on the concept of contemporary world cuisine. There are five other members of staff working in the kitchen, all from different cultural backgrounds. We can all learn from each other in terms of our different methods and styles of cooking.

The different cooking styles and methods of preparation give me variety in my job, which I really enjoy. The menu is always exciting and challenges the staff to learn how to cook new dishes.

Our customers always have high expectations of the dishes we create and we need to ensure we meet their expectations. We make sure our ideas are fresh and give a contemporary twist to traditional dishes. We often use fusions of cooking styles to produce new, exciting dishes. We need to ensure that the dishes we cook are well presented and served to a consistent standard and quality. The customers pay to enjoy good, exciting food and we need to provide what they want.

Working in this restaurant has really developed my skills and creativity in producing new dishes. I feel that it will enable me to take on more responsibilities in the future so I can progress in my career.

Think about it!

- Why is it important that the kitchen staff share their knowledge and skills with each other?
- How can you reinvent traditional dishes by adding a contemporary 'twist'? Give specific examples.

Just checking

1 What is a contemporary world food dish?

2 What factors influence the availability of ingredients?

3 What regional variations are there in Indian cuisine?

4 In which country are bamboo steamers often used?

5 Can you name a country where pasta is the staple food?

6 Why is it important to review your own dishes?

7 What are sensory qualities?

edexcel

Assignment tips

- Make sure you conduct thorough research on all your tasks. If you do not understand, make sure you ask for help from your tutor.

- When presenting information to a group, make sure you understand the information and practise your presentation before assessment.

- When you select dishes from different countries, choose ones that you will enjoy researching and cooking. Be creative with your dishes, but make sure you practise and test your dishes before assessment.

- To produce contemporary world food dishes, you need to find traditional recipes that you can change and alter to give them a contemporary twist. Do not be afraid to experiment.

- Always follow health and safety rules and adopt hygienic practices.

- Challenge yourself to progress, but set firm goals that you can realistically achieve.

11 & 12 Serving food and drink

When people go out to eat, they do not just go for the food and drink; they go for the experience. The enjoyment and fun of going out to eat includes the atmosphere and style that is created by the catering business.

Although food and drink are an important part of the occasion, the standard and quality of the service and the attitude of staff providing that service can make or break the occasion for customers. Satisfying customers is what serving food and drink is all about and this can have a key impact on the success of a business. This is important because customers have so much choice: from exotic Thai restaurants serving authentic food and luxury city-centre hotels, to gastro pubs serving traditional meals and simple high street cafés.

This unit will help you to understand and develop the personal skills and qualities needed to work in food and drink service. You will learn how to get ready for customers, prepare a service area effectively and serve meals and drinks efficiently. You will gain practical skills in serving food and drink, and learn how to review and evaluate your performance.

Learning outcomes

After completing these units, you should:

Unit 11 Service of food at table

1   Know how to greet customers and take orders

2   Know how to serve customers in a dining area.

Unit 12 Service of alcoholic and non-alcoholic drinks

1   Know how to take customer orders

2   Know how to serve alcoholic and non-alcoholic drinks

3   Know the appropriate legislation that relates to the serving of alcoholic drinks.

Assessment and grading criteria

These tables show you what you must do in order to achieve a pass, merit or distinction grade, and where you can find activities in this book to help you.

Unit 11 Service of food at table

To achieve a pass grade the evidence must show that you are able to:		To achieve a merit grade the evidence must show that, in addition to the pass criteria, you are able to:	To achieve a distinction grade the evidence must show that, in addition to the pass and merit criteria, you are able to:
P1 state the importance of greeting customers appropriately **Assessment activity 1, pages 318–19**	**P2** state the importance of giving accurate menu information **Assessment activity 1, pages 318–19**	**M1** show proficiency when preparing for food service by carrying out appropriate procedures **Assessment activity 2, page 324**	
P3 describe how to provide appropriate assistance to customers with different needs **Assessment activity 1, pages 318–19**	**P4** describe how to respond to types of unexpected situations that may occur when greeting customers and dealing with their orders **Assessment activity 1, pages 318–19**		
P5 describe safe and hygienic working practices when serving customers' orders **Assessment activity 3, page 329**	**P6** list correct condiments, accompaniments and service equipment for different menu items **Assessment activity 4, page 333**	**M2** demonstrate proficiency when providing food service on different occasions using customer service skills **Assessment activity 6, page 341**	**D1** evaluate your ability to deliver professional, safe and hygienic food service using effective customer service skills **Assessment activity 6, page 341**
P7 state the importance of arranging and presenting food in line with menu specifications **Assessment activity 4, page 333**	**P8** state the importance of maintaining the dining and service area **Assessment activity 3, page 329**		
P9 describe how to respond to types of unexpected situations that may occur when serving food at table **Assessment activity 1, pages 318–19**			

Unit 12 Service of alcoholic and non-alcoholic drinks

To achieve a pass grade the evidence must show that you are able to:		To achieve a merit grade the evidence must show that, in addition to the pass criteria, you are able to:	To achieve a distinction grade the evidence must show that, in addition to the pass and merit criteria, you are able to:
P1 identify the importance of accuracy when taking drink orders **Assessment activity 1, pages 318–19**	**P2** describe how to respond to a customer who might have special requirements **Assessment activity 1, pages 318–19**	**M1** show proficiency when preparing for drink service by carrying out appropriate procedures **Assessment activity 2, page 324**	
P3 describe different service styles that can be used when serving drinks **Assessment activity 1, pages 318–19**	**P4** state the importance of serving customers in order of arrival where possible **Assessment activity 1, pages 318–19**		
P5 state the importance of checking glassware for damage **Assessment activity 5, page 341**	**P6** state the correct temperature for storing and serving the range of drinks offered within the operation **Assessment activity 5, page 341**	**M2** provide effective drink service on different occasions using customer service skills **Assessment activity 6, page 341**	**D1** evaluate your ability to deliver professional, safe and hygienic drink service using effective customer service skills. **Assessment activity 6, page 341**
P7 describe how to serve different drinks including bottled drinks, draft beers, free pouring and optic based **Assessment activity 5, page 341**	**P8** state the appropriate types of glass for serving different drinks **Assessment activity 5, page 341**		

Unit 12 Service of alcoholic and non-alcoholic drinks – *continued*

To achieve a pass grade the evidence must show that you are able to:		To achieve a merit grade the evidence must show that, in addition to the pass criteria, you are able to:	To achieve a distinction grade the evidence must show that, in addition to the pass and merit criteria, you are able to:
P9 describe the implications of current relevant legislation relating to licensing, weights and measures **Assessment activity 7, page 344**	**P10** identify when a customer should not be served with alcohol **Assessment activity 7, page 344**	**M3** analyse the implications of non-compliance to hospitality businesses **Assessment activity 7, page 344**	
P11 describe how to respond to someone who might be under the influence of drugs or buying/selling drugs **Assessment activity 7, page 344**	**P12** state how to deal with violent/disorderly customers **Assessment activity 7, page 344**		

How you will be assessed

You will be assessed by assignments that will be designed and marked by tutors at your centre. These units have a practical element to them. You will be required to serve food and drink to demonstrate your skills. You should keep an evaluation log to support this practical work, and at the end of each practical lesson identify what you have learned.

Your assignments could require you to:

- undertake practical tasks
- give presentations
- write reports
- produce posts and leaflets.

Claudine, 15-year-old learner

I have always wanted to be a chef and that is why I started on this course. I have enjoyed the whole course so far, but I especially enjoyed this unit. It made me realise that I like working with people, and enjoy serving food and drinks to customers in a restaurant.

Of course, it's very important for the chef's food to be served to a high standard and I am thinking that I might prefer working at the front of house. The catering industry is often very busy and I really love the buzz of working under pressure, when our customers can see how I am coping with the problems that can arise.

I have learned that the industry is not just about preparing and cooking food, it also involves the whole process of cooking and serving to a high standard. We need to please our customers and keep them happy, so that they will keep coming back.

Over to you

- Think about when you have been a customer in a restaurant or café. How do you expect to be treated by the serving staff?
- What treatment would you not expect? What would make you decide not to return to the restaurant or café?

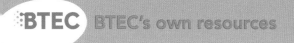

11.1 Know how to greet customers and take orders

12.1 Know how to take customer orders

Welcome

The customer experience

When you first walk into a restaurant, bar or café, how do you feel? In small groups, discuss what your feelings might be and consider what the staff in the establishment could do to make you feel at home.

In the first section of these units, we consider the basics of taking food and drink orders. We will look at:

- greeting customers
- taking drinks orders
- taking food orders
- meeting customer needs and special requirements
- dealing with unexpected situations
- personal presentation
- preparing the service area for food
- food service equipment.

Greeting customers

Customers in a restaurant or a bar need to be treated considerately to ensure they come back. If customers are not greeted properly, they will not feel welcome and may not be satisfied by any of the service provided. Imagine how you would feel if you were left standing at the door of a restaurant for more than a few moments. A poor greeting (or no greeting at all) can lead to customer complaints and loss of business. Remember that if customers walk out because there is nobody at the door to greet them properly, the opportunity for a sale has been lost.

Greeting procedures

Customers need to be made welcome and to feel at ease. Even in the most basic restaurant or café, customers need to be greeted and seated at an appropriate table or counter. This is basic customer care, which is an important area of hospitality. Many of the skills you need have been covered in Units 3 and 4 on customer service in hospitality and in Unit 7 on workplace skills.

You should speak clearly to customers when you welcome them. If you know the customers, then greet them using their names, for example: 'Good afternoon, Mr and Mrs Taylor. How nice to see you again'. Only use first names if you know the customers very well. Customers who you do not know should always be addressed as Sir or Madam.

Customers should be greeted immediately on arrival and not left standing in the doorway or entrance to the establishment. Remember, it is good manners to greet customers with good morning, good afternoon or good evening depending on the time of day.

Activity: Greeting and welcoming customers

In groups, role play greeting and welcoming customers to a restaurant. Give each other marks out of ten for your welcomes and the way you greet the customers.

Remember that customers are all individuals. As we discussed in Units 3 and 4, there are many different types of customers. You may find it useful to look back on the main customer types encountered in the hospitality industry (see pages 66–71). In food and drink service you will have internal as well as external customers. You will have to serve customers of different ages, groups and families, people with special needs and people from other nationalities and cultures. You will need to deal with customers in different ways to meet their individual needs.

Confirmation of reservation and seating procedures

After welcoming customers, it is necessary to find out what they would like. If the establishment has a reservation system, this is the time to acknowledge the booking. This can be done simply by asking: 'Can I help you?' or 'Do you have a booking?'

You should then show customers to their table or to the bar for a pre-meal drink if the customers do not want to sit straight down for a meal or if their table is not ready. It is best to walk in front of your customers to their seats, rather than to point out their table. If the restaurant is not busy, it is usual to ask customers where they would like to sit. Some customers would appreciate a table near a window if there is a view. Customers with mobility difficulties, for example someone in a wheelchair, should be seated at a table that has convenient access, such as one near the door.

Customer care policy

The customer care policy of a hospitality business is normally set by senior management. The policy usually consists of a set of rules to ensure that:

- staff know what is expected from them
- the business runs smoothly
- standards are understood and maintained
- the public image of the business is protected and enhanced
- customers get value and enjoyment from their visit.

Some rules may cover how to deal with customers. Making eye contact with customers is extremely important; it shows that you have seen them and are listening to what they say. Of course, customers should also be treated politely at all times. In a busy establishment, it is very important to serve customers in the order in which they arrive. Imagine how it feels to see customers who arrived after you being served first.

However, some customers will need to be given special attention. A business will want to reward regular customers or those who spend well. Some hotel and restaurant chains give priority cards to their good customers. These give them special privileges, like a discount or a free drink with their meal. Customers with special needs will also need prompt attention. Businesses also treat any VIP guests with special care.

Many larger restaurant chains have very thorough customer care policies and they spend a considerable amount of time training their staff to follow these procedures. Have you noticed that customers are always greeted in the same way in high street burger chains? However, many individual non-chain restaurants do not have a written policy and depend on the manager to ensure that staff are correctly trained.

Case study: Byron's restaurant

Byron's is a small city-centre restaurant. It is very popular with businessmen and businesswomen who are looking for a quick service at lunch times, and it is also popular in the evenings with families who enjoy eating at Byron's after visits to the nearby cinemas.

The manager of Byron's has been asked to review and update the company's customer care policy.

- Make a list of all the things that need to be included in the policy.

- Are there any particularly important points that need to be mentioned in every policy?

- Are there any points that only apply to this type of restaurant?

Complaints procedure

Usually, the complaints procedure is part of the customer care policy. It is important that all complaints, however small, are dealt with properly. Many hospitality businesses keep a record of every complaint and any follow-up action.

When a customer makes a complaint, you a should always follow these steps.

- Listen to the customer's complaint and apologise immediately. Remember the importance of maintaining eye contact.
- Ask questions to make sure that you have understood the complaint. It is sometimes a good idea to summarise the complaint to the customer to ensure that you have understood the complaint correctly.
- Resolve the issue. You might need to ask for help or support from colleagues or a supervisor in dealing with the complaint.
- Explain to the customer how you can resolve the issue. Hopefully, the customer will be satisfied with how you intend to resolve the problem.
- Report the complaint and the action you have taken to your supervisor.

Taking drinks orders

There are two basic situations when staff take drinks orders: at the bar when approached by customers and at the table when customers are seated for a meal or in a bar with a table service.

When taking drinks orders at the bar, it is not usual to write down the order. You should serve the drinks as the customer waits at the bar and work out the price for the order on the till. The customer will usually pay for the drinks after you have served the full order, but customers in a hotel could ask for the order to be charged to their room and those in a restaurant with a separate bar could ask for the order to be charged to their table so that they can settle their bill at the end of the meal.

When taking drinks orders at a table, customers usually know what drinks they want, so it is necessary to know what is in stock behind the bar. The way that drinks orders are taken at a table will depend on the procedures at the establishment. The main ways of taking customer orders are by:

- using a duplicate check pad – two copies are made, with the top copy sent to the bar and the bottom one kept by the serving staff
- using an electronic keypad – this is a hand-held computer terminal that has a code for each menu item and once the order is entered by the serving staff it is automatically printed out at the bar.

Getting orders right

To ensure customer satisfaction, drinks orders must be taken accurately. There are many types of drinks, and you need to understand exactly what each customer requires in order to avoid mistakes. The same basic drink can be prepared in several ways. For example, if a customer orders a spirit such as whisky, you need to find out whether that should be served with or without ice, and with or without a mixer. This is a matter of personal taste and you should not assume what the customer wants.

It is also important to find out the quantity the customer would like. If the order is for wine, ask whether the customer would like wine by the glass or bottle, and if the customer wants a glass of wine, ask whether a small or large glass is required. If the order is for a spirit, ask whether the customer wants a single or double measure.

Prices, alcoholic content and measures

It is a legal requirement to display a price list that includes the alcoholic content and measures of each drink. At the bar this is usually displayed on a noticeboard. At the table there may be a drinks list (or wine list) kept on the table or the serving staff may bring a drinks list on a tray when they come to take customers' orders.

Taking food orders

The same methods of taking drinks orders can be used for food orders from customers when they are seated at a table in a restaurant. Many establishments use either duplicate check pads or electronic keypads to take orders. Some use a triplicate check pad. Here, three copies are made: the top copy goes to the kitchen, the second is kept by service staff, and the third goes to the cashier to complete the bill.

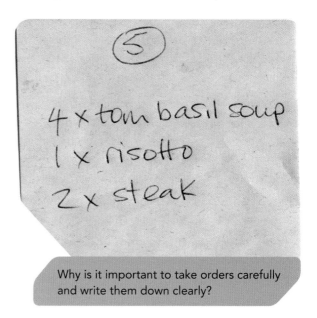

Why is it important to take orders carefully and write them down clearly?

Quite often, customers will know what they want. They might be regulars or very familiar with the type of food sold at the restaurant. It may just be a simple matter of checking that what they want is available and then sending the order to the kitchen. Other customers will need some advice, and you may need to talk through what is on the menu. It is therefore necessary for serving staff to understand fully what is on the menu.

Tips for taking a food order

- Take order pads and a pen (or an electronic keypad) to the table.
- Ask the customers if they are ready to order.
- Face each customer when taking their order and keep eye contact – it is also important to smile.
- Do not lean over customers or rest on tables and chairs.
- Answer any questions that customers might have. If you cannot deal with a query, always offer to find out the answer.
- Give suggestions if needed.
- Make sure you understand the order before you leave the table by repeating it back to the customers.
- Thank the customers for their order.

There is usually a formal procedure to take food orders to the chefs. In some outlets, only more experienced or senior staff are allowed to take orders from customers. Junior colleagues will then take these orders to the kitchen or service point, and will be expected to fetch and carry the food when it is ready.

Orders taken by waiting staff on electronic keypads can be sent electronically to the kitchen where they will be printed out. Written orders must be taken to the kitchen. When taking a new order to the kitchen, it is normal to shout 'check on'. This alerts the kitchen team that another order needs preparing. The head chef then instructs the kitchen team to prepare what is required.

Activity: Taking orders and writing checks

Collect menus from a selection of hospitality businesses. You can find many menus on the Internet, which you can download for this exercise.

In small groups, use the menus to practise writing down orders for food and drinks. Some of the group should act as customers and others as restaurant staff. Then change roles, so that everyone in the group has an opportunity to take an order. Check each other's food orders for mistakes and see if you can decide why mistakes were made.

Then continue the activity by practising taking complex orders based on an à la carte menu. Each member of the group needs to take an accurate food and drink order for a party of three people who are having a three-course lunch and beverages. The party could be other members of your group in a role play. The guests should each have a different starter but the same main course. This will be followed by three different desserts and finish with coffee.

Dish composition and cooking methods

When taking orders, you must be able to advise customers fully on the composition of dishes and how they are cooked. This means that you must understand the menu before service begins. Many restaurant managers hold a menu briefing at the beginning of each service to ensure that waiting staff understand all the dishes, especially any daily specials that may not feature regularly on the menu. If you are not sure of the composition of any dish on the menu or the cooking method for a dish, you should ask a colleague or your supervisor before service begins.

Allergies

Customers sometimes asks about the composition of a dish. This might be because they have an allergy or special dietary needs. It is very important to ensure that the information you give is accurate, as a customer with an allergy could suffer a very serious illness if served the wrong food. For more about allergies and special dietary needs, see Unit 6 (page 177).

Prices and special offers

It is a legal requirement that menus should show the correct prices. You should check the menu before you give it to customers to make sure there are no errors in pricing. If you are not sure, you should ask your supervisor.

When serving customers, you will be expected to secure customer satisfaction and to increase sales by encouraging customers to consider the special offers and any available promotions. Some establishments will also have a **specials board**.

Key term

Specials board – a list, usually on a chalkboard, of extra dishes that are not on the regular menu.

Accompaniments

You will be expected to know the accompaniments that come with each meal. This is so that you can either offer them to customers or ensure that they are available on the table. Table 1 shows the accompaniments served with some common dishes. You may have already tried some of these options.

As you can see, there are many points to consider when taking customers' orders. Good serving staff ensure that customers receive exactly what they ordered. If customers always get the exact dishes they expect, a restaurant will get fewer complaints and will be more efficient as serving staff will not have to replace dishes that do not meet customer needs. It is also important to try to increase sales by upselling items from the menu. For example, all businesses expect serving staff to offer extras to customers.

What should you do if a customer is unhappy with their food?

Starters	
Dish	**Served with**
Tomato soup with fresh basil	Croutons
Coarse game terrine	Toast and red onion chutney
Deep-fried whitebait	Cayenne pepper and lemon wedges
Chicken satay	Peanut satay sauce
Prawn cocktail	Brown bread and butter
Melon	Ground ginger and caster sugar
Pasta	Grated parmesan cheese
Main dishes	
Dish	**Served with**
Beer batter-fried fillets of pollock	Tartare sauce and lemon wedges
Roast foreribs of English beef	Horseradish sauce
Roast lamb	Redcurrant jelly or mint sauce
Grilled sirloin steak and garnish	English or French mustard
Traditional roast turkey	Cranberry sauce
Desserts	
Dish	**Served with**
Apple and blackberry pie	Cornish clotted cream
Marmalade bread and butter pudding	Custard
English cheeses and biscuits	Celery sticks or grapes

Table 1: Popular accompaniments

Meeting customer needs and special requirements

Before service, it is important to check that the information on the menu is correct. You must understand the menu and be able to pass this information on to customers. This is a basic requirement. Now let's consider other ways that serving staff can ensure customer satisfaction.

Mobility difficulties

Customers with mobility difficulties should be able to access hospitality outlets. A business should provide ramps where required, and staff should ensure that the customers are able to move around the restaurant as they wish. This might mean they are seated on a ground floor to avoid use of stairs, near the door of the restaurant or near the restrooms, so that they do not have far to walk. In a bar, consider serving any customers with mobility difficulties at their table rather than expecting them to come to the bar to order and collect their drinks.

Hearing and visual impairments

When you are serving any customers with hearing difficulties, you should speak clearly and make sure that they have understood you. Customers with visual impairments may not be able to see well enough to read the menu, so it would be helpful for you to read the menu to them or provide a version in Braille or large print. In all cases, you should be very patient with customers.

Time constraints

An important part of the role of serving customers is being aware of time. Customers do not want to wait long for:

- a table
- a menu
- the order to be taken
- their drinks to arrive
- the food to arrive
- their bill to be presented
- their payment to be accepted (if bills are settled at the table).

You can help to ensure customer satisfaction if you serve guests promptly at all stages of their visit.

Special seating arrangements

Customers will sometimes request special seating arrangements. For example, they might want a table with room for a wheelchair, they might want a highchair for a young child or they might want a table with a good view. It is important that you try to meet these requests from your customers wherever possible.

Unacceptable requests

Occasionally, customers will make requests that you cannot fulfil for legal reasons. For example, it is illegal for anyone under the age of 18 to drink alcohol in licensed premises – although 16 and 17 year olds accompanied by an adult can drink but not buy beer, wine or cider with a table meal. You cannot serve alcoholic drinks to people under the legal drinking age or outside permitted service hours. These requests must be politely refused, but you should explain to the customer why you are unable to take their order.

Dealing with unexpected situations

When you are working in a bar, restaurant or hotel, you need to be able to respond to any unexpected situations. For example, when you are taking orders, a customer might ask you a question which you may not be able to answer. At this point, you should apologise to the customer and then go and ask a supervisor to help you. Ensure that you return promptly to the customer with an answer.

If you are faced with an unexpected situation, you may not be able to handle everything on your own. You need to communicate the problem to other staff who need to know or may need to take action, such as your supervisor, the chef or the other bar and service staff.

Let's look at some of the situations you could have to deal with, including:

- pre-orders
- errors and omissions
- chance customers
- unavailable menu items
- accidents
- fire evacuations
- violent and disorderly customers.

Pre-orders

Large parties will often pre-order their food requirements. A pre-order should be given to the chef as soon as possible, so that the correct food can be prepared for the arrival of the party.

Errors and omissions

If you make a mistake on an order or leave an item off the order, you must apologise to the customer immediately and then try to put the mistake right. You might have to ask the chef to produce another dish quickly.

Chance customers

Chance customers should be accommodated if at all possible. If a table is not available immediately, you should ask customers if they would like to wait in the bar until a table becomes available.

Unavailable menu items

As dishes become unavailable for a sitting, the chef will put them on the **off board**. You should always keep an eye on the off board so that you can tell customers which dishes are unavailable before they order.

Accidents

In the event of any accident that causes an injury to a customer or a member of staff, you should inform your supervisor immediately and contact the first aider if there is one. It may be that you need to call an ambulance.

Key terms

Chance customers – customers who arrive without a reservation.

Off board – a list, usually on the wall in the kitchen, of any dishes that are sold out or unavailable.

Fire evacuations

In the event of a fire, or if the fire alarm starts ringing, you will need to help evacuate the premises. Customers may not know the way out of the building, and you should help them to leave the building safely.

Violent and disorderly customers

Unfortunately, you may have to deal with customers who are under the influence of alcohol or drugs, or who become abusive and threatening.

You can often tell that someone is under the influence of alcohol because they speak very loudly and seem unbalanced when they walk. You should always politely refuse to serve alcohol to someone who is under the influence of alcohol, not least because serving them is against the law. Someone who is under the influence of drugs will often display similar behaviour to someone who is under the influence of alcohol and, in the same way, you should politely refuse to serve them any more drinks.

Misuse of alcohol or drugs often leads to threatening behaviour. This is when someone is unreasonably argumentative or threatens staff or other guests verbally or even physically. If you feel threatened, you should remain calm. Try to keep your tone of voice neutral to avoid provoking further arguments and call your supervisor or another member of staff to assist you. Some establishments have a panic button that staff can press to get help if they feel threatened. In some cases, it may be necessary to call the police to deal with violent or disorderly customers.

Remaining calm

In all situations, regardless of how unexpected, it is important to remain calm and to try to settle the situation to a customer's satisfaction. You may be able to offer an alternative solution to customers, which they might find acceptable. Whenever there is an unexpected situation, it is important to explain what is going on to customers, so that they can understand the problem and any solution that you offer them.

However, you may not be able to deal with all situations and you may need to get advice on the solutions that you can offer. Always be prepared to call your supervisor to help you. This is especially true in the case of any violent or disorderly behaviour by customers.

Personal presentation

You will need to know how to present yourself correctly for any work that involves food and drink service. Good personal presentation and cleanliness are essential in the hospitality industry. Job roles in food and drink service involve working with the public and you need to impress customers as well as be a good colleague to your fellow workers.

Personal hygiene and freshness

You must have good personal hygiene and take particular care if you are involved in preparing and/or serving food and drink.

- You should have fresh breath. Clean your teeth regularly and use a mouthwash. Frequent visits to the dentist will ensure your teeth are in order and look good when you smile.

- Keep your hands perfectly clean and your fingernails short.

- Do not wear nail varnish, as it can flake off and contaminate the food being served.

- You should only wear a hint of perfume or aftershave. If you put on too much, the food that you are serving can taste to the customer of what you are wearing.

Appearance

You need to be clean and smart on every occasion. Your clothes must be clean and smell fresh, and they should not be stained by spills of food and drink. In many hospitality establishments, staff wear a uniform supplied by their employer. It is usually smart and well tailored, designed to match the style of the business and easy to look after. Your employer may arrange for uniforms to be cleaned regularly or you may have to do this yourself. Whatever you wear, it must be well laundered and pressed, and it should be the right size so that it fits you properly.

How can your appearance affect your customers?

Many restaurants have a dress code that you will be expected to follow. Remember:

- a well-groomed appearance is appreciated by all

- clothing needs to be well fitting and spotlessly clean

- hairstyles are best kept short and tidy

- it is best to wear very little jewellery, perfume and aftershave

- shoes need to support and protect feet.

Activity: Personal appearance

In pairs, discuss how your personal appearance could be improved. Be constructive and think about how other people might react to your appearance. Discuss your ideas with the rest of the class.

How can you make sure your customers know your mind is on the job?

Professional approach

If you look good, you will feel confident and be able to do your job well. Posture is about body position – how you hold and move your body. Good posture is needed when working in a food service outlet to prevent possible health problems, such as a bad back or strains on knees. It is a good idea to stand evenly on two feet with your legs slightly apart and arms placed at your sides when you are not walking.

Good service and proper customer focus requires developing the right attitude towards the role of serving. You need to be professional, treating customers and their requests with respect. You do not have to be servile (that is, overly willing to serve) to provide efficient service, but good skills will impress both customers and your employer. In turn, they will respect you.

Assessment activity 1 Unit 11 Unit 12    BTEC

You are the training officer for a large hotel in a city centre. Your manager has just appointed three new staff in the restaurant and one in the bar. You need to prepare a short training presentation for these staff about greeting customers and taking orders.

Prepare and deliver a presentation that:

- states the importance of greeting customers appropriately **Unit 11** P1
- states the importance of giving accurate menu information **Unit 11** P2
- identifes the importance of accuracy when taking drink orders **Unit 12** P1
- describes how to respond to customers who have special requirements and how to provide appropriate assistance **Unit 11** P3, **Unit 12** P2
- describes how to deal with at least two unexpected situations that may occur when greeting customers and taking their orders and two unexpected situations that may occur when serving food at the table **Unit 11** P4, **Unit 11** P9
- describes the different service styles that can be used when serving drinks **Unit 12** P3
- states the importance of serving customers in order of arrival where possible. **Unit 12** P4

Grading tips
Unit 11

P1 You need to state why it is important to greet customers in the correct manner when they arrive for a meal or drink. Take into account the different types of customers that are served by the hospitality industry.

P2 To help you prepare this part of the presentation, think about what information a customer might need when ordering from a menu, such as how the food is cooked.

P3 Think about the different needs that customers can have. For example, some customers are in a hurry, others have special seating requirements. Describe how you would satisfy at least two of these needs in a service situation. These are only examples; you could choose other requirements.

P4 There are many unexpected situations that can arise when greeting customers and taking orders. You need to describe how you would deal with at least two of these situations.

P9 When serving customers at the table, you might make mistakes or omissions in the order, customers might have wanted items on the menu that are now unavailable, or you might even have an accident when serving hot food. You need to describe how you would deal with these or other situations that can occur when serving customers.

Unit 12

P1 You must take into account what information customers might need to help them to order drinks, and what serving staff need to ask to ensure that they bring the right drinks.

P2 Think about the different needs that customers wanting drinks might have, such as those with mobility difficulties or those who require service outside specified hours. Describe how you would satisfy these needs in a service situation. These are only examples; you could choose other needs.

P3 The different styles of service are bar service and table service. You should describe how you would serve drinks in each situation. Think about why bar drinks service and table drinks service are different.

P2 How you would feel if other people were being served first even if they arrived after you? With this in mind, describe why it is important to try to serve customers in order.

PLTS

When you are describing how to respond to unexpected situations that may occur when greeting customers and taking orders, you will develop your skills as an **independent enquirer**.

Functional skills

When you are preparing your presentation you are developing your **ICT** skills, and when you are making your presentation you are demonstrating your **English** skills.

Preparing the service area for food

Waiting staff need to know how to clean, organise and lay tables. By keeping the restaurant or dining area clean and well organised, a business hopes to provide a good impression. That is why food and drink outlets aim to be visually as well as hygienically clean. They must smell fresh and be free from stale odours. There is nothing more unpleasant than going to eat a meal in an outlet that looks dirty, with sticky tables and chairs and soiled carpets stained with spilt drinks.

Although cleaners may be employed, it is the responsibility of service staff to keep work areas, furniture and all equipment clean and presentable. This involves tasks such as:

- dusting and arranging the furniture
- vacuuming furniture, carpets and other floor coverings
- polishing counter tops and tables
- cleaning the equipment used for serving and displaying food.

Tips for cleaning a food and drink service area

- Always clean the room before laying tables.
- Open windows to freshen up the room.
- Clean, dust and vacuum the highest things first.
- Dust before using the vacuum cleaner.
- Always use clean cloths, brushes, dusters, mops and buckets – it is difficult to clean using dirty equipment.
- Do not store cleaning equipment where it can be seen by customers.
- The floor should be the last thing to be cleaned.
- Empty the vacuum cleaner so it is ready for next time.

The method of organising and laying up tables will depend on the type of outlet and the style its owners are trying to create. Tables can be round, square or rectangular. Round tables take up more space than square and rectangular ones, but they are friendlier for groups of diners.

In many outlets, tables are fixed to the floor. To prepare for service, they just need wiping over with a clean cloth and sanitiser. If condiments, napkins and menus are kept on tables, these must be checked and cleaned and refilled or replaced where necessary.

In more formal outlets, where most customers will make a booking, tables can be arranged in the room according to the number of customers that are expected and the size of each group. The exact layout can change every day. Once tables are in position, the cloths or coverings are put on. Before they are laid with cutlery and equipment, the tables should be checked to ensure they do not wobble. A small piece of card or wine cork placed under a leg should stop any wobble.

All equipment needs to be inspected for cleanliness before it is placed on the table. A large plate can be used as a guide for spacing cutlery. This is placed in front of where each customer is going to sit, and the required cutlery can then be placed around it. Glasses and cruets (salt and pepper pots) should be put on next, with any table arrangement such as flowers last of all.

It is a good idea to check everything is in place before customers arrive. This is usually done by a supervisor or restaurant manager.

Why do different outlets have different styles of table layout?

Activity: The lay-up

Do this activity by working on your own.

1 Position and cloth a table suitable for three customers.

2 Lay the table for a formal three-course meal including bread rolls. Your three customers will be eating soup, a main course of chicken or fish, followed by a dessert.

3 Position all the other necessary equipment on the table, such as glasses, butter plate, table number, napkins and flowers.

4 Get your tutor or another member of your group to check that the table is ready for service.

Preparing a dumb waiter or service counter

The service counter is where all the equipment that is needed for serving customers is kept. Often a team of people will work from one counter. These are placed around the service area at convenient points for staff to use. Some are fitted with electrical points so that lights and food hotplates can be plugged in.

Service counters need to be kept clean and freshly stocked with cutlery, crockery and service trays, table coverings and condiments for every service. The equipment is usually stored in a specific order for ease of access by the team. Figure 2 shows a typical arrangement. The design of the counter will influence where items go.

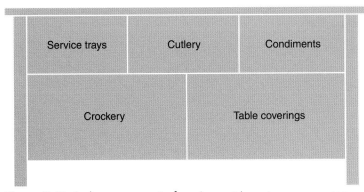

Figure 2: Typical arrangement of equipment in a storage counter

Report any problems

If you come across any problems while getting ready for service, you should report them to your supervisor. Problems with equipment and furniture need attending to promptly. If you do not deal with problems, customers may get poor service, which could result in complaints. It could even lead to accidents, which is why you must report and deal with potential hazards such as a chair with a loose leg or an electrical item with a faulty flex or plug.

Service equipment

You need to know how to prepare and handle crockery, cutlery, glassware and the other equipment used in food and drink service.

Crockery

Crockery is often heavy and difficult to move. It is best stored on shelves or in cupboards that have been specially designed to take the weight and offer some security.

- Do not make piles of crockery too high; they can topple over and break.
- Store heavy items near to the ground, so that you do not have to lift them on to high shelves, but not so near the ground that items become dirty.
- Always store crockery in a clean area.
- Use trolleys to move crockery if these are available.

Cutlery

Cutlery (knives, forks and spoons) should be stored in specially designed containers or drawers in sideboards. This will prevent damage and keep loose cutlery tidy.

Containers make it easier to move heavy cutlery around the restaurant. However, if containers are used, fork prongs and knife blades should be pointed downwards to reduce the risk of accidents, as they can be sharp.

The storage equipment for cutlery should be cleaned regularly as cutlery goes into people's mouths and therefore it must be kept scrupulously clean.

Glassware

Glasses can be broken or chipped easily. Broken or chipped glasses should never be used. It is important to check glasses before service, so that damaged glasses are not used by customers.

Glasses should be stored:

- upside down to stop dust getting into them
- near to where they are needed
- on clean surfaces free from drink spillages
- by grouping each type and size of glass together
- on specially designed racks or shelves above the bar counter at head height.

Glasses can be arranged in very attractive displays when they are being stored, which can add to the visual appeal of a bar or restaurant. For information about different types of glassware, see page 339.

Tablecloths

Tablecloths can be made from linen, cotton, polyester or a mixed fabric such as polycotton. These cloths will need to be laundered either on or

How can glassware be stored attractively?

off the premises. A good stock will need to be kept in a dry, dark and secure place.

- When laying a cloth, do not handle it too much as this causes creases, which spoils the appearance as well as leaving dirty marks.
- Tablecloths should be large enough to cover the surface of the table and hang down each side by at least 30 cm. Some of the table leg should be covered for good presentation.
- White is the preferred colour as this gives a good background to equipment, food and table decorations. Light pastel colours are also used, and these are often placed over white cloths.
- Highly patterned cloths can detract from the visual appearance of the food and the decor of the restaurant.

Sideboards

Sideboards need stocking with equipment and arranging at the start of each day or before each service. Trays and crockery need preparing and placing in the appropriate location. To avoid messy presentation, there should be enough service equipment so that all dishes can be served with separate tools.

A check needs to be made for cleanliness. There should be no build-up of dirt or waste food on the sideboards from the previous service. If there is, the sideboard needs to be cleaned properly before the start of service.

Some sideboards have electrically heated food heaters and plate warmers. These need to be turned on in time for them to reach the required temperatures. They must also be turned off at the end of each service. It is quite easy to forget to do this.

Heated service units

Heated service units are designed for particular styles of food service, such as a carvery service for roast meats or where a wide selection of hot food is offered.

- These units maintain hot foods at temperatures of 63°C or above. It is a legal requirement to keep hot food at 63°C or above to stop bacterial growth.
- They are used in outlets such as pubs, fast-food chains and shopping malls and in contract catering operations.

Did you know?

Hot food must be maintained at a temperature of 63°C or above. Cold food must be kept at below 8°C.

What kind of outlets use heated service units?

What are the advantages of refrigerated service units?

Refrigerated service units

Refrigerated service units are designed to keep food below 8°C, which is a legal requirement to help prevent bacterial growth in cold food.

- Refrigerated service units are essential for displays of salads, sandwiches, baguettes and desserts.

- In pubs, cafés and bars, they are used to display and keep wine, bottled beers and lagers, fruit drinks and bottled waters so that these drinks are chilled ready for service.

Trays

Trays come in various shapes and sizes. They are made from materials that are strong and easily cleaned. Trays should always be clean – any that are chipped or scratched should not be used as they may harbour germs.

Round trays are usually used for drink service and taking dishes of food to tables. Square and oblong trays are used for clearing away dirty crockery and glasses to service points and wash-up areas. They are also used to bring food from the kitchen to the food service point or dumb waiter. Oblong trays are also usually available at self-service counters for customers' use.

Food trays should be stored on or to the side of dumb waiters and self-service counters. Drinks trays, sometimes known as salvers, need to be kept behind or on the bar counter. Linen napkins or paper serviettes can be placed on them to help soak up any liquid spills.

Assessment activity 2

Unit 11 **M**   Unit 12 **M**   **BTEC**

This is a practical activity. You need to prepare an area for food service and for drink service. You will be observed by your tutor to ensure that you complete all tasks to the necessary standard. **Unit 11 M**, **Unit 12 M**

Grading tip
Unit 11 and 12

M It is a good idea to make a list of the tasks you need to carry out in order to prepare a restaurant and bar area for service.

 PLTS

When you are preparing a restaurant and a bar area for service, you are developing your skills as a **self-manager**.

 Functional skills

If you make a list of the different tasks you need to complete, you will be able to practise your **English** skills in writing.

11.2 Know how to serve customers in a dining area

So far we have focused on greeting customers and taking orders. In this section, we will look at the process of serving food to customers. This section covers:

- customer service
- safety and hygiene
- menu items
- maintaining dining and service areas
- style of service
- condiments and accompaniments
- arranging and presenting food
- evaluating your performance.

Customer service

It is important to know customers' needs so that they can be served properly. You need to find this out at the time you take the order, but it is also good to ask if everything is satisfactory during the meal.

It is also important to continue to give customers information during their meal, and simple comments like pointing out that the plates might be hot show customer care skills.

Teamwork

Almost all jobs in hospitality involve working with others as part of a team, often of all ages and backgrounds. Good people skills and being reliable are essential in catering.

Effective communication is a major factor in ensuring customer satisfaction. How you communicate with other colleagues in your team will impact on the standard of service customers receive and how your colleagues respond to you.

For example, when you take orders from customers these should be clear and easy to read. Kitchens are busy places and your colleagues will have to understand the order exactly. If they cannot follow your instructions, mistakes can be made and customers might not get what they ordered.

Some customers will have special requests. For example, they may ask that an ingredient is added or taken away from a dish. You will have to pass on these requests to the chef.

Activity: Pros and cons of teamwork

Think of some advantages of working in teams. Are there any disadvantages?

Timing

Just as customers should never be kept waiting too long to be seated and to place their order, they will expect to receive their food and drinks in a reasonable time, as well as their bill when they wish to leave. Some customers will be in more of a hurry than others, and you need to take this in to account when serving all your customers.

Style of service

There are several styles that can be adopted when serving food to customers.

Plate service

Plate service is where food is set out on plates in the kitchen and then carried out by serving staff and presented to customers. Sometimes food is simply plated in the kitchen for ease of serving. This might be the case in a guest house. In some upmarket restaurants the chefs require an elaborate presentation of dishes on the plate and this could not be achieved by waiting staff arranging the food from serving dishes with a spoon and fork at the table, so these restaurants also operate a plate service.

Plated food should always be served with style

Silver service

For silver service, food is served with a spoon and fork from service dishes on to customers' plates at their table. To serve meals in this style, a restaurant requires more equipment and staff as everything has to be brought to customers at the table. It is therefore a more costly approach, and it requires training staff in the elaborate serving techniques. Many luxury hotels and restaurants serve food in this way.

Counter service

In a counter service operation, customers queue in front of a counter and make a selection from foods that are already prepared or choose food to be cooked to order by staff. Sometimes the meals, such as grilled steaks, are brought by staff to the customers when they are sitting at their tables. This means customers do not have to wait at the counter while their meals are being cooked. This prevents long queues building up at the counter, and ensures that the food is served hot and fresh.

Trays, crockery and drinks are collected by customers when they make their choices at the counter. Payment is usually at a cash point at one end of the counter, where condiments, cutlery and serviettes can also be collected.

In which type of outlet are you likely to have counter service?

Self-service

Self-service is a system where customers help themselves from counters or buffets to food that is either plated in single portions or held in multi-portion containers.

Vending is also a type of self-service. Fully automated machines can dispense a wide range of snack food, drinks and confectionery. Vending is used where it would be uneconomic or impractical to have a staffed operation, such as at railway stations, in minibars in hotel bedrooms and at drinks stations in office blocks.

Buffet

A buffet offers a wide selection of foods presented on a table or a purpose-built counter. Customers either help themselves or can be assisted by staff from behind the buffet. This style of service is often used for functions. It is also used for breakfast service in many hotels.

Buffet service allows a large number of people to be served in a short period of time by relatively few staff. However, these staff must be attentive to customers and skilled in food service.

- Staff need skills in food presentation, as dishes and equipment need to be attractively displayed.
- Food service skills are needed, as customers often like food served to them while they make their choices.
- Used crockery, cutlery and glasses must be cleared away quickly and efficiently, as the turnover of customers can be quite brisk, especially at a breakfast sitting.

Activity: Type of service

Think back to occasions when you have had a meal out. What style of service did you receive? How did this affect the presentation of the food on the plate?

Food service skills

Staff need to be very skilled in serving techniques as careless serving will spoil the presentation and enjoyment of the food. Food and beverages may be served in several styles and you should be confident in all types of operation. The style adopted by an outlet depends on several factors, including:

- the type of outlet
- how much time the customer has available
- the type of food being served
- the cost of the food or meal
- the type of menu.

Safety and hygiene

Working safely and maintaining hygienic practices is essential to providing good customer care, and it is also a legal duty. Health and safety legislation applies to all businesses, those who work in them and people who visit the business premises.

General safety

Restaurants, cafés and bars can be dangerous places, posing risks not only for staff but also for customers. The Health and Safety at Work Act 1974 requires employers to ensure a healthy, safe and secure environment for the public and their employees. However, all employees also have a duty under this legislation for maintaining health and safety. You should always be observant and report anything that could be a safety problem.

We will now look at health and safety issues particularly relevant to food and drink service. There are some tips to help you work safely when serving food and drink. Follow these guidelines and you should avoid harming others and yourself.

Safe handling of food and drink

Customers are at risk of becoming ill if the food and drink they consume is not handled safely or is not cooked properly. As more meals are eaten away from the home, incidents of food poisoning have increased.

There are codes of practice and rules and regulations regarding the safe handling of food and drink. You need to be familiar with these regulations and you must comply with the requirements when you are at work. You should take care to keep food clean and take steps to prevent any food stored in the restaurant becoming dirty or contaminated.

Safe storage of items

Furniture and equipment such as trolleys, tables and chairs must be stored so that they do not cause a hazard to customers or staff.

- Stack tables and chairs in manageable piles. These should not be too high, and you should check that the piles are not likely to tip over.

- Unused equipment should not be kept in public areas where customers can go.

- Flexes on electrical equipment such as vacuum cleaners must be removed from electrical sockets when the equipment is not in use and carefully wound up. Trailing cables can be a trip hazard.

How can poor storage of furniture and equipment lead to accidents?

Clean work areas

Food and drink work areas must always be clean and tidy. They are often on view to customers and a dirty environment creates a very bad impression in a catering establishment. It is also not pleasant for staff to work in dirty and messy surroundings.

- Do not let packaging and wrappings build up – throw rubbish out regularly.

- Empty drinks bottles and cans should be placed in suitable containers, either for returning to suppliers or for disposal (which can include recycling).

- Used glasses and crockery should be taken to wash-up areas promptly. They should not be left uncollected where they were used by customers.

- Cleaning cloths and swabs should be kept out of sight. They should not be left in service areas unless they are being used.

What impression does an untidy and dirty environment create?

Hygienic working practices

Finally, not only must people use clean and safe working practices, anyone working with food and drink must pay attention to their personal hygiene. All staff working in the hospitality industry must be clean and presentable. This will help to prevent food poisoning and the spread of disease.

Activity: Restaurant appearances

Can you think of other things that make a work area look unpleasant and not very good to work in? Discuss this with your group.

Assessment activity 3

Unit 11 **P5** **P8** BTEC

Produce a poster on hygiene that could be displayed in a staff area in a restaurant. Your poster should:

- describe the safe and hygienic working practices that should be followed by staff when serving food to customers **P5**

- state the importance of maintaining the dining and service area. **P8**

Grading tips

P5 Important topics to consider here include ways of maintaining general safety, of ensuring the safe handling of food and safe storage and of keeping work areas clean.

P8 You need to think about cleanliness, safety, customer satisfaction and the costs of maintaining the dining and service area.

Condiments and accompaniments

Condiments and sauces are seasonings that are used to bring out the flavour of foods. A wide range is usually made available for customers. They should be kept on the customer's table or near the service point. Good hygiene is essential, and the tops of bottles and containers must be very clean.

- Sugars, such as demerara or brown sugar, white caster sugar and granulated sugar, are used for sweetening drinks.

- Sweeteners, such as saccharine or Candarel, are an alternative to sugar. They are used by customers who wish to consume less sugar.

- Sauces commonly available include vinegar, tomato ketchup, HP (brown) sauce, Worcestershire sauce, mayonnaise, mint sauce and horseradish sauce. The choice of sauces offered to customers will depend on the foods being served.

There are various ways of serving condiments, and the method used will reflect an outlet's style and policy. Many restaurants place **cruets** on the table for salt and pepper. Sometimes a cruet set also includes room for a mustard pot holding English (hot) or French (mild) mustard.

Salt, pepper, mustard and sauces can also be made available in pre-wrapped individual portions. These are convenient, hygienic and easy to control from a cost perspective. They are typically used in motorway service stations and fast-food outlets.

Cafés and guest houses may serve condiments and sauces by just placing the bottles and containers on the guest's table or on the sideboard. Where this is done, care needs to be taken to ensure that the tops of bottles and containers are kept clean.

Some outlets provide sugar in an open bowl. When sugar is left out in the open for a long time, it goes hard as it absorbs moisture from the air. It also attracts pests such as wasps. The sugar should therefore be put away in airtight containers after service finishes.

Similarly, sauces and mustards are sometimes placed in small glass bowls and served with a teaspoon. A plate needs to be placed underneath to hold the dirty spoon. This is quite a costly way of serving sauces and condiments as much can be wasted because a sauce like tomato ketchup cannot be put back into the bottle.

Key term

Cruets – small dispensers or containers for salt, pepper and other condiments.

As well as providing all the standard condiments and sauces, restaurant staff need to ensure that each dish comes with the right accompaniments. The accompaniments for some typical restaurant dishes were listed on pages 312–13.

Menu items

A menu is a list showing customers what is available to eat and how much it costs. Menus should be displayed near the entrance of an outlet so that potential customers can see what is available and what it costs before they go in. This is a legal requirement.

How can menus be used as marketing tools?

Menus are a marketing tool for the outlet and they should therefore be attractively presented. They can also be used to tell customers about any special deals or offers.

There are many styles of menus, ranging from a simple sheet of paper or a blackboard to elaborate printed menus with leather covers. On an **à la carte** menu, each dish is individually priced. On a **table d'hôte** menu, a complete meal is offered for one price. These are French terms, but they are widely used in the hospitality industry.

Key terms

A la carte – menus that give the prices of individual dishes.

Table d'hôte – menus that offer complete meals for a set price.

Activity: Menu design

Obtain a selection of menus. For example, when you are next eating in a café or passing a catering outlet, ask if you can have a copy of the menu. You can also find examples of menus on the Internet by visiting the websites of restaurant chains or more upmarket establishments.

Look at the menus to see how they are laid out. See what is being served. Look at the prices.

- What else is on the menu besides food and drinks?
- What are the good points of each menu?
- How could the menus be improved?

Dishes are usually organised in a menu in the order in which they are eaten, beginning with starters and ending with desserts. Drinks and beverages are listed separately.

- Bread is usually served to customers at the start of a meal, and especially with soup. It is served on a side plate with butter.
- Salads can be served as a starter or main course, or even as an accompaniment to the main course.
- Pasta comes in many shapes. The most popular types of pasta are spaghetti, lasagne and penne. Pasta is eaten with a spoon and fork, and parmesan cheese is offered as an accompaniment.
- Fish can be served as a fish course (especially at large banquets) or as a main course with vegetables. Fish is eaten with a fish knife and fork.
- Meat is usually offered as the main course and served with vegetables or a salad. Meat is eaten with a joint knife and fork
- Vegetables are mainly served to accompany the main course. Some vegetable dishes (e.g. cauliflower cheese) are served as a main course.
- Dessert is served after the main course, and it is eaten with a spoon and fork.
- Cheese can be served after the dessert or instead of a dessert. Cheese is often offered with celery, grapes, biscuits and butter, and it is eaten with a knife.

Serving coffee after a meal

A customer who orders coffee after a meal needs a coffee cup, saucer, under plate and spoon. This is known as a coffee set and it should be placed in front of the customer. Coffee can be poured from a large jug such as from a Cona machine, served in individual pots from a tray or made in a cafetière and left on the table for customers to help themselves. This is a good way of serving coffee.

Arranging and presenting food

People are said to eat with their eyes first. This means that you should always make food look good on the plate. Food should be positioned on a plate to look attractive. You should always put food in the middle of the plate. When serving a main course, it is best if the meat or fish is nearest the customer and you serve the vegetables on the rest of the plate.

Many organisations have their own quality standards that state how food should be presented. Staff might be given photographs showing the ideal layout or arrangement of each dish that is served in the restaurant.

Customers may have special preferences about how the food is arranged. For example, some may like a sauce on the side or poured on the vegetables rather than the meat. You should take these preferences into account when serving food at the table.

Assessment activity 4

Unit 11

Find menus from two different establishments.

1 Show how each dish on the menu should be arranged and presented on the plate. **P7**

2 Describe what service equipment will be needed to serve each dish. List the condiments and accompaniments that should be provided with each dish. **P6**

Grading tips

P6 You might show the required information on a chart.

P7 You can download menus from the Internet or can get them by visiting local restaurants. You must use two menus.

PLTS

When you are planning the layout of a dish, you will be using your skills as a **creative thinker**.

Functional skills

If you find your menus on the Internet, you will be using your **ICT** skills.

Maintaining dining and service areas

It is important that work areas are always clean and clear of dirty cutlery, crockery, glasses and equipment. They should also be clear of spare equipment. It is dangerous to have spare equipment lying around – it can be a trip hazard. Remember, catering work areas are busy places.

- When clearing from a sideboard or moving glasses, always use a tray or salver – it is much safer.

- When clearing crockery, do not stack it too high on trays – it can topple over and it is very heavy to carry.

Why is it important to load trays sensibly?

All breakages should be reported to your supervisor. In some establishments, there is a book for recording breakages and faults. It is important to stop other people using faulty or broken equipment. Faulty electrical equipment, in particular, can be dangerous.

At the beginning and end of service, it is a good idea to check the equipment and the general fixtures and fittings to make sure that there are no breakages or other problems that could cause a hazard.

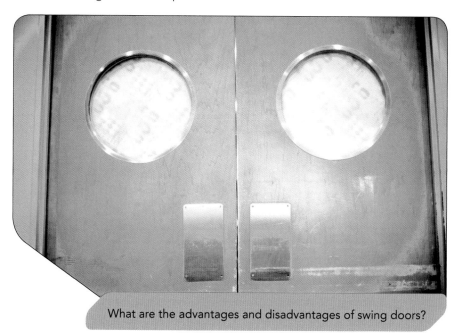

What are the advantages and disadvantages of swing doors?

Standards

All organisations have standards for cleanliness. When you work in a restaurant, you should always tidy up as you go and keep your work area clean. You should follow any departmental procedures. For example, some outlets expect menus to be stored near the door so that they can be given immediately to clients as they arrive.

Cleanliness is also very important for controlling pests. Pests are attracted to food so if waste food is not disposed of correctly, the restaurant might get a pest problem.

Maintaining customer satisfaction

When working in dining and service areas, you need to always be aware of the customers. You should not do anything that disturbs customers or reduces customer satisfaction.

- Work quietly – it is very disturbing for customers when staff are clumsy or noisily moving around with crockery and glasses.

- Using a linen napkin on a tray or salver helps to deaden any noise and prevents equipment from slipping about.

- Remember that customers can see everything that you do.

Reducing costs

You also need to be aware of costs. These should always be kept to a minimum. You should therefore always do what you can to reduce waste when you are working in a food service area. For example, cream jugs should only be filled when required by the customers, so you do not have to throw away cream at the end of service.

Evaluating your peformance

When you undertake the practical work for this unit, you will have to demonstrate your skills in serving customers. You will need to be able to evaluate your performance. To do this, you should consider several factors.

- **Timings** – prompt service is important in hospitality. You could set yourself targets, such as serving every customer with a first course within ten minutes of arriving in the restaurant.

- **Appropriateness of service style** – you can evaluate the style of service (which might be dictated by the restaurant) and consider whether a different style of service would be better in your working environment.

- **Quality and appearance of food** – when you are evaluating the success of an event involving the service of food and drink, you must consider whether the quality and appearance of the food suited the occasion. You could ask your customers what they think, using customer comment cards or by a direct approach.

- **Working methods** – you should always be thinking about ways to improve your working methods. Sometimes it is not possible to change because, for example, there is a company policy.

- **Service skills** – you need to think about whether you could develop your service skills to become better. If you feel you could do better, you need to think about what practical steps you could take to improve your skills.

- **Professional attitude** – you need to evaluate how well you demonstrated a professional attitude when you served customers. You may find that a colleague could give you some feedback and advice about your attitude.

Recommendations for improvement

A key part of any evaluation exercise is about thinking what could be done next time to make things go even better. After you have thought about the ways of judging your performance, it will be possible to decide what aspects can be improved and how this can be done.

12.2 Know how to serve alcoholic and non-alcoholic drinks

We now turn from food to the service of drinks. This section covers:

- storing drinks
- types of glass
- service equipment
- types of drink
- serving drinks
- evaluating your performance.

Storing drinks

To provide the best taste and experience, alcoholic beverages must be stored and served at the correct temperatures. Table 2 shows the correct way of storing different alcoholic drinks and the temperatures at which they should be served. Note that some people like ice in their spirits, so when serving a spirit always ask if the customer wants ice.

Beverage	Service and storage temperature	Storage needs
Red wine	Room temperature	Lying on side to keep cork moist
White and rosé wine	Chilled	Lying on side to keep cork moist
Sparkling wine	Chilled	Lying on side to keep cork moist
Bottled and draft beers	Chilled	Upright in cellar; barrels need to settle before service
Brandy	Room temperature	Upright to prevent leakage
Other spirits	Room temperature	Upright to prevent leakage
Sherry and port	Room temperature	Upright to prevent leakage
Liqueurs	Room temperature	Upright to prevent leakage

Table 2: Serving and storing drinks

Types of drink

You will need to know about the different types of drinks to work behind a bar or to be able to take orders and serve drinks in a restaurant effectively.

- **Wines** are made from the fermentation of fresh grapes. The best wines are often very expensive. Wines are divided into three main categories: red, white and rosé wines. Some white and rosé wines are sparkling. The most famous sparkling wine is champagne.
- **Beers, lagers and stout** are made from fermenting malted barley. The flavour and colour of a beer is affected by how much the barley is roasted and the addition of different amounts of hops.

- **Spirits** are distilled drinks and therefore very strong. The most popular spirits are whisky, gin, brandy, rum and vodka. Some spirit drinks are called shots. Cocktails are made from a mix of drinks, but they are usually based on one or more spirits.
- **Vermouths** are typically wine-based drinks that have been flavoured with herbs. They are often served as an aperitif before a meal.
- **Fortified wines**, such as sherry and port, are wines that have been made stronger by adding spirits.
- **Liqueurs** are flavoured and often sweetened spirits. They are usually served after a meal.
- **Mixers** are drinks, such as soda water, that are often served with spirits. Fruit juices can also be served with spirits. For example, a popular drink is vodka and orange, which is a mix of vodka and orange juice.
- **Cordials** (non-fizzy soft drinks) are occasionally served with spirits or used in cocktails.
- **Water** is often sold in bars and restaurants in bottles. Bottled water is sourced from natural springs and it is usually referred to as mineral water.

Coffee

Coffee can be made either by using the granules from a jar of instant coffee or by using ground coffee beans. The instant variety can be made directly in a mug or jug. Ground coffee comes in vacuum packs to keep it fresh. Ground coffee can be made in a variety of specialist equipment such as Cona machines and cafetières, which are glass jugs that come in various sizes suitable for one or more people.

When and where are you likely to serve tea and coffee?

Coffee machines can make a range of speciality coffees, usually from fresh coffee beans which are ground when the customer orders a drink. This is the freshest way of making coffee. Many customers have their personal favourite coffees, such as:

- latte
- espresso
- mocha
- cappuccino.

Serving coffee in well-designed mugs or cups increases the customer's enjoyment and small, tasty biscuits can be served with the drink.

Activity: Types of coffee

Visit a local coffee shop and note down all the hot drinks they serve. Find out the differences between the types of coffee served.

Tips for serving coffee
- Make sure cups and mugs are very clean.
- Make sure the coffee is hot.
- Make sure the coffee is not too weak or strong.
- Serve with hot milk or cream.
- Serve with brown or demerara sugar.

How many types of tea can you think of?

Tea

Tea can be served in several ways. The style of the outlet will influence the method of service.

Tea bags are easy and convenient to use. The amount of tea needed for a cup or serving is already measured out. String and tag is a one-cup tea bag with an identification tag which can be left outside the pot or cup for ease of service. There is a wide range of good quality teas available in tea bags.

Bulk leaf tea takes a little more time to prepare and serve, but this more traditional style of serving is enjoyed by many people.

Herbal and fruit teas also come in bags, and they are popular for those who want a healthy alternative to normal tea. Herbal teas include peppermint, camomile and rosehip. Fruit teas include raspberry, blackcurrant and apple.

Some outlets leave a variety of teas on a counter so that customers can make their own choice.

Tips for serving tea

- Make sure all equipment is very clean.
- Tea must be made with boiling water.
- Make sure the correct amount of tea is used.
- Serve with cold milk.
- Serve with white sugar.

Hot chocolate

Drinking chocolate is made from fresh chocolate granules or a powdered chocolate drink mixed with either hot water or milk. Hot chocolate can be made directly in a mug for serving. Commercial chocolate drinks usually have sugar already added, so extra sugar is not needed. Always serve a spoon with this drink as it separates out and needs frequent stirring by the customer. It can be served with whipped cream on top.

Have you ever used a drinks machine like this one?

Types of glass

We have already discussed the general steps needed to store glassware properly (see page 322). You also need to know which glasses to use for different drinks. Table 3 shows the glasses that are usually used to serve different alcoholic beverages.

Beverage	Glass for service
Red wine	Paris goblet large bowl
White and rosé wine	Paris goblet small bowl
Sparkling wine	Flute
Bottled and draft beers	Half-pint or pint glass
Brandy	Brandy balloon
Other spirits	Slim Jim
Sherry and port	Sherry glass
Liqueurs	Elgin glass

Table 3: Drinks glasses

Note that it is very important not to use glasses straight from the glass wash as they will still be warm from the washing water.

Serving drinks

Many customers will walk up to the bar to order and receive their drinks. You should serve them at the bar, remembering to try and serve the customers in the order that they arrive at the bar.

In some establishments, customers are usually served at the table. This is especially the case in hotels and restaurants. When serving at the table, you should take the order at the table, collect the drinks from the bar and take them to the customers at the table.

Service procedures and techniques

When serving beers, it is important to tilt the glass so that the head does not pour over the top of the glass. This technique is used for bottled, canned and **draft** beers. In some establishments, glasses are chilled before service. This helps to produce a good head on the beer and keeps the beer cooler for the customer.

When serving wine, it is important that you twist the bottle when you finish pouring so that the wine does not drip on the bar or the tablecloth when serving at a table.

Key term

Draft – a drink served at the bar by opening a tap; the drink travels through a pipe from the barrel, which is usually kept in a cellar. The drink is sometimes cooled on its journey from barrel to glass.

Key terms

Free pouring – a method of measuring and pouring a drink into a glass.

Optic – a device that gives a measure of alcohol from the bottle when the optic is pressed.

Measures

Many alcoholic beverages must be measured so that the correct amount is served. This is a legal requirement. This applies to any wine served by the glass and spirits.

When using a measure, you must fill the measure to the top and then pour it into the glass without spilling any of the liquid. This technique is known as **free pouring**. Some bottled spirits or wines are connected to **optics**. This is a transparent measure fitted on to the mouth of the bottle; the bottle is stored upside down, so that the optic is under the bottle. When you press the optic, it issues one measure of the drink.

Accompaniments

It is standard practice to ask customers if they would like ice in their drinks, particularly when serving spirits. Some drinks come with a slice of lemon or another garnish such as an olive.

Activity: Garnishing and decorating drinks

In groups, discuss which garnishes and decorations are most appropriate for different drinks. When do you think you should offer a slice of lemon or a cherry with a drink? Should all drinks be served with ice, or can you think of any that should never be served in this way?

Service equipment

At the beginning and end of service, it is a good idea to check any equipment used in the service of drinks. This is likely to include refrigerated units, glasses and trays. Any problems should be reported to the supervisor. In some establishments there is a book to record problems and breakages.

You also need to check that drinks menus are available for customers. These are a legal requirement, and they must show the price and alcoholic content of each drink.

Evaluating your performance

At the end of a session in which you have served drinks to customers, you should always reflect on how you have done. You will need to evaluate your performance. To do this, you can adopt exactly the same approach that was suggested for evaluating food service (see page 335).

Assessment activity 5

Unit 12

BTEC

Prepare and deliver a presentation about the service of beverages. This should be suitable for anybody new to bar work. Your presentation should:

- state the importance of checking glassware for damage **P5**
- state the correct storage and service temperature for a range of drinks **P6**
- describe the service techniques for bottled drinks, draft beers, free pouring and optic-based drinks **P7**
- state how to select the correct glasses for different drinks. **P8**

Grading tips

P5 Why is it important to check glassware for damage before service? How would you feel if you were served a drink in a chipped or damaged glass? Why would you feel like this?

P6 You might want to use a list of drinks and group them according to service and storage temperatures. They tend to be in the same groups for service and storage.

P7 This might be best achieved by listing each step of the service procedure in the correct order for different types of drinks.

P8 There is often more than one type of glass that can be used for serving a drink. However, you need to explain how you would make a suitable choice.

Assessment activity 6

Unit 11  Unit 12

BTEC

This is a practical activity. You need to serve food and drink to customers on several different occasions. This will enable you to demonstrate your skills.

1 Provide a food and drink service for customers. You must use your customer service skills. You should record what you have served and on what occasions. You will be observed by your tutor, a colleague or a supervisor in the workplace. **Unit 11 M2, Unit 12 M2**

2 Evaluate your ability to deliver professional, safe and hygienic food and drink service using effective customer service skills. **Unit 11 D1, Unit 12 D1**

Grading tips
Unit 11 and 12

M2 You should consider in advance what you are required to do and prepare yourself by reading the menu. Ensure that you understand each item on the menu and that you know what drinks are available from the bar.

D1 You should write down all the things that you did in the service of food and drink and explain what you did well and what you did less well. Provide some ideas for how you could improve. Explain what you will do in future to improve your food and drink service.

PLTS

When you are evaluating your performance, you are using your **reflective learner** skills.

Functional skills

When you are preparing and giving your presentation, you are demonstrating your **English** skills.

12.3 Know the appropriate legislation that relates to the serving of alcoholic drinks

This final section sets out the basic legal requirements that must be met when serving alcoholic drinks. It covers:

- relevant legislation
- implications of non-compliance
- responding to someone under the influence of drugs.

Relevant legislation

A primary duty of any employer is to maintain the health and safety of its staff and customers. Your employer must ensure that you and your customers are safe in the workplace. You are also obliged by law to make sure your customers and colleagues are safe. If you see any hazard or danger, it is your responsibility to report this to a manager or supervisor.

There are also some specific laws that apply to any business serving alcohol.

Licensing Acts

Over the years, various governments have introduced various measures to control and regulate the sales of alcoholic beverages. They have done this in an attempt to:

- prevent crime and disorder
- protect the public from nuisance
- ensure the safety of the public
- prevent the use of alcohol by children.

If a business sells alcohol, then there must be one or more personal licence holders. The licence holders are responsible for ensuring that the business obeys the law in respect of the sale of alcohol.

It is illegal to sell or provide alcohol to anyone under 18 in most circumstances, although 16 and 17 year olds can drink beer, wine or cider with a table meal if accompanied by an adult. If you are working in a bar or restaurant and you think a customer who asks for alcohol is under age, you must ask for proof of age. Most establishments accept driving licences or passports as proof of age, but some issue specially produced cards for young people who have proved their age.

There are other occasions when it is not lawful to serve alcohol. It is illegal to sell alcohol to someone who is drunk. It is also illegal to sell alcohol outside specified hours, although these times can be varied if licence holders apply to the licensing authorities.

It is important that licence holders do not allow the use or sale of illegal drugs on their premises. Anyone using drugs should be asked to leave by the manager. This should be done with care. People who use drugs can become violent or aggressive.

Unfortunately, alcohol can also cause some people to become disorderly or violent. Any customer who is becoming disorderly or violent should be refused any more alcohol. In this situation, tell your line manager, who will get the customer to leave. If you have to ask someone to leave the bar and they refuse to go, you should tell your line manager who should contact the police immediately. Whatever happens, you should always remain calm in the event of any problems.

Sale of Goods Act

It is the law that the prices and alcoholic content of drinks are clearly displayed. This means a bar list or drinks menu should be available to table customers and a price list should be displayed at the bar. The bar price list is often pinned to the wall.

Weights and Measures Act

Many alcoholic beverages must be served in the correct measures. These include wines served by the glass and spirits.

Spirits are served in 25 ml or 35 ml measures. These drinks can be measured using an optic. Wine by the glass can also be served from an optic (though using a larger optic than a spirit optic) or in a glass with a line to show the correct measure. Wines can be served in 125 ml, 175 ml and 250 ml measures.

Draft beers have to be measured in pints or half pints. They are usually poured into glasses that hold exactly a pint or a half pint. Some glasses have a line on the side to show when you must stop filling to supply the correct amount.

Implications of non-compliance

If licence holders do not comply with the law, they can face several penalties. They could be fined up to £5000 or receive a prison sentence. In some cases they could lose their personal licence and in very serious cases the business could be closed down. In every case of **non-compliance**, the reputation of the business can suffer through negative publicity. This could put off customers and the business could lose profits as a result.

Key term

Non-compliance – if a business or an individual obeys the law, they are compliant. If they do not obey the law, they are non-compliant.

Responding to someone under the influence of drugs

You should consult your supervisor if you are not sure how to deal with someone under the influence of drugs. The police or other support agencies should be called if necessary. However, it is best if the supervisor makes this decision. As always, you should remain calm when you are dealing with someone who is under the influence of drugs.

Assessment activity 7

Unit 12 (P9) (P10) (P11) (P12) (M3)

Prepare a leaflet on the law that covers serving alcoholic beverages. This should be suitable for new bar staff to ensure that they know and understand the law. Your leaflet should:

- describe the current legislation relating to licensing, weights and measures **P9**
- list the circumstances when a customer should not be served with alcohol **P10**
- describe how to respond to someone who might be under the influence of drugs or buying/selling drugs **P11**
- describe how to deal with violent or disorderly customers **P12**
- analyse the implications of non-compliance for hospitality businesses. **M3**

Grading tips

P9 You should cover the legal measures for serving alcohol, the laws about who can buy alcohol and the laws governing when you can serve alcoholic beverages.

P10 There are occasions when you must not serve alcohol to customers. These must be clearly stated in your leaflet.

P11 Think about the rest of the customers in the bar and their reaction to how you deal with the situation. Think about the effects on the business.

P12 Think about how to deal with the situation without impacting too much on the other customers.

M3 Think of what can happen if the business where you work does not comply with the law when selling alcohol. How will it affect you personally? What about the potential impact on the business and its customers?

 PLTS

When you are describing the implications of relevant legislation relating to licensing and weights and measures, you are developing your skills as an **independent enquirer**.

 Functional skills

Preparing a leaflet will support your **ICT** skills.

Gemma Venables
Restaurant manager

Gemma Venables has worked as a restaurant manager for three years. She was previously an assistant manager and had worked as a waitress when she first finished college. She is responsible for ensuring that guests in the hotel receive food and beverages at breakfast, lunch and dinner. She also has responsibilities in the bar, where the hotel serves bar snacks, and for room service.

Her day usually begins quite early, she supervises the service of breakfast. After breakfast, Gemma deals with emails, checks future bookings and may have meetings with the organisers of events such as conferences or banquets. She also holds regular meetings with her staff to ensure that high standards are maintained.

Lunch service is often quiet in a hotel, so Gemma may take time off at lunchtime, returning to work in time for dinner service. Gemma particularly likes the service of dinner, as customers are in less of a hurry and she has the chance to build a rapport with the guests. She has an assistant to help her through the day, as the restaurant needs to be open for breakfast, lunch and dinner every day of the week.

The most interesting part of Gemma's job is meeting people and she loves the reaction she gets from satisfied customers. She meets new people during every shift – from business people during the week to families at weekends – so she has to make sure she is always prepared for new challenges.

Think about it!

- Do you think you would enjoy working closely with people, like Gemma does in the restaurant? What sorts of people would you expect to serve?
- How would you feel serving food to people regularly? What would give you most job satisfaction when serving food and drink?

Just checking

1 List the important points that must be observed to maintain personal freshness and good presentation when working in a food and drink outlet.

2 What important points should you remember when greeting customers?

3 How should spillages and breakages be dealt with in a food service outlet?

4 List the main accompaniments that should be stocked ready for service on a sideboard.

5 What are the legal minimum and maximum temperatures for the storage of hot and cold food?

6 What information must a menu have on it?

7 List the key points for cleaning a food and drink service area.

8 List the information that must be obtained from customers when taking a food order.

9 What are the five main types of food service?

10 Give three types of people you should not serve with alcoholic beverages.

edexcel :::

Assignment tips

- Customer service is a very important part of food and drink service. You should think about the evidence that you have gathered in Units 3 and 4 to help you prepare for your assignments for these units.

- It may help you to visit some restaurants in your area to get a feel for the different types of outlets and the different ways of serving customers. This would also be a good time to collect menus that you need for some activities.

- Do not forget the importance of health and safety. You need to be sure that you deal with health and safety issues in your assignments. It may help you to list the typical hazards found in restaurants and bars to ensure that you are aware of them when doing practical work.

- When you are setting up the food and drink service area, it might be useful to keep a log of what you do. You should also do this after providing food and drink service and customer care. Your tutor or other observer will back up your log by providing a witness statement on your performance.

- You will need to show that you can evaluate your performance. You should think about timing, service style, the quality and appearance of the food, your working methods and service skills, and whether you displayed a professional attitude. From this review, you should have an idea of what you could have done better and you can make recommendations about how you could improve in these areas.

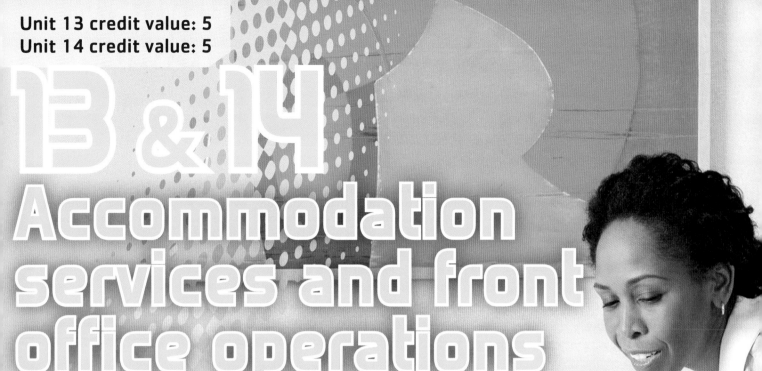

13 & 14

Accommodation services and front office operations

Accommodation services and front office operations are central to many hospitality businesses. The impressions these areas give can impact hugely on guest satisfaction and ultimately on the success of the business.

Accommodation is not just provided by hotels. It is also a service offered by self-catering apartments, halls of residence and residential care homes, as well as non-residential centres such as conference venues. In many businesses, the accommodation department is commonly known as housekeeping. It revolves around the provision of sleeping accommodation and the related activities of cleaning and servicing rooms.

Front office is sometimes referred to as reception, but you will learn that it involves a much wider range of duties. The front office handles all the activities involved in administering a guest's stay – before arrival, on arrival, during the stay and on departure – and responds to the individual needs of guests. It involves taking bookings, checking guests in and out, and administering their bills and payments, and it requires good customer service skills.

In these units, you will learn more about the roles and responsibilities of accommodation and front office staff, and you will have an opportunity to practise and demonstrate the skills needed by staff working in these areas.

Learning outcomes

After completing these units, you should:

Unit 13 Accommodation services in hospitality

1   Know the purpose of accommodation services

2   Know the job roles and responsibilities of accommodation services employees

3   Be able to demonstrate skills in accommodation services.

Unit 14 Hospitality front office operations

1   Know the responsibilities and purpose of the front office

2   Know the roles of the front office

3   Be able to demonstrate skills used in the front office.

Assessment and grading criteria

These tables show you what you must do in order to achieve a pass, merit or distinction grade, and where you can find activities in this book to help you.

Unit 13 Accommodation services in hospitality

To achieve a pass grade the evidence must show that you are able to:	To achieve a merit grade the evidence must show that, in addition to the pass criteria, you are able to:	To achieve a distinction grade the evidence must show that, in addition to the pass and merit criteria, you are able to:
P1 describe the purpose of accommodation services **Assessment activity 1, page 354**	**M1** compare the roles and responsibilities of people working in different accommodation services **Assessment activity 2, page 364**	
P2 describe the job roles and responsibilities of people working in accommodation services **Assessment activity 2, page 364**		
P3 describe documentation used to maintain standards **Assessment activity 2, page 364**		
P4 prepare and service a bedroom by carrying out the appropriate procedures **Assessment activity 3, page 369**	**M2** design a cleaning routine for the cleaning and servicing of a bedroom **Assessment activity 3, page 369**	**D1** evaluate the importance of accommodation services on the guest experience and the success of the business **Assessment activity 3, page 369**

Unit 14 Hospitality front office operations

To achieve a pass grade the evidence must show that you are able to:	To achieve a merit grade the evidence must show that, in addition to the pass criteria, you are able to:	To achieve a distinction grade the evidence must show that, in addition to the pass and merit criteria, you are able to:
P1 describe the responsibilities and purpose of the front office **Assessment activity 4, page 380**	**M1** explain the roles and responsibilities of people working in the front office **Assessment activity 5, page 391**	**D1** analyse how the flow of information between the guests and the front office can affect the guest experience and the success of the business **Assessment activity 5, page 391**
P2 describe the roles of the front office **Assessment activity 5, page 391**		
P3 demonstrate guest service skills when meeting and greeting guests and dealing with guest enquiries **Assessment activity 6, page 396**	**M2** explain what is meant by the guest cycle in relation to the activities of the front office **Assessment activity 6, page 396**	**D2** evaluate the importance of the front office on the guest experience and the success of the business **Assessment activity 6, page 396**

How you will be assessed

You will be assessed by assignments that will be designed and marked by tutors at your centre. The assignments will be designed to allow you to show your knowledge and understanding of accommodation services and front office operations, as well as demonstrate your practical skills.

Your assignments could require you to:
- make presentations
- produce written work
- demonstrate housekeeping and customer service skills
- take part in role plays.

Taru, 16-year-old learner

These units have been really useful because they taught me a lot about the importance of maintaining standards. I hadn't really realised how important the accommodation services department is and the impact it has on the customer experience. I have stayed in hotels with my parents before, and now that I have actually worked in housekeeping I really appreciate how hard the staff work to make sure everything looks nice.

I have also learnt how much other departments rely on front office to do their jobs properly. If the front office does not communicate properly, nobody else will know what they are supposed to be doing.

I enjoyed the practical element of the course. We worked as a team but there was an element of competition to see who could clean rooms to the highest standards. I also really enjoyed working in front office. I was lucky enough to work in a five-star hotel and I was really impressed with how much effort it put in to making sure that guests are happy.

These units will help me in my career. Eventually, I would like to work on a cruise ship in the hotel operations department, but I have been told that I first need to get more work experience in a four-star or five-star hotel.

Over to you
- Ask friends and family what they first notice when they stay in a hotel.
- Apart from the need to create a good impression, what other reasons are there to maintain high standards of cleanliness?
- What qualities do you think you need to work in front office?
- Media stars often stay in hotels. What special requirements do you think they might have?

13.1 Know the purpose of accommodation services

Welcome **Housekeeping roles**

List all the organisations in your area that might employ housekeeping staff. Try to identify the jobs they do.

Accommodation services revolves around the provision of sleeping accommodation and the related activities of cleaning and servicing rooms. Let's start by looking at the:

- types of accommodation services
- purpose of accommodation services.

Types of accommodation services

Guest accommodation is not just provided by hotels, it is also offered by cruise ships, holiday centres, timeshare resorts, halls of residence, residential care homes and the growing private service sector. Many organisations providing accommodation, particularly residential establishments, have a housekeeping department that is responsible for looking after the rooms occupied by guests.

Activity: Staying away from home

Make a list of all the places where someone might stay away from home. Discuss how the needs of customers in these establishments may differ.

Residential accommodation

Residential accommodation services are provided in all those places that provide away-from-home sleeping and/or living accommodation. This includes:

- hotels
- hospitals
- hostels
- holiday camps.

In any residential establishment, the accommodation services or housekeeping department must ensure that the accommodation is clean, comfortable and safe.

Let's look at the services provided by some residential accommodation providers.

Hotels

There are many different types of hotel. They differ in shape, age, size and type, factors that dictate the work of accommodation services in each establishment. For example, in a luxury hotel the range of services offered by the department may include ironing, laundry and maintaining first-class standards. All hotels need to be clean and offer a discreet service that does not disturb guests.

Self-catering apartments

Customers staying in self-catering apartments often rent them for a week or more. They may be working away from home or on holiday. The level of service offered in the apartments can vary. However, apartments will generally be serviced before customers arrive and then again once they leave. If the customers are staying for two weeks or more, their apartment may be serviced once a week during their stay.

Halls of residence

Halls of residence provide accommodation to students who are attending a university away from their home. The facilities offered vary from one hall of residence to another. In some, students have their own bathroom, and in others they share a bathroom. Some halls of residence are self-catering, with cooking and laundry facilities. Students are largely responsible for cleaning their rooms, but cleaners will be employed to clean public areas such as corridors and landings. A warden or bursar is in charge of the halls of residence, making sure that the students take care of the premises.

Non-residential accommodation

Most hospitality organisations provide rooms for the use of their customers, even those that do not offer residential accommodation. Non-residential services are provided in a variety of places, including leisure centres and conference venues. First impressions are no less important here and, as with residential establishments, these organisations must provide clean, comfortable and safe accommodation.

Purpose of accommodation services

Accommodation services can be defined as the provision of a clean, comfortable and safe environment. Let's look in more detail at what this means.

Housekeeping

Guests get their first impression of a hospitality establishment or outlet when they enter the foyer or entrance hall. This impression is largely formed by the appearance that it presents. This first impression is gained before the guests order any food and drink, or use any other service. It is vital, therefore, that the outlet provides clean, presentable, comfortable and safe surroundings.

The objectives of the accommodation department include:

- providing a clean and comfortable environment
- maintaining health, safety and security
- operating within budget forecasts
- delivering efficient and effective services.

Safety and hygiene

Every workplace should have a health and safety policy. This provides the basis from which an organisation develops its structures and procedures to ensure health, safety and hygiene. One of the objectives of the housekeeping department is maintaining health and safety. The accommodation manager must ensure relevant health and safety information is communicated to all staff and that they fully understand their responsibilities.

Activity: Accommodation hazards

Working in small groups, identify the hazards that could cause a danger to customers in residential accommodation or to staff in the housekeeping department. Share your list with other groups in the class and discuss your findings.

You have probably discovered that there are many potential hazards in residential accommodation that could cause accidents or customers and staff to fall ill. Once potential hazards have been identified, it is the responsibility of all staff to control them or to limit the risk. Later in these units, we will look more closely at how this is achieved.

Security

Crime costs the UK approximately £19 billion per year, and guests are sometimes the victims of crime when staying in hotels and other residential accommodation. Hospitality organisations have to ensure the security of their working environments and take action to prevent anything that could threaten the safety of staff and customers.

It can be quite challenging to maintain security in the hospitality industry. Consider the challenge of providing security at the London Hilton in Park Lane. This hotel is huge. It has over 450 bedrooms, numerous meeting rooms, restaurants and bars, a fitness room, barber shop, beauty salon and gift shop. Its main entrance is a large revolving door with two additional side doors. People walking through these entrances are there for many different purposes and many may not be guests staying at the hotel. This makes it very difficult to monitor people coming in and out of the hotel.

As the accommodation staff work in all areas of the hotel, they are in an ideal position to spot suspicious people or incidents. It is important that they know how to respond if they see something suspicious. They should be trained to deal with these situations.

The accommodation manager can also prevent threats to security by:

- protecting valuable stock by restricting access and issuing keys to trusted members of staff
- ensuring the care and security of the keys for guest rooms
- making sure that guest rooms are locked when they are not being cleaned
- taking steps to protect the confidentiality of customer information
- reporting any breakages, loss or faulty locks immediately
- checking the authorisation of anyone requesting access to a room.

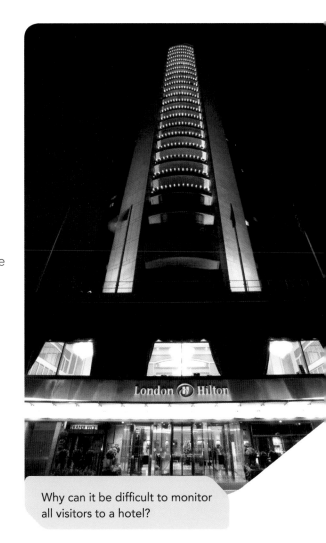

Why can it be difficult to monitor all visitors to a hotel?

Lost property

Staff in the accommodation department often find property that is left behind by guests who have already checked out or that is lost in the hotel. All lost property should be:

- reported to the supervisor
- recorded in a book
- held in a secure place
- returned to its owner if possible.

Laundry and bed linen

Residential establishments are usually responsible for laundering the bed linen and towels in the guest rooms. Some have their own laundry, but many businesses choose to use a contractor and send their washing to a commercial laundry.

Meeting customer needs

It is vital that all hospitality outlets are aware of, and strive to meet, the needs of their guests. This is no less true of accommodation services. The main aims set for accommodation services will be based on what the establishment believes its customers want.

The services offered will depend on the nature of the outlet. The service offered in a hospital or nursing home will be based on the need to operate a thorough and regular cleaning programme that does not disturb the patients or residents, or attract attention. The service offered in a hotel will be based around the need to provide a quick and thorough service to a consistently high standard.

It is worth noting that although the accommodation services team may not have much direct contact with the guests, the staff will still be expected to offer high levels of customer service.

Assessment activity 1

Unit 13 BTEC

You have been employed as a careers adviser in a further education college with a very successful hospitality department. You have been asked to put together some information on jobs and careers in accommodation services that could be used in a presentation to local schools.

To help you research these areas, visit two local hotels or providers of accommodation. Following your research, produce a PowerPoint® presentation that

describes the purpose and importance of accommodation services. **P1**

Grading tip

 Make sure you prepare a list of questions to ask before you go on your visits and take detailed notes when you are talking to people who work in each establishment.

 PLTS

You will develop your skills as an **independent enquirer** through the research that you do at each outlet.

 Functional skills

You will use **ICT** skills to identify local outlets to research and when producing a PowerPoint® presentation. You will develop your **English** skills of speaking and listening when discussing the purpose of accommodation.

13.2 Know the job roles and responsibilities of accommodation services employees

We will now consider the duties of staff that work in the accommodation departments of hotels and residential establishments. We will look at:

- job roles
- responsibilities
- documentation
- standards
- environmental issues.

Job roles

There will be several different job roles in a large accommodation services department. However, you should note that, just as the service offered differs from one type of establishment to another, the organisation of staff also varies enormously between establishments.

Managers

The way in which the management of the accommodation services is structured will be influenced by factors such as an establishment's size, type and location. However, it is the manager or housekeeper's responsibility to run the department efficiently and to meet the budget. An eye for detail is essential if you are a housekeeping manager.

As well as maintaining standards and controlling the budget, managers will usually also be responsible for:

- staff training
- staff welfare and discipline
- allocation of duties
- ensuring maintenance requirements are dealt with
- key control
- guest laundry
- lost property.

The manager of accommodation services might be known by a variety of titles depending on the type of establishment. Examples are:

- hotel – executive housekeeper, housekeeper
- hostel – bursar, halls manager, housekeeper
- hospital – domestic services manager.

What kind of checks does a housekeeper make?

As the size of the outlet increases, so the manager needs more supervisory and **operational staff**, with an assistant as a deputy or assistant housekeeper. In large outlets, the manager may be so busy that there is little time to check the work of the **room attendants** on a regular basis. If this is the case, then the deputy, assistant or floor supervisor will take on this role.

Floor supervisors

The floor supervisor will be responsible for checking the cleanliness and hygiene of allocated bedrooms, corridors and public areas, ensuring that they are cleaned and serviced to the required standards. The floor supervisor will supervise a team of room attendants, providing support and assistance, and may also have responsibilities for training staff.

Room attendants

Room attendants are allocated on a daily basis a number of rooms to service. Their role is to ensure that these rooms are cleaned and presented to the standard required by the hotel and expected by its customers. The number of rooms that a room attendant will be required to clean varies between hotels, but servicing between 10 and 15 rooms in an 8-hour shift is usual.

A room attendant's duties include:

- changing bed linen and towels
- making beds
- vacuuming floors
- treating stains, such as carpet stains, or damage to polished wood
- restocking guest supplies, such as shampoo and soap
- checking the general condition of the room and notifying the floor supervisor or housekeeper of any malfunction or damage.

Activity: How do the jobs differ?

Look for vacancies for floor supervisors, room attendants, linen porters and cleaners on the internet. Find out how the roles differ from one establishment to another.

Linen porter

The linen porter's role is to provide clean, well-laundered **linen** to the room attendants and restaurant staff. In hotels that use an outside contractor to launder their linen, the linen porter is responsible for:

- receiving linen and housekeeping deliveries
- counting and checking linen
- keeping linen records in good order

- storing linen away
- keeping the housekeeping linen room in good condition and order.

Cleaner

Cleaners are usually responsible for cleaning the public areas of a hotel. They will often start work very early in the morning so that they do not get in the way of customers who may be eating breakfast, checking out or arriving for meetings. Like all other staff in the department, they will be expected to clean and maintain the area for which they have responsibility to a given standard.

Dress code

Accommodation staff are usually provided with a uniform. This serves two purposes. It sets a dress code standard and it protects their clothes from being damaged by cleaning materials.

Cleaners have a set routine so nothing is left out. Why is this important?

Responsibilities

Now let's look a little more closely at the responsibilities of the staff that work in the housekeeping or accommodation department.

Cleaning and cleaning routines

Most staff employed in the housekeeping department undertake the practical tasks necessary to clean and service rooms. Regardless of whether they are room attendants or cleaners, they will usually follow a cleaning schedule or routine. This means that they will have a set order for doing their work. This will prevent them from missing anything out, and should ensure they are thorough and consistent in their work.

Some cleaning is carried out every day, but more thorough cleaning might be carried out on a weekly or monthly basis. A very special clean is necessary periodically. Periodic cleaning is often referred to as spring cleaning or annual cleaning. This is often carried out at convenient times depending on **occupancy**. It might include washing walls and ceilings or deep-cleaning carpets.

Activity: Deciding on a routine

In small groups, discuss what cleaning should be carried out on a daily basis and what should be done on a weekly or monthly basis.

Key terms

Operational staff – staff who carry out the day-to-day tasks of a business.

Room attendants – hotel staff who clean and prepare the guest rooms.

Linen – sheets, pillow cases, table cloths, napkins and towels.

Occupancy – the number or proportion of rooms in a hotel that have been let out. A 100% occupancy rate means that the hotel is full and all guest bedrooms are taken for the night.

Servicing bedrooms and bathrooms

The accommodation services team needs to complete its work to set standards, which may vary from one establishment to another. However, whatever that standard might be, when guests check into a bedroom they will expect it to look clean and like it has not been used before. They will not want to feel as though somebody else has slept in the bed or used the bathroom. The cleaning schedule, or order of cleaning, will help the room attendant to achieve this standard for the customer. On page 365 you will learn about the order of cleaning for a guest bedroom so that you are able to demonstrate that you can service these areas.

Pest control

Although standards of cleanliness are generally excellent in hotels and residential establishments, higher room temperatures and a lack of natural ventilation provide ideal conditions for certain pests. Failure to remove dirt, dust and food debris can encourage pests to stay in a building and breed.

The most common pests are:

- insects (for example, moths, larvae, cockroaches, flies) and spiders
- rodents, such as rats and mice.

Apart from the threat to hygiene, the presence of pests can be very upsetting to guests and give a poor impression of the establishment.

What does the presence of pests say about an establishment?

Did you know?

Cimex lectularius, also known as the bedbug, is a bloodsucking insect that travels on clothing and luggage and bites people while they sleep. News reports suggest that there has been a reappearance in hotels in the UK in recent years. In 2010, it was reported that New York was being infested by bed bugs.

Maintenance

Maintenance is the responsibility of all members of staff. People working in the housekeeping department are in an ideal position to spot and identify faults. These should be reported at once to the maintenance department and front office. The front office needs to know as it may not be able to let the room until the problem has been fixed.

Handling linen

Linen is a very expensive resource and it should therefore be treated with the utmost care. It must be kept in a secure place and there should be a system for controlling its movement to avoid damage or loss. Many hotels have a linen room that acts as a central collection, distribution and storage point. Wherever possible, soiled linen should be kept away from clean linen to avoid the transfer of germs and smells.

Replenishing supplies

Cleaning supplies should be kept in a locked store as they too are very expensive and potentially dangerous. There will usually be a system in place for their issue. This could be on an empty-for-full basis or on receipt of a requisition. In many hotels, cleaning supplies are issued at a set time each day.

Documentation

Effective communication and the control of resources are vital if the accommodation department is to meet its objectives. To achieve this, the department needs to be organised. To help with the organisation of work, a department uses a variety of standard documentation setting out work procedures, work schedules, duty rotas and maintenance schedules.

Work procedures

Work procedures detail the method that should be followed in carrying out individual tasks and the standard to which they should be completed.

Once performance standards have been set, there must be a system for checking that they are met. In accommodation services, this is usually done using checklists. Use of checklists will:

- keep staff alert and make sure that they are not tempted to slack
- show if training is needed
- highlight areas that have not been thoroughly cleaned
- identify any maintenance needs.

Work schedules

Work schedules contain the exact information necessary to service a given area, including the length of time that cleaning should take, the cleaning equipment and agents that should be used, and the correct sequence to follow when carrying out the task.

Duty rotas

Rotas are used to plan the work of the accommodation services team. They show the hours of duty, area of work and days off for each member of staff. The rotas are usually produced on a weekly, fortnightly or monthly basis. Before the rota can be completed, the accommodation manager will need to know how busy the department is going to be. It is very important that the rota produces an efficient work pattern as staff are a very expensive resource.

Maintenance schedules

It is obviously not possible to plan all maintenance because things break down, wear out or are damaged without any prior warning. However, regular maintenance should be carried out to an agreed schedule for cleaning equipment, fixtures and fittings to ensure that it is kept in tip-top condition and that it is safe to use.

Records

Once the above documents have been used, they are stored in a safe place for a period of time in case there is a query for which they are needed. The accommodation manager must also keep records relating to dealing with staff and staff training.

Standards

One of the responsibilities of the accommodation manager is to ensure that standards are set and maintained. It is important to ensure that all the staff carry out their cleaning and service tasks in a consistent manner.

Quality

An essential requirement of the accommodation department is to uphold quality. Quality can be defined as 'a measure of excellence or the state of being free from defects, deficiencies and significant variations'. To help maintain standards, the accommodation manager may make regular inspections and set strict specifications for the cleaning and servicing work.

Inspections

When a room or any area has been cleaned, it should be inspected to ensure that the cleaning meets the required standard. Checklists can be used for this purpose. Inspections are often carried out by the manager or floor supervisor. All faults or lapses in standards are noted on the checklist and fed back to the room attendant for correction.

In some hotels, room attendants are given the responsibility for checking their own rooms. This is seen as a way of motivating staff by giving them more responsibility. If this system is in place, the floor supervisor or manager may still carry out spot checks of some rooms.

Specifications

The key to consistency is to have specifications or standards of performance. These state:

- what jobs must be done
- how these jobs should be carried out.

This is an example of a standard of performance. It sets out how a hand basin in a guest bedroom should be cleaned.

Cleaning hand basins

1   Clear sinks of all toiletries and other items.

2   Remove hair from plugholes.

3   Spray all surfaces with cleaning solution including splashbacks, taps, and the inner and outer surfaces of the basin.

4   Use a damp cloth to clean all surfaces, ensuring that all marks are removed.

5   Run tap and rinse all surfaces with clean water.

6   Dry and polish all surfaces.

Activity: What jobs must be done?

Try to get an example of performance standards from a local hotel. Using it as a point of reference, write your own performance standard to cleaning an area of your school or college.

When performance standards are set by an establishment, its employees will be trained to those standards. This means they will be instructed in how to perform their tasks in the most efficient and effective manner, thereby ensuring quality. Many organisations have a standards of performance manual, which contains details of how every job should be performed.

Contract hire and specialist services

Many organisations use contractors to carry out some cleaning and servicing tasks. Contractors may be used for tasks such as:

- window cleaning
- carpet cleaning
- pest control
- deep cleaning
- servicing of equipment such as vacuum cleaners
- dry cleaning
- laundry
- waste disposal.

By using specialist contractors, organisations can often provide some aspects of accommodation services more efficiently and to a higher standard.

Legal

The safety of staff is always paramount. Although housekeeping and cleaning are not high-risk jobs, there are some risks.

It is the responsibility of employers to ensure that all staff are trained to recognise, understand and deal with health and safety risks. However, staff have a responsibility to ensure that they take note of any health and safety training and that they carry out their work with due regard to health and safety legislation.

The legislation that could impact on cleaning and servicing functions includes:

- The Health and Safety at Work Act 1974 (HASAWA)
- Control of Substances Hazardous to Health Regulations 2002 (COSHH)
- Manual Handling Operations Regulations 1992
- Personal Protective Equipment (PPE) at Work Regulations 1992
- Reporting of Injuries, Diseases and Dangerous Occurrences Regulations 1995 (RIDDOR).

In general, to ensure that you work in a safe way and comply with legislation you must:

- maintain a high level of personal hygiene and appearance
- report any hazards that you notice in the workplace.

Activity: Health and safety risks

Make a list of the health and safety risks that could be faced by those working in the accommodation services department. Discuss what can be done to minimise these risks.

Activity: Legal requirements

In groups of three or four, choose one of the laws that impacts on cleaning and servicing tasks. Produce a short PowerPoint® presentation describing the main points of the law and explaining how it applies to the accommodation department. A good starting point is the material on legal requirements on pages 28–32.

Audits

An audit is an examination of records or financial accounts to check their accuracy. They are often used within hospitality as a means of ensuring each department is following the policies or procedures of the department. For example, audits may be carried out to check that stock levels are correct or to ensure that training – especially health, safety and fire training – has been carried out.

Environmental issues

Many hospitality organisations are aware of their wider social responsibilities to reduce or limit the environmental impact of their operations. They have introduced policies to reduce their carbon footprint and some of these impact on the work of the accommodation department.

Laundry

Bed linen and towels in guest rooms are changed frequently in hotels. This is expensive and not very environmentally friendly. Managers are increasingly looking at ways to cut down on the amount of laundry they do. The frequency of linen changes can be altered so that linen in guest rooms is only changed every two or three days instead of daily.

Many hotels have introduced a towel reuse programme where guests are asked to leave their towels hanging on the towel rail if they wish to use them again, or to drop them in the bath or leave them on the floor if they want them replaced.

Reducing the amount of linen and towels laundered:

- saves water, energy and laundry chemicals
- reduces the amount of waste water generated by the laundry.

Pollution and waste disposal

The hygienic disposal of waste materials is very important. It will help to:

- control pests such as rats and mice
- prevent the spread of germs and infection
- limit the risks of fire.

Waste should be kept in tightly covered bins or plastic sacks. Bins should be emptied frequently and kept clean. Special care should be taken with the disposal of cigarette waste and broken items such as glasses or crockery.

Staff should be trained in the safe and proper handling, use and disposal of housekeeping chemicals. Dispensing systems can be used to dilute (weaken) and safely transfer chemicals from bulk containers to the refillable pump bottles used by housekeepers. Increasingly, hotels and other organisations are replacing harsh cleaning chemicals with milder and safer alternatives.

Energy conservation

Another way of being more environmentally friendly is by saving energy. Housekeeping staff should make sure the television and all lights are turned off before leaving a prepared guest room.

In some hotels guests are asked, via notes in the room, to turn off lights and adjust heating or air conditioning when they are not in the room. In other hotels the electricity supply to a room is only activated when the room keycard is placed in an electronic box. This means that guests cannot leave anything switched on when they are not in the room.

Case study: The Green Hotel

The Green Hotel and Spa is a luxury hotel and spa located deep in the heart of the English countryside. All its bedrooms and suites are comfortably furnished, with en-suite facilities, colour television, radio alarm, hairdryer and hot drinks tray. The oak-beamed restaurant has been awarded two AA rosettes and serves local and organic produce. The spa is set in the landscaped grounds and features an indoor pool, sauna, steam room, hydrotherapy spa and fitness room. There is also an all-weather floodlit tennis court, boules court and clay shooting range.

The hotel launched its 'green team' in 2009. This is a group of employees that meets regularly to promote environmentally friendly policies throughout the business. The hotel has recently achieved a gold award in the Green Tourism Business Scheme for its rigorous environmental policy and it belongs to the Considerate Hotels Association. A folder is in every bedroom with complete details of the hotel's environmental policy.

All electricity is generated from wind farms and conventional light bulbs have gradually been replaced by energy-saving bulbs. Guest room televisions cannot be left on stand-by and guests are encouraged to turn down radiators instead of opening windows. Towels are only changed on request.

The hotel recycles as much paper, plastic, aluminium and glass as possible, and it has invested in state-of-the-art equipment for the onsite treatment of organic waste, which is prepared for composting. Recycled paper is used in all stationery as well as for toilet tissues.

Water usage has been reduced by installing water-efficient fittings and equipment, such as showerheads and toilet cisterns, and by using collected rainwater. Housekeeping staff use plant-based cleaning products with rapidly biodegradable materials throughout the hotel.

1 Explain the benefits to the hotel of adopting an environmental policy.

2 Use the Internet to find out the objectives of the Green Tourism Business Scheme and the Considerate Hotels Association.

3 List the features you would include in your own 'green' hotel.

Assessment activity 2

Unit 13 **P2** **P3** **M1** **BTEC**

In Assessment activity 1 you were asked to produce a presentation for local schools. This was well received and you have now been asked to put together an information pack for schools detailing the job roles and responsibilities in an accommodation services department.

1 Research job roles on the Internet and produce a careers leaflet describing the roles and responsibilities of people providing accommodation services in the hospitality industry. **P2**

2 Produce a table that compares the similarities and differences between the various roles involved in cleaning and servicing accommodation. Describe the qualities that staff in each role need to make the stay of guests more enjoyable and explain how each role supports others. **M1**

3 Prepare an information sheet on the documentation used in the hospitality industry to maintain

accommodation standards. The leaflet should be suitable for use in an accommodation workshop for Year 10 students. **P3**

Grading tips

P2 Ensure that you use several sources when researching the various job roles. You need to show that you understand the full diversity of job opportunities.

P3 Carry out some research before completing this task. Make sure the documentation you describe is up to date.

M1 You should show that you understand how the various jobs roles differ, and you need to show that each role has a specific set of responsibilities.

13.3 Be able to demonstrate skills in accommodation services

Accommodation services is an area of work which, if carried out effectively, can have an enormous influence on customers' opinions of a hotel (or other residential organisation) and on its overall profitability. It is therefore important that staff have the required level of skill to work within the department. In this section, we will consider:

- cleaning skills
- servicing skills
- work methods.

Cleaning skills

Room attendants and cleaners often follow a set procedure when cleaning and servicing rooms, public areas and corridors. This is to make sure that they do everything that is required and that nothing is missed. In most hotels, there will be a set routine (like the one below) for cleaning guest bedrooms and bathrooms.

Cleaning schedule for a hotel guest room

1 Ventilate room.
2 Strip bed and remove dirty linen.
3 Empty ashtrays and waste paper basket.
4 Clean and restock hospitality tray.
5 Remove crockery and all rubbish and litter.
6 Remake bed.
7 Dust or damp-wipe furniture.
8 Spot-clean walls, especially areas around light fittings and doors.
9 Vacuum carpet.
10 Replace stationery and hotel literature as necessary.
11 Close window.
12 Check any defects and report.
13 Check work.

Once the room has been serviced, it will be checked. If there is anything in the room that does not meet the required standard, a note is made on the checklist and the problem is then corrected by the appropriate person.

Bedmaking

One of the most strenuous jobs of the accommodation department is bedmaking. This is particularly the case if the bed is made up with blankets and a bedspread rather than a duvet.

The room attendant may have to strip the bed and change the linen or just have to make the bed. This depends on the status of the room.

- If the room is a 'departure', the bed linen will always be changed.
- If the room is a 'stay', the room attendant may only need to remake the bed.

How often the bed linen is changed depends on the hotel. In a luxury hotel it may be changed every day, but in a hostel or hall of residence it might be changed only once a week.

There will often be a set procedure for making the bed, including a particular way to tuck in the sheets and blankets. The bed should look as if it has never been slept in before.

Why should bedrooms always be well presented?

Cleaning materials and equipment

There are many factors to consider when selecting and using cleaning materials and cleaning equipment, including:

- health and safety
- cost
- the upkeep of the area being cleaned
- the effectiveness of the product.

Cleaning equipment may include:

- mop systems for wet and dry use
- colour-coded cloths

- dusters
- bucket
- sponge and abrasive pads
- vacuum cleaner.

Cleaning materials may include:

- multi-surface cleaner
- toilet cleaner
- glass cleaner
- air freshener
- polish.

You should follow this procedure when servicing accommodation.

- Choose the correct equipment and materials for the area you are about to clean.
- Check the equipment is safe to use.
- Make sure you are wearing the appropriate uniform.
- Use the equipment and materials in line with the manufacturers' instructions.
- Store the equipment and materials safely and securely once they have been used.

Storage facilities need to be an adequate size for the handling and storage of equipment and materials. They should be secure and access should be controlled.

Activity: Practise your skills

In groups of three or four, ask a local hotel if you can spend some time shadowing a room attendant. Ask the attendant to show you how they service the room and make the bed. You may need help from your tutor to arrange this.

Relevant legislation

When you are at work, it is vital to follow the health and safety procedures of your organisation.

You will also need to understand any safety signs on display in the premises. All businesses need to display safety signs of some sort. These are the most commonly used signs.

- **Warning signs** – these have a black symbol on a yellow background inside a black triangle.
- **Prohibition signs** – these have a black symbol on a white background inside a red circle with a red diagonal line across the circle. These show things that must not be done.

- **Mandatory signs** – these have a white symbol on a blue circular background. These show things that must be in place or must be done.
- **Emergency signs** – these have a white symbol on a green rectangular or square background.
- **Fire-fighting signs** – these have a white symbol on a red rectangular or square background.

Servicing skills

Staff also need to deal with other aspects of servicing accommodation, such as dealing with waste and contractors.

The hygienic and safe disposal of waste is very important. Although most waste is non-hazardous, some waste can be hazardous. These procedures should be followed when disposing of any waste:

- wear appropriate clothing, which may include gloves
- put the waste into the correct containers, separating out any waste for recycling (if the organisation recycles its waste, as many now do)
- disinfect the waste containers
- wash your hands when you have finished.

Like many other services, some aspects of waste disposal can be undertaken by contractors. It is very important to build a good working relationship with any contractors. You need to be able to communicate with them effectively so that they fully understand the needs of your customers and your organisation.

Activity: A window-cleaning contract

Discuss what should be included in a contract with a window cleaner.

Work methods

Hospitality organisations use various methods and procedures to ensure that all work is undertaken efficiently. The use of cleaning routines and work schedules helps the accommodation department to work efficiently and to meet the required standard of performance. It is the responsibility of all staff to ensure they adhere to these procedures and are not tempted to take shortcuts.

Working efficiently and safely is extremely important. For this reason, the accommodation manager will sometimes undertake an analysis of housekeeping tasks. This task analysis will examine whether the current procedures and working practices are the best, safest and most efficient way to do the job.

Assessment activity 3

Unit 13 **BTEC**

This assessment activity is best based around a work placement, where you can demonstrate cleaning and servicing skills for accommodation operations in a real work environment. However, you can also demonstrate your skills through simulated activities in a training centre or at your school or college.

1   You will need to demonstrate a variety of skills using a selection of cleaning equipment and methods. These might include:

- dusting
- mopping
- vacuuming
- polishing
- bedmaking
- dealing with waste
- replenishing supplies.

Your skills will be observed and assessed by your tutor, or a 'buddy' within a work placement, using a checklist. **P4**

2   Design a cleaning routine for the cleaning and servicing of a hotel bedroom. It should include the tasks involved, the time required to carry out the tasks and the equipment, materials and methods of cleaning to be used. **M2**

3   Evaluate the importance of accommodation services on the guest experience and the success of a hotel or residential accommodation business. **D1**

Grading tips

P4 You will need to show confidence in using the new accommodation skills learned, demonstrating a strong understanding of routine, health, safety and hygiene and the need to maintain standards.

M2 Your cleaning routine should demonstrate your understanding of health, safety, hygiene and the need to maintain standards. One starting point would be to review the current cleaning routine for the cleaning and servicing of a hotel bedroom in your workplace.

D1 In your written answer, you should consider meeting guests' needs, the attention to detail required, the importance of guest loyalty and the contribution the housekeeping department makes to the overall business. You should take into account any experience you have of working in an accommodation department.

 PLTS

You will organise your time and resources to complete this activity and you will develop skills as a **self-manager**.

 Functional skills

You will develop your **English** skills of speaking and listening when discussing the work you are doing.

14.1 Know the responsibilities and purpose of the front office

The front office department of a hotel comprises the reception, guest services and porters. It has a great deal of guest contact and it plays a vital role in providing the services that guests expect during a hotel stay. In fact, it is often called the nerve centre of the hotel. In this section, we will cover:

- the purpose of the front office
- front office organisation
- job roles
- responsibilities
- legal issues.

Activity: Guest encounters

In small groups, list all the encounters that guests may have with the front office from the time they begin the process of choosing a hotel in which to stay until the time they leave the hotel.

The purpose of the front office

Front office staff are expected to present an appropriate image for the organisation, and they must be able to deal competently with guests and any problems they come across.

The purpose of the front office is to:

- provide guests with a good first impression of the hotel
- encourage guests to make a booking when they make an initial enquiry about the hotel
- communicate guests' needs effectively to other departments of the hotel
- encourage guests to spend their money in other areas of the hotel, such as the restaurant
- play a part in ensuring that guests are happy with their stay.

Welcome and first impression

The welcome that guests receive will help to form their impression of the hotel. When guests check in, their initial and most important impression of the hotel is provided by the receptionist at the front desk. The greeting given to guests needs to be cheerful, clear and sincere.

The appearance of the front office area is also important. If the reception area is untidy and looks chaotic, it creates a bad impression of the hotel. It may also cast doubt on the efficiency of the rest of the hotel, including areas that cannot be seen by guests such as the kitchen.

How can front office staff make a good first impression?

Activity: Greeting guests

In small groups, discuss why it is important that guests are greeted warmly and that their needs are identified and checked when they arrive at a hotel.

The guest cycle

The flow of business during a guest's stay at a hotel can be represented by a four-stage **guest cycle**.

Figure 1: The guest cycle

Before arriving at a hotel, guests must first choose which hotel to stay in. This is the pre-arrival stage. A guest's choice can be influenced by a variety of factors, including:

- previous experience of the hotel
- recommendation
- location
- ownership
- star rating
- competition from other hotels.

Key term

Guest cycle – the four stages of a guest's interaction with a hotel

The guest's choice may also be influenced by the ease of making the booking and the attitude and selling skills of the reservation staff.

All hotels need some kind of advance booking system to record reservations. Some hotel chains have a central reservations office, where staff take reservations for all the hotels in the chain. However, in many hotels there is a separate reservations department. Increasingly, customers can also make reservations online. Whatever method is used to make the reservation, there must be a system of communicating details of bookings to other departments of the hotel.

The arrival stage of the guest cycle is known as **check-in**, and it includes registration and rooming. The receptionists will carry out this function at the front desk. It is their responsibility to check the guest's needs and to ensure that these are communicated to the rest of the hotel. It is an opportunity to promote and sell other hotel services, and to make sure that the guest has everything they need.

It is at this stage that the guest's account is opened, and it is usual to ask for some kind of upfront payment or the guest's credit card details.

Activity: The need for communication

Imagine that you are working in the front office of a large hotel. A group of 30 elderly people have made a reservation at the hotel, but you have forgotten to tell other departments. Who should you have told? What should you have told them and why?

Throughout the occupancy stage, the front office represents the hotel to guests. A major objective of the front office is to satisfy guests' needs in a way that will encourage a repeat visit. As the front office is often seen as the communication centre of the hotel, it must be able to provide the guests with information about the rest of the hotel and other parts of the business, and the surrounding area.

Once guests have checked into the hotel, charges can be applied to their accounts. For example, if guests order drinks in the bar, the bar staff can add the price of the drinks to the relevant guest account rather than ask for immediate payment. This is known as **posting**, and it is done throughout a guest's stay.

The fourth stage of the guest cycle is departure (**check-out**). It is just as important to handle customers well at this stage as on their arrival. A bad experience at departure could completely spoil a pleasant stay and discourage customers from returning to the establishment.

At this stage, the receptionist:

- determines whether the guests were satisfied with their stay
- encourages the guests to return to the hotel
- presents each guest with their account for payment.

Front office organisation

The organisation of the front office varies from one hotel to another. As a rule, larger hotels are more likely to organise the front office into specialist roles. The front office might be divided into:

- reception (whose main duties include check-in and check-out)
- switchboard
- advance reservations
- **night audit**
- guest services.

In some hotels, these functions will be split between the front desk (also called reception) and back office. In smaller hotels, reception may carry out all of these functions. In all hotels, regardless of size, it is essential that the reception department is organised and staffed to maximise sales. This is because hotels earn the bulk of their income and profits from the sale of rooms.

Uniform service in a small hotel may consist of hall porters (working in the day) and night porters, but in a large five-star hotel there may also be a **concierge** on the front office team.

Activity: Organisation of the front office in local hotels

Contact a range of hotels in your local area to find out how many staff work in the front office and how the front office department is organised to provide a service to guests 24 hours a day.

Front desk and reception

Front desk consists of reception, guest services and porters. The work done here covers those activities undertaken at the arrival, occupancy and departure stages of the guest cycle. Responsibilities include:

- check-in
- guest accounting
- guest services
- customer care
- registration
- check-out
- some administration
- answering the telephone.

Back office

Back office consists of reservations and some administration. The work done here covers those activities undertaken at the pre-arrival and departure stages of the guest cycle. Responsibilities include:

- taking reservations
- dealing with booking amendments and cancellations

Key terms

Check-in – the procedures followed on a guest's arrival at a hotel.

Posting – putting charges on a guest's account during a hotel stay.

Check-out – the procedures followed on a guest's departure from a hotel.

Night audit – the process of checking the financial transactions reported by the various hotel departments during the previous day.

Concierge – the hotel worker in charge of porters and door staff.

- communicating with other departments
- night audit.

We will consider some of these responsibilities in more detail after looking at some of the job roles in a front office team.

Job roles

The organisation of the front office department will differ from hotel to hotel. Let's look at some of the typical job roles required to carry out the front office function.

Managers

The manager of the front office may be known by various titles, including:

- revenue manager
- front office manager
- rooms division manager
- front of house manager.

The size of the management team will depend on the size and style of hotel. The front office management team will have similar responsibilities to the manager of accommodation services.

Shift leader

If a hotel is large enough to have a team of receptionists working at a time, the hotel will often employ a shift leader to make sure the shift runs smoothly. A shift leader's duties will include:

- supervising the daily operation of reception
- assisting the manager in supervising the everyday operation of reception and ensuring it provides a service to the required standards
- taking the lead in the event of an emergency
- controlling and monitoring the issue of departmental keys and **floats**
- taking responsibility for the training of new team members.

Receptionist

Receptionists:

- check in guests
- answer queries
- take reservations over the counter
- post charges to guests' accounts
- liaise (communicate) with other departments of the hotel
- check out guests and balance the takings.

Receptionists may also prepare the takings for banking, but this might be carried out by the accounts department in some hotels.

Key term

Float – the amount of money in a cash till at the start of business, which can be used for giving change to customers.

To ensure that 24-hour coverage is provided where it is needed, reception staff are divided into three shifts: morning, afternoon and night reception. However, hotels with fewer than 50 bedrooms are very unlikely to provide a 24-hour reception service.

Telephonist

A large hotel will have a telephonist who operates the switchboard. The telephonist may also:

- answer enquiries
- help callers to find who they need to speak to
- take messages
- page (summon) someone in the hotel.

Reservations staff

Many hotels have a separate reservations department. This department tends to work between 8 am and 6 pm. The reservations staff are really salespeople for the hotel and they are responsible for maximising revenue (income) for the business.

Telephonists do not just answer the phones. What else do they do?

Concierge

The concierge is usually in charge of the team of hall porters and door staff. The concierge also gives guests directions to local attractions and other places, handles any special requests from guests, and can organise:

- tickets to the theatre, opera, concerts and sports events
- restaurant reservations
- car hire
- airline and train tickets.

Hall porter

Based in reception or at the porter's desk, a hall porter will:

- carry guests' luggage
- call taxis
- take charge of left property
- answer queries
- take messages for guests
- sort the mail.

A hotel porter may also assist the concierge, and help housekeeping, restaurant or banqueting staff to set up rooms or move large items of furniture. In some hotels, the porters help park guests' cars.

Many hotels have a night porter who may be responsible for:

- serving snacks and early breakfasts
- delivering newspapers
- wake-up calls to guests
- dealing with departures.

Activity: Exploring job roles

Using the Internet, see if you can find some job adverts for all of the front office roles described above. For each role, note the qualities and skills that are required.

Dress codes

Many hotels will require front office staff to wear a uniform or to adopt a standard dress code. Uniforms help to promote the hotel's image and provide the impression that staff are part of a team. They are also helpful to guests as they can quickly spot a member of staff.

Responsibilities

Let's consider the responsibilities of front office staff.

Reservations

The reservations office plays a crucial role in ensuring that as many as possible of the hotel's bedrooms are sold each night. The reservations team will try to make sales at the best possible prices. When taking a reservation, staff should follow this process:

- check that there is a room available
- take the necessary guest details and allocate a room type
- give the guest a room rate and explain what is included in the rate
- explain the cancellation policy
- relate hotel and location information
- ask for a guarantee of payment for the booking by giving a credit card number or company letter
- make sure the booking is recorded accurately.

Activity: The reservations department

Visit a local hotel to find out the system it uses for taking reservations.
- How does it record reservations?
- How are most of its reservations made?
- How does the front office communicate arrival details to other departments in the hotel?

Check-in and registration

When guests arrive at the hotel, they must check-in and register.
Registration is a legal requirement, and guests must provide their full
name and nationality to the receptionist. At check-in, the receptionist:

- greets guests
- registers guests
- takes a credit card imprint or payment
- allocates a room and issues a key or keycard as appropriate
- takes a restaurant booking if applicable
- arranges newspapers and an early morning call if required
- checks that all needs of the guests have been met
- directs the guests, or has them escorted, to their room.

Keycards can serve as room keys and as a form of identification for the
guest. Keycards and registration forms, which guests must complete
and sign when they check-in, are prepared in advance to speed up the
check-in process.

Guest accounting

The receptionist is responsible for posting charges to the guest's
account. In small hotels, the receptionist may post all the guest's
charges, including drinks in the bar, meals in the restaurant and room
service. In larger hotels, each department will be responsible for posting
charges incurred in their area to the guest's account and receptionist will
only post the accommodation charge.

Whatever system is used, the receptionist will need to ensure that
guests have not exceeded their credit limit and that all charges have
been posted. At the end of each shift, the receptionist will need to
count the takings to make sure that there is the correct amount of
money and debit or credit card payments in the till.

As the guest leaves, there are several tasks that have to be completed.
The receptionist should ensure that:

- the bill is ready for the guest
- there is plenty of change in the till
- there is a supply of pens for the guest to use to complete paperwork.

The check-out process involves the following steps:

- check and present the guest's account
- accept appropriate payment
- check that the guest has enjoyed their stay
- collect the key or keycard
- bid the guest farewell and wish them a safe journey.

Once the guest has left the hotel, the receptionist must ensure that their
account has been closed.

Activity: Guest accounting

Visit a local hotel and ask how it maintains guests' accounts and ensures that all charges are posted.

Guest services and customer care

Some hotels employ staff called guest service representatives or managers. These staff have a very similar role to the concierge. If there are no dedicated guest services staff, the front office team has a very big responsibility to make sure that guests feel welcome and relaxed. This includes:

- ensuring that guests are aware of all the services the hotel offers and how to book these services
- dealing with complaints and answering queries
- making sure any special requests (such as flowers in the room on arrival) are carried out.

How can you make guests feel pampered, not just welcome?

All front office staff play an important role in making sure that guests are happy with the service they are offered. This requires customer service skills, which were described in Units 3 and 4.

In general, front office staff should:

- display good personal skills
- have good verbal and non-verbal communication
- make sure that they always welcome guests with a smile.

Administration

There are several administrative tasks that need to be carried out in the front office. These include:

- checking that reservation documentation is accurate
- distributing reports to other departments
- preparing money for banking
- checking that guests' bills are accurate.

Answering the telephone

In a hotel, the telephone might be answered by the telephonist or receptionist. In either case, it must always be answered in a professional manner. Many hotels require their staff to answer the telephone using a standard form of words and with a 'smile' (see page 104).

Security

There are many ways in which front office staff can contribute to maintaining security in a hotel. These include:

- issuing and looking after keys
- dealing with lost and found property
- operating a safety deposit service so that guests can store their valuables
- careful handling of cash
- protecting the improper use of guest information
- reporting suspicious incidents or people to the relevant manager.

Virtually all hotels have policies to deal with the security of guests. This has become increasingly important given the threat of terrorist attacks. As frontline members of the hotel team, it is vital that front office staff are vigilant and aware of the security risks faced by the establishment.

Legal issues

The Data Protection Act came into operation in May 1986 and was introduced because of the increasing use of computer systems to store data on individuals. The act was updated in 1998 and the legislation was extended to cover all information, regardless of whether it is held on a computer or in paper-based systems.

The Data Protection Act ensures that all personal information is handled properly. This act states that anyone who processes personal information must make sure it is:

- fairly and lawfully processed
- processed for limited purposes
- adequate, relevant and not excessive

- accurate and up to date
- not kept for longer than is necessary
- processed in line with people's rights
- secure
- not transferred to other countries without adequate protection.

Under the Data Protection Act, individuals have rights in civil law to prevent organisations misusing any personal information they collect. These rights include:

- rights of access to the data
- rights to correct any information that is wrong and claim compensation for inaccuracy of data
- rights to claim compensation for loss, destruction or unauthorised disclosure of data, especially if this has caused you distress or financial loss.

Front office staff have a particular responsibility to protect the data a hotel holds on its customers. Front office staff must be made aware of their responsibilities under the Data Protection Act. The front office must be a secure area so that unauthorised individuals cannot easily access information on guests or sensitive data such as credit cards details.

Assessment activity 4

Unit 14 **P1** **BTEC**

In Assessment activity 1 you were asked to produce some careers information on the hospitality industry for use in schools. In this activity you will develop this work to cover the role of the front office.

Put together some information on jobs and careers in the front office departments of hospitality businesses. To help you research these areas, visit two local hotels or providers of accommodation. Following your research, produce a PowerPoint® presentation that describes the purpose and responsibilities of the front office. **P1**

Grading tip

P1 Make sure you prepare a list of questions to ask before you go on your visit and take detailed notes when you are there.

 PLTS

You will develop your skills as an **independent enquirer** through the research that you do at each outlet.

 Functional skills

You will use **ICT** skills to identify local outlets to research and produce a PowerPoint® presentation. You will develop your **English** skills of speaking and listening when discussing the purpose and responsibilities of front office.

14.2 Know the roles of the front office

We will now look in more detail at some of the functions of the front office team, including:

- meeting customer needs
- communication
- documentation
- standards
- statistics
- security.

Meeting customer needs

All hospitality staff must seek to do all they can to meet customer needs. Let's consider how front office staff can meet the needs of guests.

Types of room

Most hotels offer different types of rooms. When a reservation is taken, the customer will be asked what type of room they need. Table 1 shows the different types of room that can be offered by hotels. Note that many hotels will not offer the full range of rooms, but will have a limited selection.

Single	Contains a single bed and is for one guest only.
Twin	Contains two separate single beds for two guests.
Double	For two guests, with one double bed.
Family	Usually suitable for a family of four. This may contain bunk beds or a sofa that opens into a double bed.
Executive and superior rooms	Designed to provide a more luxurious environment than standard rooms. They are usually more spacious, with a sitting area in addition to the bed to provide extra comfort.
Suites and mini suites	Offers a more substantial form of accommodation. They normally consist of one double bedroom (possibly two), plus a sitting area with lounge-style furniture (sofa and armchairs).

Table 1: Types of room

Activity: Types of rooms

From visits or brochures, discuss the types of rooms found in hotels and bed and breakfast accommodation in your area.

Why should all hotels have facilities for guests with disabilities?

Disabled facilities

Some hotels have rooms adapted specifically for guests with disabilities or special needs. Here are examples of the types of adaptations that may be available:

- wheel-in showers
- raised toilet seats
- manual or electric bath hoists
- manual or electric bed hoists
- alarm systems
- vibrating alarms.

The accommodation team should be told when customers with disabilities are booked in, so that room attendants can ensure that the room is adequately prepared.

Special requests and extra beds

The front office department will usually take initial requests for any special requirements that guests might have. For example, guests might want:

- foam pillows instead of feather
- flowers or champagne in the room on arrival
- a ground floor room or a room with a view
- a special diet
- a table in the restaurant.

Another common request is for an extra bed in the room, usually for a child. The front office will need to tell the accommodation department to put the extra bed in the room. The front office should check that the hotel has an extra bed available on the nights the guest will be staying before agreeing to the request.

Activity: What special requests are made?

Pay a visit to a local hotel to find out what kind of special requests are made by guests. Find out what system the hotel has in place to make sure that guests get their requests.

Guest history

Many hotels main records of their past guests. As soon as a guest makes a reservation, a guest profile is created so that their details can be stored in a guest history. This means that if the guest returns to the hotel, reception will already have their details on record. This should improve customer service. It can help the hotel to identify if there have been any previous problems with the guest, such as non-payment of a bill or damage to a room. The details of previous guests can also be used to compile a mailing list to receive promotional offers and marketing material that the hotel sends out.

Communication

The front office department work continuously to ensure the satisfaction of guests. A lot of information needs to be communicated between the front office and the other departments in a hotel. Each department is dependent on the others – for information and/or services – if it is to meet customers' needs. This means that an establishment needs an efficient and easy-to-use method of storing and communicating information.

Reservation systems

The reservation system plays a very important part in helping to ensure effective and accurate communication between the front office and accommodation departments. It holds all the information that both departments need to ensure that the needs of customers are met.

Most hotels now record bookings on a computer, but some smaller hotels may still use a manual system. A manual system is only suitable for hotels with up to about 20 rooms. The system is based on a bedroom book, which is organised into a page per day and a line per room. The names of guests have to be entered into the bedroom book for each day that they are staying. Figure 2 shows typical entries in a bedroom book. Details of each booking are recorded on a reservation form.

DATE: ......12 January........

Room number	Room type (single/double/twin)	Name	Number of persons	Remarks	Date of departure
16	Double	Brown	2	Breakfast in room	Monday 14th January
23	Single	Peskavic	1	Vegetarian	Sunday 20th January

Figure 2: Sample page from a bedroom book

Manual systems are now becoming quite rare because computerised systems are a much more efficient way of dealing with reservations. They are essential in hotels that have more than about 20 rooms. There are many systems available, but all computerised systems can speed up the booking process considerably.

Computerised systems have many features. Room availability can be established at the touch of a button. The system can generate a reservation form. As soon as the name of the customer is keyed into the system, the computer will show if the customer has stayed at the hotel before. The system can also provide an enormous amount of information that can be used to analyse the hotel's business and to help managers plan for the future.

Activity: Enhancing communication

In groups of three or four, discuss how a computerised reservation system can enhance communication in a large hotel.

Forecasting

A forecast is a general prediction (estimate). The front office teams in many hotels make forecasts of future occupancy rates to help other departments to plan their workloads. A forecast is produced by:

- looking at the previous year's occupancy
- checking the level of advance bookings
- assessing any changes in the market, such as a new visitor attraction opening in the area that might increase demand for beds.

The forecast allows other departments to plan ahead. For example, it can be used by the accommodation services manager to complete staff rotas, to plan cleaning schedules and to ensure that there is sufficient linen, cleaning materials and guest supplies.

Reports

Each department of a hotel will use produce reports to help them operate more efficiently. Each report will serve a specific purpose. Here is a list of those most commonly used by the accommodation department:

- arrivals list
- guest list
- departure list
- special requests
- room status report/occupancy report.

Using computerised systems, departmental staff will download and update the reports they need. Front office staff need to prepare and distribute reports for any hotel that has manual administration systems.

Activity: Communication between front office and accommodation

List the information that must be communicated between the front office and accommodation departments in order to meet customer needs.

Liaison with other departments

Every department of a hotel relies on front office to let its staff know:

- how many guests are arriving and departing each day
- details of guests staying, such as names, length of stay, room number, room rate and **booking terms**
- if and when VIPs are expected
- if any special requests have been made by guests
- details of group arrivals
- any complaints or comments from guests.

Let's look in more detail at the communication between the housekeeping, maintenance and restaurant departments and the front office.

The front office needs to let housekeeping know about:

- room status
- early departures
- late arrivals.

Housekeeping needs to inform front office:

- when rooms are serviced
- room discrepancies (guests in wrong rooms)
- any damage to rooms
- lost property.

The front office needs to give the maintenance department the details of maintenance work that needs to be completed. In return, maintenance needs to issue a confirmation to housekeeping when this work is complete.

The front office needs to inform the restaurant and/or kitchen about:

- terms of bookings (so that the chef can identify how many guests have meals included in their booking)
- details of tables booked
- special dietary requirements of any guests.

The kitchen and/or restaurant should provide the front office with menus and details of any charges for food.

Key term

Booking terms – the payment and other terms governing a guest's stay in a hotel. The terms may include details of what is included in the booking (such as breakfast), payment terms, cancellation policy and non-arrival charges, as well as check-in and check-out times.

Activity: Inter-departmental communication

Discuss the means by which departments communicate with each other. Remember that communications must be timely, accurate and trackable.

Documentation

Three of the most useful documents in a hotel are the arrivals list, the departures list and the room status report.

Arrivals list

The arrivals list shows all guests that are due to arrive, and details their length of stay and any special requirements they may have. In some hotels, rooms are pre-allocated and the arrivals list will show the room number of the guests. In other hotels, rooms are allocated by the front desk when each guest arrives.

DATE: ....

4 pm release

Guest name	Room type	Number of persons	Date of departure	Rate	Room number	Remarks

Guaranteed

Guest name	Room type	Number of persons	Date of departure	Rate	Room number	Remarks

Figure 3: Example of an arrivals list

Departures list

The departures list shows all guests due to leave the hotel that day. It is usually prepared in room number order and contains a special note against any guests that are planning to leave later than the usual departure time. This is to prevent housekeeping disturbing these guests.

Room status report

The room status (or occupancy) report tells the housekeeper the status of each room. It is produced on a daily basis and used by the accommodation team each morning to prepare a list for each room attendant, with details of the rooms they need to clean that day. It gives the status of each room, specifying whether it is:

- a stay – this means the room is let and the guests will stay at least for the following night
- a departure – this means the guests will be leaving that day
- vacant and ready for letting to new guests
- unavailable owing to redecoration or repair work.

Once the rooms have been serviced, the accommodation service department must update the room status so that the front office knows which rooms are ready to let to new guests.

Standards

An important role of the front office manager, like that of the housekeeper or accommodation manager, is to ensure that standards are set and maintained.

Managers and supervisors use checklists to ensure that standards are maintained. In addition, front office staff often have a shift checklist so that they can check that they have completed all the routine jobs that need to be done on a daily basis.

Activity: Shift checklists

Visit a hotel and ask for a copy of its early and late shift checklists. If there are things on the lists that you do not understand, ask your tutor to explain them.

Because front office staff are seen as the nerve centre of the hotel, they have an enormous responsibility to ensure quality is maintained within the hotel. They can do this by:

- communicating effectively with other departments and guests
- following their own standards of performance
- feeding back any comments and complaints from guests to the appropriate department and members of staff.

Statistics

Statistics are a very useful method of identifying how a business is doing. The presentation of statistical information in a standardised form makes it easier for managers to see if a business is doing as well as expected.

Most businesses will compare actual performance against forecasted performance and check how they are doing this year against how they did at the same time in the previous year. There is little point in setting budgets if nobody checks whether they are being met.

Statistics can be used to make decisions about how to operate the business. If the managers of a resort hotel know that July is the busiest month, they will make sure that customers are charged the full rate.

Occupancy

The most commonly used statistic in a hotel is occupancy – the number of rooms sold out as a percentage of the total number of guest rooms. Levels of occupancy are of great interest to hotel managers.

To calculate room occupancy, express the rooms sold as a percentage of the total number of rooms in the hotel. For example, if the White Hart Hotel has 100 rooms and sells 85 of them, the room occupancy is calculated as follows:

$$\frac{\text{rooms sold}}{\text{total number of rooms}} \times 100$$

$$= \frac{85}{100} \times 100$$

$$= 0.85 \times 100$$

$$= 85\%$$

Occupancy will be looked at on a daily, weekly, monthly and yearly basis. It allows comparisons to be made between different periods. For example, suppose the White Hart Hotel sells a total of 2325 rooms in July. We know that July has 31 days, so can calculate the occupancy for July as follows:

$$\frac{\text{rooms sold}}{\text{total number of rooms} \times \text{number of days}} \times 100$$

$$= \frac{2325}{100 \times 31} \times 100$$

$$= \frac{2325}{3100} \times 100$$

$$= 0.75 \times 100$$

$$= 75\%$$

If the hotel had sold 1860 rooms the previous July, the occupancy would have been:

$$= \frac{1860}{3100} \times 100$$

$$= 0.6 \times 100$$

$$= 60\%$$

The manager could then easily compare levels of occupancy for the two years, and compare them against any forecasts or sales targets.

Average room rate

The average room rate shows the average price that rooms are being let for in a hotel. For example, if the room revenue at the White Hart Hotel is £6500 and it has sold 85 rooms, the average room rate is calculated as follows:

$$\frac{\text{room revenue}}{\text{rooms sold}}$$

$$= \frac{6500}{85}$$

$$= \pounds76.47$$

Figures are normally expressed excluding VAT (value added tax). Like the occupancy rate, the average room rate will be worked out on a daily, weekly, monthly and yearly basis.

Comparison against forecasts

Once the average room rate and occupancy have been established, they should be compared to the forecast to work out how well the business is doing. If the forecasted revenue is not being achieved, the reasons why will need to be investigated.

Activity: A fall in occupancy

The sales figures for the White Hart Hotel show that occupancy is down by 10% and average room rate is down by 7% on forecast. Discuss the possible reasons for this shortfall. What measures could the manager take to address this issue?

Security

Security is a major issue. Everybody likes to work in a secure environment and maintaining effective security is the concern of everyone working within a hospitality establishment. It is essential that guests feel secure and, with the threat of terrorist attacks in many areas, it is important that there are systems in place to make sure that guests are as safe as possible. Staff can only maintain security if they are aware of the risks and know how to deal with them. It is therefore essential that they receive proper training in this area.

Safe deposit boxes

Guests sometimes travel with valuable items. Many hotels provide safes in the bedrooms so that guests can keep their valuables secure during their stay. If safes are not available in the rooms, guests can usually deposit their goods in a safe deposit box at reception or in the hotel safe.

Lost property

Lost property is often reported to front office, and reception will usually hold a list of any property that has been found. This is because guests will usually phone reception if they have mislaid something.

Control of keys

There are usually three types of keys used in a hotel:

- the master key, which opens all doors
- sub-master keys, which opens a selection of doors (such as a whole floor or a set of rooms)
- individual room keys.

It is very important that there are systems in place for issuing and collecting their keys as their loss could have serious consequences.

Master and sub-master keys are often issued by the front office. To make sure that the keys can be tracked down, staff are usually asked to sign them in and out in a key book (see Figure 4). Keys should only be issued to those members of staff who are authorised to use them and the front office should have a list of who can take each key out with the key book.

Figure 4: Extract from a hotel key book

Activity: Maintaining security

List the things that the front office department does where attention to security is essential. Consider, for example, what might happen if a hotel master key falls into the hands of a thief.

Then, in groups. discuss how the front office team can ensure that its department is secure.

Assessment activity 5

Unit 14

BTEC

In this assessment activity you are going to continue preparing material for an information pack on the hospitality industry for use in schools.

1. By researching job roles on the Internet, produce a careers leaflet describing the roles of people working in the front office. **P2**

2. The job roles in the front office are very diverse. Produce a table that compares the different roles in the front office. Set out the qualities that staff in each role need to make the guests' stays more enjoyable and explain how each role supports the others. **M1**

3. Produce an information sheet that analyses how the flow of information between the guests, the front office and the accommodation department can affect the guest experience and the success of a hospitality organisation. **D1**

Grading tips

P2 Ensure that you use a number of different sources when researching job roles so that you understand the full diversity of job opportunities.

M1 You need to show that you understand how the jobs roles differ. Describe the similarities and differences between the roles.

D1 Carry out some research before completing this task. Try putting yourself in the position of a guest and imagine how you would feel if there was a breakdown in communication when you were staying in a hotel.

PLTS

You will develop your skills as an **independent enquirer** when researching job roles and analysing how the flow of information between guests and the front office can affect the guest experience.

Functional skills

You will use your **ICT** skills to research job roles and to produce leaflets. You will develop your **English** skills in reading and writing to understand different texts and to use them to gather information and ideas.

14.3 Be able to demonstrate skills used in the front office

We are now going to consider front office skills. Throughout this book we have considered the many skills needed to work in hospitality. In this section, we are going to review some of the skills specifically needed to provide front office services.

Meeting and greeting

Meeting and greeting customers is one of the most important duties that you will have to perform for your organisation.

The procedure for meeting and greeting may vary from one outlet to another, but there are some simple rules that you can follow.

- Greet customers promptly, with eye contact and a warm smile.
- Ask how you can help them.
- Listen carefully to what the customers say.
- Help the customers if you can; if not, direct them to the appropriate people, products or services clearly, making sure that they have understood what you have said.

Activity: Front office role plays

In groups of two or three, carry out these role plays.
- Check in a family of four with two small children, luggage and so on.
- Assist a customer arriving for a conference.

It might be useful to find out how the front office staff in a local hotel would deal with each of these situations before you attempt the role plays.

Handling complaints

Unfortunately, customers will sometimes feel the need to complain. Because they view the front office staff as their point of contact, they will usually address their complaint to the reception staff. When dealing with complaints, you should follow the procedures explained on pages 84–85.

Some complaints are very easy to deal with. For example, if a guest does not have enough towels, you can contact the accommodation department and ask them to provide more. In other cases, the complaint may be too serious for you to deal with and you may have to contact your supervisor for help.

Dealing with enquiries

The front desk may have to deal with an enormous variety of enquiries, so it is very important that staff have a good working knowledge of their place of work and the surrounding area. Enquiries may be made:

- in person
- by telephone
- in writing: by letter, email or fax.

Activity: Enquiries

List all the different types of enquiries you might have to deal with on a front desk.

When we communicate with another person face to face, we do so verbally and non-verbally. Verbal communication comes from what we say and non-verbal communication comes from our body language. It is very important to be aware of both aspects of communication when dealing with customers. In some cases, a customer may just want to chat. It is important that you make time for these customers, but you must remember to display a professional attitude at all times.

When answering telephone calls, remember you are likely to be the first point of contact that the customer has with the establishment. The impression that front office staff give over the telephone is therefore very important.

Enquiries in writing are usually a request for information about the hotel, and these may come in the form of a letter, fax or email. Many hotels have standard letters for replying to enquiries.

Some guests make their initial enquiry by email. It is extremely important that emails are responded to promptly. When replying to a customer by email, remember that this is a formal method of communication. The email should be checked, and any grammar and spelling errors corrected, before you send it.

Many hotels now have booking facilities on their own website or with online booking agencies. Guests can use these systems to make a booking without talking to a member of staff, so it is very important that the information on websites is accurate and up to date.

Receiving payments

It is important that customers' accounts are kept up to date. This is particularly challenging in hotels that operate 24 hours a day. There must be a system of posting charges to customers' accounts throughout the day, so that customers can pay their bills at a moment's notice.

How can you make sure your customer's last impression is a good one?

The usual time for customers to pay their bills is when they are about to leave. As this is the last chance to make an impression on the guest, it is important that this process is carried out efficiently and professionally.

Customers may pay their bills using a variety of methods. These include:

- cash
- cheque
- debit card
- credit card
- travel agent voucher.

Some bills are not directly paid by the guests but are paid on account by another organisation. For example, the bills of guests who are travelling on business are often paid by their employer.

Each hospitality organisation has its own procedure for dealing with payments, but a typical procedure is to:

- greet the customer in a warm and friendly manner
- present the bill to the guest for checking
- explain the charges on the bill
- ask the customer how they will be paying
- follow the organisation's procedure for that payment method
- check the customer is happy with the service they have received at your organisation
- thank the guest for their custom
- say goodbye.

Activity: Methods of payment

Research how to deal with each of these methods of payment:
- debit card
- credit card
- cheque
- cash.

Selling skills

Selling is an acquired skill and a key task for front office staff. It means actively promoting the services and facilities of the hotel rather than simply responding to customers' queries and requests. Front office should be aware of what makes the hotel special. This could be features such as:

- the restaurant has a Michelin star
- there is a spa
- the hotel is very close to a visitor attraction.

Appealing words should be used to describe products and services whenever possible. Explain the benefits of staying at the hotel to guests and help them to visualise your products.

Activity: Selling role plays

Collect a brochure from a local hotel or look at its website on the Internet. In pairs, role play selling the positive features of the hotel to a customer who is planning to bring her husband for a long weekend stay. The visit is a surprise present to celebrate the couple's 25th wedding anniversary.

Giving local knowledge and information

In dealing with enquiries, all members of a front office team are expected to have a good knowledge of the local area and of the hotel's products and services. It is important that you are able to talk to customers to find out their exact requirements, so that you can recommend suitable products and services.

Because the services and products offered by the organisation can change constantly and there may be many attractions and services in the local area, it may not be possible to remember everything that you might be asked. However, you should know how to answer a query quickly by using reference material. You should keep resources such as street maps close at hand to enable you to give correct and up-to-date information.

Dealing with currency exchange

Many hotels will exchange foreign currency and traveller's cheques for guests, and some even allow guests to settle their account with foreign currency.

Changing foreign currency is relatively easy if the front office computer has a program that automatically calculates exchange rates. However, without this facility, the procedure is more complex and the receptionist will need to work out the exchange rate using a calculator.

Whatever system is used, there will be a set procedure for dealing with foreign exchange. This should be explained clearly to any staff that will be handling foreign currency.

Booking travel services

Sometimes, guests may want front office staff or the concierge to book transport, such as a taxi or train. Staff need to know the best way to make the appropriate bookings.

Assessment activity 6

Unit 14   BTEC

This assessment activity is best based around a work placement, where you can demonstrate your skills when working in the front office. However, you can also demonstrate your skills through simulated activities in a training centre or at your school or college.

1 Demonstrate guest service skills when meeting and greeting guests and dealing with guest enquiries. Your skills will be observed and assessed by your tutor, or a 'buddy' within a work placement, using a checklist. **P3**

2 Explain the activities undertaken by the front office at each stage of the guest cycle. **M2**

3 Evaluate the importance of the front office on the guest experience and the success of the business. **D2**

Grading tips

P3 You will need to show confidence in dealing with guests, and you should demonstrate a strong understanding of customer service and the need to maintain standards.

M2 Your answer should demonstrate an understanding of the purpose of each activity within the guest cycle.

D2 Consider the front office role in meeting guests' needs. Reflect on the required attention to detail needed in the front office – what would be the implications for the business if this was missing? Consider also the importance of guest loyalty and the contribution the front office makes to the overall business.

PLTS

You will organise your time and resources to complete this activity and you will develop skills as a **self-manager**.

Functional skills

You will develop your **English** skills in explaining what is meant by the guest cycle and analysing the contribution of the front office to the success of the business.

Patrick Kelly
Floor supervisor

Patrick is the floor supervisor at the Brooklands Hotel. This is a brand new property with a modern, sleek style, an Art Deco-inspired interior, 250 bedrooms and conference suites. The hotel is at the upper end of the four-star category and appeals to both the local corporate market and leisure clientele.

Patrick's role involves allocating and supervising the activities of all housekeeping staff to ensure the hotel is clean, orderly and maintained to the highest standards. He has to prepare worksheets for all staff and ensure that housekeeping employees maintain appropriate standards of conduct, hygiene and appearance.

He monitors occupancy levels and ensures the staffing is sufficient. He inspects rooms and checks that all stock and linen are used correctly to avoid wastage, soiling and damage. He also responds to customer comments and feedback related to the housekeeping operation, taking action to ensure guest satisfaction.

Patrick controls housekeeping procedures such as lost and found, key and pager control, and health and safety for employees and guests. He needs to be fully aware of security and health and safety procedures and he carries out regular inspections of equipment and housekeeping areas.

Although he is enjoying the job, Patrick is finding it much more challenging than he had imagined. In the four months that he has worked at the hotel, a number of staff have left, complaining that the job is too hard. He finds it difficult to motivate some of the staff and is constantly having to ask them to revisit the rooms they have cleaned because standards are not being maintained. On more than one occasion, a member of staff has refused to do as Patrick has asked, and he has had to ask the head housekeeper to intervene.

Think about it!

- Why can it be difficult to motivate staff working in the housekeeping department?
- Identify the means Patrick could use to encourage all his staff to maintain the hotel's standards.

Just checking

1 Explain the main purpose of accommodation services.

2 List six types of establishment where accommodation services might be provided.

3 Explain three ways in which the accommodation services department can ensure it is environmentally friendly.

4 Identify the four stages of the guest cycle.

5 Describe four ways in which the front office department contributes to the success of an organisation.

6 List five potential security risks in the front office.

7 While you are on duty in reception, the following situations occur:
- four guests leave earlier than planned
- one guest moves rooms
- two guests extend their stay
- the secretary of a VIP client calls to say he will be arriving in one hour
- a cot is requested by a guest arriving that night.

Explain how you would deal with each of these situations.

8 Explain the use of a checklist in accommodation services.

9 Identify two pieces of legislation that impact on the work of room attendants.

10 Describe the procedure for meeting and greeting a customer.

edexcel

Assignment tips

- In preparing for your assignments in these units, think about what you have learned about accommodation and front office services when you have visited hotels or other establishments. Observe how well (or how poorly) they maintain standards and the systems they use to carry out their work.

- Look at hospitality and recruitment websites when researching job roles. Make sure your research is thorough and remember to look for job opportunities in a wide range of outlets, not just hotels.

- Talk to people who work in the hospitality industry and who have front office roles so that you can improve your understanding of the work they do.

- Ask friends or family members if they have ever had a bad experience when staying away from home. Find out what the problem was and try to work out what might have caused it.

- Listen very carefully to your 'buddy' when carrying out your practical activities. Do not be afraid to ask questions if there is something you do not understand.

Glossary

A la carte – menus of which the dishes are individually priced.

AIDA – short for attention, interest, desire, action. The AIDA model provides a reliable template for the design of marketing material.

Anaphylactic shock – a life threatening reaction to an allergy, often caused because the windpipe swells and the person can't breathe

Body language – the gestures, poses, movements and facial expressions that a person uses to communicate. It is sometimes called non-verbal communication.

Booking terms – the payment and other terms governing a guest's stay in a hotel. The terms may include details of what is included in the booking (such as breakfast), payment terms, cancellation policy and non-arrival charges, and check-in and check-out times.

Borsch – a soup made of beetroot or tomato, popular in many Eastern and Central European countries.

Braai – meat barbequed over a flame.

Braising – a cooking method that involves searing meat at a high temperature and then finishing in a covered pot of liquid.

Breached – broken or disobeyed the law.

Budget – the sum of money available to spend on an event or an activity. Separate budgets are often set up for the specific resources needed for an event, such as promotion and administration, food and drink, and equipment.

Calorie – a unit of energy in food.

Cassava – a root vegetable that looks like a sweet potato but has a chalk-white or yellowish flesh.

Chance customer – a customer who arrives without a reservation.

Check-in – the procedures followed on a guest's arrival at a hotel.

Check-out – the procedures followed on a guest's departure from a hotel.

Chimichurri – a South American sauce or marinade which consists of parsley, garlic, lemon juice, onion, olive oil, thyme and oregano.

Commis chef – a trainee chef. This is usually the most junior position in a kitchen.

Commodity – an item of food. For example, milk is a commodity.

Commodities – raw food products before any preparation or cooking.

Concierge – hotel worker in charge of porters and door staff.

Contingency plan – a plan devised for a specific situation when things could go wrong.

Convenience foods – bought foods that have already been prepared and/or cooked.

Counter service – food service style where customers queue at a counter to select (if there is a choice) and receive their food.

Courteous – polite and well mannered.

Credit note – a note given to cover the value of faulty goods. The customer will not be charged for these goods.

Cruets – small dispensers or containers for salt, pepper and other condiments.

Customer service – what an organisation does to meet customer expectations and produce customer satisfaction.

Delivery note – a document sent by a supplier to show what is being delivered and the amount of each item being supplied.

Draft – a drink served at the bar by opening a tap; the drink travels through a pipe from the barrel., which is usually kept in a cellar. The drink is sometimes cooled in a cooler on its journey from barrel to glass.

Empathising – to identify with another person's feelings, emotionally putting yourself in the place of another.

Expectations – what customers are expecting to get. If they have high expectations, because of everything they have heard or previously experienced, then these must be met because anything less will leave customers dissatisfied.

Fair trade – a movement that aims to help producers in developing countries obtain better trading conditions and promote sustainability.

Float – amount of money in a cash till at the start of business, which can be used for giving change to customers.

Focus group – a form of market research in which a small group of people are invited to a meeting to discuss their views and opinions on a business's products and services.

Free pouring – a method of measuring and pouring a drink into a glass before service.

Fufu – paste made by grinding down starchy edible roots.

Gender specific products – products for, or associated, with persons of one gender (male or female) to the exclusion of the other.

Gross profit – the amount of money left after the production costs are deducted from total sales.

Guacamole – a dip made with avocado.

Guest cycle – the four stages of a guest's interaction with a hotel: pre-arrival, arrival, occupancy and departure.

Haggis – a traditional Scottish pudding of sheep offal, oatmeal and seasoning, cooked in the casing of a sheep's intestine.

Hazard – something that has the potential to cause damage or harm.

Intangible goods – products that cannot be seen or touched, such as advice, friendly service and atmosphere.

Internal requisition – a document that is completed by a chef of kitchen staff to obtain food from the stores.

Invoice – a bill for goods received.

Linen – sheets, pillow cases, table cloths, napkins and towels.

Mailshot – promotional material sent out to attract customers.

Mandatory – compulsory so it has to be done.

Market segment – a group of customers with broadly similar needs and expectations.

Minutes – a written record of a meeting. Minutes are usually sent to everybody present at the meeting, setting out what each person agreed to do at the meeting.

Mise-en-place – a French phrase meaning 'putting in place'. The phrase is used in hospitality and catering to mean everything being in place.

Mystery customer – someone who poses as a normal customer but who is paid to give an organisation feedback about its services and products.

Needs – the very basic requirements that customers seek, such as good food, clean toilets, a safe environment. If these basic needs are not met, customers will never be satisfied.

Night audit – the process of checking the financial transactions reported by the various hotel departments during the previous day.

Non-compliance – if a business or an individual obeys the law, they are compliant. If they don't obey the law, they are non-compliant.

Obese – so overweight that it is dangerous to your health.

Occupancy – the number or proportion of rooms in a hotel that have been let out. A 100% occupancy rate means that the hotel is full and all guest bedrooms are taken for the night.

Off board – a list, usually on the wall in the kitchen, of any dishes that are sold out or are unavailable.

Okra – a long green vegetable, also known as 'Lady's fingers'.

Operational staff – staff who carry out the day-to-day tasks of a business.

Optic –a device that gives a measure of alcohol from the bottle when the optic is pressed by the bar staff.

Pebre – a sauce from South America which consists of olive oil, hot chillies, parsley, oregano and wine vinegar.

Period of notice – this is the amount of warning employees have to give when they resign from their jobs. Typically, staff have to give one month's notice before they can leave a business. This gives their employer time to find a replacement.

Perishable – food that can go bad very quickly.

Personal attributes – an individual's personality, qualities and characteristics.

Plantain – a banana-like fruit that is used for cooking.

Plated – standard restaurant serving method where food is served on to plates in the kitchen and then brought to the customers' table by waiting staff.

Posting – putting charges on a guest's account during a hotel stay.

Press release – information sent by businesses to media organisations (newspapers, radio stations, television channels) on their products and services, forthcoming events and other developments of possible interest.

Profit – the amount of money a business makes after taking all its costs into consideration.

Purchase order – a document sent to a supplier to order goods and services. It shows how much of each item is needed and the required delivery date.

Purchasing – another word for 'buying'. Purchasing is the term usually used in catering and the industry.

Purchasing cycle – the system used in catering to place, receive and pay for orders of food and other goods from outside suppliers.

Recession – a downturn in the activity of the economy. Spending slows and demand for goods and services is reduced, and unemployment can increase.

Recipe – a set of instructions on how to make a food dish. Recipes specify the ingredients, the amounts to be used, and the preparation and cooking method.

Repeat business – customers that have previously been guests or clients of the organisation.

Responsible sourcing – a policy by companies to take social and environmental considerations into account when dealing with suppliers.

Returns note – a note sent by a customer when returning goods to a supplier because they are faulty, of poor quality or had not been ordered.

Risk – the chance of something causing damage or harm.

Room attendants – Hotel staff who clean and prepare the guest rooms.

Room tariff – another term used for the price of a room. Tariff means price or charge.

Sales – money that a business receives from customers from selling its goods and services. This is sometimes called revenue.

Salsa – a spicy sauce, usually tomato-based.

Sautéing – cooking food over a high heat in a small amount of oil or clarified butter.

Self-employed – a person is self-employed if they work for themselves rather than for one company or business. People such as electricians and window cleaners are often self-employed. They charge their customers or clients on a job-by-job basis.

Self-service – food service where customers help themselves from counters or buffets.

Sensory qualities – taste, texture, aroma and appearance.

Silver service – high-quality serving method where food is served by waiting staff at the table from service dishes on to customers' plates.

Specials board – is a list, usually on a chalkboard, of extra dishes that are not on the regular menu.

Specification – a document that describes exactly what is required in terms of quality for food and commodities purchased by a catering establishment. Does not only apply to food.

Staff turnover – the frequency with which members of staff leave an organisation.

Statement of account – a document prepared each month by a supplier, showing items bought and the money owed by a customer.

Strapline – a slogan used to identify a brand.

Stroganoff – a Russian dish of sautéed beef, usually fillet, in a sauce made with soured cream. Can also be made with other meats such as pork or chicken, or with mushrooms.

Table d'hôte – menus that offer complete meals for a set price.

Takings – money paid to a business through its sales.

Tamales – a Latin American dish made of a starchy dough called masa, which is steamed or boiled in a leaf wrapper, and can be filled with meat or vegetables.

Tangible goods – products you can see and touch, such as food, drink and guest rooms.

Tortilla – a flatbread made from corn or wheat. Also refers to a Spanish-style omelette.

Turnover – the amount of money taken by a business in a particular period.

Ugali – maize flour ground down and boiled to a porridge or dough.

Index